The EdTech Playbook

Your definitive guide to teaching, learning and leading with technology and AI in education

**Mark Anderson
& Olly Lewis**
Edited by Liz Bury
Cover illustration by Rebecca Gray

Together we unlock every learner's unique potential

At Hachette Learning (formerly Hodder Education), there's one thing we're certain about. No two students learn the same way. That's why our approach to teaching begins by recognising the needs of individuals first.

Our mission is to allow every learner to fulfil their unique potential by empowering those who teach them. From our expert teaching and learning resources to our digital educational tools that make learning easier and more accessible for all, we provide solutions designed to maximise the impact of learning for every teacher, parent and student.

Aligned to our parent company, Hachette Livre, founded in 1826, we pride ourselves on being a learning solutions provider with a global footprint.

www.hachettelearning.com

Although every effort has been made to ensure that website addresses are correct at time of going to press, Hachette Learning cannot be held responsible for the content of any website mentioned in this book. It is sometimes possible to find a relocated web page by typing in the address of the home page for a website in the URL window of your browser.

Hachette UK's policy is to use papers that are natural, renewable and recyclable products and made from wood grown in well-managed forests and other controlled sources. The logging and manufacturing processes are expected to conform to the environmental regulations of the country of origin.

To order, please visit www.HachetteLearning.com or contact Customer Service at education@hachette.co.uk / +44 (0)1235 827827.

ISBN: 978 1 0360 0463 7

© Mark Anderson and Olly Lewis 2025

First published in 2025 by
Hachette Learning,
An Hachette UK Company
Carmelite House
50 Victoria Embankment
London EC4Y 0DZ
www.HachetteLearning.com

The authorised representative in the EEA is Hachette Ireland, 8 Castlecourt Centre, Dublin 15, D15 XTP3, Ireland (email: info@hbgi.ie)

Impression number   10 9 8 7 6 5 4 3 2 1
Year   2029 2028 2027 2026 2025

All rights reserved. Apart from any use permitted under UK copyright law, no part of this publication may be reproduced or transmitted in any form or by any means, electronic or mechanical, including photocopying and recording, or held within any information storage and retrieval system, without permission in writing from the publisher or under licence from the Copyright Licensing Agency Limited. Further details of such licences (for reprographic reproduction) may be obtained from the Copyright Licensing Agency Limited, www.cla.co.uk

Cover illustration by Rebecca Gray.
Typeset in the UK.
Printed in the UK.
A catalogue record for this title is available from the British Library.

MIX
Paper | Supporting responsible forestry
FSC™ C104740

IN PRAISE OF THE EDTECH PLAYBOOK

The EdTech Playbook is arriving at a very important juncture in the evolution of digital within our education system. *The EdTech Playbook* is a huge repository of evidence-informed insights, advice and practical applications. A highly accessible read, it's like having Anderson and Lewis sat at your side as you reflect on each of the activities shared. A must-have addition to your bookshelf.

Al Kingsley MBE, multi-academy trust chair and EdTech CEO

If you're going to read a playbook on how to successfully handle EdTech in your school, this is the book you should grab. I've known Mark and Olly, the authors, for years, and they've always been at the cutting edge of educational technology. But what sets them apart is their practical, no-nonsense approach.

In *The EdTech Playbook*, they've distilled years of experience into what they call the five Cs of digital cognition. Trust me, it's not just another set of buzzwords. These concepts – Confidence, Competence, Cognisance, Consistency and Context – are essential when it comes to actually making technology work in the classroom.

What I love about Olly and Mark's approach is that they never lose sight of what really matters: good teaching. They're not pushing tech for tech's sake. Instead, they show you how to use these tools to create more engaging, personalised learning experiences.

Whether you're an EdTech novice feeling overwhelmed by it all or a seasoned pro looking to take your digital game to the next level, you'll find something valuable here.

So do yourself a favour – pick up *The EdTech Playbook*. It's like having Olly and Mark as your personal EdTech coaches.

Leisa Grace Wilson, editorial director, Teach Middle East and Schoolfinder.ae

Technology has never moved at such a pace, nor have so many EdTech apps and services been available to schools. As leaders and teachers, how do we successfully navigate this evolving landscape?

Anderson and Lewis' *The EdTech Playbook* guides sustainable and effective cultural digital improvement, whether that be in your classroom or across a whole school. Easy to understand, this book is a great companion for those looking to improve student outcomes and reduce teacher workload. I want all our digital leads to have a copy!

Matt Lovegrove, digital learning adviser, Cognita Schools

Comprehensive, practical, sensible and balanced advice to support each reader on their digital learning journey, whatever their starting point. The focus is clearly on how to integrate technology into our everyday professional practice in order to support teaching, enhance students' learning and reduce workload. The insights shared, including the 'top tips' offered at the end of each chapter, are based on Mark and Olly's considerable experience, extensive reading and compelling commitment to evidence-informed approaches. Case studies from guest contributors provide powerful examples of innovative practice, and the book is rich in useful resources and references. Individual chapters on the use of EdTech in English, maths, science, humanities and languages should be invaluable for subject specialists and co-ordinators. This book is recommended for education professionals of all levels of experience.

Dr Jill Berry, former headteacher, now leadership development consultant

The joy of this book comes from the way it shares such a wealth of knowledge and insight in a practical, reassuring way. *The EdTech Playbook* takes a subject-by-subject approach, illuminated by thoughtful case studies, which bring the recommendations to life with a wealth of classroom examples. Mark and Olly's thoughtful and pragmatic advice continually and brilliantly reminds the reader to value what they know about analogue teaching, with 'technology should enhance, not direct, learning' as a key message throughout.

Dr Helen Drury, founder and ex-executive director of Mathematics Mastery; chair of Expert Advisory Council, Ark Curriculum Plus; dean, Maths Excellence Fund

Mark and Olly's book covers not only the technology but also, more critically, the *why* and *how*. A critical look at adoption and what it means for our implementation, pedagogical practices and cognitive processes, backed with research the whole way through, including realistic teacher chalkface tips that I will be using! Neither overly optimistic nor technologically taking us back to the dark ages. This book is just realistic about what we need to consider in using technology in classrooms and is pitched perfectly to make it an accessible read!

A masterpiece that will be joining my very, very limited collection of excellence on EdTech.

Caroline Keep, teacher, data scientist, and PhD researcher on digitalisation in education

The EdTech Playbook offers a compelling and timely guide on how and, more importantly, why we should build a more thoughtful and purposeful relationship with educational technology in schools. Packed with carefully crafted advice, this book helped me reflect on the rapid adoption of EdTech during the COVID lockdowns, which led to innovation and some great practice around instruction and feedback, but also reminded me how easy it is to revert to old habits. While the book consistently reaffirms the irreplaceable role of teachers, the focus on evidence-based practices and how technology can enhance learning for all students is fresh and exciting. As Mark implies with the phrase 'is the juice worth the squeeze?' when thinking about adoption of tech, this book certainly is worth the squeeze. A must-read for educators looking to navigate EdTech effectively.

Pete Jones, head of teaching, learning and assessment, Les Quennevais School

There have been many books written about the use of digital technology in education, but importantly, this is a post-pandemic expert view taking stock of what we've learned in that time to ensure we make the best use of what we've got, what we buy and what we might want our technology to achieve. Mark and Olly use their vast experience of what they've used, seen and advised on to bring us an easy-to-navigate roadmap that allows teachers and school leaders to ensure that technology is helping, not hindering, when it comes to enhancing the learning experiences of our students.

Whether you're looking for inspiration on using digital technology to improve your teaching and delivery skills so that students are able to understand and remember more information; curious about how technology can make assessment and feedback more effective; searching for ways to increase the accessibility of your lessons; finding ways for students to become creators and not just consumers; or searching for ideas on adding to the digital skills of both the adults and the children in your school, then this book has you covered. An essential read for teachers and leaders of all ages and phases.

Jon Tait, director of education, Northern Lights Learning Trust

The EdTech Playbook is an inspiring and insightful guide for educators eager to harness the power of technology in the classroom. Drawing on a rich history of educational technology, it offers a comprehensive view of the digital landscape, highlighting both past lessons and future possibilities.

It emphasises the importance of purposeful use of technology and provides detailed, practical examples applicable across a range of curriculum areas with the inclusion of 'top tips' at the end of each chapter for quick, actionable takeaways making this playbook not just informative but immediately useful.

'Every day is a learning day' and whether you're new to EdTech or looking to refine your approach, this playbook offers essential insights to enhance learning outcomes through thoughtful and impactful use of technology.

Wendy Brissett, head of teaching, learning and innovation,
Reaseheath College

ABOUT THE AUTHORS

Mark is an award-winning former teacher, middle leader and senior leader with more than 20 years of experience at the chalkface. He also happens to be an award-winning author, blogger, keynote speaker and strategic EdTech consultant who provides training and consultancy support for schools around the world. Renowned for his pedagogically effective practices with EdTech and AI, his last book topped the book charts on Amazon, and his blog has won numerous awards, including the UK Education Blog of the Year award. Alongside this, Mark is a founding fellow of the Chartered College of Teaching, an Independent Thinking Associate and works part-time as the head of education at NetSupport. He also co-founded www.global-edtech.com and the Global EdTech awards (an initiative that aims to support ethical approaches to awards in the EdTech space). Mark is also a serving member of the schools and colleges committee for the BCS (Chartered Institute for IT).

Olly is renowned for his innovative practice and ability to bring people on that journey in the schools he has led in and the wider world beyond. A multi-award-winning educator and leader, his influence extends beyond the classroom through his online innovations, such as the GESS award-winning LearnLiveUAE that he co-founded with Mark Anderson. He is also a GESS Awards judge (and why wouldn't he be as he has won two of them) and is recognised as being the most influential educator in the Middle East in EdTech and purposeful teaching, learning and leadership practices, also recognised as an Edruptor by ISC Research. A founding fellow of the Chartered College of Teaching, Olly has almost two decades of teaching, middle leadership and senior leadership experience covering academics, pastoral and trust-wide roles, both in the UK and UAE.

Mark and Olly have collaborated on numerous projects over the years, such as The EdTech Show and the GESS award-winning LearnLiveUAE. Through a shared belief in the power of technology to transform teaching, learning and leadership, Mark and Olly's friendship has seen them work together in many guises, which have led to them joining forces yet again to create *The EdTech Playbook*.

Mark: Being a parent is one of the greatest joys and privileges of my life and I strive every day to try and make my two amazing boys proud of me. Dougie and Oscar, this book is for you.

Olly: Stefania and Emilia, you are my joy, inspiration, encouragement and source of all love and support. This book is for you.

CONTENTS

Foreword _____ x

Introduction _____ xiii

Chapter 1: Why EdTech hasn't worked historically _____ 1

Chapter 2: Models for learning with technology _____ 11

Chapter 3: Instructional delivery methods with technology _____ 45

Chapter 4: Effective digital transformation _____ 55

Chapter 5: Cognitive science with technology _____ 79

Chapter 6: Using technology to demonstrate learning _____ 101

Chapter 7: Accessibility for all _____ 115

Chapter 8: Feedback and assessment with technology _____ 133

Chapter 9: Artificial intelligence and XR _____ 161

Chapter 10: Using technology in English _____ 187

Chapter 11: Using technology in maths _____ 201

Chapter 12: Using technology in science _____ 215

Chapter 13: Using technology in humanities _____ 235

Chapter 14: Using technology in languages _____ 253

Chapter 15: Using technology to manage learning _____ 265

Chapter 16: Online safety and digital citizenship _____ 283

Chapter 17: Digital leadership _____ 311

Chapter 18: Ambassador roles _____ 329

Chapter 19: Working with vendors _____ 339

Chapter 20: Personal learning networks _____ 367

Conclusion _____ 377

Glossary _____ 379

References _____ 387

FOREWORD

This is an ambitious project. Mark Anderson and Olly Lewis, both titans in the field of EdTech, have drawn on their considerable experience to scope the opportunities and challenges related to the use of technology in education.

To quote them both, 'Technology should always serve learning, not dictate it.' In this careful deconstruction of the EdTech space, the authors have been mindful to keep this front and centre of their work. This is a good thing because the promise of technology to transform learning through the artefacts rather than the pedagogy has been expensive and often lacking the promised outcomes.

In this eminently accessible and well-written book, Mark and Olly frequently note that it is high-quality pedagogy underpinning the use of technology that has the greatest impact on learning. For example, they note that the Education Endowment Foundation (EEF) report on learning through lockdown showed that learning was able to continue and that it performed well when classic methods of clear explanations or modelling were employed. They also make the case that there are digital divides and that more needs to be done to ensure equitable access to the tools that will support learning.

An exploration of the different models and frameworks for considering the use of technology in education is particularly useful. What is interesting is that there is a long-established history of framing the aspects of technology under different elements and lenses and for some reading the book without a deep background knowledge of this, the analysis and benefits and disadvantages of the different taxonomies are particularly helpful.

It is very useful to have the different modes in which teaching and learning can take place explained in such a clear manner: the benefits and downsides of synchronous learning, asynchronous learning, remote learning, hybrid learning and blended learning. While it can seem overwhelming to develop ongoing professional learning for colleagues, again, *The EdTech Playbook* provides a workable and realistic step-by-step approach to supporting them. Much of the authors' advice is grounded in evidence-based approaches such as shared in the work of the EEF and its work on implementing change in educational settings.

Laden with insights and anecdotes from their own practice across many schools and jurisdictions around the world, the narrative brings the work to life – the challenges, the joys and the amusing elements. For example, Mark's account of introducing personal devices to 1,300 students in 2011, when there were no mechanisms for technical management of the devices. The tips from Mark and Olly at the end of each chapter help to synthesise the main points and keep us grounded; for example, Olly says that we shouldn't be afraid to ask students for help! In my experience, they have always relished the chance to show their expertise.

The playbook makes many references to cognition and the learning sciences and helpfully shows how technology can support low-stakes quizzes, retrieval practice, spaced and deliberate practice, dual coding, direct instruction and metacognition. There are also neat suggestions for providing opportunities for students to show what they have learned, and I was particularly taken with the way that technology can support the development of oracy – podcasts, voice-based flashcards and voice-guided simulations.

There are some excellent points of clarification, for example:

> 'When asking learners to complete tasks that demonstrate their learning with technology, you must ensure you give them the tools to help them complete the task successfully. If you're going to ask students to create a timeline, then provide a timeline template. Don't make them spend time creating the timeline; you are most interested in them showing what they know, not their ability to create an attractive timeline. Equally, if you're going to ask students to generate a mind map, presentation, word cloud, spreadsheet to analyse results, or whatever it may be, be sure not to make them waste valuable lesson time creating repetitive elements that are not part of the assessment.'

The inclusion of case studies is helpful in terms of showing what high-quality technology looks like in the classroom. There are excellent examples of the use of AI to personalise learning, and of accessibility and inclusion for all, including some ground-breaking examples in alternative provision. Every aspect of classroom practice is showcased, including a significant section on the different forms of assessment and the ways in which digital mechanisms can support or hinder high-quality feedback for students. For those of us who have struggled to keep abreast of AI, there is an excellent overview and actionable points explained, together with its even more glamourous cousin XR which, I was happy to learn, is augmented, mixed and virtual reality!

To bring the conversation around to the potential for using EdTech productively within the subjects, there is a fantastic section on ideas to enhance learning, source resources and reduce workload across the curriculum. The chapter on online safety and digital citizenship is excellent and will provide a great aide-memoire for keeping this important aspect of provision front of our minds. Finally, Mark and Olly make the case for colleagues developing a personal learning network (PLN) online. As with the rest of the book, this is grounded in common sense, outlines the many benefits and provides some sage advice for getting it right!

At its heart, there is a simple mantra which Mark has articulated about making decisions about the use of technology: good use of technology will do these things – enhance learning, support teaching and reduce workload. I reckon that mantra should be on every staffroom wall!

Mary Myatt, education writer and speaker, 1st August 2024

INTRODUCTION

Why this book?

In the last few years, we have seen a catalyst in the adoption of, and attention to detail for, impactful and scalable technology. Just like our children on long car journeys, a question people often ask us is, 'Are we nearly there yet?' With so many promises of educational technology over the decades, from Banda machines to today, the unalienable truth is that we simply aren't!

While the destination for each organisation is rightly different, owing to contextualised variations, there are many common golden threads that we believe we can support through this book. Should you follow the advice, nuggets, approaches and frameworks provided, your journey should be more enjoyable, with plenty of pit stops along the way, with opportunities to explore the sights and sounds at every stage and chances to embed each element as you move through to the conclusion.

The truth is, every day is a learning day and while we will provide you with approaches, knowledge and frameworks to help you make the most of educational technology, the key determiner between success and failure is you. In the same way that as a teacher you can help your learners to succeed but their success is ultimately in their own hands, so too with this endeavour: your success is in your hands (hopefully like every good teacher).

Top issues globally in EdTech

Before we begin, a call to arms! We are united in the opinion that *education is the profession that creates all other professions*. In our ever-changing and evolving world, quite simply, technology can unleash possibilities for not only educators and students but also across all other sectors. Let us not forget, that any change or transformation, no matter how big or small, is rooted deeply first and foremost in people. It is not the technology but the empowered people that are the most important!

With this in mind, there are still many common strands relating to the world of EdTech, such as time, implementation strategies, stakeholder voice, finance, due diligence, relationships with **vendors**, and more. Our aim with this book is to tackle what we believe to be one of the most important: the educators serving in schools worldwide.

It will come as no secret to those readers who know us well that we are both hugely passionate about the force for good that technology can play in education when used strategically and with purpose. But here's the snag: just like the force, technology can be a double-edged sword. Not all tech is created equal, and we need to be mindful of how it can truly benefit us as teachers and our students' learning experiences, and how it can even help us lighten our workload. It isn't just about using technology all of the time but about making informed choices. We want you to be able to equip yourself with the knowledge to distinguish between the good, the bad and the meh!

So, for those of you who are new to us both, we hope that our passion shines through in this book and we look forward to taking you with us on our journey!

Reach out!

We both regularly share the power of a *professional learning network* **(PLN)**. We'd be delighted for you to share all that resonates with you while reading this book, whether it's an idea, something you've tried after reading this book, a new tool – anything! And if you've enjoyed the book then, of course, a review would be very well-received too!

Social channels

Please do reach out to us via our various social channels listed below and use the following hashtags: #EdTech, #EdTechPlaybook, #DigStrat, #AIinEdu.

X/Twitter

Mark: @ICTEvangelist
Olly: @OLewis_coaching

LinkedIn

Mark: www.linkedin.com/in/themarkanderson
Olly: www.linkedin.com/in/ollylewis

Instagram

Mark: www.instagram.com/ictevangelist
Olly: www.instagram.com/ollyl

Blogs

Mark: https://ictevangelist.com/blog
Olly: https://ollylewislearning.com

CHAPTER 1
Why EdTech hasn't worked historically

'Those who fail to learn from history are doomed to repeat it.'

George Santayana

To look to the future, we first need to learn from the past. And so, at the start of *The EdTech Playbook*, let's reflect on what has gone before and unpick what we can learn from it to share how we can improve, do better and *be* better.

1.1 The historical context

When it comes to educational technology, it's not like we haven't had opportunities to make it work over the years. Successive governments around the world have pumped billions into it.

EdTech is a global market with total investment, according to HolonIQ,[1] standing at $6.5 trillion in 2022. This equates to roughly 5% of the global spend on education. So why is it – even though both of us, as authors of this book, are probably two of the most ICT-savvy and pro-technology educators going – we are still left feeling like we need to ask the question, 'Are we nearly there yet?'

For all of the promise of technology, despite it having been in classrooms for many decades, we have yet to see the benefits the vendors so often have us believe are possible. 'Transform your teaching,' they say. 'Transform into what?' we ask.

In this chapter, we will explore some of the reasons why many implementations have failed to deliver – and throughout the rest of the book, we will look at some of the ways you can use technology to make multiple dents that, when aggregated, make a huge difference. The truth is, as we all know, there are no silver bullets in education! Anyone who tells you otherwise is a liar. Take the latest furore around artificial intelligence (AI), for example. 'This amazing resource took me

---

[1] www.holoniq.com/edtech-in-10-charts

under five minutes to produce,' you will hear. What they fail to share with you is that they have strong levels of confidence and competence, and are cognisant of what tools to use, where to find them, already have subscriptions to them, and know how to create fantastic resources with them. 'Mind the gap,' they say on the London Underground but, just as we teach our learners to be discerning readers of online content, we shouldn't believe everything we see being shared there either. If it seems too good to be true, you will more often than not find that it is.

In every educational setting, be it among students in the classroom or across the staff body, you will have a bell curve of experience in all manner of different topics. For any implementation to work, you need the average to move a significant number of positive standard deviations away from the mean. Any implementation is only ever as successful as your lowest common denominator.

1.2 Inherent problems with implementation

In the book, you will hear about the failed implementations of interactive whiteboards (IWBs) in the nineties and noughties, so here, let's explore more recent failures to implement correctly.

LAUSD, the Los Angeles Unified School District, spent $1B in 2012 to provide all Grade 4–12 students with an iPad, in a bid to improve student outcomes and transform learning (Blume and Ceasar, 2013). Marred with stories of chaos, the project was deemed a disaster. One of the largest issues LAUSD faced was that there was no clear plan for how the devices would actually be used in the classroom.

The secondary failing was that teachers received little or no training on how to use the devices, while there was also no clear curriculum plan or set of standards of how to embed technology into lessons to enhance learning. This resulted in teachers either ignoring the devices or students using them for non-educational purposes.

The project created further issues as devices were lost or broken, leaving LAUSD having to spend millions of dollars on repairs and replacements. In some schools, the security settings were set up incorrectly, so children were able to easily delete *mobile device management* **(MDM)** *profiles* from the devices. In addition, when things started going wrong, the parents didn't know if they were liable for the cost of the devices; some schools simply took the iPads from the students. Ultimately, the project caused more issues than it solved and was ditched, having cost LAUSD many millions of dollars and hours of learning time lost to failed implementation.

Managing technology transformation

Implementation of technology is something which has its core features embedded within the tenets of good change management. In his speech in 1991, Professor T. Knoster, Ed.D., shared a helpful change management diagram which not only highlighted the key aspects to consider when managing change but also revealed the issues that can occur when those aspects are neglected.

He stated that good change management needs to consider:

- vision
- skills
- motivation
- resources
- action plan.

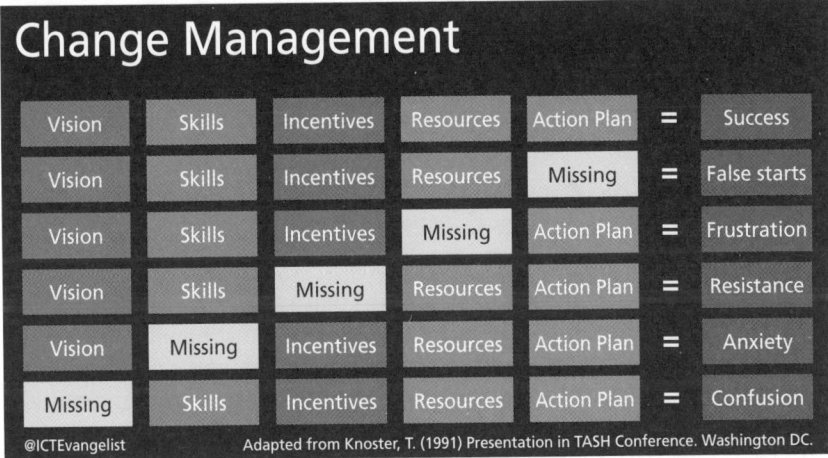

Figure 1.1: Change management

Mark has long used this framework to help guide implementation but, over the years, he learned that there was more to implementation than this. Consequently, he developed an extended version of Professor T. Knoster's diagram which included the following headings:

- vision
- community

- team
- sustainability
- environment
- continuing professional development (**CPD**)
- measurement
- learning.

Things to consider when creating your digital strategy

Vision	Community	Team	Sustainable	Environment	CPD	Measurement	Learning	=	Result
Vision	Community	Team	Sustainable	Environment	CPD	Measurement	Learning	=	Ongoing success
Vision	Community	Team	Sustainable	Environment	CPD	Measurement	Missing	=	Failure
Vision	Community	Team	Sustainable	Environment	CPD	Missing	Learning	=	No success
Vision	Community	Team	Sustainable	Environment	Missing	Measurement	Learning	=	Anxiety
Vision	Community	Team	Sustainable	Missing	CPD	Measurement	Learning	=	Frustration
Vision	Community	Team	Missing	Environment	CPD	Measurement	Learning	=	Unsustainable
Vision	Community	Missing	Sustainable	Environment	CPD	Measurement	Learning	=	Confusion
Vision	Missing	Team	Sustainable	Environment	CPD	Measurement	Learning	=	Resistance
Missing	Community	Team	Sustainable	Environment	CPD	Measurement	Learning	=	False starts

Created by Mark Anderson @ICTEvangelist   ICT EVANGELIST

Figure 1.2: Things to consider when creating your digital strategy

- **Vision** – This means ensuring that your vision is clear, articulated, regularly shared and understood by all. Fail to do this and you will experience false starts.

- **Community** – This means ensuring that all stakeholders are involved in the implementation process, from students to teachers to office staff, site staff, support staff, parents, governors/trustees and even local businesses and authorities where appropriate. For your implementation to work, all parties must be considered, involved, listened to and part of the process. Fail to involve your community and you will experience resistance.

- **Team** – For leadership to successfully manage this change, it is essential to have a good team around you – from technical to teaching and learning, to middle and senior leaders, to the teachers in the classroom and the students and their behaviour. 'Don't build your house on sandy land,' the adage goes. If you want a technology implementation to work, adding technology to a school that already has issues around teaching, learning, behaviour and attitudes to teaching/learning, means that all you are going to do is amplify rather than solve them. Fail to involve people and have a good team around you and you will experience confusion.

- **Sustainability** – Sound financial management is the cornerstone of any good school. As we share in more detail later in the book, schools are businesses and have fiscal responsibilities. You might be able to afford a device rollout now, but can you afford the infrastructure costs? Can you afford to replace devices (including staff devices) on a rolling cycle, moving forward in three, six or nine years? Fail to consider sustainability and your project will be unsustainable.

- **Environment** – You may think this is purely a consideration around infrastructure (and you would be partly right) but when considering your environment, you should also consider learning spaces, classrooms, the ability to charge devices, storage locations, and much more. Another aspect to consider is shown by the example of Chiltern Learning Trust,[2] which commits to planting five trees for every device it purchases. It is also important to consider how you will manage your IT estate. Consider what management solutions you will use to manage your devices and what IT asset management tools you will use to help shepherd appropriate use and positive etiquette for learning in the classroom and beyond. Fail to consider your environment and your community will experience frustration.

- **CPD** – Supporting colleagues with timely, effective and efficient CPD and support when they need it is one of the most important aspects to consider when implementing anything in education. Whether it's *retrieval practice*, *spaced practice* or GCSE Pigeon Studies, it doesn't really matter. As stated before, if staff don't have the confidence, competence and cognisance to consistently use the strategies within your context, then the implementation is doomed to failure. There are many ways you can support this, through **synchronous** or **asynchronous** access to training, in-the-moment support from student ambassadorship groups such as digital leaders and many more. Fail to provide quality and timely CPD and colleagues will experience anxiety.

- **Measurement** – Without measurement, how will you know whether your implementation has been successful? By setting up regular qualitative and quantitative checks on your key performance indicators (KPIs) you will be able to benchmark your journey and improvement

---

[2] https://ecologi.com/freedomtech/chilternlearningtrust

over time. Fail to measure your project and you won't know if you've been successful.

- **Learning** – When it comes to teaching and learning with technology, the technology should serve learning, not the other way around. You all know the adage, 'Fail to prepare, prepare to fail.' If you don't consider learning as the anchor upon which everything else sits within your implementation, you are doomed to failure from the start. Most things about whole-school use of technology should be centred around learning. 'Pedagogy first,' Mark often shares – and it should be your North Star around which everything else orbits.

1.3 What the pandemic taught us

The beginning of 2020 saw a seismic shift for not just the world of education but the entire world. At the onset of the COVID-19 pandemic, suddenly, the whole world went online. In the rush to do so, we quickly saw those who were ready for that move and those who were not. Those who had long sung the praises of one-to-one initiatives for students and those who were already confidently, competently and cognisantly using EdTech pivoted with relative ease. Those who had always pushed back against technology, for whatever reason, found this shift particularly difficult. These types of schools turned to the photocopier, sending out massive packs of worksheets to children at huge costs to the school – on both a fiscal front and in terms of the time taken to produce such resources. If only they had the foresight to recognise the benefits of paperless working, so much time, effort and money would not have been wasted. Many of these schools also jumped quickly to use platforms that were often inappropriate and without regard for data privacy, security and, more importantly, functionality. Mark remembers well the problems faced by his children, given the choice of platform made by their school. It was like the Wild West. Without the time to plan and map out a digital strategy using some of the ideas shared earlier in this chapter, many schools were ill-prepared.

Organisations such as the Education Endowment Foundation (EEF) rushed to support with documents such as its Rapid Evidence Assessment Report (EEF, 2020). But, for many, it was too late and leaders and teachers in these types of schools were often ill-placed to know what it was they were even looking at, let alone whether their teachers would be able to use it or families would be able to support it.

Equally, we saw key companies such as Microsoft and Google rushed to further develop products such as Microsoft Teams and Google Meet – even Zoom quickly jumped on the remote learning bandwagon. To support schools, many vendors, such as NetSupport and CENTURY Tech, started giving away their software for free in a bid to help as best they could.

With the benefit of hindsight, we would like to think that schools would have learned from this experience, yet in the time since the last (UK) lockdown, many of the schools that previously weren't prepared for remote learning have taken technology off the agenda again. We understand some of the reasons for this, particularly around the cost-of-living crisis and significantly low school budgets, but schools have always faced financial constraints. Where there is a will, there is always a way.

One of the major positives of the remote learning period was the significant upskilling of teachers with their knowledge of how to use technology appropriately. The situation meant teachers *had* to use technology to do their jobs and many saw the significant benefits that it can bring. Things such as reduced marking time through using audio feedback, more efficient and well-organised parents' evenings through remote tools like Microsoft Teams, asynchronous access to online learning resources and, despite whatever political thinking you might have, fantastic free online resources such as Oak National Academy.[3]

It is now, unfortunately, the case that many teachers have reverted to their former ways of teaching and learning without technology. It is such a shame to see this. All the hard work, professional learning and significant gains are starting to be lost. We know through our professional practice that without regular and repeated revisiting of learning, we soon forget – and without support in school where technology is high on the agenda, things can quickly fall off your radar. While we may have taken many steps forward during the pandemic, we are certainly now starting to take many steps back.

It's not all doom and gloom though! The global picture for educational technology reflects that far more schools prioritise technology as part of their ongoing curriculum models and, in more recent times, with the explosion of AI, teachers are starting to realise that while, in the short to medium-term, technology will not replace them, they will be replaced by teachers who *do* use technology to support their everyday practice.

---

[3] www.thenational.academy

1.4 Relationships and the importance of a growth mindset

Relationships are the foundation of so many things in life and we see this every day in classrooms around the world. Those teachers who take the time to foster positive relationships and mutual respect with their learners, celebrating the wins and learning from the things that don't quite go to plan, all help to create a positive learning environment.

Mark remembers his time as a form tutor and the benefits of taking time at the beginning of the academic year to touch base and make connections with the parents of new tutees in his form group. Showing a genuine interest in his students meant that every conversation he had in the future was grounded in the knowledge that he had a good working relationship with their parents and carers. Whether it was a Friday praise call or a conversation about poor behaviour in class, the parents and carers knew that he was always working to support their children as best he could, whether it was a difficult conversation or not. Never underestimate the power of positive relationships and mutual respect.

The same is true with the colleagues you work with and your approaches to your work together. According to Hattie and his research on what works in education, it continues to be the case that collective teacher efficacy has one of the greatest impacts on school improvement. He states:

> 'Collective teacher efficacy (CTE) is the collective belief of the staff of the school/faculty in their ability to positively affect students. CTE has been found to be strongly, positively correlated with student achievement. A school staff that believes it can collectively accomplish great things is vital for the health of a school and if they believe they can make a positive difference then they very likely will.' (Hattie, 2018)

It is therefore important that if teaching and learning with technology is an item of priority on your school improvement plan, then leaders must create the conditions for success where all colleagues feel (despite knowing it might be difficult) that they can use technology, use it well and consistently – with all colleagues seeking to develop their technical knowledge to make that happen.

Part of that means strong and consistent leadership, just as you would as a teacher in the classroom, by strong modelling of effort, resilience and a bit of determination to succeed – often seen as the core ingredients in what Carol Dweck calls '*growth mindset*'.

Dweck's research has shown that people with a growth mindset are more likely to succeed than those with a fixed mindset. They are more likely to take on challenges, persist in the face of setbacks and learn from their mistakes.

As someone on a journey looking to further develop your confidence, competence and cognisance of technology for teaching and learning, remember these things. Whether you're the headteacher who struggles with some of the tools your teachers will be learning to use, or you are the teacher yourself, persistence is key and role modelling is something we would argue is essential. It is through this approach that CTE will grow and, ultimately, before you know it (even though it is likely to happen through **marginal gains** when you aggregate them for yourself and your colleagues across your workplace), you'll see progress.

As a leader, getting your vision right is hard but ensuring it is heard is even more difficult. It's important to set out your roadmap and share it as often as possible in as many ways as possible. Consider the different ways you can share it while walking the talk with it in the very fabric of everything you do. It takes courage and belief, but with that, CTE can be achieved.

Challenge yourself. Don't be afraid to take on new challenges (even if you're not sure you can succeed) and be persistent. Don't give up when you face setbacks. Talk about the problems you have faced and how you overcame them with your peers. Learn from your (and their) mistakes and see them as opportunities to learn and grow together.

Be positive. A positive attitude can go a long way. Believe in yourself and your ability to succeed. You wouldn't be in the job and position you are now if you hadn't shown that you could do it before, so why wouldn't that be the case now?

As you work through the rest of this book, take it all one page at a time. Take your time. Make notes. Pick out the elements that you think will help you. Try them out. Talk about them with your colleagues. Have a go. Get them wrong. Learn.

Most importantly, as we'll discuss throughout the book, be guided by what will best help you either with your teaching, to reduce your workload, or to help young people with their learning. This approach will keep you on track and laser-focused on what will best support your work as an educator.

Finally, as you'll see below, at the end of each chapter, we have collated our top tips from it. As you progress through the book, feel free to use these as areas to focus on. You don't have to do that exactly though, as these are our choices and the areas that have worked brilliantly for us over the years. These might not be the best option or choice for you. The process of learning is a journey. We don't all start out knowing everything. Nobody does. And so, we see this as a book to help you as you start your digital learning journey.

As Mark shares widely, 'Every day is a learning day' and your learning about teaching, learning and technology will grow far beyond what you gain from reading this book.

Be bold. Be brave. But most of all, be you!

Top tips

Mark's top tips

1. Start small. Simple things like keyboard shortcuts, while small, can make a big difference to productivity.

2. Don't compare your progress or use of technology to that of others. Everyone's journey will be different.

3. Don't be afraid to ask students for help. You'll be amazed at what they know and they'll likely be thrilled that you've asked them and that they have been able to help.

Olly's top tips

1. Know your starting point (no matter how good/bad it is) and get granular about the current state of play so that you can use it as a springboard to start from.

2. It has been some time now since the pandemic. What digital skills have you developed since then? How has your school supported that growth? Have you shared these skills and any new knowledge with colleagues in your school? Now is the time to start sharing those skills and tips again. Remember, we can all learn from one another!

3. Gather data. It helps to inform, serve as evidence and steer the direction by highlighting what's needed, what's working and what isn't.

CHAPTER 2
Models for learning with technology

'Letting the pedagogy define how you use the technology, rather than letting the technology drive the curriculum, is a sure-fire way of making sure you don't leave the success of the learning in your classroom to chance.'

Mark Anderson, *Perfect ICT Every Lesson*

A cornerstone of teaching practice over the years has been taxonomies – touchpoints, if you will – that teachers have been able to use to help frame their practice and pedagogy. We all know of Bloom's and Maslow's hierarchy of needs; we might even have used **SOLO taxonomy** in our everyday classroom practice.

Yet it's surprising that there is still a lack of knowledge of the various taxonomies that people can use to help them unpick strategies around how to think about the use of technology and the effective approaches available to help frame that thinking.

Back in 2016, Mark created a flow chart[1] to help ask questions about whether an EdTech tool was pedagogically valid. It was framed from a blog post[2] that had been written by Paul Moss (@EDmerger on X).

---

[1] https://ictevangelist.com/is-that-edtech-tool-pedagogically-valid
[2] https://paulgmoss.com/2016/11/08/is-that-edtech-tool-pedagogically-valid

The EdTech Playbook

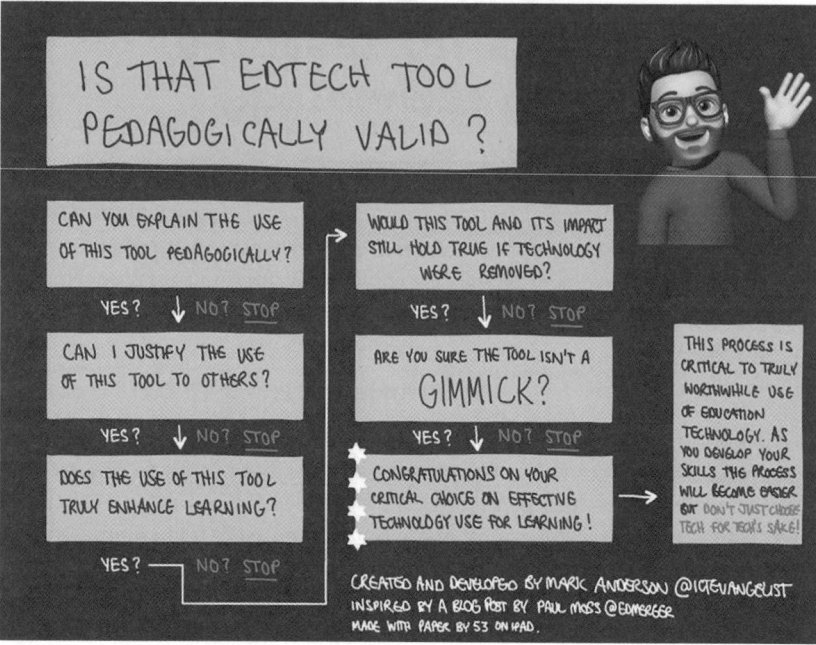

Figure 2.1: Is that EdTech tool pedagogically valid?

Of course, there's a lot more to the thinking around what constitutes a pedagogically valid approach to using technology than these questions. Firstly, there's the knowledge of teaching and learning strategies; then there's the knowledge of the different taxonomies and how they can be applied. While the flow chart might seem simple, there is a lot that should be considered within the constructs of the seemingly simple questions.

In this chapter, we'll explore some of the taxonomies linked to the use of technology, the benefits of using them, what they can mean for you as a teacher and what that might look like in the classroom. This will help frame your thinking around some of the key questions in this flow chart. In chapter 3, we'll explore different instructional delivery methods with technology which will further support your learning and thinking to enable you to think more deeply about the questions above. Then, in chapter 5, we'll explore cognitive science and what we've learned about how we learn which, when combined with the other chapters, will hopefully give you plenty of food for thought and a broader understanding of the issues and nuances tied in with each of the questions in the flow chart.

2.1 RAT

No, we aren't stepping back to the 1980s and thinking about UB40's classic about rats in the kitchen. Postulated by Dr Joan Hughes in her dissertation researching how teachers integrate technology into their teaching, her model (in a similar fashion to **SAMR** – see page 15) aimed to map the level at which a use of technology either replaces (R), amplifies (A) or transforms (T) teaching and learning.

More specifically:

Replacement	Technology serves as a different (digital) means to the same instructional practices.
Amplification	Technology increases efficiency, effectiveness and productivity of same instructional practices.
Transformation	Technology invents new instruction, learning or curricula.

Table 2.1: RAT

The model became popular because of its efforts to help answer the question, 'How is the use of technology influencing the teacher's existing practice?' It's an important question to ask, but it's equally important to recognise the question being asked. The question, after all, is not, 'How can we make better use of technology?'

This is a critical distinction to make, as the RAT framework isn't one to help us examine what a good approach is, but to reflect on the practice that we are undertaking in our classrooms already and help us characterise and examine the technology use taking place.

Jump forwards to 2020, and Royce Kimmons (an associate professor of instructional psychology and technology at Brigham Young University) postulated putting RAT alongside another framework, PIC (loosely linked to Bloom's taxonomy and where the letters stand for passive, interactive and creative). The **PICRAT** model aimed to map passive, interactive and creative (a higher-order thinking skill in Bloom's taxonomy) activities with technology against Hughes' RAT framework in a bit of a matrix:

The EdTech Playbook

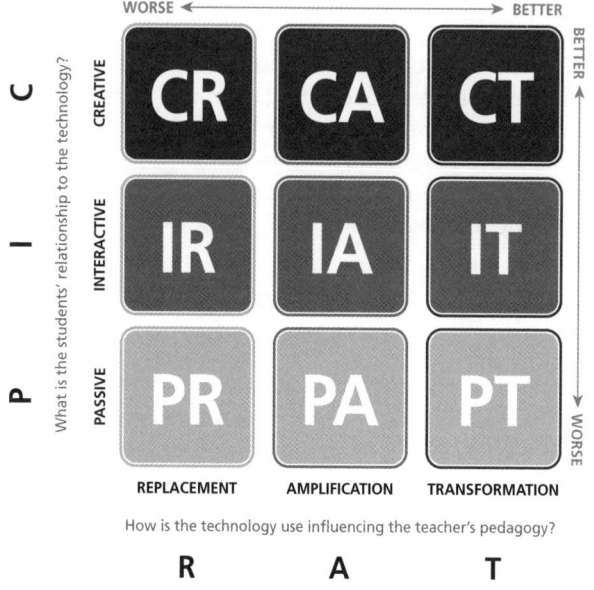

Figure 2.2: PICRAT model (source: Hughes and Roblyer, 2023)

The fact that it includes the words 'worse' and 'better' always rang alarm bells with us. As we've said, technology should always *serve* learning, not dictate it. We shouldn't try to shoehorn in the use of technology for the sake of it. So with that in mind, from our perspective, PICRAT has always caused concern.

In addition to that and its links to Bloom's taxonomy (which is really not supported by any empirical research on learning), it can leave you wondering what use PICRAT has in today's teaching and learning environments.

PICRAT does have its place in helping you to appraise the use of technology taking place within your classroom or across your wider school. It will also help you to characterise the potential uses for others to learn from as opportunities to explore what is possible. What it does not do is give a roadmap for good use. We'll explore that later on in this chapter. Being mindful of PICRAT's place and usefulness means it can be a tool in your arsenal to inform your choices about what you use technology for, but it should probably not be used to guide you on what good technology use is or should be.

2.2 SAMR

In a similar way to PICRAT, SAMR (the substitution, augmentation, modification, redefinition model developed by Dr Ruben Puentedura), was a tool that was heavily popularised during the growth of one-to-one device rollouts. It was also massively supported by the likes of Apple and educators using Apple's tablet technologies such as the iPad.

Like PICRAT, it is a useful framework upon which to think about your use of technology in the classroom. It is, however, not a good tool to try to pitch yourself to the top in terms of its use and related usefulness in the classroom.

The model looks like this:

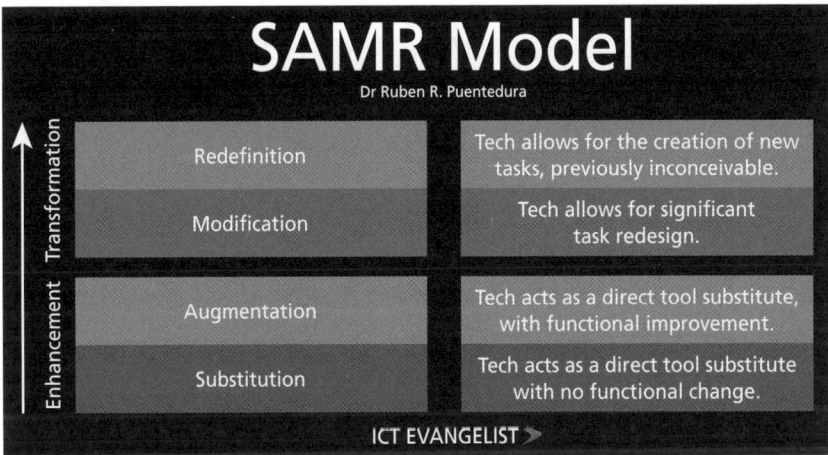

Figure 2.3: SAMR model (1)

The bottom section of the model contains the substitution and augmentation levels; these are known as the 'enhancement' levels. This is where technology is used to replace an existing analogue activity.

A good example of this might be note-taking in class. A child could, for example, simply take notes in their books each lesson and have them as a long-term record of the activities done in class. They could be interspersed with worksheets that have been completed and stuck into their book. Structure strips might have been used to help scaffold and guide the learning activities within them, but importantly, no technology has been used.

The EdTech Playbook

If a child had simply typed those notes into a document, this would be seen as a substitution activity; you're simply replacing an analogue activity with a digital one and, as Puentedura purports, there is no 'functional change'.

If the child had perhaps copied a photograph from the internet to supplement their notes, or used some of the formatting features to highlight particularly important facts or figures, then this would be seen as a functional improvement. It is, however, still seen as just an enhancement; hence, while it would now be seen as 'augmentation', it still isn't a particularly in-depth use of technology.

The following graphic develops the previous one but also includes explanations of activities that might demonstrate 'transformational' use, where note-taking is transformed using technology.

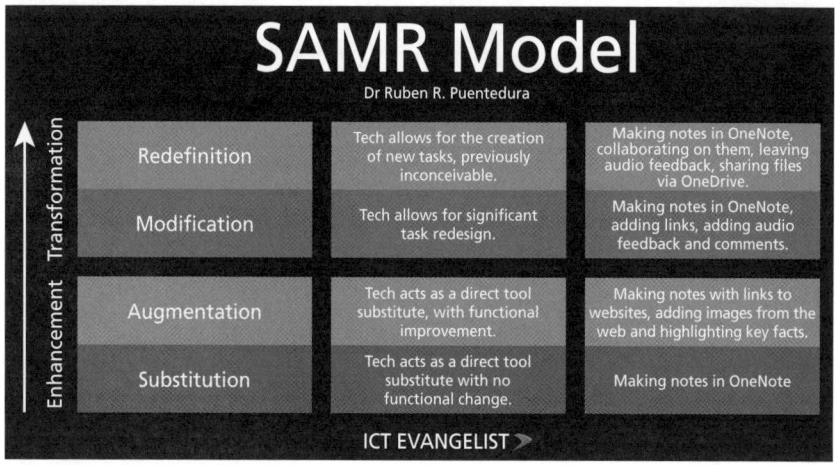

Figure 2.4: SAMR model (2)

As you can see with the transformation levels, the additional activities shown on modification and redefinition couldn't be completed in an analogue way. You couldn't, for example, leave audio feedback on your notes. You couldn't easily collaborate and share your notes with others in the room – or anywhere else in the world, for that matter.

Technology provides us with the opportunity to do things that weren't previously possible. This is a key tenet of the transformation level in the SAMR model, in that the activities shown here must use technology to do things which wouldn't otherwise be possible.

The problem with this is similar to that of RAT and other taxonomies such as Bloom's. There is a tendency to think that, because they are taxonomies and ladder-like, we should always be pushing to the top and that redefinition or activities asking learners to create something is surely the best approach. We know that simply isn't the case.

As we have grown to better understand how we learn and what makes for good technology use for learning, we now know that, like with Bloom's, ensuring our learners have a firm grounding in their subject knowledge is far more important than giving learners activities that are linked to 'higher-order thinking' skills. Equally, we now know that just because we can do something with technology (that would indicate redefinition), doesn't necessarily mean that we should.

Studies have proven time and time again that it is often not the 'super-cool' things you can do with technology that help with teaching or learning, but the more mundane, 'run-of-the-mill' activities that are most likely to have the biggest impact.

Therefore, when unpicking SAMR, just as we did with RAT, it is true that substitution activities with technology can often be just as useful (if not more useful) to learning than those that seek to be redefinition. Even simple note-taking at an augmentation or substitution level, while being supported by technologies that remove distractions, can help learners. Whether or not note-taking helps with learning itself is another matter, but the use of technology in this way brings many benefits, such as:

- access to learning content
- presentation of learning
- use of accessibility tools that are helpful to all and essential for many
- compilation of learning undertaken in classes
- organisation of notes and learning activities
- ease of access to research
- ease of feedback to the student.

When you bring these approaches together so that they are undertaken consistently across all classes, the ease of access means that you can start to enjoy these kinds of benefits at scale – for every teacher and every student in every subject they study.

2.3 So, what works?

There are many studies that have explored what works when it comes to teaching and learning with technology. The COVID-19 pandemic brought a laser focus onto this at its height when lockdowns and the associated requirement of remote learning was in place. In April 2020, the EEF brought together its 'Rapid Evidence Assessment' report (EEF, 2020a) which, at 29 pages long, summarised the findings from 60 systematic reviews and meta-analyses answers in the following areas:

- remote teaching and learning
- *blended learning*
- *computer-supported collaborative learning*
- *computer-assisted instruction*
- *games for learning.*

It shared five important key findings which are just as pertinent today as they were then – in fact, post-pandemic, it could be said that many of them are even more important.

1. Teaching quality is more important than how lessons are delivered

'Pupils can learn through remote teaching. Ensuring the elements of effective teaching are present – for example, clear explanations, scaffolding and feedback – is more important than how or when they are provided. There was no clear difference between teaching in real time ("synchronous teaching") and alternatives ("asynchronous teaching"). For example, teachers might explain a new idea live or in a pre-recorded video. But what matters most is whether the explanation builds clearly on pupils' prior learning or how pupils' understanding is subsequently assessed.' (EEF, 2020a)

This goes to reinforce the adage that good teaching is good teaching. No amount of technology can change that. Ensuring good pedagogy is of paramount importance. This also reinforces comments made earlier in this chapter considering the different characteristics of PICRAT and SAMR. Just because you *can* do something with technology doesn't necessarily mean that you *should*. It's important to keep the main thing 'the main thing', which is ensuring solid and grounded teaching practice.

2. Ensuring access to technology is key, particularly for disadvantaged pupils

'Almost all remote learning uses digital technology, typically requiring access to both computers and the internet. Many reviews identify a lack of technology as a barrier to successful remote instruction. It is important that support is provided to ensure that disadvantaged pupils – who are more likely to face these barriers – have access to technology. In addition to providing access to technology, ensuring that teachers and pupils are provided with support and guidance to use specific platforms is essential, particularly if new forms of technology are being implemented.' (EEF, 2020a)

Post-pandemic, we have seen economies hit hard, not just in the UK but globally. There has been a big hit on school budgets and here in the UK there have been massive inflation rises resulting in a crisis for many families where they are having to make hard choices just on the basics for everyday life, such as heating and eating.

The gap has grown considerably between the haves and the have-nots; more children live in poverty in the UK than ever before. The point made here about ensuring 'support is provided to ensure that disadvantaged pupils ... have access to technology' has never been more pertinent, yet ironically, it is those most disadvantaged pupils who would stand to gain the most benefit from having access to technology to support their learning.

3. Peer interactions can provide motivation and improve learning outcomes

'Multiple reviews highlight the importance of peer interaction during remote learning, as a way to motivate pupils and improve outcomes. Across the studies reviewed, a range of strategies to support peer interaction were explored, including peer marking and feedback, sharing models of good work, and opportunities for live discussions of content. The value of collaborative approaches was emphasised in many reviews, although notably many studies involved older learners. Different approaches to peer interaction are likely to be better suited to different age groups.' (EEF, 2020a)

This is an activity that, post-pandemic, we can more easily engage in with our learners as they are most likely now learning in the same space within a classroom. However, there are still many ways we can use technology to facilitate peer interaction in the classroom:

- peer feedback
- collaborative research
- brainstorming ideas
- creating low-stakes quizzes
- virtual group work
- project planning using online tools
- digital artefact creation.

The key is to make sure that the technology doesn't dictate the learning activity but enhances it as part of the content and pedagogy you are delivering to bring the outcomes your learners need.

4. Supporting pupils to work independently can improve learning outcomes

'Pupils learning at home will often need to work independently. Multiple reviews identify the value of strategies that help pupils work independently with success. For example, prompting pupils to reflect on their work or to consider the strategies they will use if they get stuck have been highlighted as valuable. Wider evidence related to metacognition and self-regulation suggests that disadvantaged pupils are likely to particularly benefit from explicit support to help them work independently, for example, by providing checklists or daily plans.' (EEF, 2020a)

Metacognition and *self-regulation* are key to successful learning outcomes for pupils, and, as you'll discover, there are many ways that technology can help with both.

5. Different approaches to remote learning suit different tasks and types of content

'Approaches to remote learning vary widely and have different strengths and weaknesses. Teachers should be supported to consider which approaches are best suited to the content they are teaching and the age of their pupils. For example, games for learning were found to have a high impact on vocabulary learning in foreign languages, but there is less evidence relating to their use in other subjects. Likewise, using technology to support retrieval practice and self-quizzing can help pupils retain key ideas and knowledge, but is not a replacement for other forms of assessment.' (EEF, 2020a)

There are some great caveats shared here, but without wanting to repeat things, it is important to note some of the key points.

Context is key. Just like no two students are the same, no two schools are the same either. We have best bets for learning of course, but as you'll learn later in this chapter when we explore **TPACK**, good teaching and learning with technology is about developing your technological knowledge and knowing when to use technology or not (as sometimes that's the best choice).

It does lead nicely on to thinking more deeply about methodologies that work. Throughout the book, we highlight lots of evidence-informed approaches – and we wanted to share another seminal and exceedingly useful document from the Education Endowment Foundation.

In March 2019, it released its 'Using Digital Technology to Improve Learning' guidance report (EEF, 2020b) which shared four approaches, three of which are worthy of deeper exploration here.

The report is broken down into four sections:

1. Consider how technology will improve teaching and learning before introducing it.
2. Technology can be used to improve the quality of explanations and modelling.
3. Technology offers ways to improve the impact of pupil practice.
4. Technology can play a role in improving assessment and feedback.

The EdTech Playbook

It summarises them in this graphic:

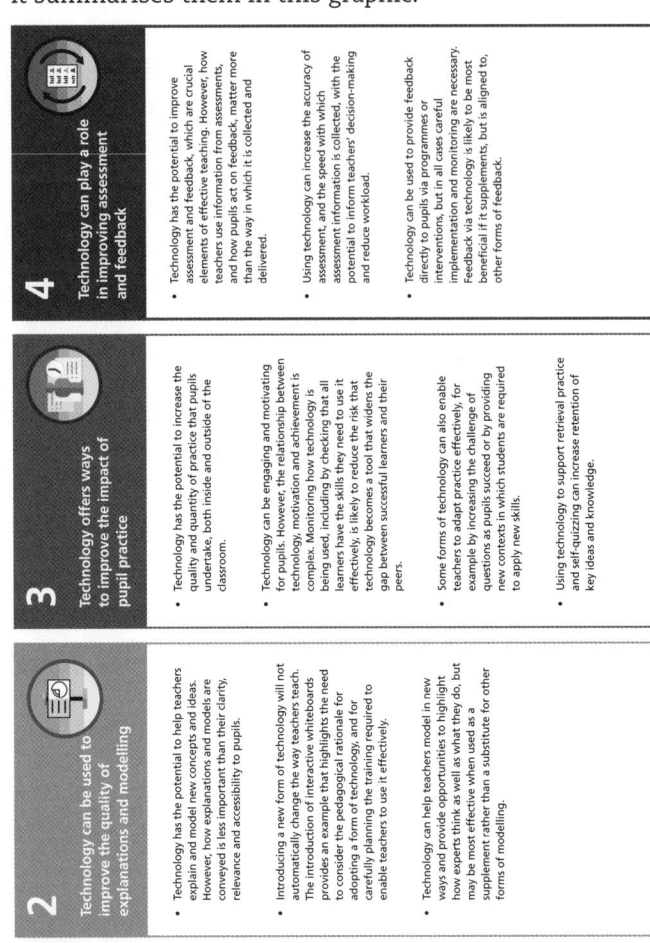

Figure 2.5: 'Using Digital Technology to Improve Learning' (source: EEF, 2020b)

Section 1 is the best advice out of the four, and marries nicely with the fifth point shared in the EEF's 'Rapid Evidence Assessment' report.

Its point about how technology can become a solution in search of a problem is key. Technology purchasing and subsequent use in education should always come from a clear and identified need. This seems like absolute common sense but how many schools have you worked in where you find previous technology purchases in a cupboard at the back of the classroom gathering dust?

Let's dive more deeply into points 2 and 3, which ask us to consider how technology can improve explanations and modelling and the impact of pupil practice.

Improving explanations and modelling

Explanations and modelling are essentials of good teaching and learning. And, as one of the pioneers of **direct instruction**, Siegfried Engelmann, said: 'Direct Instruction, the greatest educational intervention ever designed'. Passing over his obvious arrogance at a statement describing his own intervention strategy(!), it has been found to have considerable benefits, particularly for students who struggle academically.

Direct instruction is just one part of the picture though. Explanations and modelling shared with learners which are methodical, accessible, memorable/engaging and clear (Wittwer and Renkl, 2010) are the most likely to be high-quality and effective. Of course, these don't need to include technology but, when we do use technology to enhance and support our practice where those explanations and modelling are aligned to the pedagogical principles at play, we may be more likely to see benefits. Implementation is, as always, the determiner of success.

In its report, the EEF states the oft-quoted example of IWB implementations.

> 'In the early 2000s, the government funded a large-scale pilot introducing interactive whiteboards to Primary classrooms in England. One of the goals of the pilot was to raise attainment in literacy and mathematics, particularly through the use of 'whole class interactive teaching' (Reynolds and Mujis, 1993). Teachers were offered some support and training on how to use whiteboards effectively.
>
> 'An accompanying evaluation explored the impact on classroom practice and attainment (Higgins, 2010). The evaluation found that whiteboards did change teacher practice – for example

increasing the pace of lessons and the number of open questions teachers asked – but these changes were not sufficient to bring about clear improvements in learning. The evaluation found no clear evidence that the attainment in the schools involved in the pilot improved relative to a matched group of similar schools.

'Interactive whiteboards were introduced in a large number of schools and are now very common. Not all schools will have provided training and support as in the pilot, so even the shifts in classroom practice observed in the pilot may not have been achieved in other schools.

'It could be argued that it was wrong to assume that introducing interactive whiteboards would improve attainment, and there are strong arguments for the other benefits of introducing whiteboards. But this case does provide an example of where an expensive new piece of technology was introduced to the classroom with ambitious aims that do not appear to have been fulfilled.' (EEF, 2020b)

There are a number of ways that technology can be used, however, to successfully support teachers' modelling and explanations:

Technology used	Example
Visualiser/mirroring from your touch device/wirelessly via camera on your device	Worked examples. Annotate a poem. Highlight an extract. Demonstrate a technique. Success criteria marking.
Presentation tool, e.g. PowerPoint/Slides/Keynote	Explain steps in a process. Zoom/pan to key points. Explain relationships between different parts of a system. Explain how something changes over time. Explain historical context in a timeline in chronological order.

Table 2.2: How technology can support modelling and explanations

Reducing cognitive load

Another way that technology can help (as alluded to in the examples in the previous table) is in reducing *cognitive load*. Many will have heard the phrase 'death by PowerPoint' and we've all been subject to terrible presentations where a lecturer or teacher will simply display a slide full of text, most likely including many difficult concepts.

Dual coding is a particularly useful technique for displaying information in meaningful ways. When it comes to using presentation tools to support explanations and modelling, it is particularly important to consider:

- what you display
- how you display it
- when you display it.

Just *using* technology isn't going to improve anything. Mark's Bananarama principle – 'It ain't what you do, it's the way that you do it, and that's what gets results' – fits in perfectly here.

The key point of Cognitive Load Theory (CLT) is that there is a limit to how much information can be processed at any one time. This limit is determined by the capacity of working memory, which is a temporary storage system for information being processed.

Use of presentation tools to support and enhance explanations and modelling can be greatly improved when we consider using instructional techniques that reduce the amount of processing required. There are a number of these that can be used to reduce extraneous load, including:

- **Using worked examples:** Worked examples are illustrations of how to solve a problem or complete a task. They can be used to reduce cognitive load by providing students with a model to follow such as with a visualiser.
- **Chunking information:** Chunking is the process of grouping together related pieces of information. This can reduce cognitive load by making it easier to store and process information either by introducing groups together as part of an animation or on individual slides to reduce cognitive load.
- **Using multiple representations of information:** Multiple representations of information, such as text, diagrams and images, can help students to understand and remember information more effectively.

By introducing worked examples, chunked information or multiple representations of information in methodical and sequenced ways using animations through the technology we have, we are much less likely to hinder students and we create opportunities for instruction which are more effective and efficient.

It makes sense; if we use a simple whiteboard and marker, we don't display all of the information to our learners at once, do we? We dual code our display of what we are showing with the visual we are creating and the words we are using. Therefore, translate that digitally by introducing the different elements of your instruction at the right time (particularly in presentation tools) by using simple animation sequences, all of which are easy to set up in every popular presentation tool you will have access to in your school.

Improving the impact of pupil practice

In its third piece of advice on where use of technology can enhance learning, the EEF report states that, 'teachers can use technology to increase the benefits of practice to improve fluency or retention of information' (EEF, 2020b).

A simple example many teachers will be aware of where technology can quickly and easily increase how often pupils practise is through the use of quizzing tools. Whether that's on dates in history, keyword definition checks or vocabulary in languages, it doesn't really matter. There is plenty of evidence related to this approach linked to many subjects such as English, maths, science and languages.

The report highlights that it is difficult to untangle whether the technology itself is the determiner of whether the impact of practice is successful or if the practice in and of itself, regardless of technology, would yield the same results. It does not say either way, but it does say:

> 'Understanding the complex links between engagement and achievement is important. Monitoring how technology is being used, including by checking that all students have the skills they need to use it effectively, is likely to reduce the risk that technology becomes a tool that widens the gap between successful learners and their peers.' (EEF, 2020b)

The EEF also cited some research (EEF, 2018) on the impact that using tools you wouldn't normally associate with pupil practice can have on improving it. It states (and subsequently advocates) that technology can be used to support pupil practice outside of the classroom – not by pupils using technology beyond the classrooms themselves, but by using communication strategies to parents and carers, with reminders and prompts about homework and revision, to improve attendance and attainment.

What else?

Within this domain, adaptive and spaced practice also come into play. As AI becomes more and more prevalent, automated tools that recognise *forgetting gaps* and can pivot to support learners will become available. Some systems currently available purport to do this, but not to the extent that their advertising and PR would have you believe.

According to the EEF report, there are strategies to enhance teaching effectiveness by harnessing technology's potential to facilitate retrieval and spaced practice through low-stakes assessments. By using existing systems that we are already familiar with, we increase the likelihood of our students making meaningful connections and improving their ability to recall information. Furthermore, this approach saves us time by providing convenient access to resources we have previously developed and employed in our teaching.

As teachers, we already have a significant number of tools at our disposal that, with discipline, we can use to help us plan and map out our curricula, scheduling when we choose to (and do) use some of these strategies with our learners. Through using tools such as reminders, calendars and planners, we can more easily map out the 'how, what and when' we choose to revisit topics on a whole-class basis for our planned spaced practice.

It will undoubtedly be the case that in the not-too-distant future, personalised learning platforms for pupils will become more readily available in the education space; however, at the time of writing, there were none that we were happy to recommend based upon the unsubstantiated claims of such companies.

Gamification

It would be remiss of us to not mention *gamification* at this point in the book. This isn't to say we think we should start bringing gaming consoles into the classroom, extol the virtues of Mario Kart, link Business Studies lessons to Sim City or promote exercise with Tekken. Gamification is the approach whereby you take the methods used within games and apply them in the classroom for benefits such as engagement, personalising learning, motivation, learning from feedback and more.

When you purchase a game and play it for the first time, you are often onboarded to help you learn how to play the game. For example, if you had purchased a Spider-Man game you'd be taught how to shoot webs, swing from buildings, fight, climb walls, etc. You don't natively know how to do these things. Equally, at the start of the game, when you don't have these important skills, you aren't presented with particularly difficult things to achieve – that would make the game too hard.

Thinking about this as a 'Goldilocks effect', where skills have the opportunity to develop and challenges are pitched and set at the right level so they aren't too hard or too easy, are all hallmarks from games that we can apply to the classroom under the umbrella term of gamification.

What does this look like?

There are a number of areas where gamification as an approach to supporting learning and teaching can assist your efforts in the classroom. It's likely you've been doing some of these things for years without even realising they're classed as gamification strategies, such as:

- badges and achievements
- house points
- rewards and achievements
- personalised learning
- adaptive resources
- digital escape rooms
- role-playing scenarios
- storyline integration

...the list goes on.

As you can tell, these aren't about introducing games into the classroom, but taking what we know from the world of gaming. (There's a reason why they're so popular with young people!)

And so, as we consider the previous taxonomies and how they can support learning and teaching, it is important to consider how we make choices about how we combine *what* we know we have to teach, what we know about *how* to teach and how technology might come into the mix. Enter TPACK!

2.4 TPACK

In all of Mark's years of sharing about teaching and learning with technology, and certainly plenty of Olly's, TPACK has been a pillar of our thinking to frame what good teaching and learning with technology should look like.

Originally formulated in 2009 by Koehler and Mishra, as a development of Shulman's (1987) pedagogical content model (PCK), TPACK sought to further develop the idea that good teaching and learning occurs when you combine your pedagogical and your content knowledge.

With the explosion of new technology, Koehler and Mishra were seeking an approach which kept the teaching and learning at the heart of their thinking while further developing a technological domain which enabled teachers to make informed decisions around their choices and use of technology for learning in the classroom.

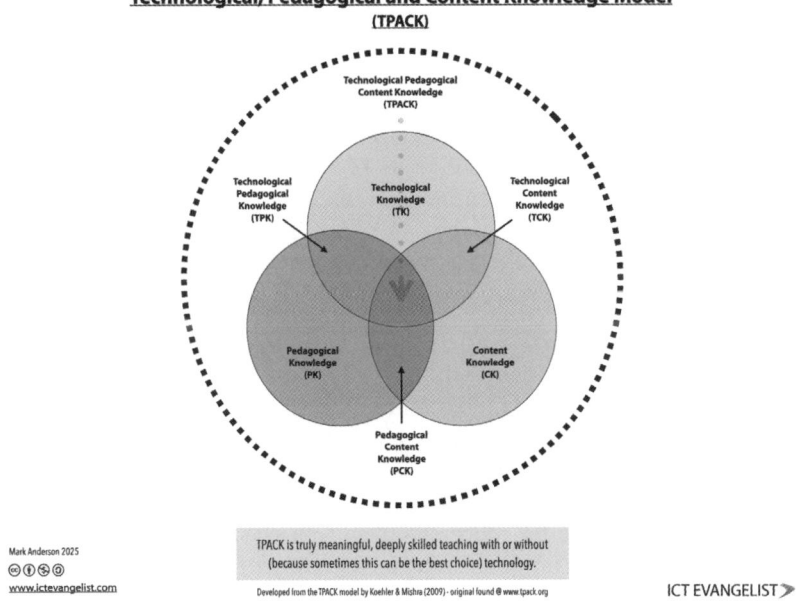

Figure 2.6: TPACK model

The EdTech Playbook

There are a variety of domains in the TPACK model:

- **PK:** This is your pedagogical knowledge; what you know about teaching. All of the various facets of your teaching toolkit come into play in your pedagogical knowledge. As teachers in the classroom, you know when it is best to use, or not use, a different strategy. Often combined with your content knowledge (CK), PK is usually determined by two key factors: the learning activity you are undertaking and the content you are trying to teach.
- **CK:** This is your specialist subject/content knowledge; the domain-specific content knowledge you often learned and studied about in detail when completing your subject specialism degree.
- **TK:** Many teachers have PK and CK ingrained into their everyday practice; an area that often needs considerable training and support is the development of teachers' technological knowledge (TK). Frequently, this isn't necessarily training on how to use software – many teachers already know how to use tools such as Microsoft **PowerPoint** and **Word** or how to surf the internet. What they lack is the knowledge of how to combine that technological knowledge with their PK and CK. Much of the training and support that Mark has delivered over the last decade and more has been around this: how to successfully integrate technology into everyday practice so that teachers can make informed decisions about the different ways technology can be used to either support their teaching, enhance student learning, or reduce their workload. For sure, technology can be thrilling, exciting even, but if its use doesn't serve one of those three key domains of teaching, learning, or workload reduction then it is unlikely to reap the gains you may be seeking.

It is often easy to confuse technology for teaching and learning with subject-specific technology. Please don't do that. For example, in design and technology lessons you will likely use tools such as **Tinkercad** (www.tinkercad.com), **SketchUp** (www.sketchup.com) and **Photoshop** (www.adobe.com). Don't get us wrong, these are powerful pieces of software, but they are far more useful in that specific subject than they might be in, let's say, languages. Now, you might find a company telling you how its software can be used in geography, let's say, and sure, this might be a fun piece of software to use in that subject, but if children don't have the requisite skills to use it in class, valuable curriculum time will be wasted. There are more useful tools that have wide-ranging uses which are far more subject specific. Couple this with budgetary constraints, teacher confidence, competence and cognisance and the fact that these teachers would also need considerable training to use the tools on what would likely be rare occasions, and the juice isn't worth the squeeze.

- **PCK:** Links to pedagogical and content knowledge to bring about learning that is built upon your strong subject knowledge and all of the teaching and learning strategies that you have in your toolkit.
- **TPK:** Links technological and pedagogical knowledge to aim to help bring learning opportunities that are built upon a strong understanding of technology and teaching and learning strategies that can be enhanced by it.
- **TCK:** Links your technological and content knowledge together to help bring about learning that is grounded in strong subject knowledge and a mastery of 'more than the subject [you] teach' (Koehler and Mishra, 2009).
- **TPACK:** This brings together the three domains of your TK, PK and CK. Koehler and Mishra (2009) class this as being 'truly meaningful, deeply skilled teaching with or without (because sometimes this can be the best choice) technology. It differs from three individual concepts because to embrace all three simultaneously requires a deep understanding of how all three can work together to bring about the best technologically and pedagogically sound learning based upon a deep understanding of subject matter.'

As we move into a new AI era, many talk about the need for AI literacy, and quite rightly so; but we advocate for making sure technology isn't used for technology's sake. TPACK is a superb foundation for supporting the idea that teacher voice, expertise and experience frame any outputs from AI. It's imperative that we keep the 'human-in-the-loop'. Otherwise we run the risk of dumbing down the profession and offering a weaker 'one-size-fits-all' approach to teaching and learning, which, of course, we know isn't fit for purpose. Using TPACK to interrogate outputs from AI will always help keep learner progress and teaching efficacy at the heart of our thinking.

2.5 How to build your TK

One of the biggest issues that anyone leading on technology faces with supporting teachers in this area is helping them to improve their confidence, competence, cognisance and consistency.

In Mark's 2013 book, *Perfect ICT Every Lesson*, he talked about Mandinach and Cline's (1992) work that explored teacher confidence and competence in the use of technology. In his book, he took their four levels of survival, mastery, impact and innovation and explained what each of those levels might look like from a teacher's perspective.

This work has been copied and used many times since then as a benchmark for measuring where teacher confidence and competence lies. Those in schools who have responsibility for leading professional development have used it with teachers to personalise professional learning so that it matches their confidence and competence levels. The low-stakes nature of this framework means that CPD leads often ask teachers to self-select where they feel they are on that scale.

Upon seeing Mark sharing this on social media, Canadian educator Sylvia Duckworth, now renowned for her popular sketch notes, took Mark's expansion of Mandinach and Cline's work and created the following sketch note which has been shared widely since 2014.

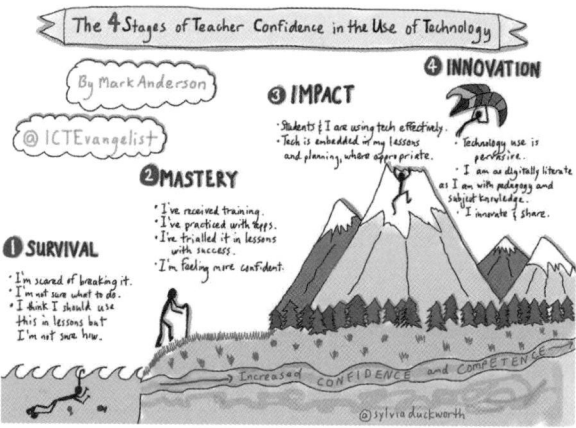

Figure 2.7: The 4 stages of teacher confidence in the use of technology

Moving forward to 2024, our knowledge about what works with teaching and learning with technology has significantly advanced. The COVID-19 pandemic taught us many things, and when it comes to this particular area, we know that it is far more than just confidence and competence that shapes the success of technological implementation in the classroom.

2.6 TAM and TIM

The technology acceptance model (TAM) was originally proposed in 1989 and was based upon research undertaken by Fred Davis, where he explored the factors and likelihoods of technology adoption.

The TAM aims to explain and predict individuals' intention to use and adopt new technologies, particularly in a workplace context. The core constructs of the TAM are 'perceived usefulness' and 'perceived ease of use', which are believed to be the primary determinants of an individual's intention to use a new technology. It is an extension of the Theory of Reasoned Action and has been widely used and built upon in technology adoption research.[3]

It is useful in education to consider those two important elements of 'perceived usefulness' and 'perceived ease of use'. Often, thinking about barriers to adoption, if a teacher thinks something is difficult to use and is unlikely to help with a need (perceived or otherwise), they will be unlikely to want to spend the time familiarising themselves with and ultimately using the software or hardware.

When considering technology and its implementation in your setting it is, therefore, important that you check products for their ease of use and, even more so, the usefulness of the product to solve the problem that you are aiming to solve with it. By asking questions about this, you will not only make sure that products are fit for purpose but you will be helping the overall success of the implementation, as you will be able to elucidate for colleagues these two important factors when explaining why and how they should be using the product within your setting.

The similarly named TIM (technology integration model) goes beyond the elements of the TAM. It was developed because later researchers felt Davis' work did not clearly explain the effective ways of integrating technology.

> 'TAM contains several variables such as perceived usefulness, perceived ease of use, external variables, attitude and behavioral intention as precursors of technology adoption and use (Davis, Bagozzie and Warshaw, 1989). However, the variables which predict technology adoption have been shown to differ from the variables which predict continued technology use (Limayem, Cheung and

---

[3] https://www.usersense.io/knowledge-base/usability-metrics/technology-acceptance-model-tam

Chan, 2003). For example, a person's attitude towards a technology before adoption is often influenced by perceptions of usefulness, ease of use, result demonstrability, visibility and trialability, whereas attitudes after adoption are influenced by instrumental beliefs of usefulness and perceptions of image enhancements (Karahanna, Straub and Chervany, 1999). As such it appears that continued technology use is not just a continuation of technology adoption, but a phenomenon within itself. This raises additional questions regarding the suitability of TAM and successive extensions when measuring continued use.' (Shaw, Ellis and Ziegler, 2018)

To that end, TIM was developed by Shaw, Ellis and Ziegler (2018) to unify and build upon existing theories (such as TAM) that attempt to explain technology adoption and use.

TIM is complex and has broad coverage. It does, however, reflect the depth and complexity of thinking required when integrating technology. While its focus is not specifically on education, the 14 key variables held within the model help frame thinking about technology integration. The variables, which incorporate thinking from existing technology, use theories that, when combined, can be used to develop this comprehensive approach to considering technology integration. The 14 key variables are:

Variable	Explanation for school context
Ease of use	**Teachers:** The simplicity with which technology can be implemented in lesson plans. **Leaders:** The ease with which staff can adopt technology, influencing training and support structures.
Effort expectancy	**Teachers:** The perceived effort required to integrate technology into teaching methods. **Leaders:** The effort leaders anticipate needing to encourage and support technology adoption.
Intrinsic motivations	**Teachers:** Motivations based on personal satisfaction or pleasure in using technology. **Leaders:** Driving engagement by highlighting the personal and professional growth opportunities with tech.

Variable	Explanation for school context
Habit	**Teachers:** The formation of consistent patterns in using technology for teaching. **Leaders:** Establishing regular routines and protocols for technology use in school operations.
Social influence	**Teachers:** The impact of colleagues and the educational community on technology use. **Leaders:** Leveraging peer influence to enhance technology adoption among staff.
Facilitating conditions	**Teachers:** Availability of resources and support for using technology. **Leaders:** Creating an infrastructure that supports technology use, including training and IT support.
Performance expectancy	**Teachers:** The expected improvement in teaching outcomes due to technology use. **Leaders:** Anticipating how technology can enhance school performance metrics and learning outcomes.
Attitude towards use	**Teachers:** Overall sentiment about the usefulness and appropriateness of technology in education. **Leaders:** Shaping positive perceptions and attitudes towards technology in the school.
Behavioural intention	**Teachers:** The intention to use technology based on its perceived benefits. **Leaders:** Strategic planning to foster a culture that embraces technology willingly.
Use behaviour	**Teachers:** Actual usage of technology in classrooms and for preparation. **Leaders:** Monitoring and encouraging effective use practices across the school.
Perceived usefulness	**Teachers:** Belief that technology will enhance their teaching efficiency and effectiveness. **Leaders:** Convincing staff of the tangible benefits technology brings to their roles.

Variable	Explanation for school context
Perceived ease of use	**Teachers:** How user-friendly technology is perceived, affecting willingness to adopt. **Leaders:** Selecting and promoting technologies that are straightforward and intuitive for staff.
Extended self	**Teachers:** The integration of technology as part of a teacher's professional identity. **Leaders:** Encouraging teachers to see technology as an extension of their teaching capabilities.
Cost-benefit decision and situational context	**Teachers:** Evaluating whether the advantages of using technology outweigh its costs, considering the teaching environment. **Leaders:** Assessing the overall impact and feasibility of technology initiatives within the school's specific context.

Table 2.3: 14 variables of TIM

Often confused with each other, the technology integration model (TIM) and the technology integration matrix (also abbreviated as TIM) are distinct frameworks, each with a specific focus and development background.

The technology integration model aims to predict the continued use of technology. As shown in Table 2.3, it integrates interdisciplinary insights from computer science and psychology to understand and enhance the human-computer relationship.

On the other hand, the technology integration matrix, developed by the Florida Center for Instructional Technology at the University of South Florida, provides a framework for describing and targeting the use of technology to enhance learning. This matrix is particularly focused on educational settings and offers a structured guide across five levels of technology integration, from entry to transformation, detailing how technology can be integrated into teaching and learning effectively.

Singing to our thinking around the use of technology in education, this 'TIM' aims to keep the focus on effective, research-based pedagogy rather than just the uses of technology. The technology integration matrix is specifically educational, providing actionable guidance for teachers and leaders.

What we like about the technology integration matrix is that it is a strong combination of some of the models that we have discussed previously.

It balances the need for solid training (CPD) along with confidence against the ways in which technology can be used in different teaching and learning scenarios.

The five levels of technology integration are laid out as being:

1. **Entry:** Technology is used by students for the first time in a straightforward, teacher-directed manner.
2. **Adoption:** Teachers begin to use technology tools regularly but still in traditional ways, primarily to support existing teaching practices.
3. **Adaptation:** Technology use becomes more student-centred, with students starting to make choices about how they use technology tools.
4. **Infusion:** Technology is integrated seamlessly with the curriculum, and students regularly use it as a tool to help them achieve their learning goals.
5. **Transformation:** Technology allows for new and transformative educational methods, creating learning experiences that were not possible before.

Mark wrote clearly on his blog that SAMR is not a ladder, as alluded to above, which is a key issue with approaches such as SAMR and RAT. While TIM is ladder-like, its structure is all about integration. That said, while we like this, it is somewhat problematic and draws out some issues with the practicalities of students making choices about their use of technology.

There clearly is no 'one-size-fits-all' approach with this and so, informed by elements of the models above, we developed our 5 Cs of *digital cognition* which we hope will help you achieve impact within your context.

2.7 The 5 Cs of digital cognition

With evidence and research-informed approaches being so prominent in the thinking of schools and on initial teacher training courses, we would love to see a time when digital cognition – the idea of teachers having cognitive knowledge of what types of technology help and enhance learning – is part of the knowledge base of all educators.

We expect teachers to have understanding of a range of pedagogical strategies as part of their teaching and learning toolkit, so why should technology be any different? We certainly don't want to find ourselves in the situation we encountered at the beginning of the COVID-19 pandemic, with significant gaps in teachers' confidence, competence and cognisance of what works.

The evidence bases for cognition and cognitive science driving learning are compelling. The base for digital technologies should be equally so, but unfortunately can be less so. As our use of technology in society accelerates (in education, we are more critical), how can we confirm that the ecosystem we operate in ensures we are aware of the best approaches to using technology in education?

Over the years, we have both been asked to speak about cognitive science and digital learning. These are two topics we are both passionate about and have spent much time reading around, reflecting upon our practices and the practice of those in the lessons we have observed, along with seeking out opinions from respected individuals in the field.

They are two fairly heavy areas of research to examine and distil into tangible actions for teachers. Coupled with this, there are two areas in education that leaders should be (in our opinion) zeroing in on, with a critical eye and a view to sustained system change.

Luckily, previous models of learning with technology are helpful, like the ones discussed in this chapter. TPACK and its developments thereof, such as with TIM (the technology integration model), highlight the importance of digital cognition that helps educators know when it's right (or not) to use technology to support or enhance learning or teaching.

Digital cognition therefore is the professional understanding of educators to make informed choices about how and when technology can improve, support or enhance learning.

Our 5 Cs framework that we have developed in recent years has become, for us, a new standard to help inform our collective work – whether that's Mark's work supporting school leaders and teachers, or Olly's work leading on digital transformation in his former multi-academy trust (MAT).

1. **Confidence:** This is not just about a teacher's confidence in using technology but, as outlined in the TPACK section, it is about a teacher's confidence in how to successfully blend their TK, PK and CK. Teachers gain confidence by developing their technological knowledge; not just knowledge of how to use different pieces of software or hardware, but how they can be used to support teaching and/or learning and when they can be useful.

2. **Competence:** This is about a teacher's ability to use the software/hardware/EdTech tool they need to use to do their job effectively. It is likely to include key ecosystem software (such as those provided by Microsoft or Google) plus other essential software such as their management information system (MIS), IWB, visualiser, etc.
3. **Cognisance:** This is about a teacher's ability to successfully make informed decisions about when to use, or not use, technology to aid learning as per the central pillar of TPACK.
4. **Consistency:** This is about a teacher's ability to consistently use technology linked to a school's core set of technology tools for teaching and learning.

Digital cognition: Combining the above four Cs help bring about true digital cognition, where a teacher is able to confidently, competently, cognisantly and consistently use technology just as easily as they might use different questioning techniques or other pedagogical practice(s) (or not, as sometimes that's the best choice).

5. **Context:** The problem with all of the above is that context is paramount. We need to always remember to be cognisant of where our colleagues are on their digital teaching and learning journey. This is where the fifth C of **context** comes in. (Anderson and Lewis, 2023)

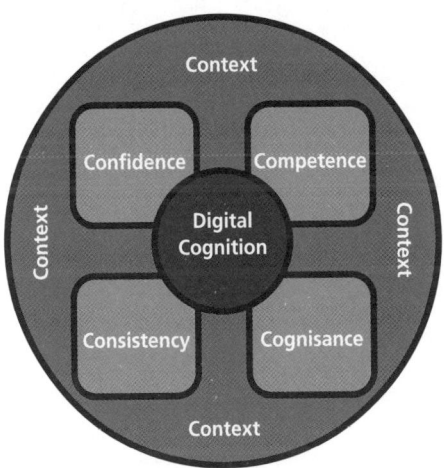

Figure 2.8: The 5 Cs of digital cognition

2.8 Is the juice worth the squeeze?

All of the above is, of course, really useful but the truth is, using technology in the classroom can be a daunting prospect for many teachers. While the taxonomies and ideas shared are useful and helpful in your journey to successfully using technology with your students, when we break it down, there are a few north stars we can use to help guide you to whether you should be using technology at all.

Something that Mark learned pretty quickly as a practitioner when working with colleagues on technology implementation was that there are just three priority areas that teachers should focus upon as they decide whether to use technology in the classroom or not.

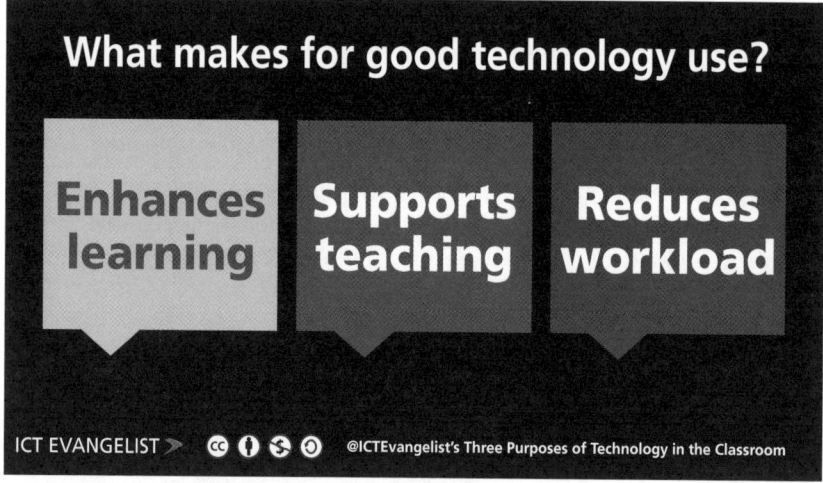

Figure 2.9: What makes for good technology use?

Yes, there are many other reasons why you might be using technology with your class. For many subjects, such as computing, design and technology, music, art and more, technology use is a curriculum essential for writing code, composing digital music or art, or working on 3D models. You might even want to be injecting some creativity or awe and wonder through the use of XR, such as augmented reality models. We have no issue with those uses and love seeing them used but, for many, these are nice-to-haves when the time available for teaching a crowded curriculum is so limited.

If we are to make the best use of technology so that it enhances rather than distracts from learning (being mindful of cognitive load and more!), it is essential we keep these three pillars as guiding lights in our choices around our technology use. Therefore, before considering using technology in your classroom, consider these three questions:

Question	Examples
Does the technology you're seeking to use enhance learning in some way?	Is there a digital resource you can access that wouldn't be otherwise easily available? Is there a model you can use that will help improve your explanations to aid student understanding of a difficult concept? Is there a tool your learners can use that will help them with their practice with learning content?
Does the technology support your teaching in some way?	Is there a resource, software or hardware that can help you with your explanations and modelling or that could support and deliver more timely or effective feedback?
Are there ways you can use technology to reduce your workload?	Are there any tools you could use (such as AI or approaches such as keyboard shortcuts, dictation or automation) that can help give you quicker and clearer insights into student progress?

Table 2.4: Three questions for classroom technology use

Using technology effectively can sometimes take considerable preparation time. Therefore, it's important to ask yourself the question: is the juice worth the squeeze?

By this, we mean: is this use of technology worth the time and effort required for you to be able to use it to its desired effect; namely, to help learning, support your teaching or reduce your workload? Sometimes the answer is yes, despite that in the initial stages it may take you or your learners a fair while to gain confidence and skill in using the desired approach. Sometimes, however, it definitely isn't!

One model that has proved useful for us in our thinking around this and for our colleagues is that of the impact/effort prioritisation matrix.

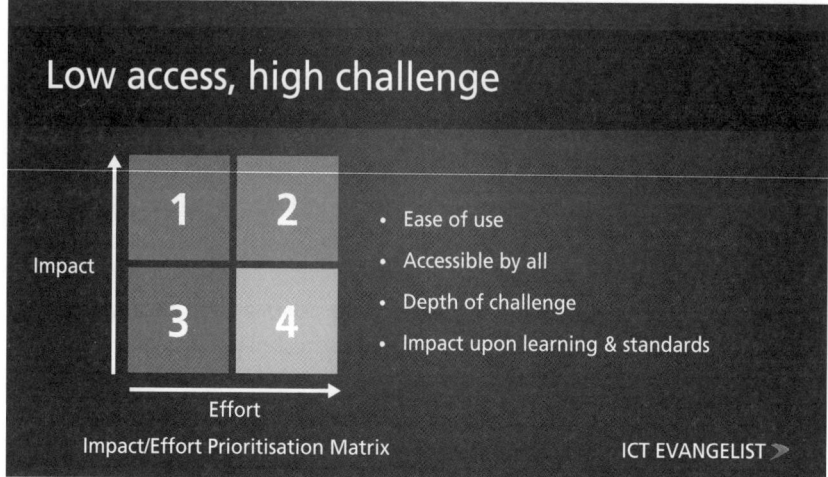

Figure 2.10: Low access, high challenge model

We share it with the title 'low access, high challenge' by placing your thinking into two clear domains when questioning your use of technology before you use it with a class:

1. Is the tool you're looking to use easy to learn, manipulate or gain skill in using?

2. Is the tool or approach you're looking to use going to keep the depth of challenge in supporting your students' learning or the task you're going to ask students to complete?

Therefore, if a tool is likely to be high effort but low impact (on improving teaching or learning or reducing workload), it is likely you wouldn't want to use it. If, however, it is low effort but high impact, then it is definitely something worthy of consideration.

'Low effort, low impact' and 'high effort, high impact' approaches will be the calls that you are best placed to decide upon and discuss with your colleagues.

Either way, the matrix is useful to help you decide the all-important question of whether your choice of technology is worthwhile or not. After all, as we discussed earlier, good technology use isn't just about using technology all of the time; it's about having cognisance of what works and whether or not (because sometimes that is the best choice) you should be using any given technology for your chosen teaching or learning activity.

Top tips

Mark's top tips

1. Good teaching is good teaching, whether or not it includes technology. Use the frameworks above (particularly the impact/effort prioritisation matrix) to decide whether or not your choice is worthwhile, and consider the uses that will most benefit all learners in your class, e.g. using a visualiser to demonstrate live marking, while recording it for playback and repeated viewing for those who might want it.

2. Remember, good use of technology for learning is sometimes about not using technology at all. Develop your confidence and competence in technologies to help you gain cognisance of what works and talk with colleagues about what's working for them to help you gain a better understanding of things you and your learners will be able to make good use of.

3. Remember, there are no silver bullets. Simple things, such as learning keyboard shortcuts, can help massively in reducing your workload and help you to gain more confidence in your uses of technology – plus, it'll help you to clear your workload even more quickly.

Olly's top tips

1. In your next department or school meeting, collectively brainstorm what opportunities you have as a school to do things differently and how technology can support you, then put it to the test against one of the frameworks.

2. Pedagogy is often assumed within the profession; it is likely worth some time being invested into reviewing the different types of pedagogy as you start to reshape your vision and values for learning and teaching in your school.

3. There are several important references in this chapter. Share them with colleagues across the school so that they can get up to speed with the range of taxonomies and research we have signposted.

CHAPTER 3
Instructional delivery methods with technology

'If we teach today as we taught yesterday, we rob our children of tomorrow.'

John Dewey

The truth is, one of the best things about teaching is that no two days are ever the same. We defy anyone to ever have the same two lessons. Mark remembers well that some years he would have upwards of four different classes within the same year group, teaching the same content to those four classes – let's say, Year 7. Given the dynamics of the class, from interests, behaviours, coughs, colds, the weather, aptitudes, attitudes and so much more, it's not just that no two lessons are ever the same; no two *students* are ever the same. It's part of what makes the job so enjoyable while simultaneously so demanding.

When we think about how and when we incorporate technology into our practice, we need to take into consideration many of these factors. As OECD Director for the Directorate of Education and Skills, Andreas Schleicher, shared, 'Technology can amplify great teaching, but great technology cannot replace poor teaching' (OECD, 2015). Throughout this book, a key theme is that while technology is amazing, solid and grounded teaching practice trumps it – not just every day of the week but in every lesson you teach.

Rewind your mind to 2020 and, no doubt, many different emotions will resurface. Olly remembers well going from being face-to-face with his classes one day to suddenly being fully virtual the next; a pivot that occurred across the educational landscape.

Not only did we adapt and adjust to suddenly sitting down in front of a laptop all day to carry out our core business of education, but we also adjusted to working at home with our families and children in the next room, amidst live teaching or meetings. Many of us, Olly included, failed at the early stages of teaching in the online classroom. Our pedagogical choices weren't fine-tuned but we were resilient and did our best, even when the Wi-Fi went down, our laptops froze or we played (and many of us still do to this day!) the bingo call of 'Can you see my screen?', 'Can you hear me?', 'Is my camera on?', 'Sorry, my camera isn't working today'. All those early feelings of speaking into the void while waiting for a response from students, only for us to move on before we'd given them a chance to pluck up the courage to give us the response we so desperately craved. We lost a little piece of ourselves in that time, the piece that all teachers truly enjoy in the classroom: human connections.

We whisked ourselves and our learners through content and lessons quickly, while we had even fewer social cues than we are accustomed to in our normal classroom setting, in the hope that content coverage was king when, at this point, less was actually more for everyone involved. We justified it by comparing our curriculum coverage and trajectory relative to in-person teaching, so we knew we weren't making students miss out on core knowledge in our subjects. Truth be told, we should have spent more time here building human connections and collaborating.

While the learning curve for everyone was steep, it most certainly wasn't linear in nature. If we take anything away from the experiences of lockdown and learning, it's that there is another way. We innovated, found new norms and different approaches, and changed how we thought and solved problems.

There are many different types of learning with technology and each has its benefits and drawbacks. The person best placed to decide which approach to take, and when, is the person who knows their class the best: the teacher. Sadly, this is not always possible, as the decisions that directly impact the chosen type of learning happen on a school, local or even national scale – and we saw this during the pandemic in 2020 and beyond.

Fast forward to the tail end of 2020 and education found itself navigating between five more common types of learning with technology:

1. synchronous learning
2. asynchronous learning
3. remote learning
4. hybrid learning
5. blended learning.

3.1 Synchronous learning

Synchronous learning happens in real time while students and teacher(s) are together, whether that be face-to-face or online in a live conference call during the time that their lesson is timetabled to take place.

The most common example of a digital synchronous lesson is one that is live-streamed over a platform such as Microsoft Teams or Google Meet, where students attend virtually. Teachers and students can then effectively collaborate by making use of their video cameras, microphones and classroom resources such as presentations, along with the tools baked into the video conferencing software, like breakout rooms, reactions and the chat feature.

While this type of learning can be engaging and has a structure more akin to a typical face-to-face lesson, it can in equal measure be disruptive (despite the student not needing to travel) due to the plethora of distractions in the home. All stakeholders can get and give faster feedback, and teachers can also pick up on students' verbal and non-verbal cues.

This type of learning can also help to maintain the sense of community you typically see within a face-to-face lesson owing to the opportunity that the technology brings, enabling the continuation of collaboration and communication.

Benefits	Drawbacks
Continues to foster a sense of belonging and connections for students.	Needs a good and reliable internet connection along with a distraction-free space.
Allows real-time interaction with teachers and peers.	More challenging to deliver support to all students.
Immediate feedback from questioning.	
Opportunity for students to ask questions and receive immediate answers.	Follows a set schedule.
	Higher stakes – for teachers and students.
More structured approach.	
Supports social interaction and community.	Students need to have the confidence to speak up.
	Can be difficult to manage large groups of students.

Table 3.1: Benefits and drawbacks of synchronous learning

3.2 Asynchronous learning

Asynchronous learning is a type of learning where students can work at their own pace (once the teacher has provided the learning materials) and respond to tasks at a time that suits them, thanks to the flexibility of this approach.

A typical example of an asynchronous lesson is where a teacher pre-records new material and shares this with students. The students watch the video, access any additional resources and complete an activity (e.g. complete a quiz or post a comment on a discussion board) to show their engagement with the lesson content and their understanding of the new material.

This type of learning is often seen as being more flexible, as students have greater autonomy when working towards deadlines. However, it also means students need to have a greater degree of metacognitive and personal awareness so that they can thrive in this approach, as there is often a greater time delay (compared to synchronous learning) for receiving/giving feedback and communicating with their peers/teacher.

Benefits	Drawbacks
More flexible approach and allows self-paced learning.	Students can feel isolated and disconnected through a lack of social contact with peers.
Easier for many students to manage and work at their own pace.	Lack of immediate clarification and feedback.
Easier for parents and teachers to support.	Requires strong self-discipline and time-management skills, with more opportunities for distraction.
Provides access to pre-recorded lectures and materials.	
Students have more time to digest new material.	Potential for reduced engagement and motivation.
	Limited availability for immediate support from the teacher.

Table 3.2: Benefits and drawbacks of asynchronous learning

3.3 Remote learning

Remote learning is a type of learning where the teacher and students are not present in the same geographical location. This has been a requirement and a necessity for a long time, particularly in regions of the world where people live in geographically disparate places. Mark remembers well when he visited Texas on a government research trip in 2002 (exploring citizenship education in Texas to help inform the new UK National Curriculum programmes of study for citizenship), just how important remote learning was for their learners.

For students at Texas Tech University (now a world-leading university in using virtual reality to help train its medical students in surgical procedures) and at some of the local high schools, remote (or distance) learning was a necessity, as many students lived in areas where it was more than an hour's bus ride just to get to school. Here, even back then, they were leveraging (what is by today's standards) simple technologies to help ensure learning was possible. Mark remembers the video conferencing room, all set up to ensure learning could take place, where teachers would go to teach to cameras and students would dial in to watch or listen to their lessons.

Yes, there were days in the week when students would make their long journeys to and from school, from farms and other far-reaching areas of Lubbock ISD (Independent School District), thus making it more akin to 'hybrid learning'. However, without the tools shared here, much of the curriculum (and therefore learning) would have been out of reach for many families across the vast region.

A further example of remote learning was Olly's experience during the COVID-19 pandemic. Like many educators across the globe, he pivoted from being in school one day to being remote/online the next and replicating a full teaching timetable through his laptop from the confines of his makeshift 'office desk' on his dining room table.

Some facets of remote learning worked well, while others did not. One example that springs to mind is science practicals. These were challenging for some learners as they simply did not have the capacity for thinking outside the box as to how they would be able to conduct a scientific investigation from their homes – and that, ultimately, had a negative effect on learning.

A second example, which was more positive, was making use of quizzing to support understanding through the use of a simple tool called **Quizizz** (www.quizizz.com). While the live or recorded elements of Olly's lessons were for instruction and question/answer sessions, through using Quizizz he could assess what stuck, what did not, and what needed

49

reviewing and re-teaching. By setting the quizzes on Quizizz, he was able to set a timescale for learners that allowed them to complete the quizzes at a time that suited them, rather than instantly. Many students in his classes said that they felt 'Zoom fatigue' after spending many lessons in live calls or watching recorded content and they preferred having longer breaks between lessons to digitally detox.

Benefits	Drawbacks
Continuation of learning regardless of geographical location, so long as you have an internet connection.	A lack of social opportunities outside of lessons.
Ongoing opportunities for accessibility.	A challenge for learners who prefer socialisation and swifter support.
Flexibility as students can 'dial in' from anywhere and complete tasks at a time that suits them.	Limited opportunities for face-to-face interactions.
A tailored approach for individuals.	Requires self-motivation and discipline.
A more positive experience for learners who prefer independent approaches.	Can increase stress levels owing to technical difficulties or a lack of independence.
Reduces travel costs and commuting time.	Increased potential for distractions.

Table 3.3: Benefits and drawbacks of remote learning

3.4 Hybrid learning

Hybrid learning is a type of learning that combines more traditional in-person teaching and learning with online learning. This approach is the most flexible of all, as it allows students to attend some classes for in-person instruction while other classes will be online. The learners have the benefits of both real-time face-to-face instruction and self-paced learning at a time and place that suits the learners.

The hybrid learning approach was more commonly found during the latter stages of the pandemic, when children of key workers attended school while others were at home. It was sometimes expanded further where social distancing required children in school to be separated. Olly remembers delivering lessons where he had children in his classroom, others viewing from home on Microsoft Teams, and socially distanced students participating from other rooms within the school, also using Microsoft Teams. Here, the technology facilitated all children receiving the same asynchronous learning opportunity while still being able to participate in collaborative classroom activities as if they were together, despite being geographically distant. This is a great example of technology enhancing and supporting, but not dictating, the learning and teaching.

A typical example of an approach to hybrid learning is where learners will attend a lesson for in-person instruction and then complete a range of tasks, e.g. an online quiz, access extended reading or curate a resource, to evidence their learning at home.

An additional benefit is that it can be a more cost-effective way to deliver education at scale across a school (or group of schools) where there are not enough specialists to teach multiple classes at once. In a world where we are currently facing teacher shortages, this is likely to be an approach we see more of. Additionally, this strategy can be more beneficial for learners living in remote areas (reducing their travel costs) and can be more accessible for those with disabilities.

While there are many positives of hybrid learning, there are also drawbacks – such as it often being put in place as an emergency response so that learning can continue.

Hybrid learning is technology-dependent and, due to equity of access and the digital divide, often those who need the continuation of education most are the very learners who do not have the technology at home to grant them access to it.

For the learners who do have the technology, issues can still arise. Often, schools and children won't have the same solutions, and children may not have the skills to manage their own software; both of which present another layer of challenge for hybrid learning.

Benefits	Drawbacks
Increased opportunities for social interactions.	Some learners benefit best from in-person instruction.
Increased access to resources.	Requires strong digital literacy skills.
Provides a balance between in-person and online learning.	Not as easy to group (and support) learners with common misconceptions.
Reduced distractions in many instances.	Not all schools or students have the necessary software or skills to support and manage their learning/attention.
Cost-effective.	
Increased access for learners.	It requires all learners to have access to the internet and similar devices which might not be available.

Table 3.4: Benefits and drawbacks of hybrid learning

3.5 Blended learning

Blended learning is very similar to hybrid learning in that it involves some in-person teaching and learning, some remote, and some independent work. However, the big difference is that *all* learners participate in both in-person *and* online learning.

In a blended learning environment, the online component is usually used to supplement the in-person component, where students are provided with additional resources, opportunities for practice, online quizzes, online discussion forums, or access to synchronous or asynchronous video lectures. In a blended learning environment, the online and in-person components are thoughtfully integrated, ensuring that learners engage with both modes as complementary parts of the course. This approach gives students a cohesive experience where digital and face-to-face interactions enhance and reinforce one another.

This strategy has been commonplace in universities, colleges and further education establishments for a long time now. Perhaps this is because adults have more freedom and access to using transport than younger people or they recognise the maturity older students have around managing their time and their commitments to their learning. Either way, blended learning has been used as a vehicle for teaching and learning in these spaces for some considerable time.

Benefits	Drawbacks
Combines face-to-face and online learning.	Potential for inconsistency in teaching quality.
Promotes active learning and student engagement.	Increased workload for instructors.
	Requires strong digital literacy skills.
Allows for personalised learning experiences.	Requires access to technology and internet connectivity, which may be variable between households/students.
Provides opportunities for collaborative activities.	Possibility of lack of face-to-face social interaction.
Opportunities for flexibility in scheduling and location.	

Table 3.5: Benefits and drawbacks of hybrid learning

A commonly heard phrase during the COVID-19 pandemic (adapted from Plato's *Republic*) was: 'Necessity is the mother of invention'. It means that people are more likely to come up with new ideas and solutions when they are faced with a difficult need or problem. The pandemic made it necessary for people to have to use technology and think differently about how they approached teaching and learning.

All of these different models of learning with technology have their place. As we learned in the last chapter with the 5 Cs model, the gravy of the meal that brings together the other 4 Cs is that of context. This is very relevant here! Your choice of instructional delivery method has to be linked directly to your context. For example, successful blended learning would be difficult to enact in a setting with younger students. They have yet to develop the metacognitive and organisational skills required to be successful in such an environment. Similarly, students in a K-12 (Key Stage 1–4) setting, as we found in the pandemic, find it difficult to succeed in asynchronous and hybrid settings.

Keeping in mind your context (and of course the necessity brought about by the situation you find yourself in) will help you to decide which of the different types of learning are the most appropriate and fitting for your setting at any given time.

Whichever way you look at it, when it comes to all of these things, as the author, speaker and education consultant, Michael Fullan, says, 'Pedagogy is the driver, technology is the accelerator'. Successful use of technology is very rarely about the technology itself (yes, of course, the infrastructure and access to technology are essential); it is more about people. Do they have the relevant confidence, competence, cognisance and consistency of use to enable them to teach and learn appropriately, given the circumstances they find themselves in?

What we find is that if people have these qualities, then they can flourish regardless of the mode of learning they are presented with. This is why older students are more able to be successful in blended and hybrid learning environments than their younger counterparts.

Top tips

Mark's top tips

1. Be flexible – offer opportunities for learning support that match the needs of your learners.

2. Be cognisant – you know the tools, resources and activities that best fit the topics you're teaching. Use them.

3. Remember it's all still about people more than technology. Make sure your learners can (and know how to) access any opportunities for learning that your teaching is asking them to.

Olly's top tips

1. Good teaching and learning is still good teaching and learning in a face-to-face, blended or hybrid approach, so keep on checking for understanding, providing feedback to learners and using low-stakes quizzes to inform your next teaching steps.

2. Make it a habit to record your explanations and modelling so that you can reuse them time and time again to support learners and reduce your workload.

3. Focus on ensuring both you and your learners develop your confidence and competence with technology so you can use it when you, as the teacher, decide it's appropriate for it to be used.

CHAPTER 4
Effective digital transformation

'Change is not made without inconvenience, even from worse to better.'

Richard Hooker

For transformation to take place it is important to take the time to reflect and consider the past and what lessons we can learn from it. In this chapter, we explore the key components of effective digital transformation. You will learn how you can apply these components to your practice if you're reading this as a teacher or at a whole-school, trust or district level. The key elements are the same regardless of the size or scale, the only difference is that it is more difficult to ensure consistency across all colleagues when exploring these things at scale. Don't worry though, we'll explore that too!

4.1 Pause for reflection

The summer term is a great time to reflect upon how things have gone with your classes across the academic year. We remember well the department subject reviews we had to write when we were subject leaders. Sure, there were accountability questions to cover, but the best part for us was the reflection on our practice and that of colleagues which helped to inform what professional learning we wanted to engage in for the next academic year.

Of course, as you'd expect from us, taking control of our professional development is something we've always advocated for. Even before the COVID-19 pandemic, there was so much in the way of freely available learning content from blogs, educational books, podcasts and, of course, from creating your professional learning network (PLN). Even as far back as 2011, Mark was sharing the power of Twitter and its impact in helping support professional learning, networking and professional development.

Professional development, however, isn't free, whether it's free to access or not. One of the key issues for teachers being able to participate and act upon professional development is time. Therefore, taking the time to plan, design and be selective in choices which are most likely to lead to impact will help ensure any investment, financial or otherwise, is an investment well made.

If we're going to map out our CPD for the next academic year, it should aim to be as effective as it can be for you while fitting in with the context of the school. To help with that, the EEF has some great recommendations (EEF, 2021):

1. When designing and selecting professional development, focus on the mechanisms.
2. Ensure that professional development effectively builds knowledge, motivates staff, develops teaching techniques and embeds practice.
3. Implement professional development programmes with care, taking into consideration the context and needs of the school.

We have found this to be fantastic advice with the work we do supporting schools with technology implementations. Just like good professional learning to support the effective use of technology is the cornerstone of any quality technology implementation, so it is the same when looking to lead professional development across a school for all facets.

With this in mind, let's examine what the EEF means by this and how you can take on board this advice on a micro, as opposed to a macro, level.

We share this because your SLT member with responsibility for teaching and learning will most likely have mapped out the whole staff CPD through a macro lens, looking at whole-school performance and unpicking target areas for improvements, where there are opportunities for aggregated marginal gains. Taking control of your own CPD is about self-improvement, exploring how you can best support yourself, to make improvements that you see as being relevant and important to your practice.

So, what are the mechanisms?

Well, when the EEF talks about the 'mechanisms', what it does is break down what we already know good teaching and learning looks like, but then apply this to learning for adults as opposed to what we know about teaching young people. Have a look at the four key areas it states as being the 'mechanisms of PD':

1. **Building knowledge:** This is essentially good teaching and learning: namely, managing cognitive load and revisiting prior learning.
2. **Motivating teachers:** This is about setting and agreeing goals, sharing credible sources and providing reinforcement after progress.

3. **Developing teaching techniques:** This covers instruction on how to do something, arranging support, modelling, monitoring with feedback and rehearsing; all good teaching and learning practice.

4. **Embedding practice:** This is providing prompts and cues for colleagues, action planning, encouragement of monitoring and prompting repetition in areas that require it.

While this is aimed at being explored at a macro level, there is plenty here that should be bread and butter for you as a teacher. Within your subject specialism, it's easy to see how this is applied by you daily with the classes you teach. The difference is that here, you're the student!

So, what can I do?

Now that we have a grasp of what CPD looks like on a whole-school level, what can you do to map out your CPD for the next academic year? Here are five things to consider:

1. Keep, grow, change

One practice for reflection shared with Mark by a former colleague, the brilliant Jim Smith (*Lazy Teacher's Handbook*), was a development of the WWW/EBI (what went well/even better if) activity you'll be likely to have come across as an activity with your learners. With keep, grow, change, you reflect upon your experiences across the year and think about what you'd like to keep (WWW), grow (develop, i.e. EBI) or change (consider doing completely differently). This self-assessment activity never failed to help Mark plan out his targets for development and identify his professional learning needs and was vital to help set meaningful targets for the upcoming year.

Another aspect is to take on board feedback from your students. They are experts at working with you, and so ask them what worked for them, what they might like to keep, grow or change – you'll be surprised by what they say! We are confident they'll give you both glowing and interesting feedback to help you work out some areas you could focus upon.

2. Set SMART targets

You will likely be familiar with this acronym too, but following on from your keep, grow, change activity, you'll have identified your areas for growth so it's now time to set some SMART (specific, measurable, achievable, relevant and time-bound) targets. These goals will guide your CPD journey, help you to prioritise what should be done and help to ensure that your choices for professional learning are targeted and effective. For example, instead of vaguely aiming to 'improve cold calling', set a goal like 'plan for cold calling activities with each class at least once by the end of the first term'.

A technology-linked opportunity to improve and aggregate marginal gains might be to see how technology can bring about efficiency savings such as by using software such as **classroom.cloud** (https://classroom. cloud) to launch specific websites or apps for your students, rather than waiting for them to type in the URL or blanking their screens to get their attention back to you immediately. A SMART target of using software such as this to reduce time wasted in class is a simple yet powerful way to enhance and support time-saving in the classroom.

3. Explore a variety of learning opportunities

Variety is the spice of life and the same goes for professional learning. Don't limit yourself to traditional CPD courses or workshops; it's likely your CPD lead may have these set out for you already. Taking control of your own CPD means you can choose whatever you want to consider for a blend of formal and informal learning opportunities, such as:

- Online courses and webinars – try **FutureLearn**, for example.
- Peer observations and feedback – ask your CPD lead who already demonstrates good practice in one of your target areas to arrange for a drop-in.
- Professional learning communities or networks – ahem, BlueSky, Twitter/X and LinkedIn anyone?
- Reading research articles and books – check out your school's CPD library or approach your CPD lead or PLN to ask for recommendations.
- Collaborating with colleagues on projects or initiatives – ask your CPD lead if anyone else in the school is targeting similar areas to you. Could you collaborate and work together?

By diversifying your learning experiences, you'll gain a broader perspective and a richer understanding of your chosen topics.

4. Stop, collaborate and reflect

Research shows that collaborative and reflective learning experiences are more likely to lead to lasting improvements in practice (Darling-Hammond et al., 2017). So, don't go it alone!

As shared in point 3, if you are engaging with colleagues exploring similar professional learning as you, engage with them! If not, consider engaging with colleagues to share your goals and what you've been learning, and seek feedback on your progress. Perhaps there's time in your weekly staff briefing or in a department meeting for you to share or there may be professional learning communities in your school you can participate in. One of the reasons Mark began blogging was for reflective practice when these opportunities didn't exist. You could use your blog to discuss ideas, share resources, and use your writing to reflect on your learning as well as evaluate your progress. If blogging isn't for you, then journalling can be helpful as an alternative approach. It's both cathartic and rewarding as an activity. Learn from others' experiences and don't forget to regularly reflect on your learning journey, evaluate your progress and adjust your goals as needed.

5. Put it into practice

Now that you've learned these new things, it's important to try to put them into practice. Part of the process here is to not try to do too much. Marginal gains and small wins that are aggregated are lower stakes and more likely to be successful. You'll have your SMART targets, but don't try to achieve them all at once. The most crucial step in making your professional learning impactful is applying it in your classroom. Don't worry if you don't get it right the first time or if it doesn't bring the intended impact.

You may find that it's not just you who needs to learn techniques; sometimes you'll have to teach your students how to engage in the approach that you're working upon. For example, if it's a new quizzing technology, your students will need time to familiarise themselves with their use of the tool too. Don't worry if things don't work perfectly the first, second or even third time – after all, practice makes perfect! Experiment with new strategies, techniques or tools, and observe their effects on your teaching and your students' learning. Be prepared to iterate and refine your approach based on your observations and feedback from colleagues or students. Importantly, if it still isn't working after some time, reflection can help you pivot or even re-evaluate whether the approach is still worthwhile.

The summer term provides numerous opportunities to spend time reflecting upon your practice. Hopefully by taking on board some of the advice we have shared, you'll find areas of improvement that will be of help to you and will give you focus to help you plan for your effective professional learning and development in the upcoming academic year!

4.2 A model for sustainable staff training and development

As with all training and development, we are often not our own allies within schools when designing sustainable training and development plans. This is for the inherent reason that schools themselves, and education as a whole, are incredibly busy places and there's often a time misalignment in proportion to the scale of the priority (or priorities) at hand.

The more priorities, goals, plans or aims there are within an institution, the more diluted the available time becomes for reinforcing messaging, training, embedding and so on; all reducing the chances for success. This is all too true and, on the face of it, seems both counterintuitive and counterproductive, especially so given that we are in the business of learning and development, aka education.

While this will likely resonate with many in the education space, no matter the phase or sector (whether state or private education) – it is certainly an experience we have both had in our own educational careers – there's surely a better way.

Less really is more. On the face of it, this sounds like perhaps you wouldn't be getting as much bang for your buck or meeting your goals in a shorter time frame. The truth is that frequently in schools, we are overburdening colleagues with the number of initiatives we are expecting them to freshly implement and embed relative to the training and development time they've received. The more initiatives we push at any one time, the more we dilute the quality of what is happening. Pick a sole focus and work continuously towards it. CPD (or *continuous* professional development) should be just that: continuous.

It should be the mission for everyone to become highly adept at one or two new skills/processes before moving on to the next. Balancing this against the expected rate of pace of adoption and mastery, everyone will move at different paces. So, it is important to factor in multiple opportunities to deliberately space out practice with new opportunities for revisiting, checking in and re-teaching core elements.

Many schools highly recommend Communities of Practice (CoP)[1] as being paramount to their success in this area. A Community of Practice is where small groups of educators with commonality in an area of interest regularly collaborate, learning from and with one another through the building of knowledge collectively. CoPs work best in clearly defined practice areas where colleagues' purposes align – building similar capabilities and outputs that foster enhanced practices across their team.

Another model, originating in Japan, that is more intensive in terms of the time required to successfully facilitate it, is jugyokenkyu (where 'jugyo' means teaching and 'kenkyu' means study), more commonly known as 'Lesson Study'. An Education Endowment Foundation report (EEF, 2017) highlighted 'no evidence of impact' for such an endeavour, while also noting that, 'This result does not show that all activities related to Lesson Study are ineffective'. Pjanić (2014) concluded that, 'Besides individual professional development, research lessons contribute to spreading new content and approaches, connect individual teachers' practices to the school goals and broader goals, create demand for improvement, shape national policy and teach teachers to understand children better.'

David Weston, Chief Executive of the Teacher Development Trust, wrote an informative post titled, 'Does Lesson Study Work? A look at the new EEF trial' (2017) on what a school would need to put into place for this initiative to be successful: an expert in lesson study itself, plus high-quality and supportive research engagement.

Further to this, Sarah Seleznyov wrote an enlightening article for the Chartered College of Teaching's *Impact* magazine titled, 'Learning through research: the case for Japanese lesson study' (2021), which identified modes of translation to apply lesson study to schools in a UK context. She advocated that schools should 'make rational and informed choices about how best to adapt it to their context … not to invest in an "off the peg" model, but to take time to develop a school-specific model that remains true to its critical components, while meeting your school's needs.'

The EEF report titled, 'Effective Professional Development' (2021), impresses three recommendations in the area of effective CPD:

1. When designing and selecting professional development, focus on the mechanisms.

---

[1] https://www.communityofpractice.ca

2. Ensure that professional development builds knowledge, motivates staff, develops teaching techniques and embeds practice.
3. Implement professional development programmes with care, taking into consideration the context and needs of the school.

All are sensible and relatively common-sensical. Yet, we still aren't paying homage to this and we return to our previous point of less being more. Take the time to really drill down and have a laser focus on the specific needs of the school as a whole and then design a programme that fits your context. There is no panacea, just a contextually driven form that enables coherent mechanisms for improved practices.

Secondly, ensure that it is sustainable and timely in its delivery. Give the respect that the development time needs by protecting it at all costs. Remember, you are in it for the long game; quick fixes are an ill-afforded illusion.

For schools that operate on one hour per week for professional development, a successful model might look like this:

- **Session 1, week 1:** Local context and understanding – why this is the developmental need followed up with specific knowledge-building training.
- **Session 2, week 2:** Time to develop techniques within small departmental teams.
- **Session 3, week 3:** Embedding practice.

Repeat the cycle, adding in new skills/procedures when identified as being the optimal time for successful understanding and interoperability.

Caveat: The trainer/s should be available to visit the individuals/teams during weeks two and three so that they are on hand for ongoing and sustained support.

4.3 Digital leadership

As with all leadership, regardless of titles, it is everyone's responsibility to ensure that the change is enacted and realised. While the senior 'leader(s)' will be responsible for the strategic direction and strategy itself, we are all leaders in education and effective leadership is the ultimate key to leveraging technology's potential in education.

Another important facet of successful technology leadership in schools is having a senior member of staff who is responsible for technology implementation and has a 'seat at the top table,' so that they have total oversight and overall decision-making at the highest levels within and across the organisation.

Leadership (more specifically, digital leadership within an educational context) is considerably more complex than simply adopting some new digital tools within the classroom. It involves strategic planning and vision beyond the normal four walls of a school, carefully curating a culture of innovation and growth mindset, while also bringing multiple stakeholders together to form a fruitful partnership at just the right time. Not to mention the ongoing commitment to developing digital literacy across all stakeholders in the organisation and getting professional development right.

There has been a fair amount of talk in recent times about there being no need for a digital strategy. We disagree with this. Strategies are a cyclical and iterative process. Some advocate for a digital vision, while some have said that a strong digital culture negates the need for a digital strategy; again, we disagree. A good digital strategy will and should be something which intertwines with all aspects of school life. It isn't something which sits purely with pedagogy or operations or marketing, etc.; it's all part of enabling the overall vision of your context, be that in FE, HE, Primary or any other stage within an educational setting. Just as curriculum or safeguarding or teaching and learning are strands that help you achieve your vision, so is a digital strategy.

In recognition of this and its importance, the Department for Education (DfE) recently updated (May 2024) its 'Meeting digital and technology standards in schools and colleges' (2022) guidance for digital leadership and governance standards to include the requirement that a member of SLT has responsibility for digital. It says:

'Schools and colleges need a member of their SLT to:

- have strategic oversight of all digital technology and how it fits with their development plan
- create and manage the digital technology strategy led by the needs of staff and students, not the technology itself
- help all staff to embed digital technology that meets staff and student needs.'

It also says that schools and colleges should: 'Have a digital technology strategy that is reviewed every year.'

What hasn't been mentioned yet is the importance of making data your ally when it comes to digital leadership. Data tells the story which informs areas for development and decision-making next steps; keeping your fingers on the data pulse is vitally important. An evidence-based and evidence-informed process will not only help guide and shape decision-making but also enable the allocation of resources to where they are most needed, while the organisation remains adaptive and responsive.

This includes all data relating to the organisation's asset register, information asset register, digital data, equipment and systems. All licences, contracts, software and hardware should also be tracked. This data will enable an organisation to know when reviews are needed and to evaluate the value of contracts both financially and in terms of organisational needs (educational or otherwise).

Getting digital leadership right is a crucial part of navigating the complexities of successful and sustainable technology integration. Tapping into teacher agency is another important enabler for leaders to empower teachers through supportive and autonomous mechanisms that encourage innovative methods of collaboration, effective resourcing, coaching and mentoring, and capacity building at scale.

4.4 Getting IT right

The development of Knoster's change management model by Mark, shared in chapter 1 (figure 1.2), helps unpick the key characteristics of the elements you need to ensure successful implementation. Getting IT right is about ensuring you are laying down the foundations and conditions for success.

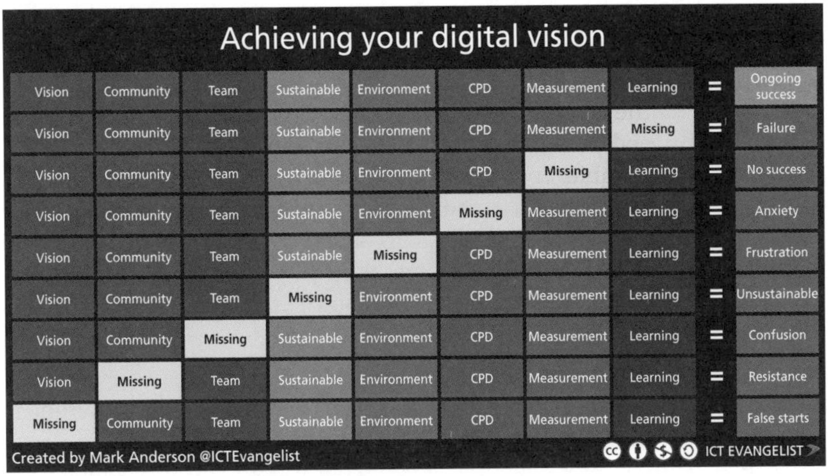

Achieving your digital vision

Vision	Community	Team	Sustainable	Environment	CPD	Measurement	Learning	= Ongoing success
Vision	Community	Team	Sustainable	Environment	CPD	Measurement	Missing	= Failure
Vision	Community	Team	Sustainable	Environment	CPD	Missing	Learning	= No success
Vision	Community	Team	Sustainable	Environment	Missing	Measurement	Learning	= Anxiety
Vision	Community	Team	Sustainable	Missing	CPD	Measurement	Learning	= Frustration
Vision	Community	Team	Missing	Environment	CPD	Measurement	Learning	= Unsustainable
Vision	Community	Missing	Sustainable	Environment	CPD	Measurement	Learning	= Confusion
Vision	Missing	Team	Sustainable	Environment	CPD	Measurement	Learning	= Resistance
Missing	Community	Team	Sustainable	Environment	CPD	Measurement	Learning	= False starts

Created by Mark Anderson @ICTEvangelist   ICT EVANGELIST

Figure 4.1: Achieving your digital vision

To secure the conditions and mechanisms for success, you need to ensure that you are achieving each of the key areas in figure 4.1.

- **Vision:** A clear vision not only gives clarity on what you are trying to achieve but also a steer on the actions that you need to take to get there. Without clarity of purpose, you will be left with false starts and misalignment across the organisation.

- **Community:** Ensure you involve the entire community – from teaching to support staff, students and parents. Not just leaders in isolation. Effective buy-in and the development of efficacy and culture are bought for and paid for by your timely approach to listening to all stakeholder voices, plus the mechanisms for collaboration within and across the whole community. Without this, you are susceptible to resistance which, ultimately, will derail any change management and jeopardise getting IT right.

- **Team:** Aligning your team (and teams) not only helps to get IT right but also helps to foster an innovative and collaborative culture among colleagues and the wider school community. Without this, confusion will set in and compounding this with resistance and false starts will only lead to ineffectiveness and inefficiencies.

- **Sustainable:** As previously mentioned, any change management process must be sustainable for everyone involved. Without it, you won't be able to keep the main thing 'the main thing' – an often underappreciated and misrepresented action.

- **Environment:** Leaders set the tone and lead by their example; 'walking the walk' you could say, by guiding with your values and behaviours as opposed to just with your words. Are you modelling the behaviours you wish to see in your teams? When you do lead by example, you not only drive developments towards excellence but you are actively and consciously demonstrating those positive practices and aligning habitual practices, routines, behaviours and core values. What about when you get it wrong? Own it, as to err is to be human. The purpose of leadership is to be the change that you would wish to see in your school. Without such environmental conditions being carefully curated, frustration will soon set in.
- **CPD:** Targeted, sustained, developmental – and the truth is, it isn't all about what you do. It is how you do it that makes the difference. Choose that which serves the needs of your school/organisation and be responsive to the evolving needs. Poorly planned and incoherent CPD will only lead to increased anxiety and poor performance, so don't leave it to chance.
- **Measurement:** Over time, education has become fantastic in its attempts to measure progress and performance for learners, yet measuring other facets of education still often lacks clarity, leaving ambiguity and failure. After all, without measuring the initiative and benchmarking key moments in time, how will you know how far you've come on a micro and macro scale? Measurement is not a stick to beat people with but a driver for information and being evidence-informed. Let's ensure we are changing the narrative here, as data is useful but what we do with it is even more crucial to the recipe; data is only useful if you use it.
- **Learning:** If technology isn't being used to support learning within and across your organisation, then what is it being used for? Technology should enhance but not dictate learning.

With all of the above conditions accounted for, you will be hard pressed to *not* get IT right!

4.5 Little and often – marginal gains

A little-and-often approach to transformation helps to support its adoption. From promoting consistent messaging around the change, driving progress, celebrating successes along the way, and having a transparent process to review and adapt your progress, this approach makes it easier to maintain momentum and motivation among colleagues.

It takes time to change and build new habits. However, it is worth the effort as it will reduce the risk of staff feeling overwhelmed while enabling seismic and lasting positive changes.

More often than not, despite rigorous planning and strategising, transformation involves navigating and adapting to any challenges that arise. The little-and-often approach enables flexibility and responsiveness to the needs of your project which, in time, leads to a more sustainable transformation, thanks to ongoing marginal gains.

The theory of marginal gains first hit the educational sector through Dr Zoë Elder[2] (@fullonlearning on Twitter/X) and was inspired by the same philosophy that drove the Team GB cycling team to success at two Olympics. The premise is simple: the aggregation of well-developed small actions leads to larger gains, and thus impact, on an organisation.

As with any initiative, we must ensure, from a due diligence stance, that we allow sufficient time for the design of each checkpoint in learning as well as time to reflect upon it, so that we are truly drilling down to answer the root of the question of procedural analysis at a micro level to further develop high-quality practice.

When we combine the components of transformation – pausing for reflection, getting IT right, digital leadership and a sustainable approach to staff development – the marginal gains approach offers a specific starting point for the novice and expert alike, as it is both contextual and can build on Sir John Whitmore's GROW coaching for performance model,[3] which is specific for each individual while also building on SMART targets/goals. Ultimately, we want each individual in our schools to be productive, learn new skills and be happy at work, and this approach helps curate such a culture.

The GROW model is a powerful framework for supporting the structuring of your coaching. It aids in setting out the journey by helping you decide on your goal and establish the current reality. It then prompts you to explore your options and any obstacles to the intended goal and then asks you to commit to the journey.

The GROW model can be seen in the following table with some example questions:

---

2 https://marginallearninggains.com/about
3 www.coachingcultureatwork.com/wp-content/uploads/The-GROW-Model.pdf

GROW	Some examples of GROW coaching questions
GOAL	What are you trying to achieve?
	What does that look like?
	What will that enable you to do?
	What new elements are in place?
	What is different?
REALITY	What is happening now?
	How important is this to you?
	What resources do you have/need?
	What are you doing that takes you towards this goal?
OPTIONS (or Obstacles)	What ideas can we come up with to achieve the goal?
	What alternatives do you have?
	What if this obstacle was removed?
	What worked in the past?
	What steps could you take?
	Who could help you with this?
	Where can you find out the information?
	How could you do that?
WILL (or Way forward)	What can we commit to?
	Who will do it, and by when?
	Who will you talk to?
	Where will you go?
	Is there anything you need to put in place before that?
	How committed are you to taking that action?
	What will it take for you to commit to that?

Table 4.1: The GROW model

The imperative question to return to when using the GROW framework is that of target setting: what is the time frame for this and when shall we meet again? This question keeps the discussion rooted in reality and provides a check-in for progress, along with accountability. It is worth mentioning, for the avoidance of doubt, that if the original plan turns out to be not achievable, there's also an opportunity to adapt and manoeuvre the approach to ensure success.

Marginal gains, in unison with the GROW coaching model and SMART targets, enable organisations to not only offer the mechanistic conditions for effective transformations but also to encourage the development of a positive culture through providing sufficient challenge and support, a sense of purpose, a culture based on thinking and reflecting, psychological safety, collegiality and a sense of belonging.

4.6 Common misunderstandings

Often in school, leaders will give a message and operate under the assumption that the message was both received and understood by the intended audience – a signal-to-noise ratio, you might say. In science (engineering to be specific), this is a measure that compares the levels of desired signal to the levels of background noise; the ratio of signal power to the noise power, more commonly expressed in decibels (dB). Has your message, as the leader, been heard or has it caused a range of reverberations offset against the original message's echoes?

Another issue that can wreak havoc is if a leader provides no clear guidelines or frameworks from which the audience is expected to operate, which can leave teachers and other leaders formulating their own interpretations of the message.

The knock-on impact of both of these common occurrences is the formulation and evolution of a range of mutations and subsequent mutated implementations across the organisation. Here lies, but also breeds, inconsistency, which to unpick and realign is costly and weighs heavy on the organisation.

A third common mistake is that of misalignments in time. We have got ourselves into a quandary somewhat in education with a mindset or culture of 'change must happen now and we must see the impact immediately'. While positive changes can occur in a narrow time frame, sustained and lasting change that is effective can take effort, focus and time to get right.

The remedy?

Fundamentally, as we've hinted at but perhaps not made as explicit as it could/should have been, we are talking about effective change management. All transformations are rooted in this being done well.

When it comes to articulation of your vision, it is important to share this information regularly and in different ways. As we discussed in chapter 1, collective teacher efficacy is 'the collective belief of the staff of the school/faculty in their ability to positively affect students',[4] which comes from sharing key messages frequently and in different formats. It is only through consistently sharing and modelling the key aspects of your vision as a leader that you will be able to bring your staff body on that journey.

Years ago, at the start of a whole-school transformation process (after years of poor results, poor behaviour of students and many other indicators of a poor school), one of our (new to the post) headteachers shared to an audience of 80+ teaching staff that the school would become the best-performing school. Most of the audience didn't hear the claim, but some did – they laughed and didn't believe it. Three years later, with repeated messaging (and the school ranking highest within the county in terms of results, a new school uniform, house system, vertical tutoring and many more transformations), not only was that vision still shared outwardly by that headteacher, but it was believed, realised and heard – not just by the teaching body but by the whole school community including parents, carers, governors and, most importantly, students.

4.7 Digital skills for all

We all need digital skills in the current day and age. This is certainly not going to change as time moves forward. One argument against this could be that the rise of AI will negate the need for us to have as many skills in the digital arena. We would argue against this idea and that, in truth, we will need digital skills that are inclusive of AI. To be a cognisant user of technology, you still need the necessary knowledge and skills so that you can make sound, informed decisions.

This doesn't mean you need to know everything about every tool/platform out there, but certainly a base level of understanding across a few tools is essential. Take, for example, our working lives in education right now: schools are typically using either a Google or Microsoft ecosystem. Educators therefore need a basic set of skills to navigate this environment, along with a working knowledge of the device that they are using.

---

[4] https://visible-learning.org/2018/03/collective-teacher-efficacy-hattie

An example of a base set of digital skills can be seen in this table:

Skill type	Digital skills
Basic computer skills	Knowledge of operating systems, file management and file organisation, menu navigation, how to work with interfaces, curating tabs and bookmarks, keyboard shortcuts, using the ribbon and setting system preferences.
Ecosystem navigation	Finding and using applications native to the ecosystem. For a Microsoft ecosystem, this would be switching between Word, Excel, Outlook, PowerPoint, Teams, OneDrive and SharePoint.
File management	How to manage files and documents within the ecosystem, inclusive of creating, saving, renaming, sharing, copying, moving, deleting and editing file permissions.
Document creation and editing	Creating and editing documents in applications such as Google Docs, Google Sheets, Google Slides and Google Forms. Tracking changes, adding comments and using the editing features in each application.
Collaboration	Making use of tools such as document and folder sharing, real-time co-authoring, permission setting, access controls, feedback via comments and editing.
Communication	Using tools such as Outlook for emails, the calendar for scheduling, Teams for virtual meetings, and SharePoint communication sites for school-wide or group-wide data and information.
Storage	Successfully using OneDrive or Google Drive for the storage of data. Knowing how to sync said data/files and how to access files from alternative locations. How to set up backup and recovery options so that the files/data are protected. How to set passwords onto files to ensure their privacy is protected.
Data and reporting	Make use of tools like Google Sheets for data analysis, formatting spreadsheets, entering and organising the data, using formulas, performing calculations and turning data into visual aids such as graphs/charts.
Presentation skills	Creating engaging and interactive presentations using tools such as Google Slides, Microsoft PowerPoint and Canva. Making use of presentation tools to deliver effective presentations synchronously or asynchronously.

Table 4.2: Digital skills

These options and skills are important, but what about a curriculum? As mentioned above, and inspired by the paper by Hamilton, Wiliam and Hattie (2023), this begs the question that we need to be incorporating AI literacy for all, both staff and students alike.

While digital and AI literacy are going to be ever more fundamental in the future, now is the time to build a curriculum for staff and students. Yes, they might start out with some similarities in terms of key content, definitions and foundational elements but, over time, they will likely diverge, given the needs of stakeholders and the nature of the makeup of a digital cognition curriculum. It is clear that a new approach to what it means to use technology as a teacher and as a student is needed. Therefore, we advocate for a curriculum for learning, professional or otherwise, that incorporates digital citizenship, digital literacy, AI literacy, and computer science.

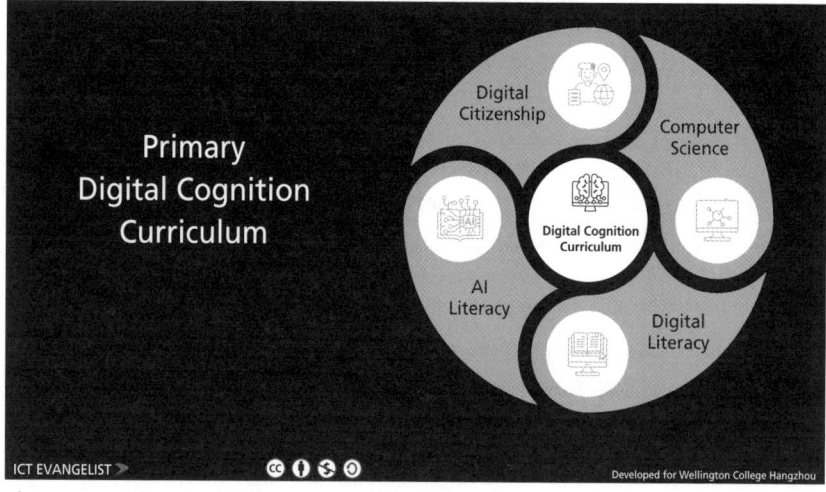

Figure 4.2: Primary digital curriculum

A great starting point for a digital cognition curriculum would be exploring what good digital citizenship is (and is not), from etiquette and respect to cyber awareness and prevention, protecting personal information, accuracy of information, an awareness of one's digital footprint, and the overall positive engagement and contributions online.

Digital literacy is the ability to efficiently and effectively evaluate and create with digital technologies, both ethically and competently, from having a working knowledge of software applications and competence in using digital tools and platforms for communication and collaboration purposes, to assessing and selecting reliable information sources, leveraging a range of digital tools to support productivity and learning, and maintaining a positive online presence.

AI literacy is our understanding and ability to effectively and critically evaluate technologies that have AI baked into them – or AI technologies themselves. It involves the knowledge of AI concepts, tools, applications and ethical considerations so that individuals can meaningfully and critically interact with AI – from grasping fundamental AI concepts and its applications, to identifying how it can positively (or negatively) impact on our lives, enhance productivity and creativity, and be responsibly used to assess outputs – and understand its limitations.

Finally, we come to computer science literacy. For all of the above, we also need to have a working understanding of and ability to use computer systems and software. That doesn't mean we all need to now be able to programme in Python (although AI can help with this!); however, it does mean we need to have a working knowledge of these things so we can check the code generated by AI. We also need to know how algorithms work, how to store and access data, how to think and work in the computational domain, how hardware works and how software interacts with it. Additionally, we should understand how to secure and protect systems and information from threats, be able to test vulnerabilities, interact with databases, troubleshoot networks, and more.

It begs the question: with all these mentions of different types of literacy, in a world where *prompt* crafting is increasingly important, is it not the case that we need to reconsider what is meant by 'literacy'?

The purpose of all this isn't to shock you, as there is a lot of detail here, but to help develop an appreciation of the brevity and depth of a digital cognition curriculum.

Yes, there's plenty to get stuck into, but it is just that: a curriculum which extends over time and across year groups. Carefully sequencing the core competencies and knowledge is the most important part, so that each layer builds on the former. Next is an example of what this might look like in a primary school for each of the four key areas which cover the NCCE computing curriculum, ISTE standards for students and an AI literacy curriculum borne out of Mark's work with Wellington College Hangzhou.

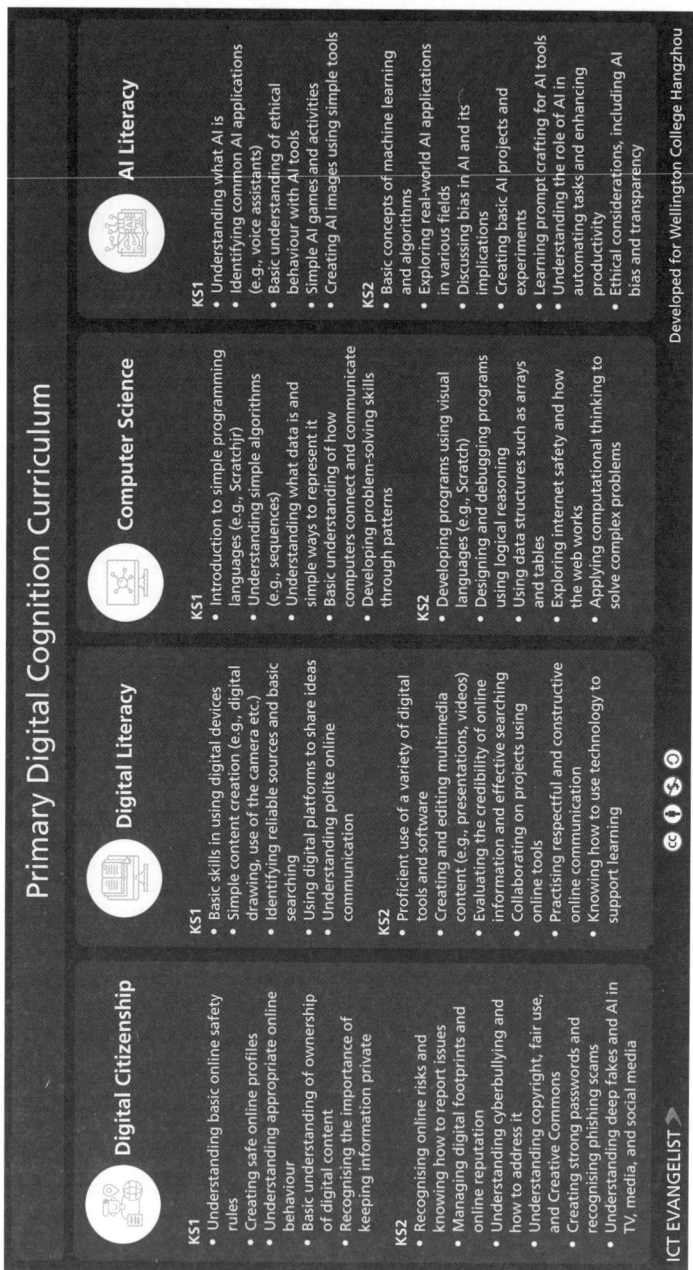

Figure 4.3: A potential Primary digital cognition curriculum

Whichever way you approach it is entirely up to you. However, as you can see from figure 4.3, the skills and knowledge are built upon across the key stages for each of the four key domains across the curriculum: digital citizenship, digital literacy, computer science and AI literacy.

4.8 Using technology to manage your IT estate

This book isn't, by any stretch, a book about technical IT management, but it is important that, as educators, we have an appreciation of how all of this 'magic' happens.

Mark remembers well, when rolling out one-to-one devices to 1300 students back in 2011, it wasn't easy! Back then, an iPad was a personal device. It simply couldn't be managed. Technical teams who were used to being able to manage devices (such as Windows desktop machines) across the school were reticent to roll out devices that they couldn't so easily support, from a technical and a safeguarding point of view. Systems, training and support for key stakeholders, particularly parents and students, was paramount. Of course, as teachers, we needed to have clear etiquette on how devices could be used in the classroom. Forget classroom management tools to lock screens with a tablet in the classroom. A lot of time was spent focusing on student behaviour (not just with devices).

Looking back, it was very much like the Wild West then. It's funny how hindsight can change a viewpoint.

Of course, nowadays, things are much more rigorously controlled in IT environments and there are a number of ways to do it. A key part of the jigsaw puzzle that we'll talk about in a number of ways throughout the book is a type of technology called an 'MDM' or 'mobile device management' solution.

It's often linked to your MIS and your ecosystem's tenant, be it Microsoft, Google or Apple. On Apple devices, things can be a little bit more complicated as it's likely you'll both want to manage the device, but also have a Google or Microsoft ecosystem running on it. That said, the MDM is now an essential part of making IT work in the classroom for teachers. Through these platforms, IT teams can:

- push apps
- administer IT policies
- enrol devices

- manage devices
- monitor devices
- support cross-platform compatibility
- support safeguarding
- provide content filtering

...and much more.

While as an educator (or leader) you'll (likely) never be asked to do this work, it's important to know that these things exist, so the next time you want an app on a device or to check what a pupil has been doing with their device, your technical team will be able to assist more readily, because of these amazing pieces of software.

In summary, effective digital transformation is a bit like lining up dominoes. It requires you to look at the whole piece in both a macro and micro view. We've covered many of these aspects in this chapter, but recognise that this could be a book in and of itself. We hope that we've given you, as a classroom practitioner or leader, enough scope to know what a good one looks like and signposted enough for you to explore more depending upon your interest and role.

As move forward in the book, we'll continue to explore more teaching, learning, cognitive science and other key aspects you should consider to make the most of the EdTech you have in your setting.

Top tips

Mark's top tips

1. Take time. Work out what collective teacher efficacy with digital should look like in your setting and aim towards that target.

2. Recognise that technology is often the easiest thing to get right; it's the mechanisms that are the most difficult. Focus on setting the conditions for success and tend to them like a gardener would the contents of their greenhouse.

3. Don't try to achieve everything at once. Time is the thing people need most, so build it into your plans.

Olly's top tips

1. Rome wasn't built in a day! Sensibly work through your curriculum so that you can work towards achieving your targets in the four areas across the digital cognition curriculum.

2. Focus on getting the foundations right and get them right as early as you can so your digital skills are constantly built on and reinforced.

3. Tap into teacher agency and foster opportunities for collaborative work! Also, don't be shy to learn from and with students.

CHAPTER 5
Cognitive science with technology

'Cognitive science is a rapidly developing area, so it could be that there are some surprises around the corner. That does seem to be kind of where the trend line is leading.'

Louis Menand

It has been a delight in recent years (certainly, since Mark studied at university on his B.Ed), to see cognitive science become de rigueur as part of the conversation about what works when it comes to teaching and learning. In Brian Simon's 'Why No Pedagogy in England' article back in 1981, he wrote passionately about how learning science simply didn't exist in England, 'reflecting deep confusion of thought, and of aims and purposes, relating to learning and teaching – to pedagogy' (Simon, 1981). Not so much anymore!

We only have to look at the number of books on offer from our publisher, Hachette, to see the massive growth in the conversation and thinking around the science of learning. The impact of incorporating its learnings into teachers' everyday practice has been huge – and quite rightly so.

In this chapter, we will explore many of the key cognitive science approaches that have become standard food for thought among teachers when considering learning design and how technology can help you achieve some of your aims.

We do not propose to make this a chapter that tries to teach you about these different strategies and the research behind them. Yes, we'll explain them in some detail, but that's not what this book is about. For that, there are many other excellent titles out there. This book is *The EdTech Playbook*, so therefore we will concentrate on the approaches and how technology supports them.

5.1 Retrieval practice

Retrieval practice is a learning strategy whereby students recall information from their long-term memory. (It's supported by plenty of research, such as the work of Dr P. Agarwal,[1] Professor R. Coe,[2] Dunlosky et al.,[3] E. Furst,[4] the Learning Scientists,[5] and many more.) This recall strengthens the memory, thanks to the learner having to locate it actively. It is designed to help negate the impacts of what Ebbinghaus called the '*forgetting curve*'.

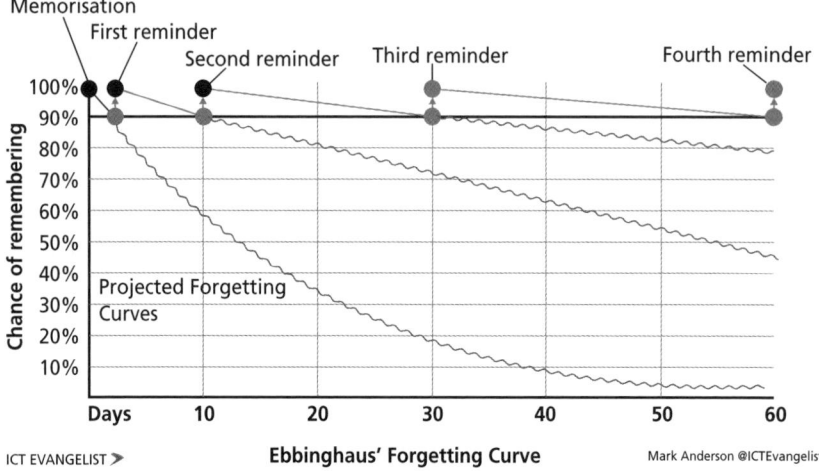

Figure 5.1: Ebbinghaus' forgetting curve

Retrieval practice is based on the 'testing effect' that states that the performance of long-term memory can be enhanced when it is practised. Through the action of recalling the information, a learner can actively identify any knowledge gaps and, therefore, take the necessary steps to practise using the information again in the future in a similarly relevant scenario.

While not a direct form of assessment, it is a method for improving performance when recalling information required in the future. The strategy has proved to be highly successful due to the effort invested in recalling the pathway to where the memory is stored. Thus, when retrieving information, we will rehearse an entire pathway, rather than a specific subset of information.

---

1 www.poojaagarwal.com
2 https://educationendowmentfoundation.org.uk/news/does-research-on-retrieval-practice-translate-into-classroom-practice
3 https://pcl.sitehost.iu.edu/rgoldsto/courses/dunloskyimprovinglearning.pdf
4 https://sites.google.com/view/efratfurst/home?authuser=0
5 www.learningscientists.org

By triggering prior knowledge, we activate the pathway for new learning. This deepens our understanding of that prior knowledge, which in turn has a cumulative effect on schema development. The introduction of connective cues supports conceptual thinking (which aids knowledge assimilation and the development of richer schema) while also enabling strengthened connections to prior knowledge.

The key elements of successful retrieval practice are that it should:

- be meaningful
- take effort
- offer feedback
- be timely
- be supportive of the learner.

The mental challenge involved with retrieval practice ensures that long-term memory becomes more durable and efficient over time. Retrieving information should involve thought that is deep and promotes challenge. If it is easy, the opportunity for memory reconstruction will not take place and the retrieval will be, in essence, ineffective in promoting long-term storage access. Thus, meaningful and effortful retrieval builds on the associated memory pathways and supports the development of rich(er) schema.

Some of the best bets for effective use of retrieval practice are ensuring that:

- it is low stakes
- it is used as a supportive learning strategy
- there are frequent and timely opportunities for feedback
- it is not simply used for factual retrieval, but also for connecting, contrasting and comparing learning.

Technology to support retrieval practice

Many EdTech tools can support retrieval practice in the classroom. Given the different types of retrieval, we've created a table sharing some of the tools that can support the activity across the range of types.

Type of retrieval	Purpose	EdTech tools to support
Quizzing	Retrieving facts or definitions, self-testing, and checking.	▪ Quizizz ▪ Quizlet ▪ Kahoot ▪ Mentimeter
Compare, contrast, connect	Supporting the development of schema.	▪ Quizizz ▪ Quizlet ▪ Kahoot
Generative learning activities	Learners use their memory to explore what they do and don't know (without the use of prompts) to enhance their learning.	Content creation tools, e.g.: ▪ Adobe Express ▪ Microsoft PowerPoint ▪ Apple Keynote ▪ Google Slides ▪ Apple Clips ▪ iMovie
Self-explanation	A student-led mental explanation is checked.	Voice notes.
Demonstration or modelling	A means for learners to show they know a technique, process or procedure.	▪ Visualiser ▪ Microsoft OneNote ▪ Loom ▪ screen-casting ▪ simulation tools
Elaborative interrogation	Answering 'how' and 'why' questions in pairs or individually.	▪ Mini White Board (MWB) ▪ content creation tools
Explanation rehearsal	A process for describing, explaining or simply telling the story where details are the foci.	▪ MWB ▪ content creation tools

Type of retrieval	Purpose	EdTech tools to support
Mind mapping	Checking learner capacity to make links.	■ Visualiser ■ Microsoft OneNote ■ Microsoft PowerPoint ■ Google Slides ■ Apple Keynote ■ paper and pen(!) ■ MWB
Summarising	A less precise strategy for checking but useful nonetheless.	■ Visualiser ■ Microsoft OneNote ■ Microsoft PowerPoint ■ Google Slides ■ Apple Keynote ■ Microsoft Word ■ Apple Pages ■ Google Docs ■ paper and pen ■ MWB

Table 5.1: Technology to support retrieval practice

Key point to remember: It's not about the tool you use to support retrieval practice but how you incorporate it to facilitate the retrieval that is important!

5.2 Spaced and deliberate practice

Spaced practice involves multiple learning opportunities that are deliberately distanced over time. It enables a learner to break down material and promotes the retention of information for long-term learning. This strategy allows the learner to almost forget prior learning before they revisit it.

The steps for effective spaced practice are to:

- plan for regular intervals between study sessions
- keep the sessions specific and focused

- review the learning before recalling the material at the first spacing interval
- continue to recall at intervals along the determined timeline.

Simple but easily accessible technology can help with the planning stages for spaced practice, with a wide variety of calendaring tools available – from those that come as standard with your ecosystem (such as Google **Calendar** or **Outlook**) to those within your operating system (such as the **Calendar** app on MacOS and iOS). Many students and teachers alike find it useful to have separate calendars for different subjects, to help organise and highlight different subjects in different colours when mapping out activities for spacing their practice.

Deliberate practice is a strategy whereby activities are designed to improve a specific aspect of an individual's performance through repetition and successive refinement. For educators, deliberate practice aims to segregate a specific pedagogical practice which can then be rehearsed and improved through feedback, in much the same way that we would model to a learner and then use further prompts, questioning, feedback and scaffolds to develop their performance.

Forget to remember!

While these methods are already well-documented, it is important to note that, while it sounds counter-intuitive to forget before you remember, these strategies are supported by those leading their fields in education research and cognitive science.

Technology to support spaced and deliberate practice

Spaced or deliberate practice	Purpose	EdTech tools to support
Spaced	Recall over time.	- Quizizz - Forms - Century TECH - Tassomai - UpLearn
Deliberate	Improve a specific aspect of performance.	- Quizizz - Seneca - Microsoft/Google Forms

Table 5.2: Technology to support spaced and deliberate practice

5.3 Dual coding

Allan Paivio's dual coding theory has, in recent years, been expertly explained by Oliver Caviglioli in his book *Dual Coding with Teachers* (2019). This seminal book brings together research, theory and experience that highlight the benefits of how visuals support and reinforce learning through diagrammatic explanations. (As an aside, an excellent summary is provided by Global EdTech speaker, Greg Hughes, in his blog on LinkedIn.[6])

In an educational setting, the two most frequent stimuli are verbal and visual; these are what learners use to encode information into their memory for it to be retrieved later on. The combination of these stimuli supports the formation of working memory, and yet, while they are separate information channels, they work in unison. Despite verbal stimuli being processed sequentially and visual stimuli being processed synchronously, their links occur simultaneously to aid learning.

Why visuals support constructive memory-building

Visuals assist constructive memory-building as they support directing attention, trigger prior knowledge, manage cognitive load, aid schema formulation and make transfer easier between long-term and working memory – plus, they motivate learners.

Visuals that are well-designed and thought-out draw our attention to their key elements and thus avoid any obscurity or confusion. The clarity of well-crafted visuals aids the connection with prior knowledge and supports new learning while ensuring no mental faculties are wasted. This organisation supports the encoding into our long-term memory and builds affluent schema.

---

[6] www.linkedin.com/pulse/dual-coding-digital-technology-greg-hughes

Technology to support dual coding

Strategy	Purpose	Tech to support
Infographics	Distilling complex information into more easy-to-understand and accessible formats.	▪ Piktochart ▪ Canva ▪ Adobe Express.
Mindmap	Organising and linking concepts visually, helping in the creation of relational and hierarchical structures in learning material.	▪ Popplet ▪ Coggle ▪ Lucidchart.
Storyboarding	Storytelling techniques help to sequence ideas and information as a narrative, which can aid in memory and understanding.	Software that enables easy creation of storyboard templates, including: ▪ Microsoft PowerPoint ▪ Microsoft Excel
Video curation	Explainer videos that slowly walk through complex content.	Software that enables video creation, including: ▪ Canva ▪ Microsoft Stream ▪ Screencastify ▪ Loom
GIFs	Explaining in sequence a variety of elements to help with the understanding of complex subject matter.	Presentation tools whereby you create animated elements which can be exported as a GIF, including: ▪ Microsoft PowerPoint ▪ Apple Keynote ▪ Canva
Visual organisers	Giving clarity to complex information.	Visualiser or well-constructed presentation slides with appropriate animations so that information is added incrementally so as to not add cognitive load.

Table 5.3: Technology to support dual coding

There are other strategies you may decide to employ in the classroom to show a sequence or complex array of interlinked information, such as using timelines or hierarchical information – technology can support this too. Technology can reduce cognitive load, thanks to its ability to bring information to the fore in small chunks, e.g. via transitions/animation functions in presentation software (e.g. Google **Slides**, Microsoft **PowerPoint**, **Prezi** (www.prezi.com)) to show the build-up of a system of knowledge and/ or the delineation of a process. This allows students to focus their attention on the teacher's explanations. The key here is to ensure each slide isn't overloaded with content, otherwise students' attention will be split, as they'll be reading the slide and not listening to you!

5.4 Direct instruction

Direct instruction is the 'model for teaching that emphasises well-developed and carefully planned lessons designed around small learning increments and clearly defined and prescribed teaching tasks. It is based on the theory that clear instruction eliminating misinterpretations can greatly improve and accelerate learning.'[7]

There are five key principles for direct instruction:

1. All learners are taught.
2. All learners can improve academically (and their self-image).
3. All teachers, with sufficient training and resources, can succeed.
4. Disadvantaged and low-performing learners should be taught at a faster rate compared to typical rates for high-performing peers.
5. All instruction details are controlled to minimise misinterpretations and misconceptions – plus maximise the instructional effect.

More recently, direct instruction has been referred to as 'explicit instruction'. However, there is a difference between the two approaches. Direct instruction's approach is teacher-centred and focuses on skill acquisition, whereas explicit instruction is a type of direct instruction that is characterised by:

- **clearly defined learning objectives:** The teacher clearly states what students are expected to learn.
- **step-by-step instruction:** The teacher breaks down the learning task into small steps and provides explicit instruction on each step.

---

[7] www.nifdi.org/15/index.php?option=com_content&view=article&id=52&Itemid=27

- **active student participation:** Students are actively involved in the learning process, either through hands-on activities or through verbal responses.
- **immediate feedback:** The teacher provides immediate feedback on student performance.
- **opportunities for practice:** Students have multiple opportunities to practise the skills they are learning.

Either way, both approaches are teacher-led with a deep engagement and focus on well-designed, structured, scripted and resourced lessons to maximise learning.

Explicit instruction has been identified as being effective for students with additional needs or those struggling to learn, in teaching a variety of skills, including reading, writing and mathematics.

Why visualisation works

Visualisations work with both direct and explicit instruction. They enhance understanding by providing a visual representation of a key piece of information or concept. They also help learners to visualise a complex or abstract concept so that it becomes more tangible. This visual clarity supports critical thinking and higher-order cognitive skills. Visualisations also help information to be processed and stored more effectively when both the visual and auditory channels are used in tandem, making the taught concept more concrete.

While visualisations can capture the learner's attention, they can also foster inclusivity in the classroom environment, providing access to learners with a diverse range of abilities and needs – including those who are partially sighted.

It is worth noting that the overall effectiveness of visualisations, irrespective of direct or explicit instruction, depends upon the quality, relevance and alignment to the learning at hand. Any visualisation used should be specific to the learning objective and form a part of the instructional process so that it impacts learning.

Technology to support direct instruction

Direct instruction requires you to be able to demonstrate live to learners. At its simplest level, you can just use the whiteboard in your classroom. Purveyors of interactive whiteboards (IWBs) will have you believe you *need* to use their devices; however, technology provides us with the opportunities to do far more than just use an IWB. Technologies that enable you to project to your board can be far more useful for direct instruction, whether it's through a visualiser or via wireless mirroring technology that allows you to beam content from your device to your class instantly.

The key to success is two-fold. Firstly, it's about finding the right technology to match the activity you are trying to undertake and demonstrate as part of your (direct) instruction. For example, if you are an art teacher trying to demonstrate a particular brush stroke or a science teacher trying to demonstrate how to dissect a frog, then using the camera on your device is great. You could amp it up by recording a video and the audio of your explanation for later viewing. Secondly, it is important to think carefully about what software/hardware will best suit the learning activity. We say this because while a camera on a visualiser is a useful tool, it does not allow you to annotate digital work to demonstrate augmented reality models or other types of digital content important to your direct instruction.

The best-case scenario for a class teacher wishing to use direct instruction as part of their teaching and learning toolkit is to have a set-up that provides the flexibility to pivot to the pedagogy and content they are trying to cover with their students.

Given budget constraints in schools, it is likely that a single device that incorporates a camera with the added dexterity of a visualiser would be the best-case scenario. Often, schools will purchase a grip or stand built to match their single device that will enable the dual functionality. Popular software solutions often found in schools to support these kinds of activities are: Microsoft **OneNote Class Notebook** (www.onenote.com/classnotebook), **Explain Everything** (www.explaineverything.com), Apple **Keynote** and Microsoft **PowerPoint**.

What else and so what?

Given the overarching theme of this chapter is focused on learning and how technology can support and enhance it, it is only right to include our thoughts on what a good example looks like.

For us, the principles of effective teaching and learning with or without technology remain the same and are underpinned by the works of Sweller (2011), Rosenshine (2012) and Kirschner.[8] They are:

- Present new information in small chunks.

---

[8] https://scholar.google.com/citations?user=6c3HTBIAAAAJ&hl=en

- Provide worked examples.
- Check for understanding frequently, supported by low-stakes testing.
- Provide feedback regularly.
- Employ peer and teacher collaboration.

Both Olly and Mark have long communicated this and it was part of their key messaging during the COVID-19 pandemic when learning moved online. The environment changed but the principles of effective learning and teaching did not.

Next is an example that Olly shared back in 2020 (Lewis, 2020) which links to the metacognitive process to enhance learning.

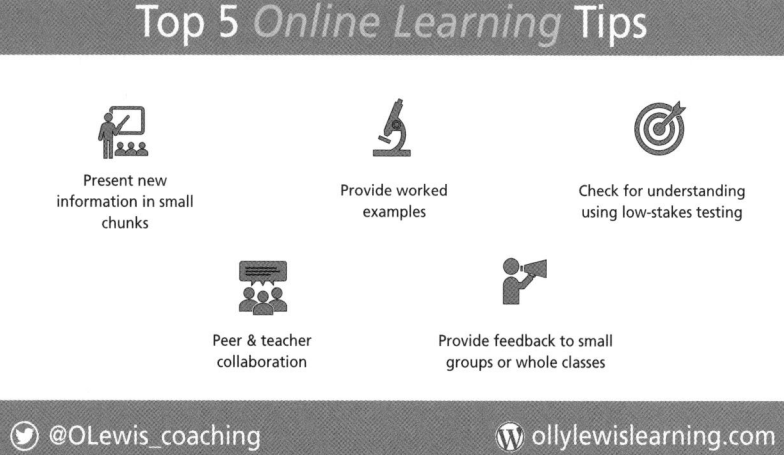

Figure 5.2: Top 5 online learning tips

5.5 Metacognition

The Cambridge Dictionary defines metacognition as 'knowledge and understanding of your own thinking'.[9] Metacognition is our ability to regulate our thinking processes, the monitoring and control of our cognitive processes, our awareness of our internal thoughts and self-talk, and our understanding of how we learn. It's directly linked to our self-awareness, self-monitoring and self-regulation.

Evidence from a study conducted by the Education Endowment Foundation focusing on 'Metacognition and Self-regulated Learning' (EEF, 2021)

---

[9] https://dictionary.cambridge.org/dictionary/english/metacognition

suggests that the successful use of metacognitive strategies can be worth seven additional months of progress. Yet still there is a deficit in knowledge as to how to apply such strategies effectively.

Because technology can support learning as much as it can teaching, as we alluded to earlier in the chapter, we believe children should learn how to use technology that helps them learn. As children should learn about metacognition and how best to learn, they should also be taught how to use technology to support their learning.

To add extra insights, we asked metacognition author and expert, Anoara Mughal, the author of *Think! Metacognition-powered Primary Teaching*, to share her thoughts on the subject in the form of a case study. Given that Anoara is the founder of #ThinkMPPT, registered writer for *Headteacher News*, fellow of the Chartered College of Teaching, former senior leader, consultant, and founder of Inspire Metacognition (@IMetacognition), we thought she would be perfect to share her thoughts. You can find Anoara online on X @anoara_a.

Case study: Anoara Mughal

Background: Ali is a Year 6 pupil who is one of the novice learners in class. He is often distracted and finds regulating his emotions a challenge. He also finds focusing a challenge in a traditional classroom setup. He struggles to identify his strengths and areas to develop, and he is unsure about the learning processes and how to improve on them.

The objective was to encourage Ali to develop metacognitive skills using technology.

Intervention

Ali's teacher focused on developing three metacognitive skills:

- identifying strengths and areas to develop
- identifying mistakes in writing and correcting
- reflecting on learning.

She started off using an app called **Quizlet** (www.quizlet.com) to help Ali identify strengths and areas to develop. The second strategy was to use **DraftBack**[10] to help identify mistakes in writing and to correct them. The third strategy was to

---

[10] Available from the Chrome web store.

promote reflection on learning, through writing in a group and publishing class blogs online.

A. Quizlet: Quizlet, an educational technology application, was introduced to Ali. Using this app, he could create his own study sets that made learning personalised and more engaging. He would test his knowledge and track his progress within the app, improving his understanding of his learning process.
B. DraftBack: Ali was also encouraged to use DraftBack, an extension that plays back the revisions made on Google Docs. It allowed Ali to rethink his writing process, identify his mistakes and learn from them – critical for the development of metacognitive thinking.
C. Reflective blogs: Year 6 pupils were also introduced to blogging as a tool for reflection. Each half-term, a different group reflected on their learning journey, recorded their thoughts and wrote and published class blogs online.

Progress and observations

1. Improved behaviour and concentration: There was a marked improvement in behaviour and concentration. Ali was able to transfer self-regulation strategies into the classroom setting; his behaviour improved and he became less distracted.
2. Improved motivation: Ali became more engaged and motivated to learn in the classroom. As his confidence grew, his teacher noticed Ali taking part in classroom discussions more.
3. Improved awareness and understanding of learning: Ali showed a marked improvement in understanding his own learning strategies through the tools used. The Quizlet app helped him identify his strengths and the areas he needed more work on. His error percentages helped him track his improvement, leading to more focused studying.
4. Better writing skills: By using DraftBack, Ali was able to visually witness his thought process during writing, allowing him to better understand his writing structure and improve it. He noticed patterns in his errors and developed strategies to counteract them.
5. Development of critical thinking: Writing reflective class blogs promoted critical thinking, as Ali and the Year 6 group began not only to discuss what they had learned but how and why they learned it. This turned out to be a practical method for them to express their thoughts, further reinforcing their metacognitive skills.
6. Improved confidence: With an improved understanding of how he learns, Ali became more confident in his academic abilities. He made huge progress and he was more actively engaged in class.

Conclusion

This case study highlights that using technology can be a powerful tool for nurturing metacognitive skills in students. Observing Ali's progression, it became evident that incorporating modern technology tools in an education setting has the potential to transform a student's learning experience, making it more reflective, personalised, self-regulated and, therefore, more effective.

As we can see from Anoara's case study, it's important to explore each use case on its own merits. Here, a critical analysis of the student's needs resulted in finding technology that specifically addressed those needs.

The case study also highlights the importance of student buy-in, whereby they need to be a part of the iterative process when developing their answers as this helps build confidence while building skills and knowledge. These things don't happen by osmosis; they happen with regular reviews and critical and helpful feedback.

5.6 Poor proxies for learning

Proxies are a way for us to identify or, at the very least, judge if something is happening or has happened. Students thinking hard about a problem is a good proxy for learning. Poor proxies for learning are identified as failures in capturing subject knowledge in depth and being able to transfer knowledge and skills. Poor proxies may give the appearance that learning has happened, yet they fail to do so or to capture that learning is happening for students. Typical poor proxies include:

- a calm and ordered classroom
- curriculum coverage
- memorisation without understanding
- performing well on low-level tasks
- completing work without any evidence of truly understanding the content
- being busy engaging in the work
- some students get some of the answers correct.

These are all related to learning but they are not learning in and of themselves. If you haven't already done so, we advise you to read

Professor Rob Coe's work[11] on this topic. Not only will it likely challenge your thinking, but it will also ask you to re-evaluate what you do in the classroom to establish if learning has happened at a deeper level or not.

So, where does technology come into this?

At a basic level, we all know how important basic engagement was to supporting learning during the COVID-19 pandemic.

When technology is poorly integrated or a task is poorly designed, it is often a poor proxy for learning given that students are likely paying attention but not deeply engaging in the subject matter. The technology itself becomes a vehicle to engage and entertain but the students are not understanding what they are seeing.

You don't have to be gimmicky with technology to ensure learning is meaningful. Take, for example, feedback. A good way of keeping children interested in their work is to close the feedback loop in a timely fashion. Another way might be to offer authentic outputs using technology to inspire things such as creative writing. As always, keep pedagogy at the front of your thinking, but consider how technology can enhance the learning activity. Using technology as a gimmick devalues you as a teacher, devalues the technology and, ultimately, devalues what you are doing in the classroom. Keep the challenge.

5.7 Conditions for success

It is well-documented, and increasingly so in more recent years, that the work of Rosenshine and the impact of his Principles of Instruction (Rosenshine, 2012) can have a largely positive impact on educational outcomes and learning. The 10 key principles can be expanded to 17 key principles from his seminal work. Here, we highlight eight of the 17 areas and discuss how technology can support them.

Principle: 'Begin a lesson with a short review of previous learning'

'Do now' activities are a great way to actively review content as learners come into your lessons and can be accessed via a **QR code** or via a hyperlink on your learning management system (LMS). This reinforces retrieval and a host of other powerful learning routines.

---

[11] https://profcoe.net

At a simple level, students and teachers can make use of scheduling in the calendar so that they have a reminder of what is being reviewed and when, whether organising this for a class or for personal revision/memorisation activities. Many online platforms can also be integrated into your LMS so that timings and scheduling align, helping as a reminder to practise.

Principle: 'Present new material in small steps with student practice after each step'

Visual aids, interactive demonstrations, multimedia resources, digital displays and whiteboards can all be used to support explanations and scaffold understanding while complementing verbal instruction. Well-designed presentations, void of clutter, can be used to introduce new material in digestible chunks to scaffold student understanding.

A key point in this is making sure that the content being shared is chunked and presented in stages so that it mirrors the words you are using, and you are explaining it. This relates directly to concrete examples and dual coding, and can be easily achieved with most presentation tools using animations.

Alternatively, visualisers are great for helping present new material in small steps just as you would using your whiteboard but at a micro level from your desk, allowing you to check for understanding as you go using a range of questioning and *formative assessment* techniques.

Another way of supporting student practice after each step would be to use one of the many low-stakes quizzing tools we have shared throughout the book.

Principle: 'Give clear and detailed instructions and explanations'

Thinking back to what we learned in chapter 2 from the EEF 'Using Digital Technology To Improve Learning' report, the second recommendation openly states that 'technology can be used to improve the quality of explanations and modelling' (EEF, 2020). We won't write about this again here but do check back in that chapter (section 2.3) for ideas on how to use technology to give clear and detailed instructions and explanations.

Principle: 'Provide a high level of active practice for all students'

Research shows that active engagement in one's learning means you are more likely to retain information in your long-term memory. While engagement through fun is a poor proxy for learning, bringing your subject alive using digital techniques such as AR models, green-screening and virtual-mapping makes activities more authentic for learners thus prompting active engagement in the learning itself. By tying in AaL (Assessment as Learning) and AfL (Assessment for Learning) along the journey you will help to ensure engagement is checked along the way with formative assessments.

There are a variety of ways that technology can support opportunities for practice such as online quizzes, simulations, educational software through your LMS, or online platforms that offer students the opportunity to practise independently or through AI *chatbots*.

Further examples where students (and teachers) can practise their learning can be recorded in Microsoft **OneNote Class Notebook**; the 'replay' features allow a learner to review the steps taken for a key skill or modelled explanation so that they can review and use the model to guide their own practice examples. Given the infinite pages in **OneNote**, students have ample space to digitally ink examples and record orated explanations which can be seen and heard by the teacher, allowing opportunities for further feedback. Similar approaches can be achieved using tools such as Apple's **Freeform** app, Canva's **Whiteboard** (www.canva.com) and **Padlet** (www.padlet.com).

Principle: 'Provide systematic feedback and corrections'

Technology is a great accelerator for feedback, from automated grading tools natively built into online quizzing and assessment platforms such as **Century, Tassomai, Toddle** and more.

Voice feedback is another example of providing learners with a greater depth of feedback in a shorter time frame while reducing teacher workload. This can be achieved through technologies such as **Mote** (www.mote.com), **Showbie** (www.showbie.com), and Microsoft **OneNote Class Notebook**.

Timely feedback is a cornerstone of student engagement in their learning which we will discuss more in chapter 8, which focuses on assessment and feedback.

Principle: Engage students in regular review

Spaced repetition that is built into the algorithms of many online platforms allows for regular and repeated review.

Spaced repetition, as discussed earlier in this chapter, is deliberate practice that is spaced out over time to help reinforce learning and key concepts.

Tools such as **Anki, Quizizz, Seneca, Kuizical** and **Century** can be utilised for this.

Principle: 'Ask students to explain what they have learned'

The sky is the limit with the plethora of new technologies available and the types of artefacts your students can create to evidence either their learning or a particular skill, from curating a website or coding a robot to creating a video or writing an essay. All of this evidences the learning, be it a new concept or the solution to a problem. The most important thing here is that the new learning is front and centre.

Claude AI's **Sonnet** can even be used to help create an easily sharable artefact, but you still need to give Sonnet the relevant knowledge and details so that it can make the artefact for you. Examples of this can include outputs such as code, markdown documents, HTML, SVG images, mermaid diagrams (flow charts) and react components (a JavaScript library for building user interfaces), all of which can be moderated and iterated.

For more examples that demonstrate how students can explain what they've learned, check out chapter 8 (section 8.5) which explores screen-recording techniques and *oracy*.

Principle: 'Monitor students when they begin independent practice'

If you are asking students to complete work using technology, then classroom management software, whereby you can view the screens of all of the devices your students are using, is a no-brainer piece of technology to incorporate into your teaching and learning toolkit. The ability to jump in and give some quick formative feedback as students work on whatever they are focusing on will help keep them on track, avoiding distractions, while enabling you to help them as they need it, 'in the moment'.

In summary, while many of these strategies can positively enhance teaching and learning practice, remember that technology is not a panacea. It is important to remember the adage that the tail should not wag the dog. Consider carefully how and when to use technology when it enhances. Analogue activities are important to blend into your practice, so make sure you consider all approaches that best fit your classroom. A technology-rich classroom is one where cognisant choices are made, not one where you use technology for every activity.

By developing digital cognition as part of the 5 Cs approach (see chapter 2) and incorporating the deeper thinking shared in this chapter, more informed choices can be made where technology keeps the main thing 'the main thing', thereby improving outcomes and progress.

While making meaning and linking concepts to new learning should be effortful for the learner, technology should serve to support this and not further complicate matters, as the learner foci should be firmly on developing their learning. Where technology serves as a distraction, is poorly embedded in the task design or detracts from the learner's cognition, then we should question whether we should be using technology for the task at hand. Enhance and support, rather than detract and distract.

Educational technology use that is grounded in the principles of cognitive science can significantly enhance learning when it manages cognitive load, encourages spaced and distributed practice, promotes active learning, leverages dual coding, provides timely feedback and supports metacognition. Remember why you have cognisantly chosen to use the technology you are planning to use and be critically clear on how the tool supports both cognitive processes and learning.

Top tips

Mark's top tips

1. While there is a lot to consider, there are many things which go across what we know about what works – take visualisers and their use, for example. They work with Rosenshine's principle of 'clear explanation' and they support direct instruction. While digesting the content, look for low-hanging fruit that is easy to grasp and ticks lots of boxes for supporting broad pedagogical benefits.

2. While seeking big-ticket items that work for lots of things, try to also focus on those elements which can support marginal gains, such as expert level use of software, particularly including keyboard shortcuts for optimal efficiency.

3. Back up your choices of approach with lots of support, training and time to discuss wins (and problems) in communities of practice, both within and outside faculties, to share best practice and what works.

4. Bonus: Don't forget to consider how AI tools can leverage many of these approaches to help with the resources you create. Seek out integrations which benefit many of these cognitive approaches and which can help you with your teaching, resource creation and management of learner data analytics to inform your planning.

Olly's top tips

1. Whatever you do, make sure to work towards consistency as we are only as good as our lowest common denominator. Take collective and repeated action to support all stakeholders.

2. Don't be shy to survey colleagues – it is useful information. Make the results transparent so that everyone knows what you need to work on and why.

3. Don't throw the kitchen sink at it. Select one tool to support learning and hone your skills on how to use it.

CHAPTER 6
Using technology to demonstrate learning

'Today, we don't just use technology; we live it. It's woven into the fabric of how we express, understand and share knowledge in our classrooms.'

Mark Anderson

In this chapter, we're looking at how to use technology to demonstrate learning. There are several reasons why you would want to ask learners to do this, but assessment (in varying guises) is usually the starting point.

As we know, thinking always starts with the pedagogy of the situation you find yourself in. There are many different forms of assessment and, to wrap around all of those, you'll likely want some kind of LMS to act as a place for you to manage, set, record, receive, retrieve and feed back on those assessments.

It can seem quite daunting but, don't worry, it's not! We'll dive into the different forms of assessment and ways to do it with technology in a moment, but for now, we'll talk about managing all of these assessments using an LMS.

6.1 Learning management systems

We'll explore real-life examples and more depth of workflows later on in the book, but here we'll cover the basics and define what learning management systems are and what you are likely to have access to within your context.

An LMS is a software application for the administration, documentation, tracking, reporting, automation and delivery of educational courses, often to classes, training programs, materials or learning and development programs.

LMSs are used in a wide variety of settings beyond schools, including corporate training and government. There are standalone systems that you can buy into that often come with lots of fantastic curriculum resources, although it is fair to say they often are found and work within one of three ecosystems: Google, Microsoft and Apple.

Within those ecosystems, you will have access to a variety of tools to facilitate productivity and the completion of tasks, often used by teachers for teaching and students to demonstrate their learning. They work in similar ways and have similar tools to facilitate similar tasks.

Activity	Microsoft	Google	Apple (iPad)
Storing files	OneDrive	Drive	Files
Email	Outlook	Gmail	Mail
Word-processing	Word	Docs	Pages
Spreadsheets	Excel	Sheets	Numbers
Presentations	PowerPoint	Slides	Keynote
Note-taking	OneNote	Keep	Notes
LMS	Teams	Classroom	–

Table 6.1: LMS ecosystems

The features and functionalities of each of these different tools are *very* similar. The things you can do in one tool will be very similar to what you can do in another. Many of them have interoperability, where you can use one file type, e.g. Microsoft **PowerPoint** files, in other ecosystems. For example, if you created a presentation in PowerPoint, you can upload that file to Google **Slides** and continue working on it there. Similarly, you can open a PowerPoint file in Apple **Keynote** and work on it there as well.

The conundrum with Apple is that it does not have a specific LMS, although it can make use of those from other providers, such as Microsoft **Teams**, Google **Classroom** or other platforms such as **Showbie**. For that reason, we will save that deeper dive until later in the book where we examine workflows with an LMS, where we have some great case studies from schools that do all of that using third-party tools to great effect.

Learning management systems have common features. They allow you to:

- share resources
- group classes together
- create courses

- manage content
- set assignments
- assess and give feedback on assignments
- access built-in reporting and dashboards
- use communication options such as chat.

Considering two of the most popular options, Microsoft **Teams** and Google **Classroom** both facilitate and allow for all of the above to happen. So, whether you're a Microsoft or Google school (or an Apple school using a third-party solution), you can easily ask your learners to complete different activities to demonstrate their learning for a variety of assessment methods and successfully collect, assess, track and report on it.

Discussing LMSs in this chapter is important as it is via an LMS that you will manage your classes digitally. It is within your LMS that you will receive the different assessments and digital artefacts you've asked your learners to complete, such as essays, videos, presentations, podcasts, posters and quiz results, among many more.

Let's now examine the different forms of digital assessments that learners can complete to demonstrate their learning and progress.

6.2 Formative assessment in your LMS

When it comes to learners demonstrating what they know, formative assessments – those which help give us, as teachers, the feedback we need on what students have learned – are a cornerstone of every teacher's practice and an LMS is a fantastic place to capture assessments, gain analytics and give that all-important feedback.

In a world without technology, we might use mini-whiteboards, cold calling, 'think, pair, share', or exit tickets (although we also like entry tickets for retrieval practice). However, for the whole class (and to reduce workload and paper!), we believe that technology has much to offer. Ultimately, the goal of formative assessment is to help learners learn more effectively by identifying their strengths and weaknesses and providing them with the opportunity to untangle areas of misconception to help them focus on the areas in which they need to improve. An LMS is a brilliant place and space for all of this to happen.

Technology allows us to do things more efficiently. If we're using an LMS to undertake our formative assessments, we can benefit from:

- speed of access
- speed of completion
- automated marking
- libraries of questions to save time
- analytics of areas of misconception
- personalised feedback options for students

...and more.

We all have our favourites, but the key points to consider when choosing a tool for formative assessment are:

- Does it work in our ecosystem?
- Will it integrate with our LMS?
- Does it mark the questions for me?
- Does it give me the analytics to resolve misconceptions?
- Will it resend questions to students to support retrieval?

Quizzing tools are one of the most popular types of tool for this kind of assessment. Bearing in mind that learning is meant to be hard and distractions don't help, some types of quizzing tools appear to be more like a pub quiz than a serious class quiz. Some platforms offer the fastest-finger-first type of competitive-style quizzes. These, we would argue, do not help with learning; they encourage random choices instead. We prefer quizzes that allow students to think, reflect and perhaps use a pen and paper to calculate their answers. Retrieval can be difficult and we want it to stretch them. So, just because a quizzing tool might be fun, it doesn't mean it helps with learning. We suggest saving those tools for house competitions in the hall.

6.3 The camera

Given that cameras are bundled with many devices that students and teachers use, it is a great starting point to consider how we can demonstrate learning in different ways.

It could just be that the camera is used to take photographs of written work so that it can be saved and shared straight into your workflow solution ready for assessment and feedback. However, it doesn't just take photographs; it can also record video, so it is very useful for recording video evidence of learning taking place. This is particularly handy for Early Years and Key Stage 1 settings where you need to record and evidence progress in areas that will not be covered by writing in books.

A significant number of the ideas we share involve the use of the camera on the device. Whether you are green-screening or using slow-motion video to capture things happening for science or PE lessons, the camera, coupled with the microphone, is an extremely powerful tool that is a big help to demonstrate learning within the classroom.

During the COVID-19 pandemic, use of cameras and microphones on our devices was essential to bring learners together when they were geographically distanced. While it might be deemed inappropriate now in no-lockdown scenarios, many of the video conferencing tools we used then, such as Google **Meet**, **Zoom** and Microsoft **Teams**, rushed to create interesting additional features to their offerings: virtual backgrounds and the ability to wear virtual costumes or disguises such as pirates, witches and animals, all became readily available. Yes (and quite rightly), under normal circumstances, these features aren't appropriate (although for some creative learning activities they can be really helpful), but it goes to show how helpful and adaptable technology can be to ensure engagement in learning.

The point is that your knowledge of your context and how you use technology will determine why you choose to use a particular tool at a certain time. You know your learners and the context within which you are teaching, so you are best placed to choose the appropriateness (or not) of the tools you use.

6.4 Timelines

Several subjects require learners to have an understanding of the sequence of events, such as in history and geography, where it is helpful to know the order in which things happen and the impact previous events have on subsequent ones.

Chronologies are also present in other subjects. For instance, in computing, you learn about the development of technology over time. In science classes, you learn about evolution or how medicine has developed. Similarly, timelines appear in PE, design and technology, art, music, English and maths; in fact, they are often a focal point.

There are various ways to present timelines to encourage engagement. For example, in history lessons, you could choose to ask students to create a timeline using the above/below-the-line approach to demonstrate opposing views or to show activities from different sides.

Let's say, for example, you're asking students to show their knowledge of both sides of the Second World War. Details about the Allied troops could be placed above the timeline and information about the German forces could be placed below the line. If you were showing the life cycle of a plant as a timeline, you could put daytime activities (photosynthesis) above the line and night-time activities (respiration) below the line.

Whatever approach you take to timeline creation, there are tools to help. Teachers commonly ask learners to create them using presentation tools such as Google **Slides**, Microsoft **PowerPoint** or Apple **Keynote**. Other types of software, such as virtual whiteboards, mind-mapping and note-taking tools where learners can draw with a stylus or their finger, are also useful for their creation.

6.5 Promoting oracy

It has been fantastic to see the growing prominence of evidence around the impact of oracy in learning in recent times. The work of Voice 21 (www.voice21.org) has played a huge part in this. Whether you're a proponent of 'talk for writing', a user of 'think, pair, share' or 'Socratic questioning', or whether you simply ask students to pass a book around the classroom, taking it in turns to read a paragraph each, speaking and active listening have been central in classrooms for as long as we can remember, whether as educators or as avid learners in classrooms as children ourselves.

Student voice is important for empowering and engaging students in education. It helps to give them a sense of agency and allows them to express themselves. Learning how to use one's voice in different settings can also have the benefit of helping students achieve a wider range of tones to work with in everyday life.

When you bring technology into the mix, it can further enhance the learning experience. Speech-to-text technology, for example, has been found to help many teachers and students unlock opportunities for literacy. It can help in transcribing the spoken word into written text, aiding in the development of writing and language skills. Using technology and your voice to demonstrate what you have learned can help hugely in retention – and practising sharing what you've learned can also be helpful for retrieval.

Another foundation of the modern EdTech classroom is presentations. Both of us have asked students to create presentations to show their learning many times in our careers. However, in the post-pandemic world of AI where you can now use tools such as **Canva** with its 'magic design' feature to automatically create your presentation for you, a great way to ensure students know their topics and practise their knowledge (rather than them use AI to help them cheat!) is for them to use their voices, recording themselves delivering their presentations! Yes, you can use Canva to create presentations you can talk over, but do you want to trust your students to follow that option? Instead, why not consider, for example, Adobe **Express** (www.adobe.com/express) where, with the video option, learners can create different slides and record their voice over each slide, which saves as a video? Sure, Canva is a great tool, but cognisance with technology (that all-important element of your technological knowledge within TPACK) is about knowing which tool to use for which learning activity, at what time, within your context.

So, what if you don't have access to Adobe Express in your setting? Similar features appear in Microsoft **PowerPoint**. Or alternatively, why not consider asking your learners to use the presentation tool of choice for your school instead? They can screen-record themselves speaking over each slide, save that video and submit it as evidence of their learning. Perhaps that might not work for your school's ecosystem, but don't fret – the great thing with technology is that there is always another way. So, in this instance why not try **Mote**, where children can leave voice notes on their slides? Alternatively, your learners could use your class Microsoft **OneNote Class Notebook** and, with the infinite canvas of each note in their Notebook area, they can add a section and record a voice note directly onto their notes. There are, as they say, many ways to skin a cat; cognisance of what tools are available to support the pedagogical outcome you want is paramount.

For students to demonstrate what they have learned using technology with their voices, here are some more approaches you might like to consider:

Approach	How?
Podcasts	Create your podcasts using freely available tools such as GarageBand, if you have an iPad in your school. If you don't, why not have a look at Audacity (www.audacityteam.org), a free audio recording tool with which you can create your own podcasts.
Voice-based flashcards	Create voice-based flashcards using tools such as Quizlet (www.quizlet.com) or Anki (https://apps.ankiweb.net). Record the question on one side of the virtual card and the answer on the other. Practise by verbally stating the question and checking if the answer matches. This method can be particularly helpful for language learning and memorising key facts.
Voice-guided simulations	Language learning apps like Duolingo (www.duolingo.com) use voice recognition to assess pronunciation and provide instant feedback. This approach allows for hands-on practice and immediate correction. Similarly, tools such as Microsoft's Reading Progress/Reading Coach offer similar instant feedback to a student's voice following the reading of a text.

Table 6.2: Technology and oracy

6.6 Stop-frame animation

One of the easiest ways for your youngest learners to evidence their learning is to create *stop-frame animations* using tools such as Adobe's **Animate from Audio** (https://new.express.adobe.com/tools/animate-from-audio). Students can select a character and then record their voices. The application will then make the mouths move in sync with when the student's voice is playing. This helps on two fronts: developing oracy and ensuring safeguarding (as the students are not on video themselves).

Students could use this to support their explanations of key events, practise saying keywords, talk through timelines, showcase newly learned language, produce news reports and so on, in a low-stakes way – all while developing their oracy and evidencing their learning. You can see an example from Mark on his YouTube channel at www.youtube.com/ictevangelist.

There are many more apps with additional features you can explore for stop-frame animation for older learners. One of our favourites is the free **iMotion** app available on iOS from the Apple app store.

6.7 Green-screening

Following on from the ideas for using your students' voices, one of our favourite ways to engage young people in their learning is by using one of the many green-screening tools available for education.

Green-screening (also known as chroma-keying) allows you to replace the green background recorded with any image or video with any background you wish to have instead. This means you can easily transport your students to exciting virtual environments anywhere in the world – or the universe! You can even use multiple green screens (blue also works brilliantly) to create fantastic special effects.

The opportunities for demonstrating learning with green-screening are huge and you can use the technique for lots of other approaches to support learning too.

Here's Erika Sandström, an American educator and world-leading expert on green-screening (known on X as @GreenScreenGal), with a case study on the topic.

Case study: Erika Sandström

Educators are constantly seeking innovative tools and techniques to engage students and foster deeper learning experiences. One such exciting approach is green-screen technology which, when combined with creative media, offers a multitude of benefits for supporting all subjects while being mindful of pedagogy. By leveraging this technology, educators can promote oracy, facilitate knowledge acquisition and empower students to become active participants in their own learning.

Please find samples of all projects mentioned below via the following QR code and use it as your guide to a creative green-screen experience.

Figure 6.1: QR code resource

Enhancing learning

Students can use green screens to transport themselves to historical events, any global location they have learned about or fictional magical worlds, sparking their imagination in writing, storytelling and enthusiasm. We also love green screens for science, as students can use voice-overs and stop-motion animation, and climb into their projects to show how things work through movement and animation. We even love time-lapse and slow-motion photography to share a scientific process, create a rap about perimeter or even run from a sandstorm!

With the freedom to experiment, students can indulge in outtakes and re-filming, fostering their creativity and encouraging them to take risks. Outtakes are our favourites, as the laughter is contagious! Through collaborative scriptwriting and video production, they develop not only a deeper understanding of the subject matter but also essential skills like teamwork, problem-solving and resilience.

Fostering STEAM learning

Green-screen technology and creative media are perfect for fostering playful learning in science, technology, engineering, arts and mathematics (STEAM) subjects. Students can use green screens to create virtual environments that simulate science experiments, architectural designs, engineering marvels or artistic masterpieces.

By allowing for experimentation and exploration, green screen projects encourage students to think outside the box, embrace failures as part of the learning process, and find innovative solutions. This approach promotes curiosity, critical thinking and a love for discovery – essential qualities for success in STEAM fields. All, of course, while having a ton of fun trying to figure out how to climb into our STEAM creations, such as homemade aeroplanes, rockets and even trampolines made out of homemade colanders!

Supporting SEL and mindfulness

Green-screen and creative media offer an avenue for supporting social and emotional learning (SEL) and mindfulness in the classroom. Through video creation and role-playing, students can explore and express emotions, developing self-awareness and empathy. Collaborating on green-screen projects fosters positive relationships, effective communication and conflict resolution skills, all while having fun. Additionally, creating calming and immersive scenes against green screens provides students with the opportunity to practise mindfulness techniques, promoting emotional wellbeing and stress reduction.

Additionally, the social, emotional learning that happens naturally will astound you! I often swoop in as a facilitator to teach SEL skills such as the 'I statement'. Our favourite activity is to create personalised breathing bubbles we call #MyBreathingBubble. We also love to teach other breathing techniques using creative media and, of course, the green screen, such as five-finger breathing and how to create and use a glitter-jar meditation.

SEL skills such as 'negative self-talk' can prompt wonderful productions, especially when you hear students in the hallway using the new language of, 'Put your brakes on that negative self-talk!' My heart explodes with pride and joy every time I see the positive aftermath of such productions, even with students who do not take my class.

Empowering pedagogy

Green-screen technology and creative media empower educators to embrace an engaging pedagogical approach. Their flexibility allows for adaptations and personalisation of instruction. Multimedia elements such as visual effects, animations and quizzes add an element of surprise to lessons, captivating students and promoting active participation.

The green screen takes all these teaching methods to a whole new level of creativity. For example, we love to make animated transparent GIFs of ourselves to give directions in a game/activity, climb into our artwork and projects or even share an inspirational GIF (#GiftaGIF) to cheer someone else on.

Promoting oracy and knowledge acquisition

Green-screen and creative media create a light-hearted environment that supports oracy skills and enhances knowledge acquisition. Students can script and perform their presentations, debates or interviews against imaginative virtual backgrounds, adding an element of fun to their communication. Through this process, they improve their articulation, critical thinking and persuasive abilities. For example, I had a wonderful time collaborating with the languages department when we created video postcards with speaking and writing skills.

Moreover, green-screen projects encourage active participation and knowledge acquisition as students immerse themselves in the subject matter through research, scriptwriting and content creation, often accompanied by laughter and shared excitement. Let's face it, these kiddos learn differently and are very visual creatures. They are masters at video and social media, so, as educators, the green screen will help us reach and *go to where they are* while having a blast ourselves.

> I always say, 'It is easy being green!' The best part is that you can create a green-screen studio for less than $10. You will never look back once you take the plunge – and the pure joy it fosters and the positive climate in your classroom will be worth it!

Erika's case study highlights how exploring certain EdTech tools can open up creativity and enable learners to showcase their learning meaningfully. Whether you're asking students to take you on a virtual field trip to a landmark they have to cover as part of their curriculum (despite being too young to go on an actual field trip – true story!) or jump into a book to retell a popular story or create a stop-frame animation that explains a key process, the learning is always the main component; technology is there to serve as a vehicle to support and enhance it.

In Dylan Wiliam's book *Embedded Formative Assessment* (Wiliam, 2011), he identifies that students' time is well spent creating quiz questions with answers, compared to revising. It is a great activity for students to showcase what they know (and don't know) alongside the opportunity to make their questions challenging for their peers. They will work hard to ensure they get their work right and provide a high level of rigour for their classmates, in turn, investing directly into the activity of learning.

Here are the types of activities teachers often set and the tools that support them.

Activity	Tools to facilitate
News reports	Tools that allow video or audio recording such as Adobe Express and Canva.
Virtual tours	Tools that allow video recording such as screen recording a tour you've made using Google Earth or Google Arts and Culture.
Fake news	Students make fake profiles for famous figures using any document application.
Presentations	Canva, Microsoft PowerPoint, Apple Keynote, Google Slides, Prezi.
Stop-frame animations	Applications like Adobe Animate, I Can Animate and iMotion.
Videos or voiceovers	Loom, Screencastify, Adobe Express, Microsoft Stream, or simply screen recording using the built-in software in your operating system.

Table 6.3: Learning activities and tools to facilitate them

6.8 A word of caution

The vast majority of the readers of this book will likely be teachers of subjects other than ICT and computing. Therefore, when asking learners to complete tasks that demonstrate their learning with technology, you must ensure you give them the tools to help them complete the task successfully. If you're going to ask students to create a timeline, then provide a timeline template. Don't make them spend time creating the timeline; you are most interested in them showing what they know, not their ability to create an attractive timeline. Equally, if you're going to ask students to generate a mind map, presentation, word cloud, spreadsheet to analyse results, or whatever it may be, be sure not to make them waste valuable lesson time creating repetitive elements that are not part of the assessment.

The ways in which you can ask students to demonstrate their learning while using technology are far from exhaustive. We could have written a book just on that! Whatever approaches you choose, the key is to remember that you are asking students to demonstrate their knowledge of *what they've been learning*, not their ability to use technology well.

Top tips

Mark's top tips

1. Choose the tool to match the activity, not the activity to match the tool. Think cognisance and context.

2. Consider using tools that are accessible and ensure students have equity of access to complete the task.

3. Remember to continue to ask students to complete analogue activities as they are equally important, particularly writing, as this requires stamina as well as practice.

Olly's top tips

1. Keep the focus on learning. Try, where possible, to ensure any tool that is used means the students can retain focus on the main activity rather than having to learn a new tool or app.

2. Don't be shy to learn from students and ask them what tools work for them (and why) when evidencing their learning. You might be surprised at what they say and they may even share something new with you.

3. Celebrate your students' work by sharing the artefacts they create on the school website/blog/social channels.

CHAPTER 7
Accessibility for all

'Accessibility is not a luxury, it is a necessity.'

Tim Berners-Lee, *inventor of the World Wide Web*

7.1 Why accessibility matters

Accessibility is important. It isn't just about making things more available for those who need it; it's important so that the world is inclusive for absolutely everyone.

One of Mark's favourite quotes about accessibility is one often shared by Patrick (Paddy) McGrath, head of education for EMEA at the fantastic accessibility company, Texthelp (www.texthelp.com), where he describes accessibility as 'necessary for some, useful for all'.

Certainly, when it comes to accessibility tools, it is important to have available tools such as screen readers and dictation, but there's so much more to accessibility than that.

Accessibility by design

The idea of accessibility by design was first talked about by people such as Judy Brewer of the World Wide Web Consortium (W3C),[1] who argued that accessibility should be considered 'at the outset of the design process, rather than as an afterthought'.

The premise is a design philosophy that emphasises the importance of considering accessibility right from the outset of the design process. This means that accessibility is not an afterthought, but rather an integral part of the design.

There are some great benefits to working from this mantra. Firstly, it can help ensure that products and services are accessible to people with a disability right from the very beginning. This can save time and money in the long run but it can open a product or service up to a much wider market too.

---

[1] The W3C Web Accessibility Initiative (WAI): www.w3.org/WAI

This is particularly important for education products. We know how vital it is that learning in school is inclusive, and what better way to make sure that a school chooses to take on a product than by making sure it is open and accessible to all learners?

A good example we came across recently was with a popular school wellbeing product: YouHQ. This is an online portal that helps schools and colleges track and improve the wellbeing of their students and staff. It does so with methods such as surveys, goal-setting opportunities, resources on wellbeing for students, staff and parents, a communication hub and so much more. So why mention it? Well, baked right into the portal is what it calls the 'accessibility genie'. This is a feature that gives those who need it essential support, and for those who don't, it can be helpful too.

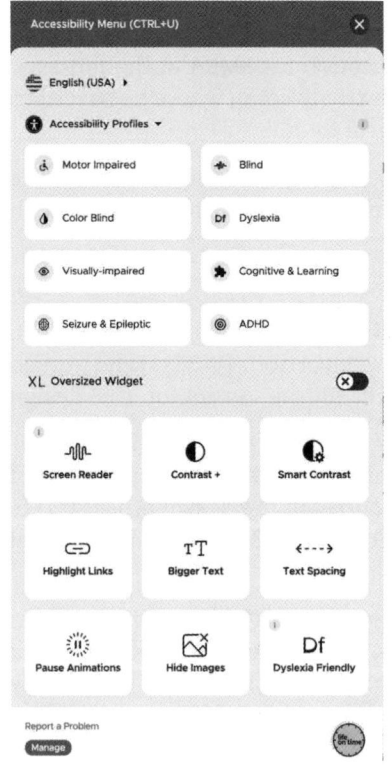

Figure 7.1: YouHQ's accessibility genie

Secondly, accessibility by design can help to improve the usability of products and services for everyone. A large part of that is because accessibility principles often focus on making things clear, concise and easy to understand. We saw this in chapter 5, where we explored dual coding.

Finally, on a moral front, accessibility by design helps to create a more inclusive society, something which we should all strive for. When people with a variety of learning needs can access technological tools, they are more likely to feel included in their learning and therefore more likely to progress when their most basic needs (according to Maslow's hierarchy of needs) are satisfied.

Someone else who agrees with this is Paddy McGrath, whose quote we shared at the start of the chapter. On telling him about our book, Paddy was keen to share his thoughts on the topic.

Case study: Paddy McGrath

Everyone's different. If there's one simple fact that every educator can attest to, it's that in any class they've ever stood in front of, every single pupil is unique. Individual. Different.

EdTech has helped immeasurably with personalised learning, enabling many students to be engaged and supported, providing effective means for formative assessment and feedback and, ultimately, offering flexible learning paths.

We need to do more, much more, to ensure we embrace the true diversity and differences in our classrooms. Put simply, education, learning and the materials and resources we use must be accessible to all. We tend to think about accessibility exclusively in the context of those pupils with SEND or with individual needs. Accessibility is much more than that, and something that as we develop our use of EdTech, we need to think about in much wider terms and embed it as a standard into our everyday practice.

Think about an iceberg and how this compares to the diversity in any classroom. There's just 10% of that iceberg showing above the water. This 10% is what we see, what's visible. Now think about this in the context of your class. You'll typically have that percentage of pupils with identified needs and targeted support with specific plans. Is this who you think about when it comes to accessibility? Probably, and rightly so. But what about every other pupil? The 90% of your class under the waterline who don't have any obvious or identified challenges. Those who struggle in silence, those who simply aren't formally assessed, those with challenging home backgrounds or those who simply don't engage. These are pupils who also need accessibility for learning. Take **dyslexia** – it's often quoted that approximately 2% of any class has identified dyslexia. Studies show that, in reality, this could be as high as 17%. That's 15% of your class who need accessible content and potentially aren't getting it.[2]

When we provide true accessibility, everyone can benefit because we enable equity of access – access to the incredible range of tools and technologies that can embrace and support the differences in all of our classrooms; access to learning.

True accessibility requires a new way of thinking. It requires us to take on the responsibility for change. It needn't be onerous though, or require huge shifts in what we do. We can start small – because those small changes can deliver huge wins. Simply changing your standard default font on every document that you and your pupils create to something that's dyslexic-friendly like Lexend (www.lexend.com) takes five minutes, just once. Now, those documents are more readable for everyone. More accessible. And not just for those with dyslexia. Double spacing your lines on a document has the same effect – another one-minute change. Adding alt text for images is now just a simple right click and a few extra words typed. There are also tools that can take your PDF resources and automatically make them accessible. Small changes. Huge wins for all of your pupils.

With an accessible foundation as standard, the power of EdTech is there for all. Tools like text-to-speech are built into many platforms today and available in external apps so they can be used anytime they are needed. For that 10% of identified needs, through to those pupils who just need to check their answers more rigorously, suddenly it's not just the technology that's accessible, it's the learning.

Accessibility and EdTech are not just a powerful combination. They're a necessary one.

The reality is that everyone is indeed different. As educators, it's our responsibility to remove barriers to learning where we can. Recognising that accessibility is important to all is our first step. By making just a few changes, we can ensure accessible practice becomes standard practice and move towards a truly inclusive classroom, leveraging technology for all.

---

[2] All Party Parliamentary Group for Dyslexia, October 2019. See www.bdadyslexia.org.uk.

7.2 Accessibility baked in

As we saw in the previous section, many technology tools have accessibility options built in by default. We have seen this improve dramatically over the last five or so years with the development of tools such as Microsoft's **Immersive Reader** becoming ever more pervasive in Microsoft products.

Originally, Immersive Reader was only found inside its browser, but now, it is found in many of Microsoft's products, including but not limited to **Word, Excel, PowerPoint, Outlook, OneNote** and **Teams**.

What is Immersive Reader?

Immersive Reader is a powerful tool that can help people with dyslexia, reading difficulties and other learning disabilities to read and understand text. It provides a variety of features that can make text more accessible, including:

- **Text formatting:** Immersive Reader can change the font, size and colour of text to make it easier to read.
- **Read aloud:** Immersive Reader can read text aloud, which can be helpful for people who have difficulty reading or who prefer to listen to text.
- **Picture dictionary:** Immersive Reader has a picture dictionary built in to help learners who have English as an additional language (EAL) or English for speakers of other languages (ESOL) but equally for other languages. It supports more than 120 different languages.

Of course, there are many other tools similar to Immersive Reader, many of which have even more features to help make text more accessible. Texthelp's popular **Read/Write** is one such example.

7.3 Accessibility models

When it comes to teaching, there are a variety of strategies that we, as educators, can use to deliver content in the classroom. We discussed many of them in chapter 5, but as we know from our pedagogical knowledge (PK) of PCK and TPACK, as practitioners, we use our PK to help inform how we deliver learning to our students.

Being mindful of the various needs within our classrooms, it is incumbent upon us to consider the best approaches to support our learners. This isn't about personalising learning for every child like we used to be asked to around differentiation. It's about making learning accessible using the approaches we have in our teaching and learning toolkit to best support and serve them. This is adaptive teaching.

> 'In-class differentiation, through providing differentiated teaching, activities or resources, has generally not been shown to have much impact on pupils' attainment.
>
> 'On the other hand, adapting teaching in a responsive way, for example, by providing focused support to pupils who are not making progress, is likely to improve outcomes.' (Ofsted, 2019)

With this in mind, let's explore some of these approaches and how technology can support and help them.

Universal design for learning

A universal design for learning (UDL) is an inclusive educational framework for designing classroom instruction that is accessible to all learners. It involves using multiple means of representation, engagement and expression that assist in accommodating individual learning differences. This isn't to be confused with the well-debunked 'learning styles' debate. This is about ensuring all learners can access the curriculum.

UDL is based on the premise that, by providing multiple means of representation, action and expression, and engagement, all learners can succeed.

The three main principles of UDL are:

1. **Representation:** Provide multiple ways to present information and content. Depending upon the needs of learners, this can include using different modalities (e.g. visual, auditory, tactile), different formats (e.g. text, images, video) and varying levels of complexity.
2. **Action and expression:** Provide multiple ways for learners to demonstrate what they know. This includes providing different tools and materials, different ways to interact with the learning environment and different ways to communicate their learning.
3. **Engagement:** Provide multiple ways to motivate and engage learners. This includes creating a sense of purpose, providing choice and offering opportunities for collaboration.

UDL is not a one-size-fits-all approach. It is a framework that can be adapted to different learning contexts and different learners. However, the basic principles of UDL can be applied to any learning environment to create a more inclusive and accessible learning experience for all students.

If you're reading about this for the first time, you might be (like we were) mindful of the increased workload that adopting these approaches could bring. However, with technology, there are ways you can help to provide support for all learners by using software.

Here are some examples of how technology can support UDL in the classroom:

- **Representation:** You could provide a text-based resource for the classwork, but by allowing the use of a screen reader or text-to-speech tools, you would allow students who learn best by listening to have access to the same information as students who learn best by reading, without creating any additional work. You're just providing the means to access the content in different ways.
- **Action and expression:** You could give students a choice of how to demonstrate their understanding of a concept. For example, students could write an essay, but you could allow others to create a presentation or make a video. This would allow students to express their learning in a way that is most comfortable for them.
- **Engagement:** You could create a game-based learning activity based upon low-stakes quizzing by using a simple EdTech tool that facilitates easy creation but is designed to motivate students and keep them engaged. This would help to ensure that all students are interested in the learning content. Many readily available tools such as **Quizizz** (www.quizizz.com) can help with these kinds of activities.

Things to remember with UDL:

- It is not 'learning styles'.
- It does not have to mean additional work.
- It can sit alongside your other practices.
- The key is focusing on accessibility for the learners in your class who need it.

Co-teaching

Co-teaching is a teaching model in which two or more teachers work together in the same classroom. This can be a great way to provide support for students with disabilities, as one teacher can focus on the content while the other teacher provides individual or small-group instruction. We often see this in the role of a teaching assistant (TA) working with a teacher.

One of the difficulties with making these scenarios work is that often, teachers and TAs do not (particularly in Secondary/high school settings) cross each other's paths very frequently, so time to prepare lessons together is limited. Here, technology can help again. By using cloud tools and their collaboration features (as seen in Microsoft and Google online spaces), you can easily work together, share resources and collaborate on planning for lessons asynchronously, without the need for regular face-to-face meetings.

Mark used this approach to great success when he was head of department in one of his schools and took it further into other schools. By including TAs in shared online areas, such as folders or channels in Microsoft **Teams**, they were part of the team and could be kept in the loop. This ensured they knew what lessons were coming up and gave them time to consider approaches and accommodations they could provide to help the learners they were supporting in the classroom. Rolled forward as a whole school approach, this meant communication and planning was facilitated without these important colleagues having to be present in every department meeting.

Peer tutoring

Peer tutoring is a strategy where students work together to help each other learn. This can be a great way for students with disabilities to get the support they need, while also providing the opportunity to practise their skills and knowledge.

Peer support has been a cornerstone of both Mark and Olly's practice over the years – and technology can help here too. From using tools linked to a management information system (MIS) to create helpful seating plans or collaborative activities such as peer assessment and feedback in online spaces (e.g. Microsoft **OneNote Class Notebook**), to lower tech tools such as mini-whiteboards, peer support can be facilitated in the classroom in many ways and helps provide opportunities for retrieval and memorisation for those both providing and receiving support. It is also an approach which can support metacognition where students become better custodians of their own progress while supporting the progress of others.

Accessible assessment

Accessible assessment is the practice of making assessments accessible to all students. Taking into account non-technological methods, this can involve all manner of support, such as providing alternative formats for assessments, e.g. audio recordings or Braille, or it can involve providing accommodations, such as extended time or a quiet environment.

With technological methods, there is a choice of tools to provide accessible assessment. One such tool that has been particularly useful in recent years has been the **C-Pen** from Scanning Pens (www.scanningpens.com). This useful tool is available with a plethora of features in its full form, but the **C-Pen Exam Reader** is a pen-sized device that provides text-to-speech support for exam conditions.

7.4 Enhanced learning for all

Technology is advancing all the time and there are incredible tools available to support all manner of learning differences. From the aforementioned C-Pen to the ultra-expensive **OrCam** (www.orcam.com) devices that will attach to the side of your glasses and read whatever you look at (and even describe the room around you and more!), there's something to support everyone, whatever their need.

Here are some of the different types of technologies that can support learners in your classroom.

Type	Explanation	Additional information
Text-to-speech software	Reads aloud digital or printed text.	Can be used by partially sighted students, students with dyslexia or other reading disabilities.
Speech-recognition software	Converts spoken words into text.	Can be used by students with physical disabilities that make it difficult to write.
Specialised keyboards	Keyboards with larger keys, different layouts or other features that make them easier to use.	Can be used by students with physical disabilities or learning disabilities that affect their fine motor skills.
Braille displays	Devices that display text in Braille.	Can be used by students who are blind or partially sighted.

Type	Explanation	Additional information
Screen-readers	Software that reads aloud the text on a computer screen.	Can be used by students who are blind or partially sighted.
Zooming software	Software that allows users to magnify text and images on a computer screen.	Can be used by students who are partially sighted or who have learning disabilities that affect their ability to see small print.
Audio-recorders	Devices that record audio.	Can be used by students to record lectures, class discussions or other important information.

Table 7.1: Accessible tools for the classroom

Academic researcher and senior leader in the alternative provision sector, Dr Alexandra Gray, has lots of experience in this field. Having designed and run accredited behaviour-management training and qualifications for education and third-sector organisations, Alexandra's work advocates for a needs-based model for managing challenging behaviour. She's even found the time to develop an MIS geared towards supporting students in alternative provision (for whom normal systems aren't geared up to best support) called **Learntrek** (www.learntrek.co.uk). Given her knowledge and experience in the space, she kindly shared some thoughts with us on how we can use a variety of technologies to support behaviour management.

Case study: Dr Alexandra Gray
Manage your state

The concept of state comes from neuro-linguistic programming (NLP) and proposes that we are all affected by psychological, physiological and environmental factors in any challenging situation we find ourselves in. If we don't manage our own state well by paying particular attention to these factors, we are likely to make challenging situations worse.

Using technology to manage state can help combat the accumulation of negativity surrounding challenging behaviour. Wellness apps like Apple's **Happier**[3] and **Meditopia** (www.meditopia.com) offer support to prevent and

---
[3] https://apps.apple.com/us/app/ten-percent-happier-meditation/id992210239

manage the long-term effects of stress, as well as great ideas for techniques to help manage your breathing in the moment when things are kicking off.

Changing up the atmosphere in your environment can be helpful – most devices (phones, watches, fitness trackers, etc.) allow you to set targets for movement to incorporate into your day. Get pupils involved by setting movement targets for the whole class using a fitness app and connecting it to some kind of shared reward.

Co-regulation with pupils can work especially well using apps like **CalmKids** (www.calm.com) or **Headspace for Kids** (www.headspace.com – free for those working in education) to model techniques and get pupils to demonstrate them with you. Options that work well with a desktop include **DreamyKid** (www.dreamykid.com) and video meditation site **Gaia** (www.gaia.com), while Apple's **Calm Counter** works particularly well with autistic pupils. The best use of this I have seen was in a pupil-referral unit where students in 'seclusion' for fighting lay on their backs with their feet in the air listening to guided breathing – I was amazed they were so up for it!

However you decide to manage your own state, acknowledging that it is an important piece of the behaviour management puzzle is key. Technology can help prepare us for dealing with challenging behaviour, to practise self-care and to encourage pupils to do the same.

Plan for behaviour

In most education settings, there is a focus on lesson planning that emphasises preparation for the content of lessons with careful consideration of differentiation for pupils who struggle. What happens less often is preparation for behaviour management on a whole-class or whole-group scale. Rather than planning by differentiating only the subject content for individual disruptive pupils, try to plan for meeting the (sometimes competing) needs of all pupils using a behaviour plan. The plan can be created for each class/group and adapted as and when new information comes in or in response to ongoing behavioural issues. This requires you to:

- think about the activities you'll be delivering and how pupils could possibly respond
- consider what past behaviour tells you about the needs of your students
- be proactive about possible solutions – don't wait for challenging behaviour to just happen
- pay particular attention to the edge that technology can provide in combatting challenging behaviour by meeting pupils' need for fun!

Software such as **Class Charts** (www.classcharts.com) can be adapted to plan for behaviour using the notes function of its seating plans, whereas behaviour-specific tracking options like **BehaviourWatch**[4] or **BehaviourSmart** (www.behavioursmart.co.uk) can also be annotated to show planning for behaviour. Apps designed for planning like **Figma** (www.figma.com), **Planboard** (https://.app.chalk.com), **Evernote** (www.evernote.com) and **Planbook** (www.planbookedu.com) offer a free trial or free version and can be used to create a class behaviour plan by plotting students or groups of students and colour-coding for helpful prevention and intervention ideas. While there are a number of technical solutions to planning for behaviour, getting into the habit of proactively planning for potential behavioural incidents by adapting existing technology will allow you to improve outcomes without overcomplicating things. For example, look at whether your existing MIS or safeguarding or behaviour software system allows for annotations at the whole-class or whole-group level, or create a separate plan for behaviour (using free software) at the class level. You can then continually revisit your plan with new information as things change over time and you learn what works (and doesn't work) for your pupils.

Using technology to meet the need for fun should always be part of your planning for behaviour. Build into your plan frequent opportunities for students to develop digital skills that bring them into contact with emerging technologies. For instance, gamified learning through apps like **Pear Practice** (www.peardeck.com/products/pear-practice) can be accessed via desktop and built into most subjects. I love using AI-powered apps like **Face App** (www.faceapp.com) as a fun way into discussion around race, culture and identity, and my favourite **ChatGTP** (https://openai.com/index/chatgpt/) prompt so far has been 'Write me a rap in the style of...' which can get some very funny results.

Divert from challenging behaviour

One of the best techniques for managing challenging behaviour (both preventatively and in the middle of an incident) is to have plenty of diversions up your sleeve. It is important that all incidences of poor behaviour are challenged so that pupils know that it is not OK and staff are consistent. However, challenge alone often doesn't create a path back for the pupil(s) and can put staff in situations they can't back down from. This can be especially difficult when it involves pupils who are so constantly being challenged about poor behaviour that they have ceased to register it.

---

[4] https://eduspot.co.uk/product/behaviourwatch

Always create a win-win situation when you challenge poor behaviour by calling it out and offering an 'out' to the pupil – allow them a way to comply without losing face by switching up the conversation. Don't keep challenging them repeatedly, rather ask them to do something else or force the class's attention elsewhere, giving them time to think about what you've asked them to comply with.

Technology now offers us a range of options for distracting pupils from challenging behaviour, and whether we build this into our planning to avoid issues, or have it ready to go when things start to get out of hand, it is a must.

Designing subject-appropriate quizzes for your class, group or one-to-one is a fun and personalised way to capture the attention of a whole group and switch things up. Using free applications that utilise devices (like **Kahoot** (www.kahoot.com) or **Survey Monkey**'s quiz maker app (www.surveymonkey.com)), or polling software (like **Gimkit** (www.gimkit.com) and **Plickers** (https://.get.plickers.com)) that can be used on desktops can help. If pupils don't have access to devices, free quiz software options such as **EdApp** (www.edapp.com), **TriviaMaker** (www.triviamaker.com) or **Quizlet** (www.quizlet.com) can help you put together some highly competitive distractions that you can run on a screen (or have pre-printed) with a moment's notice. For working outside the classroom, these can be a lifesaver in a queuing situation!

Using wellness technologies can also work as a distraction, whether for a whole class or an individual student. Apps like **DreamyKid** can be ready and loaded onto a device with headphones, as can brain-training games like Google's **Cognifit** (www.cognifit.com) or **Readlax** (www.readlax.com). I have had some great low-tech success sending a pupil to the corner of the room to do some shredding for me when he was highly triggered in the classroom, so try setting up a repetitive technical task somewhere (inputting into a spreadsheet, for example) for that pupil who would otherwise be sent outside of the classroom and/or put in isolation.

Using technology as a diversion can help give you something to reach for when all is getting out of hand, and planning for it will help you feel calm and able to manage your own state in a positive way.

The truth is, everyone is different and inclusion is important, so when it comes to trying to make your classroom more inclusive, don't forget to think about how technology could and probably would help some if not all of your learners.

7.5 Making school accessible

Just as we heard from Dr Gray, for some learners, school and everything it involves can be a struggle. Schools require conformity from students for them to succeed, but what if the constraints surrounding that requirement ostracise a learner due to their additional needs? How can technology help make school more accessible to those who struggle to be there?

Certainly, safeguarding learners and helping keep them on track using classroom management software such as **classroom.cloud** or Apple **Classroom** can be part of the picture, but as alluded to by Dr Gray, sometimes schools aren't fit for purpose for some.

Here's Nina Jackson, author of *Of Teaching, Learning and Sherbet Lemons*, Independent Thinking associate director and expert in mental health and emotional wellbeing.

Case study: Nina Jackson

In the classroom and at home, assistive technology can be used to support challenges in areas including communication, mobility and learning. When the correct assistive technology is available and implemented, students with learning and living differences can perform and complete tasks that may previously have been too difficult to access or even finish. It also supports independence, self-esteem and self-confidence, and our learners can then be empowered to complete tasks with greater success and efficiency.

The importance of routines and rituals for SEND/ALN learners

Routines and rituals play a crucial role in the lives of individuals with special educational needs and disabilities and additional learning needs (SEND/ALN), and the effective use and incorporation of technology into these practices can enhance an individual's overall wellbeing and learning development.

Here are some key reasons why routines and rituals, along with technology, are important for our SEND/ALN learners. Think of how you can adapt and meet these needs with reasonable adjustments in your classrooms.

- **Predictability and structure:** Learners with special and additional needs often thrive in environments that offer predictability and structure. Routines and rituals provide a sense of order and stability, reducing anxiety and promoting feelings of safety. Technology can be used to create visual schedules, timers and reminders that help learners to anticipate and understand what comes next, making their daily lives and learning pathways more manageable.
- **Skill building:** Routines and rituals present regular opportunities for skills development. For individuals with special and additional needs, repetitive tasks can aid in learning and mastering new abilities. Technology can serve as a valuable tool for skill-building, offering personalised learning experiences, interactive games and educational apps tailored to the individual's needs and preferences.
- **Communication and social interaction:** Many learners with special and additional needs can sometimes face challenges in communication and social interaction. Routines and rituals that involve technology can facilitate communication by using augmentative and alternative communication (AAC) open tools, speech-generating devices or social apps that encourage interaction with peers and caregivers.
- **Emotional regulation:** Special and additional needs learners may have difficulty managing their emotions. Consistent routines and rituals, supported by technology, can help them develop emotional regulation skills by providing a sense of comfort and familiarity. Technology-based tools, such as mindfulness apps or sensory calming applications, can also aid in managing anxiety and stress. Integrating these into the routines and rituals in classroom learning can aid and support positive behaviour which will, in turn, help with communication skills.
- **Independence and autonomy:** Routines and rituals promote a sense of independence and autonomy for individuals with special and additional needs. Technology can empower them to complete tasks on their own, fostering self-reliance and confidence. For instance, assistive-technology devices can support daily living and learning activities, such as managing equipment, homework, self-study, research and even the organisation of their belongings.
- **Personalisation and flexibility:** Technology allows for the customisation of routines and rituals to suit the specific needs and preferences of the learner. Whether it's adjusting the level of difficulty in educational apps or tailoring visual schedules, technology can adapt to the person's changing requirements over time and through their learning journey.

- **Motivation and engagement:** Incorporating technology into routines and rituals can make learning and daily activities more engaging and enjoyable for those who may have challenges due to their special or additional needs. Gamification elements, interactive content and multimedia elements in educational apps can enhance motivation and keep the individual interested and focused. Make sure that every time you introduce these tasks, the routines and rituals are embedded in everything you do, as this will really support the learners.
- **Data collection and progress tracking:** Technology can help collect data on an individual's performance, progress and achievements. Analysing this data can provide valuable insights into areas of improvement and areas of strength, aiding parents, caregivers and educators in developing target interventions and support plans for the essential part of routines and rituals in using EdTech – both in and out of the classroom.

In conclusion, routines and rituals, when combined with appropriate technology, offer immense benefits for individuals with special and additional needs. They provide structure, promote skill development, improve communication and emotional regulation, foster independence and enhance motivation and engagement.

As technology continues to advance, its role in supporting individuals with special and additional needs is likely to become even more impactful and empowering. Let's ensure that routines and rituals are an everyday occurrence in their learning journey.

And that, for many, is the key. Accessibility is just that: making things accessible for learners and being mindful that, while we may have learners with specific, identified learning needs, all of us are unique. In that way, we are able to best support all of the learners in our classrooms.

Top tips

Mark's top tips

1. Remember to consider accessibility from the start. By incorporating it into your instructional design from the outset, you are more likely to make learning accessible to all.

2. Accessibility benefits everyone. Remember that accessibility principles focus on making things clear, concise and easy to understand, which benefits all users, regardless of their specific needs.

3. Technology can support accessibility and often, while some technological tools are essential for some, they're also useful for all.

Olly's top tips

1. In your next department/team meeting, put accessibility on the agenda. Spend time delivering departmental CPD so that everyone in the team has a sound understanding of a common tool, such as Immersive Reader, so that they can upskill all students.

2. The second agenda item in your team meeting should be to look through your planning and make sure that you are redesigning/planning lessons with accessibility in mind.

3. Reach out to colleagues in your school/district to ask for advice and support on the accessibility strategies they are using successfully and share them with your team/department.

CHAPTER 8
Feedback and assessment with technology

'Feedback is the breakfast of champions.'

Ken Blanchard

Good feedback should bring us food for thought and action. It is an essential element of growth and improvement, although equally essential is acting upon it to ensure that growth.

Many have written about feedback over the years, such as Wiliam, Hattie and others. We won't, of course, try to replicate their work. Their work informs what we do, so that we keep pedagogy front and centre in our thinking in line with what we know works with technology as we apply our 5 Cs in the classroom.

Wiliam suggests that effective feedback should be more about triggering students' thinking and providing cues for improvement rather than merely grading or providing correct answers:

> 'The first fundamental principle of effective classroom feedback is that feedback should be more work for the recipient than the donor. The shorter the time interval between eliciting the evidence and using it to improve instruction, the bigger the likely impact on learning.' (Wiliam, 2011)

The truth is, feedback is the cornerstone of learning; without it, you don't know how, if at all, you've been successful in your learning endeavours. In this chapter, we will explore the different types of feedback, assessment and how technology can help you achieve efficiencies, support your teaching and ultimately, help learners with their learning.

8.1 The role of feedback in learning and teaching effectiveness

Without feedback, our learners do not know how well they have done in their learning or what they don't know or understand. More importantly, they also don't know what they need to do to improve. Students will have aims and aspirations to achieve levels of knowledge within the different subjects they learn. Sometimes, those aims will be linked to achieving a certain grade in an exam or a specific test score. Sometimes, it will be to demonstrate progress from a starting point. It might be lots of things; however, without feedback, none of that is possible.

Not only does feedback guide learning but it can enhance motivation and engagement, facilitate reflection and self-assessment and promote a culture of continuous improvement. By receiving feedback, learners can reflect on their learning process and the outcomes it has generated for them – and regular feedback shared in a timely fashion can engage and enthuse them.

We can well remember those teachers who were slow to give feedback when we were young. Reflecting upon that now, as adults, we can almost plot the decline in interest we had in the work we submitted on a daily basis from the date it was submitted onwards.

As adults who are now teaching professionals, it is much easier to understand, empathise and sympathise with the pressures of teachers and why, sometimes, feedback might be slow to return, if at all. As children though, the lack of feedback in and of itself can sometimes be misconstrued and they interpret the lack of feedback as a lack of interest in them, which in turn can lead to apathy for the subject. 'Why should I bother trying if my teacher doesn't bother to tell me how I'm getting on?' is one such memory Mark has from when he was a child.

Feedback can come in a variety of formats:

Type of feedback	Purpose	Characteristics	Effort for educator
Formative feedback	To provide ongoing feedback during the learning process to improve the learner's performance before the final assessment.	Often verbal, immediate and focused on the task and process of learning rather than the final outcome. Also, often the outcome of low-stakes testing.	Low

Type of feedback	Purpose	Characteristics	Effort for educator
Summative feedback	To evaluate a learner's competency after an instructional period, often through tests, projects or other forms of assessment.	Summarises the learning at a specific point in time and is more about the outcome than the process.	High
Peer feedback	To involve learners in giving and receiving feedback among themselves, and foster a collaborative learning environment which also helps reinforce their knowledge and understanding.	Can provide diverse perspectives on performance and understanding, encouraging reflection and deeper engagement with the material.	Low
Corrective feedback	To correct errors or misconceptions in students' understanding or performance.	Can be immediate or delayed, specific to a task and focused on guiding students towards the correct understanding or method.	High
Descriptive feedback	To provide detailed information about what the student did well and what needs improvement, without judgement.	Focuses on specific elements of the work or performance, offering concrete suggestions for improvement.	High
Evaluative feedback	To assess the student's work or performance against a set of standards or criteria, often resulting in a grade or score.	Summarises the quality of work but most likely does not guide how to improve.	High
Self-feedback	To encourage students to reflect upon their work and performance to self-identify areas of strength and areas for improvement.	Prompts self-assessment and metacognitive skills, helping learners become more autonomous, independent and reflective.	Low

Table 8.1: Types of feedback

A cornerstone of our practice for as long as we can remember has been tied into the feedback loop:

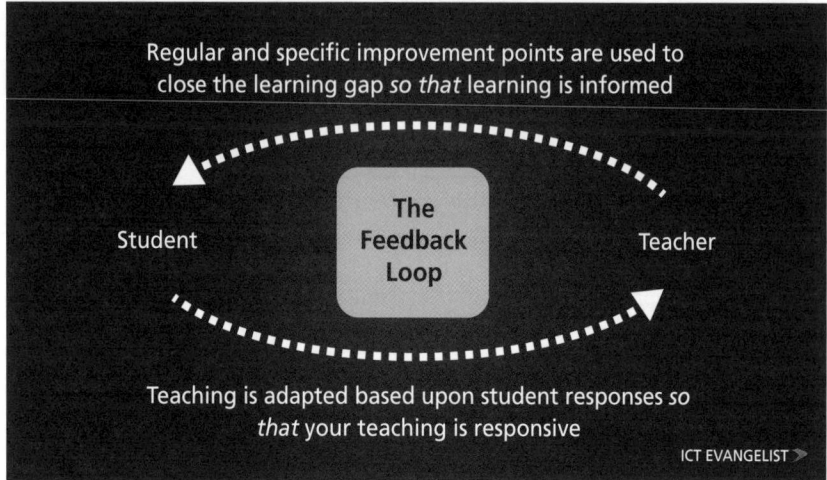

Figure 8.1: The feedback loop

Regularly shared in more keynotes and inset days than he can remember, Mark has long advocated for feedback approaches that make the most of technology to help close the feedback loop as quickly as possible.

Linked directly to the impactful quote from Hattie's work, feedback should be:

> '…just for me, just in time, just for where I am in my learning process, just what I need to move me forward.' (Hattie, 2011)

When planning out our learning sequences, it is important to factor in regular and specific improvement points to help close the learning gap so that learning is informed.

We factor in the regular and specific improvement points to counter Ebbinghaus' forgetting curve (see chapter 5) so that, if required, we can adapt our teaching and our support so we are responsive to our learners' needs.

8.2 Challenges in providing effective feedback

The biggest barrier to pretty much anything in a teacher's day-to-day work is time and workload. When you look at the overriding reason why so many teachers leave the profession, it is more often than not linked to this. A significant part of a teacher's workload comes from marking, assessment, feedback, planning and preparation – and that's before you add in the largest time factor of all: contact time with your classes. With time constraints, the impact is that feedback can be delayed which in turn might be less effective, or could lead to more generic feedback which doesn't address individual student needs.

It's also difficult for teachers to balance the quality versus the quantity of feedback. Finding that 'Goldilocks moment' of sharing feedback that is 'just right' (helpful, while not too much to make it confusing or overwhelming) is a difficult balance to strike. Often, it is also difficult to engage learners in their feedback. If students ignore feedback, especially if they don't understand its value or how to use it to improve, this is disheartening for the teacher who has taken the time to give it. It also reduces the feedback's potential to improve learning.

Another challenge around feedback is providing it in a way that maintains or boosts confidence while still addressing the need for improvement. If feedback is received as being overly critical or negative, it can have the unwanted effect of demotivating students and lowering their self-esteem, enjoyment of and ultimately their success in the subject matter. On top of this, ensuring that feedback is aligned with learning goals and outcomes requires careful planning. Feedback that doesn't link up with shared learning outcomes can also confuse students, so striking that balance is essential. Students can also misinterpret feedback depending on their starting points, backgrounds and experience. This can also lead to confusion, frustration and misdirection in their learning efforts.

Couple all this with the fact that while technology can help address and overcome many of the issues outlined above, lack of equity of access to technology, both in and out of school, can lead to feedback not being accessed at all.

Clearly, there's an awful lot to consider and plan for when it comes to effective feedback. It requires careful attention, knowing your learners and their needs, the content you teach, how you teach it, learning criteria, and the method of assessment and associated feedback that best suits what you are covering.

Fortunately, technology can help with all of the different types of feedback outlined in figure 8.1 to improve the efficiency of your delivery, offer access to knowledge that will help you understand better where your learners are, and reduce some of the administrative burden of assessment, so you can focus on the insights gained from that assessment to speed up the feedback process.

8.3 Leveraging technology for effective feedback

There are plenty of technological platforms, tools, apps and approaches to help with feedback delivery. Ensuring its effectiveness isn't always as easy as we've alluded to, but hopefully, by the end of this section, you'll see some light at the end of the tunnel in the ways it can support your endeavours.

We will dive further into learning management or workflow systems later on in chapter 15, where we look at using technology to manage learning, but as you'll come to learn, systems which integrate into your central ecosystem – whether Google, Microsoft or Apple – can really help.

Line up your dots…

Ensuring that you have systems in place where students can submit their work easily will help with the feedback process immensely. Platforms which auto-grade or generate dashboards to present insights for you as a teacher are widely available, particularly those which you might use for low-stakes quizzing.

Choosing tools which talk with your ecosystem to feed into your MIS and learning platform of choice is, for us, something which is critical.

Many tools outside of your central ecosystem will facilitate single sign-on (SSO) using the Microsoft or Google login you and your students use to access tools *within* your ecosystem. This is enormously beneficial, not least because it will also allow you to integrate assessments and the results of assessments that can be automatically assessed, directly to your central hub for recording results.

A good example of this would be the tool **Quizizz** (www.quizizz.com). It's similar to Microsoft or Google **Forms** and enables you to easily create low-stakes quizzes. (The benefits of using Quizizz over tools such as Microsoft or Google **Forms** are many, but we aren't here to sell Quizizz!) The point is, just like with Microsoft or Google **Forms**, when students complete assessments using this platform, the results feed through into your LMS (such as Google **Classroom** or Microsoft **Teams**), so you can see your class results. You can also view the results and historical views of your students' results on their platform.

Note that not all tools have this sort of functionality, so it's worth checking out those that do. By bringing assessment results into one place, it is much easier for you, as their teacher, to gain insights into student progress over time and for your colleagues to see progress across classes, year groups and the whole school. Another reason why 'consistency' as part of the 5 Cs is useful!

To help with thinking about what tools are available and the different types of approaches you can adopt, it's helpful to reflect on the different types of feedback. Earlier in the chapter, we examined the different types of feedback, their purpose, characteristics and the amount of effort required for the teacher.

To help understand how those different types of feedback can be supported by technology, let's revisit them:

Formative feedback

Given this is often verbal, immediate and focused on a task rather than a final learning outcome, you could use audio feedback tools within your ecosystem such as those built into Microsoft **OneNote Class Notebook** – or **Mote**, which can integrate into Google **Classroom**. In an Apple ecosystem, **Showbie** provides similar functionality.

Of course, in a classroom setting, it's great to use your voice to speak with learners in real life. Using some of the formative assessment tools we have talked about, you can, of course, talk with students, but the quick insights these tools give enable you to make these comments in the moment, on an individual, group or whole-class basis, depending upon the information you've been given from the platform.

Classroom management software is also useful as you can see the work students are undertaking 'in the moment' on their devices, all from your screen. Tools such as **classroom.cloud** are perfect for observing students as they work so you can intervene in a timely, personalised and formative way to support learners when they need it.

Summative feedback

Increasingly, summative assessments are being supported by technology. For a long time, the multiple-choice or short-answer questions in summative assessments have mostly been able to be assessed by digital systems. Historically though, technology has struggled to consider the long-response questions that tend to give higher marks, meaning that teachers have had to mark these by hand. As AI has developed, tools have been (and are being) developed that can handle these more prose-based responses.

Take **sAInaptic** (www.sainaptic.com), a Cambridge-based start-up that has developed a tool that can read, respond and give feedback to students on extended-answer questions in science. The teacher has complete control and can, on the occasions the platform misinterprets a student's response, alter the feedback or score and see the results of the entire class at a glance on the dashboard. It is only a matter of time before more tools like this will be available across the board for all subjects.

Peer and self-feedback

Peer and self-feedback are great approaches that can certainly help with self-reflection, critical thinking, metacognition and self-regulation. For this, it's about providing the conditions and the opportunities with the tools you have at your disposal that can support the feedback activity.

Certainly, while some of the tools we've mentioned, such as the audio tools, can be helpful, it's about ensuring students have the means of sharing their work with peers or for them to share the results of their self-reflection with you. It's also important that students have the frameworks for assessment available to them so they know how to give effective feedback and what to feed back upon.

A good text-based approach is to consider using the commenting tools available in many word-processing applications such as Microsoft **Word**, Google **Docs** and Apple **Pages**. In these environments, the use of the 'suggestion' mode is also a useful way to offer some feedback although, as you'll see in a moment, it's a great approach to use for corrective feedback.

Another approach would be to use a classroom management solution such as Apple **Classroom** where you can share a student's digital work with the entire class and guide the feedback process.

Alternatively, if students have completed work with a pen and paper, the visualiser (a popular digital device for the classroom) is a great tool to enable the entire class to see a piece of work by a peer for feedback and improvement purposes.

This research summary by our good friend José Picardo,[1] suggests that visualisers can help with 'improving the efficacy of feedback' while

---

[1] https://my.chartered.college/research-hub/using-visualisers-to-give-whole-class-feedback

allowing you to deliver 'targeted feedback to a whole class at once'. Picardo's research summary is just one of many that promote the use of these handy little classroom tools.

Many, however, point to two things of importance:

1. The quality of the feedback is down to the person delivering the feedback.
2. The quality of the visual is important, meaning a good-quality visualiser is required along with good lighting. It's important to note too that if the projector quality is poor, it doesn't matter much if the visualiser is high-quality – nobody will be able to see it!

Corrective and descriptive feedback

The purpose of corrective feedback is to correct errors or misconceptions. With descriptive feedback, it's important to give detailed information about what went well with a piece of work, but equally to feed back on what didn't and what needs improvement or adjustment. Either way, for the feedback to be effective, it's just as important that students know what they did wrong as it is for them to know how to improve.

The 'suggestion' mode available in word-processing tools is a great way of giving corrective feedback and modelling improvements. Equally, the commenting tools are also useful, as are the audio-feedback tools available in different applications. The point is, whatever you choose to use when it comes to corrective feedback, it should be focused on guiding a student towards the correct understanding rather than telling them it is incorrect or simply giving them a poor mark.

Whichever way you look at it, assessment and feedback are important cornerstones of every teacher's practice. With workload being such a big issue and technology, for the most part, being widely available, it makes sense to make assessment and feedback *with technology* a focal point for a school's development plan and digital transformation/ implementation strategy.

By taking a strategic approach to how you utilise technology to support teaching and enhance learning, you'll not only improve how teachers teach and how students learn, but, critically, you'll help make learning and feedback more effective, timely and personalised – while simultaneously reducing workload. Now, that can't be a bad thing, can it?

8.4 Assessment

Luckily, technology can help with assessment too. Wiliam suggests that, once a student has received their feedback, they disconnect from the process:

> 'As soon as students get a grade, the learning stops.' (Wiliam, 2011)

From this, we can assume that feedback linked to assessment should be a core pairing if we want learners to improve and make progress from their starting point to where they achieve the success they are aiming for.

There are several different modes of assessment, primarily assessment *of* learning (AoL), assessment *as* learning (AaL), and assessment *for* learning (AfL).

Given that teachers will make hundreds (if not thousands) of decisions relating to their teaching and the subsequent student learning in a lesson and during a day, there are aspects of assessment which are not always caught or as readily tangible. Still, assessment *of*, *for* or *as* learning all give the teacher valuable insights.

Formative and summative assessments are hugely valuable in their own right. When used together, they provide us with a comprehensive understanding of achievement and progress – with technology playing a supporting role, enabling teachers to respond and adapt at an ever-faster rate.

Within the different modes there are different types of assessment and, while not exhaustive, these can be broadly characterised as:

Type of assessment	Purpose	Characteristics	Effort for educator	Mode
Diagnostic assessment	To identify students' knowledge and skills before instruction.	Informs teaching strategies and interventions and sometimes activities such as grouping.	Moderate	AfL
Formative assessment	To monitor student learning and provide ongoing feedback.	Informal. Integrated into daily learning routines.	Moderate	AfL

Type of assessment	Purpose	Characteristics	Effort for educator	Mode
Summative assessment	To evaluate learning at the end of an instructional period or the end of a course.	Formal. Includes tests, exams and coursework.	High	AoL
Performance assessment	To assess students' ability to apply skills in realistic scenarios.	Project-based, practical application.	High	AfL/AoL
Peer assessment	To engage students in evaluating each other's work.	Encourages metacognition, collaborative learning and critical thinking.	Low	AaL
Self-assessment	To encourage reflection on own learning.	Promotes metacognition and self-regulated learning.	Low	AaL
High-stakes assessment	To make important decisions based on student performance.	Outcomes are critical and present high pressure.	High	AoL
Low-stakes assessment	To guide daily teaching and learning with minimal pressure on learning.	Used frequently, often with little to no grade impact, but to inform interventions and to support learning.	Low	AfL
Portfolio assessment	To collect and evaluate work over time to show growth or to present final pieces of work.	Ongoing collection and reflection of student work.	High	AfL/AoL

Table 8.2: Types of assessment

8.5 Formative assessment with technology

We assess formatively to help us know where students' learning is on any curricula they are following. Formative assessment works best when it's low-stakes and, according to Hattie, linking into feedback, it should be:

- just in time

- just for them
- just for where they are in their learning
- just what they need to move forward

...to help close the feedback loop. (Hattie, 2011)

Dylan Wiliam's work on embedding formative assessment (Wiliam, 2011) is also important, as it highlights that it takes place during the learning process and enables teachers to continuously move learning forward. Teachers monitor student understanding and provide feedback for timely instructional adjustments – it informs the teacher and guides learning.

Formative assessment strategies identify three key aspects:

- where the learning is currently
- where the learner is going
- how the learner can get to the destination.

All of these help to lead us to a point where our pedagogy can inform our approaches to using technology to support assessment and feedback.

Therefore, in a lesson, a teacher might decide to use a quick multiple-choice quiz to gauge student understanding. This will inform the teacher of where each learner is and the next instructional steps they need to take to fill any knowledge gaps. Typically, teachers use online quizzing tools for this activity. However, these can become more game-based and students can lose focus.

This goes counter to what we know about cognitive load and, as teachers, we want to give students the chance to show what they know and 'catch them in' rather than 'catch them out'. This way, we'll understand far more clearly what support students need with any misconceptions they might have. This is far more desirable than us thinking students know something, when in reality they do not – they've just been overloaded with a 'fun' quiz without spending the necessary time thinking carefully about their responses in a low-stakes, formative assessment.

By successfully coupling a pedagogical and technological approach – using low-stakes quizzing tools to canvas students' levels of understanding with a simple scale, multiple-choice questions, or as entry or exit ticket – gives you immediate insights into student learning without distractions or any gamification; it keeps pedagogy and technology focused on assessing learning. Students can access these by scanning a QR code or clicking on a shared link posted in your LMS (as we explained in chapter 6).

Alternatively, you can use these tools to great effect for knowledge checks with open or closed questions, or ask students to elaborate on a statement or well-crafted question. These get your students thinking hard while yielding instantly useful information for you, as the teacher. The technology reduces the time it takes to receive this and, ultimately, you can act and support students faster. No gimmicks, just a learning-centred approach.

Similarly, again with TPACK in mind, asking students to use voice-noting tools like **Mote** to capture their discussion or elaboration to a question, captures formative assessment in action. Tools like **Padlet**, the collaboration space in Microsoft **OneNote Class Notebook, Whiteboard** in Microsoft **Teams**, **Freeform** using Apple devices, Google **Slides/Docs**, or **Mentimeter** (www.mentimeter.com) all capture thinking and subsequent learning through a blend of technological and pedagogical knowledge.

With a lens of developing (and formatively assessing) understanding, knowledge application and oracy in the classroom and beyond, consider tools that help students showcase their knowledge which teachers can then assess.

Feedback can be in the form of written text or audio – again, offering versatility and supporting formative assessment in meaningful and creative ways.

Audio

Using audio notes or feedback can provide depth and detail to students (and teachers) in a timely and efficient manner, while bringing the warmth and timbre of your voice to help with understanding, compared to written feedback. It can also be useful for students to elaborate on their answers and provide further details to help unlock their schema and bridge any learning gaps.

Of course, you don't just need to use audio for feedback purposes; you can also use it as part of your teaching and learning toolkit.

Language subjects can use audio to practise the pronunciation of words and/or phrases. Students can listen back to their recording to compare to a model example, reflecting on their progress – or they can exchange their audio notes for peer assessment. Listening comprehension forms a large part of many courses, so audio notes provide authentic opportunities while also exposing students to a range of accents, speeds of speech and sounds to encourage active listening and develop the skill of extracting key information from spoken language.

In an English classroom, students could record themselves reading to practise adjusting tone, narration, intonation patterns, phonetics and more. Students can curate and create recordings of their work to encourage the development of oral expression skills, such as pacing and articulation. Students can record re-enactments of historical events, with dialogue and background sounds, or perform a reading of historical speeches to help develop their immersion in and deepen their understanding of past events.

Students orating their learning and teachers providing constructive and detailed feedback at the tap of a button is more effective than long, written communications.

The opportunities are vast and you'll see many of these ideas reinforced in the later chapters, where we explore case studies from teachers across different subjects.

Tools with audio capacity include **Mote**; Microsoft **OneNote Class Notebook**, **Word** and **PowerPoint**; Apple **Keynote** and **Pages**; Google **Slides** and **Docs** – and many more.

It would also be remiss of us to not mention Microsoft's **Reading Progress** and **Reading Coach** assignment tools that are built directly into **Teams** assignments. Reading Progress puts reading directly in front of students for them to read into their device, which tracks fluency, pronunciation and more. Once completed, the tool gives both teacher and students feedback and, when coupled with Reading Coach, students have the opportunity to practise the predetermined focus, such as pronunciation, of the words they found difficult to read.

Screen recording

Coupled with audio is the option to provide screen-recorded content that supports formative assessment and feedback, making it a powerful ally to formative assessment strategies. In addition, when students use a combination of audio and visual tools to evidence learning, they have greater agency and it helps to deepen understanding through meaningful connections.

Asking students to screen-record enables the teacher to observe processes and identify areas for improvement. It also provides insights into the problem-solving strategies the student has adopted and how they might go about iterating and refining their work.

Practically speaking, students (or teachers) could provide screen recordings that:

- detail procedural understanding
- process assessments
- demonstrate interpretation activities
- demonstrate experimental design
- model work
- demonstrate problem-solving
- explain concepts
- record reading fluency
- document processes (e.g. planning an essay or mathematical calculations)
- practise oral presentations
- practise using digital maps to evidence map skills

...and more.

As you can see, there are so many possibilities where technology can support formative assessment strategies and you could use tools such as Google **Slides**, Apple **Keynote**, Microsoft **PowerPoint**, and screen-recording software such as Microsoft **Stream**, **Screencastify** (www.screencastify.com), **Explain Everything**, or **Loom** (www.loom.com). Many operating systems have screen-recording functionality built in, which means that regardless of the tool you're using, you're often able to record your screen.

Another creative solution with a subject-specific example might be the use of **Minecraft Education Edition** in geography, which can be used to incorporate collaboration, problem-solving and critical thinking while, for example, creating a virtual landscape based on processes and land formations students have previously learned.

As a physics teacher, Olly's modus operandi has been to use Microsoft **OneNote** for modelling worked examples of challenging concepts with students. He also ensures he records the examples so they are saved for future use – reducing his workload in the long run and serving as a resource for students to use time and time again.

147

Where common misconceptions are identified – or even if it is beneficial for students' overall learning – short, explanatory videos enable key concepts to be accessed asynchronously, and embedded into OneNote for further review and discussion in future lessons.

This increases the efficiency of class time as each student gets exactly what they need, when they need it, as opposed to waiting for 20-plus minutes in a lesson for Olly to get to the question that they needed explaining and subsequent help with reviewing. This enables feedback to be personalised and timely. It builds in time within lessons for reflection and follow-up activities so each student makes more progress.

Here is a screenshot from one of Olly's Year 12 physics classes:

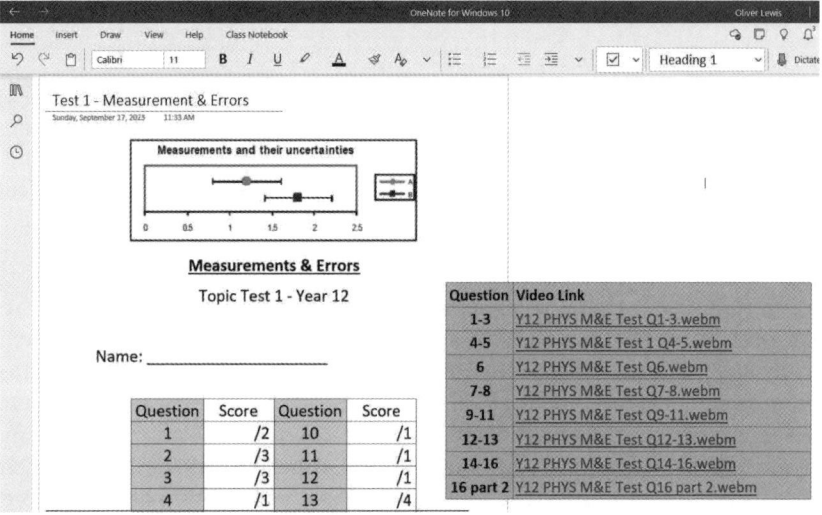

Figure 8.2: OneNote screenshot from a physics class

While this might not seem particularly innovative, it demonstrates what good use of technology can look like in a low-stakes and high-impact way. Remember, when it comes to using technology to support learning and feedback, solid, granular feedback that zeroes in on the specifics is about the pedagogy leading the technology use, not the other way around.

Interestingly, many schools worked in this fashion during COVID times and then reverted to whole-class teacher-talk feedback, which is often less efficient for each individual in your classroom. Which seems better to you when you reflect on this?

Many technological tools can help with formative assessment, but the good ones tend to have certain things in common. When you're looking to see which tools will work best for you, consider the following:

- Can it increase opportunities for communication efficiency?
- Can it reduce workload or save time?
- Can it provide opportunities for deeper sharing?
- Does the tool offer more opportunities for personalisation?
- Does it help a diverse range of skills to be assessed?
- And importantly, does it support accessibility for those learners who may need it?

Whichever way you look at it, making sure you can positively leverage a blend of pedagogical approaches from your choice of technological tools is key. Why? As a modern educator looking to make the most of technology to support your teaching and their learning, you should be able to be adaptive and responsive to your learners' needs.

8.6 Summative assessment with technology

Summative assessment is typically evaluative in nature and falls at the end of a learning cycle in the form of a topic test or exam. The initial learning has already taken place and the summative assessment is measuring the students' overall achievement relative to a set of learning objectives or criteria.

Technology can support summative assessment in a multitude of ways; for example, tools like Microsoft **Forms**, **Socrative**, Google **Forms**, etc. can be used equally well for formative or summative assessment. The challenge for both comes in ensuring that your students cannot access other content – like the internet(!) – so you ideally need a platform like **classroom.cloud** to mitigate this, that has the functionality of being able to lock students into certain tools or limiting internet access in the classroom.

Another example of how technology supports feedback is the use of quizzing tools. These provide instant scores, responses and, in some cases, feedback to students, which helps identify areas for improvement and reduces the time taken for the feedback loop to be completed. Ultimately, this helps students in a quicker and more meaningful way while also reducing teacher workload.

When designing your summative assessments and considering how technology should be used by your students, consider:

- Does technology increase accessibility for students?
- Can students showcase their learning in a timely fashion using the technological tool?
- Will it improve the efficiency and efficacy of the assessment?
- How can you ensure the validity of the student's work?
- What other ethical considerations do you need to consider?
- What are the long-term requirements: licensing costs, hardware requirements, ongoing support costs and sustainability of the tool itself?
- Do the students have the necessary digital literacy skills to complete the assessment digitally?
- Accessibility: do all students have access to technology and to the tools that aid assessments?

What's more important is how you use the technology, given the context of the learning taking place at the point in time in your lesson or cycle of learning.

Technology can play a vital role in supporting summative assessment in an array of subjects; for example, video-analysis software allows teachers to analyse student performance and techniques in subjects such as PE, performing arts and DT.

Tools like Microsoft's **Reading Progress**, **Goodreads** (www.goodreads.com) and **Accelerated Reader** (www.renaissance.com) give teachers insights into students' reading and comprehension skills and abilities, which then informs teaching and provides ample opportunities for feedback. Common tools such as **Turnitin** (www.turnitin.com) or **Grammarly** (www.grammarly.com) can also give feedback on spelling, grammar and writing styles.

Programs like **AutoCAD** (www.autodesk.co.uk) and **Tinkercad** or 3D printers and laser cutters allow students to design and create product prototypes in which teachers can assess their technical-design skills along with problem-solving skills.

Python (www.python.org) and **Replit** (www.replit.com) allow students to create code and/or programs which demonstrate their computational and programming skills, which teachers can then assess. Tools alongside this like **PyCharm** (www.jetbrains.com/pycharm) can help to solve some of the problems of missed parentheses when coding.

What needs to remain front and centre when selecting technology for summative assessment is that it should align with and enable your specific learning and assessment objectives, while also offering support to students. These things are crucial for integrating technology into assessment processes effectively.

8.7 Digital artefacts as assessment

Education is constantly evolving, so we cannot overlook the potential of digital artefacts when it comes to assessment. Not everything needs to be done formatively or summatively; assessments can be iterative over a longer time frame and be supported by technology.

Howard Gardner's multiple intelligence model[2] tells us that students have a diverse array of cognitive strengths as opposed to a single general intelligence: some are more linguistic, some visual-spatial, some interpersonal and some naturalistic, while others are more logical.

(**Warning!** This is not to be confused with the debunked learning styles theory, which refers to an individual's preferred way of processing information. Multiple intelligences purport a broader and diversified range of intelligences beyond simply academic abilities.)

Gardner's model also teaches us that people are not born with all of the intelligence they will ever have; we all have a range of strengths and limitations which we can develop to become a more well-rounded individual. This is important, as it's not just about academic achievement, but includes a range of abilities and strengths, our capacity to develop self-awareness and self-esteem and, ultimately, pursue our interests.

With this in mind, surely it is time we open up the realms of possibilities for digital artefacts for assessment purposes. Digital artefacts can make assessments more student-centred and offer them the chance to be more creative and authentic in their output, as Erika Sandström advocated for in her case study shared earlier (section 6.7). While authenticity does often breed engagement, striking a balance that allows learners to demonstrate their learning while not detracting from the learning

---

[2] www.simplypsychology.org/multiple-intelligences.html

content, nor them spending valuable curriculum time learning how to use technology rather than the content, is important.

Digital artefacts open up a plethora of possibilities for students to demonstrate their learning of real-world concepts and solve complex problems. This is especially true when students are enabled to form projects on topics they are passionate or curious about. Having said that, it wouldn't take much of a mindset shift to move to digital artefacts as a means of assessment in many curriculum subjects.

Here are some examples of how you could make use of digital artefacts for assessment purposes:

- **Video playlists:** Students curate a video playlist that showcases their knowledge and understanding of a topic, process or technical development. Alternatively, they could document their coursework as it has evolved.
- **Blogs:** Students write blogs to demonstrate their learning in a particular area of the curriculum, charting their development, which is then shared publicly.
- **Mixed media:** Creating with tools like **Canva** or Adobe **Express**.
- **Journals (digital):** Students use a range of digital tools to curate a digital journal of their learning and work.
- **Digitally annotated compositions:** Students digitally annotate work from other classes to provide feedback that shows that they can critically evaluate subject content.
- **Discussion boards:** Students create discussion boards to showcase their strengths and challenges while also showing their progress.
- **Websites:** Students curate a class website to house all of the above suggestions.

All of these provide opportunities for sharing within and outside of the school to garner more feedback from a multitude of stakeholders. Don't forget to consider artefacts you can create with AI, such as Claude AI's **Sonnet** that we mentioned earlier (section 5.7).

8.8 How technology can hinder assessment

While this book is about technology and the many benefits that it brings, we are distinctly aware that there are times when it is not appropriate and is not the right tool for the job at hand. We do hope that this has come across in the book – we both openly advocate for technology while, at the same time, bang the 'just because you can, it doesn't mean you should' drum!

Yes, the technology itself can cause issues such as technical problems or glitches, raise questions of academic integrity (and thus authenticity), be reductive in terms of interactivity (in certain instances), cause inequity around access or lack thereof, be unable to meet the challenge of assessing soft skills, and so on. While all of these can be true, they are not our biggest concerns.

What is often overlooked is how we might go about mitigating any of these points when using technology to support assessment strategies. Yes, technology can be a great resource, but it is vital to find a balance of more traditional and digital methods regarding assessment.

At this point, it is also worth noting that some quizzing tools which are used for assessment purposes do not always elicit the most effective responses for these reasons:

- They reward speed.
- Their fast-paced nature can promote more superficial, as opposed to deep, learning.
- They reduce the need for problem-solving or critical thinking.
- They increase the likelihood of a student cheating.
- They provide limited feedback.
- They promote social norms that are not in the best interests of learning, such as overstimulation or excitement.

While this is not true for many quizzing tools, it does exist, so choose your quizzing tool wisely and ensure that pedagogical and learning decisions are at the forefront as you do.

8.9 A case for online exams – what if?

In October 2023, exam boards announced that they would trial digital exams in some subjects (Woolcock, 2023) and AQA released a long-term roadmap for digital exams (Norden, 2023). While this is, in our opinion, a good move for many reasons, it does bring to the fore the need for education to move to a more inclusive model where inequity is addressed and any systemic barriers are removed.

While our world is becoming ever more digital and schools strive to always do the best they can for their young people, the truth of the matter remains that, in the world of work, the vast majority of adults will interact with technological tools daily. It is almost inescapable. It is, therefore, our moral imperative to ensure that we are building digital skills and digital literacy, while navigating digital interfaces with proficiency within and across our curricula. We do this so that our young people are as prepared as possible for the future, no matter what walk of life, sector or job they end up pursuing.

We know that, at the time of reading this many of you, like us, will likely be thinking of all the reasons not to have digital exams at such pivotal points in education, such as security and integrity issues. But, what if:

- those digital exams did indeed level the accessibility and inclusivity playing field in terms of having features like text-to-speech, adjustable text size and other accessibility tools that enable learners with specific difficulties to be empowered? Would we still say no to this as a sector?
- assessment timelines were rapidly reduced with automated grading which gave individual and personalised feedback to every candidate? What would this mean for curriculum and class time?
- What would digital exams mean environmentally across the sector? Would it lead to a long-term move to a more sustainable future?

There could be lots of positive arguments for moving towards digital exams, but we appreciate that to reach this point, it is most definitely a marathon and not a sprint to the finish line.

Those exam boards that are planning online exams are forward-thinking and this is somewhat of a milestone in education, regardless of what happens next. If we stick with what we have always done, we will get what we have always had. What if something new *actually* worked for the better?

8.10 Consider 'how can AI help?' instead

In recent times, artificial intelligence (AI) has spread rapidly across the globe. While it is true that it has been a part of our lives for a considerable time now (making recommendations on platforms like Netflix and social media, for example), its place in education is still young in the grand scheme of things. Nevertheless, is it now the time to overhaul assessment in education in an efficient, sustainable and scalable manner or simply approach assessment differently now that large language models (LLMs) are accessible?

AI has the potential to personalise, automate, increase the range of areas assessed, provide faster feedback, increase the frequency of assessments, provide appropriate challenge and consistency over time, stealth test, virtually tutor and, ultimately, over time enable students to progress more quickly.

While all of this is possible, there will certainly need to be considerable research and investment into these areas, given the ongoing concerns around data privacy, ethics, bias and the hallucinations (fake information being created that appears plausible) that occur with AI. Currently, hallucinations in tools like **ChatGPT** cause challenges to assessments that require written responses, leading to a loss in academic integrity and honesty.

Is now the time we finally look at assessment differently?

Firstly, we should educate our students on what they can and cannot use AI for. Secondly, schools can create an AI framework which highlights acceptable uses and methodologies for developing answers which are then used to inform a student's final piece of work. Thirdly, we can reframe how we assess students.

Banning AI isn't the answer. It's here, largely accessible, and not going anywhere. As educators, we need to teach the good, the bad and the ugly so that our young people are wiser and more informed. Therefore, clear guidelines on what are acceptable and unacceptable uses in schools are critical. Take the time as a staff body to codify this at a school and then subject level; this way, there's no hiding and there is a clear line in the sand.

Creating an AI framework which highlights strategies for acceptable use across the school and curriculum will support staff and the curriculum while also enabling students to use it as a reference point. In the same way that a teacher will model their expert thinking aloud in a lesson, a framework gives the bounds within which students can operate, acting as a supportive and structured approach.

Assessment doesn't need to be overcomplicated simply because AI is around. Rather than written text, you can ask students to label a diagram, complete a fishbone diagram or complete missing details from a timeline of events; we can be creative in how we assess without AI.

As indicated in Australia's 'Assessment reform in the age of artificial intelligence' (TEQSA, 2023), many assessment types are at risk to AI. Therefore, it is important to address the nature of assessment with *generative AI* so that, as a sector, we can overcome this issue. Now, this will no doubt ruffle some feathers, as historically analogue exams have worked, so why change anything at all? We would argue that in a highly technological world, it is imperative to change with the times. At the very least, we must consider the opportunities and adapt and/or pivot to meet our learners' needs.

An interesting piece of work in the areas of AI and assessment has come from Leon Furze and his counterparts, Dr Mike Perkins,[3] Dr Jasper Roe[4] and Dr Jason MacVaugh,[5] at British University Vietnam. They have developed an AI assessment scale (Furze, 2023) which aims to explore the problems with many existing assessment strategies that a world with AI in it brings to educators.

The AI assessment scale is an attempt to help educators decide what is and what isn't cheating when considering the use of AI by students in their learning activities.

---

[3] www.linkedin.com/in/mgperkins
[4] www.linkedin.com/in/dr-jasper-roe-sfhea-894571102
[5] www.linkedin.com/in/dr-jason-macvaugh-a44661165

1	NO AI	The assessment is completed entirely without AI assistance. This level ensures that students rely solely on their knowledge, understanding, and skills. **AI must not be used at any point during the assessment.**
2	AI-ASSISTED IDEA GENERATION AND STRUCTURING	AI can be used in the assessment for brainstorming, creating structures, and generating ideas for improving work. **No AI content is allowed in the final submission.**
3	AI-ASSISTED EDITING	AI can be used to make improvements to the clarity or quality of student-created work to improve the final output, but no new content can be created using AI. **AI can be used, but the original work with no AI content must be provided in an appendix.**
4	AI TASK COMPLETION, HUMAN EVALUATION	AI is used to complete certain elements of the task, with students providing discussion or commentary on the AI-generated content. This level requires critical engagement with AI generated content and evaluating its output. **Students will use AI to complete specified tasks in the assessment. Any AI-created content must be cited.**
5	FULL AI	AI should be used as a 'co-pilot' in order to meet the requirements of the assessment, allowing for a collaborative approach with AI and enhancing creativity. **Students may use AI throughout the assessment to support their own work and do not have to specify which content is AI generated.**

Figure 8.3: The AI assessment scale

The model is particularly useful because it doesn't shirk away from recognising that students will be using these tools, whether they are allowed to or not. It is helpful to educators and students alike. We would advocate for its inclusion as part of the AI literacy strands of the digital cognition curriculum we discussed earlier in chapter 4 (section 4.7).

For those braver colleagues who wish to use AI as a means of assessment *of* learning, *for* learning or *as* learning, your challenge is to share with us the assessment modes you are using which involve AI and tag us on X or LinkedIn, using the hashtag #EdTechPlaybook!

In the meantime, while remembering that AI tools are assistants and not substitutes, you could try one of the following strategies:

- Give students an AI-generated piece of work which has purposeful errors contained within. Ask them to assess its quality, while giving feedback on a specific area (e.g. knowledge content, accuracy of information, links made, etc.).

- Ask students to write prompts that give feedback to the AI so that it generates a higher-quality piece of work with improvements in the identified areas.
- Ask students to generate content that is contextually specific to their current learning, then ask them to assess any biases found within it.
- Use AI tools to generate quizzes that assess specific learning objectives from the course.
- Use an AI tool to generate a quiz from media such as a course-specific **YouTube** (www.youtube.com) video.
- Develop grading rubrics.

At the time of writing this, it is worth noting that AI assessment tools are constantly expanding. The focus should still always be on your students and their learning, improving the quality and frequency of feedback while also empowering learners. At the very least, why not ask the students which AI tools they are using and ask them to teach you how they use them so that you can develop your insights?

In a world where we model what we want to see in our young people, surely now is the time to be open and transparent and demonstrate trying something new to see how it may (or may not) enhance your teaching and their learning.

Top tips

Mark's top tips

1. Use formative assessments strategically, ensuring they're frequent, low-stakes and designed to give students feedback that will help improve their learning. Consider technological tools that can make that process simple.

2. Consider how you can space the formative assessments that you give to support retrieval practice that counters the forgetting curve and reinforces long-term retention of learning.

3. Read up further on assessment and feedback strategies that work with the great, accessible resources shared by the team at the 'learning scientists' on the website www.learningscientists.org.

Olly's top tips

1. Give it a go! Pick one tool that aligns with your learning goals and see how it can enhance learning, whether by increasing feedback, reducing the time delay of feedback, reducing your workload or offering a new way to assess the students.

2. As technology now enables us to make ever-improved digital artefacts, why not set students a project to create an artefact that evidences their learning less traditionally? Caveat: Let them know you will share it with the world so that they make it their best work, rather than just making it 'good enough'.

3. Involve the students in the journey so that you have unique user voices and can help chart the right path for them and your school in terms of AI adoption.

CHAPTER 9
Artificial intelligence and XR

'If not now, when?'

Hillel the Elder

It would, of course, be remiss to not have a chapter dedicated to the use of AI in education. It will, of course, most likely be the singular type of technology that will have progressed the most between the publication of this book and the time you actually read it. That's fine. We aren't worried. Let us explain why.

While AI and the associated tools, features and functionalities of the technology are being updated and improved almost daily, the rules about how we approach its use make it just like any other technology. Just because it is ground-breaking and particularly helpful in targeting the three impactful ways of supporting teaching and learning around reducing workload, helping to teach and helping to learn (alongside many other improvements to workflow and efficiency), how we approach it to make a difference to our daily practice is just the same as any other EdTech.

Of course, AI isn't the only cutting-edge technology we'll explore in this chapter – we'll also dig into XR.

Not sure what XR is? XR stands for 'extended reality'. It is an umbrella term that encompasses virtual reality (VR), augmented reality (AR) and mixed reality (MR). In the context of educational technology:

- **Virtual reality** (VR) offers a fully immersive digital experience where users are transported into a computer-generated environment.
- **Augmented reality** (AR) overlays digital content in the real world through devices like smartphones, tablets or AR glasses.
- **Mixed reality** (MR) is a blend of both AR and VR, where real-world and digital objects interact, such as through experiences you can explore using Microsoft's **HoloLens** headset or Apple **Vision Pro**.

Given the advancements in educational technology, XR has the potential to revolutionise teaching and learning, offering immersive and interactive experiences that can enhance understanding and retention. Like many technologies though, according to the Bananarama principle, 'It ain't (so much) what you do, it's the way that you do it, and that's what gets results'. And so, in this chapter, we'll explore each of the different forms of XR and some of the case scenarios for it to be used successfully. Some are more mainstream, others more niche, but that's what helps, right? Knowing what to use, when it can be useful and whether or not the 'juice is worth the squeeze'.

9.1 What is AI?

Artificial intelligence (AI) encompasses tools that aim to emulate human intelligence. There are different forms of AI, namely:

- **Simple LLMs (limited learning models):** These foundational tools are akin to specialised instruments – like a calculator tailored solely for arithmetic – performing a singular function with precision.
- **LLMs (large language models):** Models like **ChatGPT** or **Gemini** sit on the more complex end. Picture an entity absorbing a vast library's worth of information. LLMs are trained on extensive datasets, enabling them to craft human-like text. While they can respond based on their training, they don't 'understand' as humans do; they simply identify patterns in the data to deliver a response.
- **Machine learning (ML):** Think of teaching a child to identify animals. After numerous examples, they'll recognise a 'cat' or 'dog' on their own. ML algorithms learn from data, discern patterns and make predictions. For instance, Netflix suggests TV shows by analysing your viewing habits.
- **Natural language processing (NLP):** The technology that sits behind Siri and Alexa, NLP enables machines to comprehend and articulate human language. Pose a query to Alexa and it interprets, processes and responds in a coherent fashion (or at least you hope that it will!).
- **Image recognition:** Using machine learning (ML), modern operating systems such as iOS employ AI to detect objects in photos. Try searching in the Photos app for 'dog' or 'car' and see what happens! ML algorithms analyse vast amounts of image data, learning to identify patterns associated with specific objects or faces. Over time, these algorithms become adept at categorising images or recognising familiar faces by scrutinising pixels and patterns.

Now, you might be sitting there thinking, 'So, what about the Terminator?!' Many of you might picture self-aware machines from films like this.

While compelling and great cinema, many think we are far from achieving such sentient AI. Current models such as ChatGPT operate based on algorithms and patterns – genuine emotions or consciousness remain elusive, despite how clever they might seem.

That said, according to Hamilton, Wiliam and Hattie (2023):

> 'We should work on the assumption that we may be only two years away from artificial general intelligence (AGI) that is capable of undertaking all complex human tasks to a higher standard than us and at a fraction of the cost.'

Their working paper is at best somewhat positive, and at worst Orwellian and scary, but we hope these things are listened to, so as to give us time to plan for the huge shift in AI, AGI and the inevitable ASI (artificial super intelligence) that will likely appear in the coming decades, potentially within the time frame of current toddlers finishing their compulsory education (2040).

Five ways AI is already revolutionising the classroom:

1. **Personalised learning:** Adaptive learning platforms modify content based on individual student performance, offering customised learning experiences.
2. **Automated administrative tasks:** AI can handle administrative chores, allowing educators more quality time with students.
3. **Assistance for diverse needs:** Tools powered by AI can offer real-time translations or aid students with learning disabilities.
4. **Interactive smart content:** AI can generate interactive content, from digitised textbooks to customised learning modules.
5. **Predictive analysis:** By analysing student data, AI can predict which students might be at risk, allowing timely intervention.

Like all good technology use in education, embracing AI should be, for the most part, about leveraging available tools to support equity, accessibility, learning, teaching or reducing workload. The truth is though, despite lots of influencer furore on social media, getting the results you want from using AI tools can be tough. While influencers will tell you how amazing AI is and how much time you'll save using it, the truth is that, often, you don't get the results you want. One of the best things you can do to help is to work on developing your approaches to creating prompts for these kinds of tools.

A word of caution about social media and educational technology

Linking back to the comments above about influencers on social media and AI (and any educational technology for that matter), we'd like to take a moment to focus on what influencers share. The fact is that many of the tools, approaches and *amazing* things they talk about are because those posts are sponsored.

Not all influencers are equal. According to the rules set out by the Advertising Standards Authority in the UK, influencers should indicate clearly that their posts are sponsored and are, in essence, adverts.[1] Many, however, don't say it at all – or bury it deep at the bottom of a long thread.

I guess what we are trying to say is, don't believe the hype. We'll discuss this in more detail in chapter 19, where we talk about the importance of a good procurement process – but, given the large number of edu-influencers sharing about AI (in particular) at the moment, we felt we had to mention it in this chapter too.

Another good example to illustrate what influencers communicate on social media is around some of the compelling statistics they share that might incite you to start using a technology such as AI. Recently, Boston Consulting Group did some research on its employees, where it found a 40% increase in productivity for people who use AI compared to those who don't (Pontefract, 2023). Now that is pretty compelling, right? What the influencers sharing these results didn't mention is that when you dig deeper into the report, they found that 19% of those people using AI were 'more likely to produce incorrect solutions in such scenarios'. This is more helpful and highlights the importance of not believing the hype. Regularly sharing this in his work, Mark goes further to explain what this helps us to do about the problem, because it makes it very clear that to counter this issue we should consider the importance of:

- CPD and time to learn how to use AI effectively
- cognisance of what works and when to use AI
- planning so that AI enhances rather than diminishes the human element.

Of course, the irony is that this is true for all technology use in education, as we have shared many times throughout this book.

---

[1] www.asa.org.uk/news/influencer-marketing-key-advice-resources.html

9.2 Generative AI

Generative AI is a branch of AI that comes into its own in helping its users to create new content. We've already heard about a generative-AI tool, **ChatGPT** (www.chatgpt.com). At the time of writing, some of the most popular tools are:

- **ChatGPT** which, on the paid-for version (**ChatGPT 4**), currently incorporates **DALL-E 3** (an image generation tool) and Bing Search
- **Claude** (www.claude.ai)
- Google **Gemini**
- **Perplexity** (www.perplexity.ai)
- Microsoft **Copilot**.

Many educators have rushed to use these, particularly ChatGPT, to help in key areas such as workload reduction and resource creation. The AI's ability to interrogate text, assimilate that information and then pump out an output is staggeringly quick. That is useful because, as educators, we often have to do that ourselves, particularly around lesson planning and creating resources.

Generative AI represents a paradigm shift for educators both in how we approach content creation and how we assess our learners, when they, for example, can just work with a tool to create brilliant essays, perfect model answers to exam questions, and more. Its integration into education can be transformative. Students can work with AI to serve as a collaborative learning partner where they can pose questions, explore ideas or even brainstorm with AI and receive immediate, helpful and informed feedback. AI's ability to create content quickly means that resources for students in your class can be tailored quickly to their reading age or incorporate accessibility features that help them in their learning journey. Need to analyse some complex progress data? Don't worry, AI can analyse vast amounts of data, providing quick insights into student performance, learning trends and areas of misconception.

Generative AI and image generation

While generative AI's capabilities in text are fantastic, tools like Open AI's **DALL-E 3** (www.openai.com/dall-e-3), **Midjourney** (www.midjourney.com) and Adobe **Firefly** have extended this potential into the ability to generate images. Other tools such as **ideogram** (www.ideogram.ai) are also useful in this regard. These tools translate a text description into detailed images based on the words provided. For example, crafting a prompt that describes 'a bustling market in eighteenth-century London' should result in a vivid portrayal of that scene.

The ability to use AI to generate amazing imagery truly democratises creativity and can help make us all fantastic designers. It is important to understand however that, while AI tools generate images from text prompts, the process isn't about replacing traditional art forms or foundational learning – quite the opposite. Having foundational knowledge in subjects such as art and photography improves the quality of the prompts we can write and the output from these tools immeasurably. This is, in part, why we chose to work with Rebecca Gray[2] for the illustration on the cover of this book. It would have been very easy for us to use one of the many tools available to create something for it. The results AI can create are stunning; however, they do not replace the brilliance of human artistry.

Rebecca's work and her knowledge of painting, design, layouts, brush strokes, colour and more, enable her to create amazing designs which make her a successful artist in her own right. That said, when she applies that knowledge to the prompts she crafts using these tools, her results will automatically generate better quality images because she has that significant experience and beyond foundational knowledge. Thus, deeper success will only occur with a firm understanding of specific domains of knowledge. Her illustration on the front cover reinforces the notion that AI tools complement the knowledge and skills acquisition she already has, so that her outputs are vastly improved as a direct result of that knowledge.

The use of AI to generate outputs is significantly improved through the foundational knowledge users have. This applies to the literacy students and teachers have in their ability to write clearly, by being analytical and employing critical thinking skills so that they get the most out of these AI tools and systems. Never before (we think) have knowledge, skills and metacognitive attributes been more important to the process of learning.

People sometimes say, as per Ian Gilbert's book, *Why Do I Need A Teacher When I've Got Google?* Why do you need a teacher when you've got **ChatGPT**? Clearly, the teacher's role is equally as important as the knowledge, skills and metacognitive skills of students – and without the support of the teacher to reinforce these, the use of these transformative

---

[2] Learn more about Rebecca and her work at https://rebeccagrayart.com.

tools will be superficial at best and, at worst, less effective than learning and working without them.

On a more basic and cross-curricular level, however, when looking to either reduce workload or find the perfect resource to support your lesson, when you incorporate tools like **DALL-E**, students and educators can quickly visualise abstract concepts with the minimum of effort. Results can be easily tailored to students' individual needs and, whether it's at varying complexities, topics or languages, creating bespoke resources for your classes has never been easier. From generating illustrative images for a history lesson or conceptual diagrams for complex scientific theory, the tools now at your disposal are extremely helpful and the results are copyright-free.

All of this helps hit those three key areas where technology can make an impact in the classroom, from reducing workload to helping teaching, and supporting and enhancing learning.

9.3 Prompt craft or prompt engineering

Getting the most out of your use of AI isn't an easy undertaking, however. Just as with any tool, as we've shared repeatedly in the book, while generative AI is special, it is just like Microsoft **PowerPoint** or **Excel**, i.e. just another tool in your EdTech arsenal. Discerning use and teacher insights are crucial.

Just like any child in your classroom, you need to check its work.

AI makes mistakes. It gets things wrong. In its eagerness to provide responses, it has been found to make up facts, research papers and much more. These are called hallucinations and they happen frequently. In June 2023, two US lawyers were fined for submitting fake court citations generated by **ChatGPT** (Milmo, D. et al., 2023). Steven Schwartz, a US lawyer, admitted that ChatGPT invented six cases he referred to in his case against the Colombian airline, Avianca.

Fundamentally, a prompt is the text you write using a generative AI tool to ask it to create or do something for you. Creating a good one is a bit of an art form in itself, with new phrases like 'prompt craft' and 'prompt engineering' entering regular conversations– yet more examples of careers beginning that didn't exist previously! At a basic level, you could write:

> 'Write a lesson plan for my Year 7 class on the topic of tidal forces.'

This prompt will enable that tool to create a lesson plan for you – but you won't get what you want. High levels of specificity will garner far more useful resources for you, and you can instruct the tool to do far more than just creating the lesson plan. A prompt which says...

> 'Develop a lesson plan focused on tidal forces for a 50-minute lesson. Include objectives, direct instruction elements and assessment methods for Year 7 students in England studying geography. Create a multiple-choice quiz for the class (including answers) and link that to Bloom's taxonomy.'

...will create a much better response to the original prompt. Prompt craft/engineering takes precision and patience. It is important to know that while these tools are useful, they should at best be seen as a starter for ten and you shouldn't just copy and paste its responses onto your lesson plan proforma. Remember also that there often comes a point in time, while iterating the response to help you achieve what you want, where it becomes quicker for you to take over the heavier lifting that the AI tool will struggle with. Focusing on trying to get the perfect response may well be likely to take longer than doing the last 10% of the work yourself.

In computing, there is a term, GIGO, which is relevant here; it stands for 'garbage in, garbage out'. It conveys the idea that the quality of output is determined by the quality of the input. You should also remember that the quality of the output will only ever be as good as the training data the tool has been developed upon and, because it has mostly learned from us (humans), it is inherently likely to have the same biases and limitations as we do.

When it comes to using generative AI which is predominantly text-based, it's important to remember the importance of our sound subject knowledge, strong literacy skills and mindfulness of these inherent biases, so you can get the best output from the system you are using. Strong literacy skills have always been important but, in a world of AI, never before have these and other skills such as resilience and knowledge been so vital. You can't sense check an output if you don't have a scheme upon which to check it.

If you're looking for some good generalised examples of prompts for different subject areas, you might like to refer to Mark's book, *The Little Book of Generative AI Prompts for Teachers* or *TheLittle Book of Generative AI Prompts for Senior Leaders* (Anderson, 2023, 2024) – resources that are freely available on his website.

STAIR model

The ability to craft effective prompts is an important element to consider when you're working with generative AI. To help with this, back in 2022, Mark created the **STAIR model** which aims to offer a structured approach to creating your prompts.

- **Specific:** Precision in your language helps to narrow the AI's focus, helping to ensure accurate content generation so when creating your prompts, aim to be as specific as possible.

- **Tell:** Beyond specificity, clarity in your instructions is vital. Therefore, like you would with a student, give lucid, unambiguous guidelines to deliver the desired output.

- **Actionable:** By giving the AI the complete context of what you want to do, you help it to create a more comprehensive narrative and take a more rounded approach to what it creates. By asking it to do more than just one thing you're going to get better results, as the AI will weave together the different strands of the whole task rather than looking at elements in isolation. Therefore, create prompts that ask for the complete set of activities you require from it.

- **Iterate:** It is imperative to understand that it is always highly unlikely that the AI will give you the result you want the first time. Iteration is almost always essential. Therefore, perseverance and persistence are crucial to getting what you want. Equally, as we've mentioned, there will come a time when finishing off the activity will be better done yourself. Don't spend more time iterating the output than you have to.

- **Role:** Finally, contextualising the AI's role, such as behaving like 'the best, most thoughtful, kind and caring Year 6 teacher in all of Britain' can influence both content and style, so make sure to set the scene for your AI so that it gives you the response that you need. Of course, many AI tools allow you to have a baseline of 'custom instructions' to save you that effort, but if the tool you're using doesn't have that, make sure you give it a role as part of your prompt design.

The STAIR model therefore can be summarised as:

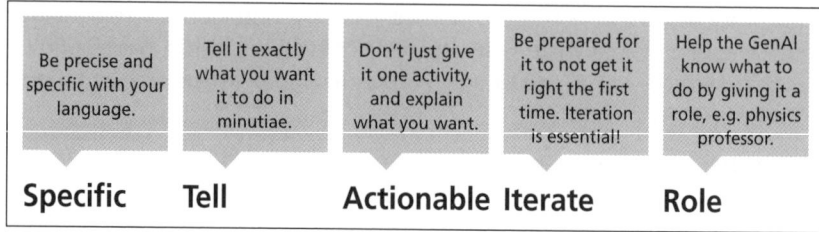

Specific   Tell   Actionable Iterate   Role

Figure 9.1: STAIR model

While generative AI tools such as **ChatGPT, Gemini, Claude, Firefly** and **DALL-E 3** present a world of possibilities and opportunities for educators and students alike, they work best in tandem with traditional learning, just like any good educational technology in the classroom.

As Dr Zoë Elder[3] shared with Mark many years ago, technology should enhance, not dictate learning – and generative AI should do just that. By valuing and integrating both traditional learning and digital learning, educators can provide a richer, more comprehensive learning experience for students while simultaneously saving a tonne of time with their workload.

Plugins

Increasingly, generative AI tools are gaining the ability to bring in third-party plugins that give them even more usefulness. Currently, there are a number of tools, such as **ChatGPT**, that have access to plug-ins which enable them to interrogate PDFs, search the internet, analyse data sets, pull in documents from storage areas such as Google **Drive (Gemini)** for analysis, provide help from given images, such as photos or screenshots – and lots more.

Imagine getting an updated syllabus from your exam board or a new government guidance document that needs assimilating and the key elements being summarised. It happens all the time in education, particularly for those in middle and senior leadership. And what if you, as part of your prompt asking AI to summarise that document, ask it to create an email draft for colleagues to share the important things they need to know? Simultaneously, you can also ask the tool to craft a similar email for students and parents about key elements that they need to know, all in your voice because you've trained the generative AI tool how to write

---

[3] https://x.com/fullonlearning

and sound like you. Of course, you won't just copy and paste it, because you need to check its work, but how much time will that have saved you?

How about, instead, you take a photograph of a page from the syllabus you're teaching and ask it to do some planning and resource creation for you? Sound unreal? It's not. Using the 'Advanced Data Analysis Feature' in **ChatGPT Plus**, we were able to use the following prompt based on this screenshot from the AQA GCSE French (8658) syllabus:[4]

3.4.1.7 Using common patterns between French and English

There are thousands of words in French which, although not having exactly the same form as the English word, can easily be understood with the application of a few, simple rules. When words which can be understood using the rules below occur in context, students will be expected to understand them.

Rule	Examples
The French word adds an 'e'	*branche, liquide, signe, vaste*
The English word adds an 'e'	*futur, masculin, paradis, pur*
Words which end with 'e' or 'é' in French and with 'y' in English	*beauté, liberté, mystère, armée*
Words which end with 'i' or 'ie' in French and with 'y' in English	*économie, parti, tragédie*
Words which end with *aire* in French and with 'ar' or 'ary' in English	*grammaire, militaire, populaire*
Words which end with *el* in French and with *al* in English	*individuel, officiel*
French adverbs ending with *ment* which end with 'ly' in English	*complètement, généralement, spécialement*
Verbs which add 'r' or 'er' in the infinitive in French	*admirer, confirmer, inspecter*
Verbs which end with *er* in French and with 'ate' in English	*assassiner, cultiver, décorer*
Words where 'o' or 'u' in English is replaced by *ou* in French	*approuver, gouvernement, mouvement, bouddhiste*
Words where a 'd' is added in English	*aventure, avance, juge*

Figure 9.2: Common patterns between French and English languages (from AQA GCSE French syllabus)

---

[4] https://filestore.aqa.org.uk/resources/french/specifications/AQA-8658-SP-2016.PDF

Our prompt:

> 'From this extract from the GCSE French syllabus, create a series of six 50-minute lessons for Year 10 French GCSE that are creative but promote opportunities for listening, speaking and writing to practice the content shared in the syllabus. Create a 20-question multiple-choice quiz (with answers) linked to Bloom's taxonomy and an extended writing task for students with a mark scheme.'

At the time of writing this, there are (as with most technology) many ways to skin a cat, so while this was completed using ChatGPT Plus, you can perform this task equally as well in **Bing Chat. Gemini**, unfortunately, struggles at this stage with this kind of task, although a similar prompt which asks AI to interrogate the PDF of the syllabus did produce some promising responses. It was, however, not even close to the level of what was created by Bing Chat or ChatGPT. As time progresses though, the abilities of all of these tools will only improve.

You can see the results of the activity using ChatGPT at https://bit.ly/gcsefrenchexample. As you'll see, iteration was of course required, and the subsequent resources will need copying and pasting into relevant formats and platforms. The quiz, for example, will need to be added to your platform of choice, but the heavy lifting has been done. Time has been saved and, of course, as the education professional in the room, you can tweak and add your personal touches or flair to the results.

The limits of what is possible with the use of a photograph or a document that an AI tool can interrogate and feed back on, given its ability to quickly and easily assimilate, decipher and analyse, are limited only by our demand, need and creativity. While the results differ on different platforms, the fast pace of the developments means that this is only going to improve.

As such, the introduction of generative AI tools into education has been transformative – more than we've seen with any other technology for decades, probably since the introduction of the internet, and look how much that transformed people's lives and continues to do so every single day.

9.4 Getting started with AI in the classroom

Getting started with any new technology requires you to dip your toes in the digital water – and it's no different with AI. As you'll have read earlier in the book, a good place to start is with having a defined need. AI can certainly help in many ways but having a defined destination in mind is always helpful in charting your journey.

Here are just some of the ways AI could help you:

1. Use AI to help generate ideas, lesson plans and content that align with curriculum standards, saving time in lesson preparation.
2. Leverage AI tools to adapt existing lesson content to fit diverse classroom needs, enhancing adaptive teaching without extensive manual effort.
3. Utilise AI to suggest supplementary resources (videos, articles, quizzes).
4. Use AI to generate quizzes based on lesson content directly within Microsoft **Word** or **Excel**, saving time in assessment preparation and providing instant feedback to students.
5. Use AI to draft emails or reports.

Once you've done this, a good next step will be to investigate what tools you already have access to in your school. It's likely that you'll have some access, either to Microsoft **Copilot** or Google **Gemini**. Whichever tool you look to investigate first, it is important to remember to consider a few key factors, such as:

- **Data privacy:** Do you have permission to use this tool, particularly if you're using personal data, either of your own or that of your students?
- **Bias:** Are the outputs being generated by the tool you're using biased in any way?
- **Hallucinations:** Is what the AI tool is sharing with you factually correct?

These are important considerations and are all part of AI literacy, i.e. knowing how to use AI effectively, safely and within the remit of your organisation.

It's also important to consider that sometimes the use of AI is a bit like using a sledgehammer to tap in a nail and, as we've alluded to many times in the book, cognisance is vital. Considering the environmental impact of AI, we should be mindful of the fact that, for each query made using a generative-AI tool, it is estimated to take 500ml of water to cool the processors in the data centres. Using AI responsibly means ensuring that the benefits justify the ecological costs and is something worthy of consideration.

England's Department for Education shared helpful advice around AI literacy[5] in a policy paper back in October 2023, which is well worth reading, wherever you are in the world. It is essential to know that it is incumbent upon teachers to know whether tools and any activities undertaken on them are compliant with data protection and privacy policies. We wish that all schools did their due diligence on this, but experience tells us that this is not always the case. It is, of course, good to err on the positive, but our strong advice is to make sure you know the answers before you start using any third-party tools, whether they are AI or not.

It isn't just us that think this either. Former director of digital learning at Berkhamsted School, Laura Knight, shared her thoughts on AI in education with us.

Case study: Laura Knight

What are the potential benefits of AI for teaching and learning?

Making the most of teacher time: We are all too busy, and often our admin and prep work needs a lot of time. AI can help to build capacity for teachers and support them in the 'heavy lifting' tasks. It's like having a virtual research assistant, TA and content creator on hand all the time: you do the thinking, and AI does the doing.

Personalising learning: AI can help to tailor the learning content, challenge, style and feedback to the individual needs, preferences and goals of each learner, based on their data and performance. This is superb for creating accessible lesson materials for all your students. There is huge potential here to raise attainment for students using AI with Socratic questioning and mastery techniques in the same way a 1:1 tutor would; a strategy that can help students perform **two standard deviations** better than students learning in a conventional classroom setting. Check out *Bloom's two sigma problem*[6] to find out more about this.

Innovative learning opportunities: AI can help to create new learning opportunities and experiences that are engaging, interactive and immersive. AI can simulate realistic scenarios or environments, and bring meaningful contexts to lessons for problem-solving and decision-making.

---

[5] www.gov.uk/government/publications/generative-artificial-intelligence-in-education/generative-artificial-intelligence-ai-in-education
[6] https://en.wikipedia.org/wiki/Bloom%27s_2_Sigma_Problem

What are the challenges and risks of using AI? Is it safe?

As teachers, we need to take care that our use of AI is responsible and appropriate in our professional context. There are some key issues that are worth considering:

- accuracy and validity
- data and privacy
- integrity, transparency, and honesty
- regulations and laws
- inclusion, equity and accessibility
- bias (gender, ethnicity, language, age – just as a starting point)
- environmental impact.

We have a crucial role in ensuring that AI is used in a responsible, inclusive and fair way in education and that it supports and extends human intelligence rather than replacing it. Let's model using these tools *well* for our students.

9.5 The benefits of modelling with XR and AI

As mentioned in chapter 2, the Education Endowment Foundation recommendations in its report, 'Using Digital Technology to Improve Learning' (EEF, 2020), specifically discuss how 'technology can be used to improve the quality of explanations and modelling'. Both AI and XR bring about many opportunities to improve the quality of explanations and modelling. At a simple level, just using a generative AI tool to give us alternative explanations to concepts that students find difficult, is a simple way to improve your explanations to help them.

AI can help at a much deeper level than offering alternative explanations to concepts, for example, with powerful dynamic modelling tools to allow complex concepts to be visualised and interacted with in real time. AI-driven simulations can help provide students with hands-on learning experiences where, by manipulating variables, they can see the results of their changes in the moment.

Alternatively, combining AI with XR technologies can offer teachers some exciting possibilities. Take, for example, the light detection and ranging (LIDAR) technology available on iPad tablets. This uses remote sensing technology to measure the distance of an object from the tablet's camera and, with it, you can map classrooms, objects and (powered by AI and AR modelling software) view objects you've designed on your tablet in situ within your classroom. And, as if by magic, because of the speed at which these calculations are made, it can all take place in seconds.

Tools like the **Measure** app (which comes as a standard app on iPad) will scan your surroundings and almost instantly work as your virtual tape measure. It's a fantastic tool to use in the classroom to help students learn about distance, shape, area, perimeter and many other mathematical concepts.

Arthur C. Clarke famously said in his essay 'Hazards of Prophecy: The Failure of Imagination', which was part of his book *Profiles of the Future* (Clarke, 1962): 'Any sufficiently advanced technology is indistinguishable from magic.' This quote has become a staple concept, not just in science fiction but also in technology, innovation and, of course, education.

Technologies such as XR and AI, which incorporate much of the most advanced technology available to educators today, might seem like magic to many, particularly younger learners who can see their designs come to life right in front of them. They might be forgiven for saying, 'That's magic!' – a phrase Mark has heard on numerous occasions in his work with students and teachers around the world. Even his own children have asked him, 'Daddy, can we do the magic?' when referring to one particular AR tool.

Augmented reality tools in the classroom

Blending the traditional with the digital is an interactive and educational experience that is particularly popular with early years settings and older students alike. For example, **Quiver**[7] is a popular 3D colouring AR app from QuiverVision (formerly known as colAR Mix) that helps teach concepts such as the sea, land masses and continents. Once students have coloured in their maps with pencils or pens, they can scan the page with the Quiver app on their iPad and it brings the drawing to life in 3D to lay over the top of the physical drawing, complete with the colours the child used.

Beyond that, amazing AR tools such as **Merge Cube** (www.mergeedu.com), which places 3D models on top of the physical cube, or **AR Makr** (www.armakr.app), which allows you to place, using LIDAR technology, your 2D designs in a 3D space, can help to facilitate some amazing experiences to promote oracy around the models or work created and then placed in the real world.

---

[7] https://play.google.com/store/search?q=quiver&c=apps

One example Mark has shared the world over is using the AR Makr app to create a virtual art gallery of a student's digital media with the student standing next to their design. Here, promoting oracy and demonstrating their understanding of the topic and the concepts used in creating the digital artefact, students explain how they've made their design and what they've learned in the process.

Many AR apps, such as the aforementioned Quiver, require a real-life trigger for the apps to know when to respond. Another fantastic AR app, **Halo AR** (www.haloar.app), enables you to turn anything into its own trigger image to launch the AR experience. Another popular example of Mark's is to use the app to turn the covers of books into triggers within the app. The idea behind this is that, upon being triggered within the Halo AR app, a video of a child delivering a review of the book becomes visible.

This activity is a modern way of encouraging oracy while students deliver their book reviews. It requires a number of higher-order thinking skills to promote learning at many levels. Students need to read the book. They need to write the review. They need to have the confidence to speak clearly and remember the key concepts from the book they wish to share. It's something children love to do and it can help blend digital and analogue while helping to promote a love of reading and providing another reason to go to the library. It also helps others learn more about library books and can encourage students to read books they might not otherwise read – after all, we shouldn't judge a book by its cover!

Mixed and virtual reality tools in the classroom

Mixed and virtual reality opportunities for learning in the classroom are still relatively niche. Certainly, in further and higher education, the modelling opportunities to practise things such as surgery for surgical training or pilot or ship navigation training can be done exceedingly well using mixed and VR headsets. Both technologies have, however, struggled to gain much traction in educational settings. This could be down to the significant costs of the technology involved.

The term 'mixed reality' isn't just tied to thinking about visual *and* audio. London-based multi-award-winning EdTech company **Now Press Play** (www.nowpressplay.co.uk) has a fantastic immersive-audio tool that uses (pink) headphones to bring the world to life for its users. With a smorgasbord of curriculum-aligned resources, it is a powerful tool that can be used to great effect in the classroom. Olly has rolled this tool out both in Trusts and in his school in Abu Dhabi, with fantastic feedback from teachers and pupils alike.[8]

XR has also landed well through companies such as **ClassVR** (www.classvr.com), which provides headsets and an ecosystem of highly tailored VR experiences. This seems useful, as it removes much of the need for specialist teachers and equipment to be purchased and managed by teachers within the educational setting.

One thought leader on the use of VR in the classroom is Dubai-based educator Steve Bambury. In 2019, he shared the second version of his model on the depths of virtual reality. The diagram is a useful tool to consider what level of virtual reality might be beneficial for your learners if you're thinking of using it in the classroom.

---

[8] https://nowpressplay.co.uk/case-study-amity-international-school-pupil-engagement

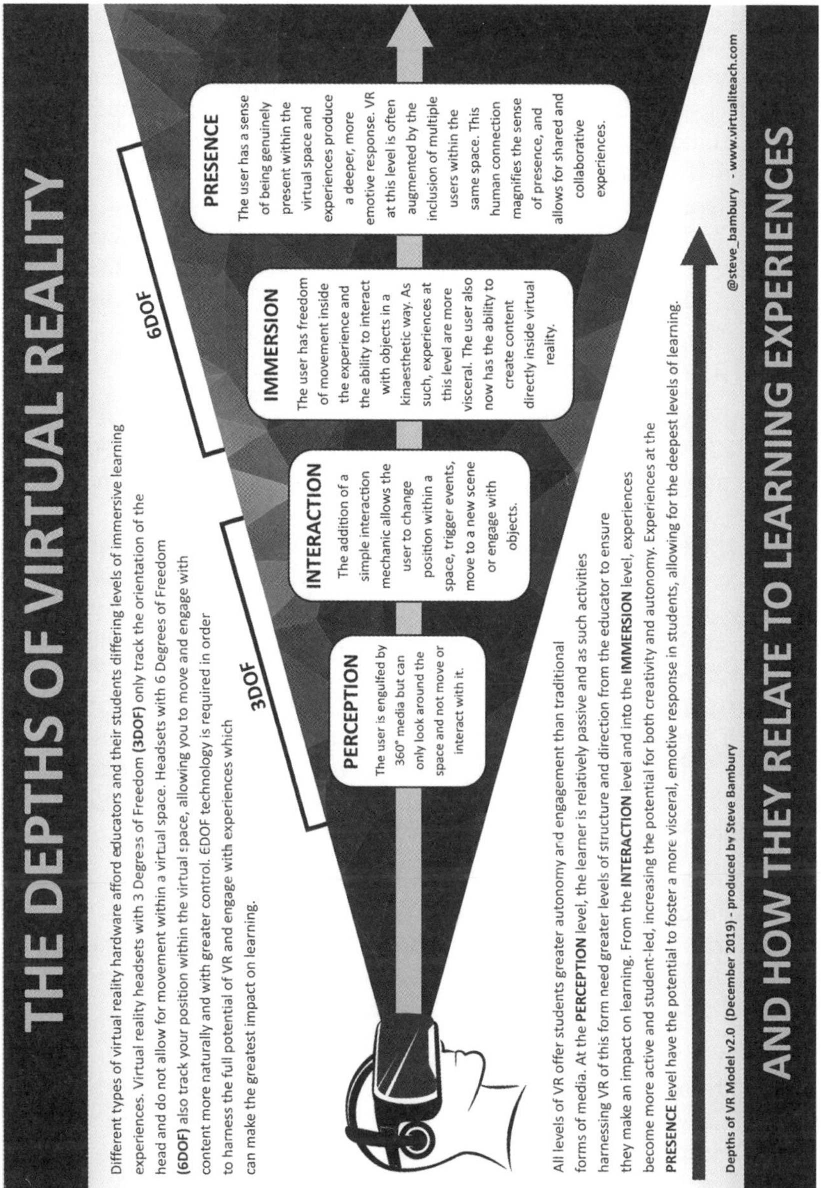

Figure 9.3: VR in the classroom

Of all the technologies available to support and enhance teaching and learning in the classroom, if we were to follow Ruben Puentedura's modification and redefinition levels from SAMR to think about using 'technology to do things that wouldn't be possible without the technology', then virtual reality definitely falls into that space. However, while its use is potentially transformative, with it being relatively cost-prohibitive, the barriers to access and the lack of compelling research to inform its efficacy and impact makes VR an area of educational technology still to make its mark quite as much as, let's say, generative AI has since the launch of **ChatGPT** in November 2022.

9.6 The risk and reward of AI

While AI in education brings much promise, it would be remiss of us to not do some future gazing, particularly in light of the paper from Hamilton, Wiliam and Hattie (2023). One area they spend time focusing upon is the concern of over reliance on AI by teachers, particularly those who are new to the profession. They suggest that while AI in and of itself will be useful to all teachers, just as we have seen with the historic de-skilling in areas such as farming (due to farming machinery developments), mental arithmetic (particularly linked to the invention of the pocket calculator) and map reading (linked to the availability of mapping apps on smartphones), overreliance on AI, particularly by novice teachers, will lead to a reduction in their skills. Conversely, expert teachers, who have (and this is an important thing to note) schema upon which to reflect on the quality of the output, will be far more likely to succeed and will, as the authors put it, 'become Elite by riding the machines'.

There is much we can unpack from this. Just like an expert teacher might give feedback to a student in class, an expert teacher will be able to pick up on errors, inconsistencies, hallucinations and more in the output from an AI system, which a novice teacher may struggle to notice. It then becomes a self-defeating activity.

Therefore, just as Mark has shared in his work on the topic around digital literacy, and with literacy having never been so important, it is the case that teacher skills, knowledge and experience have also never been so important. It is therefore, we would suggest, incumbent upon school leaders to ensure as far as possible that early career teachers are supported with their professional learning, while trying to make sure that there isn't an overreliance on these tools so that they end up being de-skilled.

The synthesis of research and thinking in Hamilton, Wiliam and Hattie's paper make it essential reading for all involved in education and beyond; it truly is a stellar piece of work.

Top tips

Mark's top tips

1. Always keep the focus on learning, teaching, reducing workload or any combination of those three.

2. Whatever tools you choose to explore, consider safeguarding and data protection principles before engaging in the use of anything and if unsure, seek advice.

3. Remember 'GIGO' when working with AI tools – the quality of your output will depend upon the quality of your input. Use the STAIR model to help you and be prepared to iterate!

Olly's top tips

1. Avoid the temptation try to use a multitude of tools at once. Select one, develop your use of this and evidence impact with it before choosing a second tool.

2. Gather a group of educators and students in your school to form a 'guiding group' or 'test pilots' on the use of AI and XR in education so you can be sure you are harnessing the best of what is out there.

3. As the saying goes, 'If at first you don't succeed, try, try, try again'. Well, now perhaps we should say, 'If at first you don't agree, prompt, prompt, prompt again'.

Subject-specific EdTech field guide

INTRODUCTION

With teaching and learning with technology, some things work for almost every subject. A good example might be low-stakes quizzing. Informed by what we know about retrieval practice and implemented aligned with our spaced practice, this is an excellent strategy for using technology that will work with practical subjects, knowledge-based subjects and everything in between.

There are, however, some strategies that are more suited to particular subjects. For example, what might work in geography might not be appropriate in a language subject.

To that end, in the following few chapters, we offer you our mini field guide, where we will explore:

Chapter 10 – Using technology in English

Chapter 11 – Using technology in maths

Chapter 12 – Using technology in science

Chapter 13 – Using technology in humanities

Chapter 14 – Using technology in languages

Chapter 15 – Using technology to manage learning

We recognise that we haven't included all subjects – it is already quite a hefty book – however, we hope that in the future, we can dive deeper into creating shorter books that focus on each subject area.

In each of these chapters, we have included our thoughts and experiences from our work in schools over the years. Additionally, we have included short case studies from teachers of these subjects, plus coverage from both Primary and Secondary educator perspectives.

Teachers are some of the most creative people. While we hope the ideas shared will be helpful, it is not an exhaustive list. Naturally, a lot of your choices will (and should be) informed by your knowledge of the content you're teaching (CK) and how to teach it (PK). Using your creativity with the tools as you develop your 5 Cs (TK), along with the approaches advocated for and shared in the book, will, we are sure, bring many dividends. Just remember to keep true to the golden rules by asking three simple questions:

1. Will the use help my teaching?
   - Creation of resources
   - Help with explanations
   - Reduce my marking

2. Will the use help with learning?
   - Support retrieval
   - Reduce cognitive load
   - Improve feedback

3. Will the use help reduce my workload?
   - Speed up feedback
   - Speed up processes
   - Make me more efficient
   - Give me easier access

CHAPTER 10
Using technology in English

'Such stuff as dreams are made on.'

William Shakespeare, *The Tempest*

10.1 Technology for the English classroom

There are several different types of learning activities which can take place in an English classroom. Commonly in an English curriculum, we see:

- **Reading:** Students read a variety of texts such as fiction, non-fiction, poetry and plays.
- **Writing:** Students write things such as essays, stories and poems, and do so creatively, often demonstrating different genres.
- **Speaking:** Students often participate in classroom discussions, learn about and practise debating, deliver presentations and read aloud from books.
- **Listening:** Students listen to others reading, e.g. podcasts and audiobooks.
- **Viewing:** Students watch film representations or adaptations of books and plays, e.g. *Romeo and Juliet*.

In class, students learn things such as:

- vocabulary
- grammar
- comprehension
- composition
- speaking and listening skills.

Many different technologies are available to help and support their learning and demonstration of that learning. There are various digital outputs that students can create using technology to demonstrate their learning such as:

Type of output	Tools that can be used
Essays, stories and poems	▪ Microsoft Word ▪ Google Docs ▪ Apple Pages
Presentations	▪ Google Slides ▪ Microsoft PowerPoint ▪ Apple Keynote ▪ Canva for Education
EPUBs	▪ Microsoft Word ▪ Apple Pages ▪ Book Creator
Podcasts	▪ Audacity ▪ GarageBand
Artwork (graphical representation of written work such as a poem)	▪ Adobe Express ▪ Canva for Education
Newspaper articles	▪ Microsoft Word ▪ Google Docs ▪ Apple Pages ▪ Adobe InDesign

Table 10.1: Technology tools to demonstrate learning in an English lesson

The types of learning activities and outputs that are used in an English classroom will vary depending on the specific goals of the lesson or unit.

Accessibility tools, such as those discussed in chapter 7, are also particularly useful to students in the English classroom and, while essential for some, could be useful for all.

10.2 Using AI in the English classroom

As we learned in the last chapter, new tools incorporating AI are being developed daily that can help with teaching and learning – and English is a subject that can be supported as much as any other.

Interrogate texts

From the latest syllabus to the books you're reading with your class, uploading PDFs or transcripts into generative AI tools such as **Gemini** and **ChatGPT** will be sure to give you a plethora of time-saving opportunities.

Let's say you have just received the updated syllabus for your GCSE English course as a PDF. There are many things that you could ask the tool to do for you which could save you significant time.

Prompts such as:

- Summarise the key points in this document.
- What implications are there in this document for a teacher of this course?
- List the units of study in the syllabus.

...will save time and effort, but you can go many steps further. This prompt, for example, elicits a more helpful response:

> 'I am a fantastic teacher of the subject of English and I want to help the students in my classes. Analyse the attached syllabus and create a table with two columns. One with the keyword and the other with a definition for all relevant terms that all my students should know.'

Mark: I am a fantastic teacher of the subject of English and I want to help the students in my classes. Analyse the attached syllabus and create a table with two columns. One with the keyword and the other with a definition for all relevant terms that all my students should know.

ChatGPT: Used **AI PDF**.

Based on the provided syllabus, here's a table of keywords and their definitions:

Key word	Definition
Critical Reading and Comprehension	Identifying and interpreting themes, ideas, and information in literature and other high-quality writing.
Summary and Synthesis	Identifying the main theme or themes; summarising ideas and information from texts.
Evaluation	Assessing a writer's choice of vocabulary, form, grammatical and structural features.
Writing	Producing clear and coherent text for different purposes and audiences.
Writing for Impact	Selecting, organising, and emphasising facts, ideas, and key points in writing.
Spoken Language	Presenting information and ideas, responding to spoken language, and using spoken Standard English.
Standard English	A form of the English language that is considered the norm, free from regional variations.
Figurative Language	Language that uses figures of speech, like metaphors or similes, to be more effective, persuasive, or impactful.
Grammatical Terminology	The set of terms used to describe and analyse the grammatical functions and structures in language.
Linguistic Conventions	Established practices in language usage, including grammar, punctuation, and diction.

This table provides a concise overview of the key terms and concepts that students should be familiar with based on the GCSE English Language syllabus.

Figure 10.1: Example AI prompt for an English teacher: keywords and definitions

You can do so much more. A prompt such as:

> 'I am the head of an English department. Analyse the PDF and create a draft email to my colleagues outlining the key features of the syllabus. Include a list of each of the units broken down with bullet points explaining what needs to be covered in each unit and an explanation of what the different assessment objectives (AOs) are.'

Mark: I am the head of an English department. Analyse the PDF and create a draft email to my colleagues outlining the key features of the syllabus. Include a list of each of the units broken down with bullet points explaining what needs to be covered in each unit and an explanation of what the different assessment objectives (AOs) are.

ChatGPT: Of course! Here's a draft email to your colleagues based on the analysis of the GCSE English Language (8700) syllabus:

Subject: Overview of the GCSE English Language (8700) Syllabus

Dear Colleagues,

I hope this email finds you well. I wanted to provide a comprehensive overview of the key features and assessment objectives of our new GCSE English Language (8700) syllabus.

Key Features:

Dynamic and Engaging Content: The syllabus offers two equally balanced papers, with reading sources related to the topic and theme of writing tasks. Each paper has a distinct identity to support high-quality provision and engaging teaching and learning.

Units Breakdown:

1. Paper 1: Explorations in Creative Reading and Writing.
   - **Section A: Reading**
     - Literature fiction text from either the 20th or 21st century.
     - Genres: Prose fiction with extracts from novels and short stories.
   - **Section B: Writing**
     - Students' own creative text, inspired by the topic they've responded to in Section A.

2. Paper 2: Writers' Viewpoints and Perspectives
   - **Section A: Reading**
     - One non-fiction text and one literary non-fiction text.
     - Sources from the 19th century, and either the 20th or 21st century.
     - Genres: Journalism, articles, reports, essays, travel writing, and more.
   - **Section B: Writing**
     - Single writing task related to the theme of Section A.

Figure 10.2: Example AI prompt for the head of an English department: syllabus key features email for colleagues

Of course, this isn't the full output, but the speed at which the tool can do this sort of thing is amazing. At the time of writing, there are many ways to achieve the results shared here but, with AI tools improving all the time, we are positive that there will be more ways of achieving similar results from a wide number of tools.

(To achieve our results, we used the premium version of **ChatGPT** from OpenAI.)

Teachers are often rightly concerned that students will use tools such as these to do the work for them. Mark recently delivered an inset session where a teacher, pretending to do just this, asked ChatGPT to write an essay on a topic. The results were poor, to say the least.

We know that with better prompt design, the output could have been better. Strong literacy is key when using text-based tools such as generative AI but, rather than try to make the output better with a stronger prompt, a great learning activity can take place when you have a conversation with your class about the essay that the tool has created.

- Why is it poor?
- What hasn't it included?
- What could it have done to make it better?
- What mark would you have given it?
- What would it have to do to improve it from that grade to a grade 5/6/7/8/9?

By having conversations with students about the output, you are helping them learn, practise and then embed these skills from the mark scheme and requirements of the course so that their outputs will be better from the activity.

Other examples could include the following areas.

Text analysis

Use AI to analyse themes, symbols and writing styles in a given text. This could be a student's writing or another piece of a given text. Students could use this to check against their understanding. Alternatively, teachers could (so long as it's anonymised for data privacy reasons) do this to assist with student writing assessments.

Grammar, spell check and comprehension

AI-powered tools such as **Grammarly** (be honest, who isn't already using this?!) can be easily added to devices at a whole-school level to help improve writing accuracy and assist with vocabulary expansion. Similar tools, such as 'Simplify' within Texthelp's **Read&Write** (www.texthelp.com), can also help with reading comprehension by simplifying reading texts and removing distractions that can be a barrier to comprehension for some children. Other tools can help introduce and reinforce new words and phrases.

AI image generators

One great tool that has always had the target of 'Making writing ridiculously exciting!' is **Pobble** (www.pobble.com). The Pobble 365 tool has a long history of success in sharing writing prompts to promote great writing alongside other activities to improve writing standards, particularly in Primary settings.

Using tools such as **Dall-E** from OpenAI (embedded directly into offers from Microsoft, e.g. Microsoft **Designer** and **Copilot**), and **Firefly** from Adobe (embedded into Adobe Express), you can create brilliant images that can be used to inspire writing.

These tools offer opportunities to help young people think carefully about what they write to generate the images. Iteration (as shared in the STAIR model in chapter 9) is key to getting the output you want. This activity helps children to reflect on their language choices – from the adjectives, verbs and nouns they use, the opportunities are vast.

Another way you can use these kinds of tools is to promote discussion around themes inherent in texts you are going to study with learners before reading them, such as the example below. Here, we've used the image generator to create an image we can use to promote discussion and learning about the madness of King Lear and the use of the literary device 'pathetic fallacy' in Shakespeare's play.

Figure 10.3: An image generated using Microsoft Designer to reflect the madness of King Lear

10.3 What about in Primary?

Technology can play a significant role in teaching English in the Primary classroom. Over the years, Mark has worked with many schools, delivered training and spoken about it at many events – such as those with Rob Smith of the Literacy Shed and at literacy conferences organised by The Education People and Reading Solutions.

Someone Mark came across while working with schools and speaking at events is former Primary school teacher, Dominic Traynor, who has kindly shared his thoughts and ideas, with four ways to use technology to help young people improve their writing skills.

Case study: Dominic Traynor

Dominic Traynor is the Education Evangelist for Adobe. Before joining Adobe, Dominic found his passion for combining literacy with digital skills as a teacher both in the UK and internationally. From there, he was part of the first cohort on the accelerator Emerge Education, where he started LitFilmFest which worked with YouTube Kids, BBC Worldwide, Houses Of Parliament and www.change.org to inspire young people to write and create media.

He won the EDUCATE award from the Institute of Education for a four-month research project into improving writing using digital skills. His book, Literacy Beyond The Classroom, *was published in late 2020 by Bloomsbury Education and shows how to bring writing to life using technology.*

Persuasive pitch deck – Google Slides

Rarely have I seen such writing with passion in the classroom as when I have engaged young people in a real-life issue that lights them up. Social, political or environmental – whatever it is, the more real and personal you can make it for them the better. I don't shy away from negative things but, obviously, be sensitive with your choice of issue.

Use all the writing techniques at your disposal to persuade your audience to bring about change. Allow your students to be vitriolic, to be emotional, to believe in their ability to make a change, to be heard.

Be open to sharing their work both with your local school community as well as the wider community via social media and other means. Invite local councillors, relevant business people and community leaders to your school to talk about the issue. Share their work with relevant people both in person and through social media. You will often be amazed by the responses they get and make sure to celebrate their wins, no matter how small they may be.

Tech recommendation: Using Google **Slides** allows students to use professionally designed templates for visual impact. People are used to swiping through a pitch deck and each slide can be seen as a step in the storytelling journey and path to change. They can also be shared via a URL, making the reading experience similar to an e-zine. Encourage students to play around with layouts to make sure their writing hits the reader right between the eyes. Include images or videos where appropriate to highlight the issue they are campaigning about.

Poetry voiceover video – Adobe Express

Free-verse poems have no structure and often don't have any particular rhythm or rhyming. They are just 'free'. This brings freedom to your students' writing and helps them to express their ideas without getting distracted by form. This is also a superb way to improve your pupils' oracy skills through creating voiceovers of their poetry – much easier and less daunting than performing poetry on camera.

I usually like to use the theme of 'play' for this project because it has very positive vibes and yet can mean something different to different people, allowing for a range of interesting outcomes. Play invites discussions on physical and mental benefits. Play often has sounds, repetition, rules or conventions associated with it which can also help with style and vocabulary building.

Tech recommendation: Adobe **Express Video**'s best features are its voiceover button and built-in, safe image search library, making it perfect for voiceover poetry. I've stood by as 6-year-olds make their poetry come alive using Express Video with next to no help from me and seen GCSE students create pieces that have left lasting impressions on me. Selecting the perfect soundtrack from the in-built library is another feature which can take a good piece of poetry to new levels.

Travel brochure – Book Creator

One of the best projects I've ever done as a teacher was around creating a travel brochure. Although many young people travel with their families to far-flung destinations, there is nothing more exciting than researching places that seem like other worlds. Whether it's the Arctic, Australia or the Atacama desert, students are fascinated by places that seem to offer a version of reality so different to their own.

I can't think of many writing genres that wouldn't fit into a project like this and it works as a way to combine English, history and geography. It's also a great way to inspire children to write at length before taking them through the editing process to distil their key ideas into something much more punchy and more suited to a brochure.

Tech recommendation: Use **Book Creator** (www.bookcreator.com) to create a mini-brochure full of different writing styles, focusing on simple but attractive layouts and making good use of white space. Vary layouts by using both single and double-page spreads, and use call-out boxes in your design to showcase hyperbole or interesting facts. Record simple, bitesize videos to embed in key sections of your brochure.

Fan web page – Adobe Express

There's nothing young people like more than telling the world about the things they love the most. Whether it's a sports person, team, music act or hobby, they can go on for hours about all the reasons why they love it so much. Being so personal, it's a rich area for writing which doesn't require much heavy lifting in terms of inspiring them to record their thoughts. It's also a very good way to include lots of different styles of writing: persuasive, non-chronological, questioning and opinions.

Given that our students were all born since the birth of the internet, this gives them access to a world of rich digital media which they can use to bring their chosen subject to life. Images, videos and relevant websites are all easy ways to engage your writers even further.

Tech recommendation: Use Adobe **Express** to create a simple visual webpage without needing to code anything! A style often used by news outlets like the BBC when publishing a longer form article with stunning pictures, Adobe Express Page allows students to enhance their writing with images, embedded videos, text formatting and buttons to external web pages where readers can dive deeper into your students' chosen subject. The Glide Show layout is particularly pleasing.

As you can see, there are many ways you can use third-party tools to promote and enhance the subject of English in Primary.

Improving results or even engagement, however, isn't all about using tools way outside of your core ecosystem. Sometimes it's about thinking, 'How can we use the tools we've got to best suit the needs of our learners?' This is exactly the approach that Cat Chowdray, deputy head at Taaleem Charter Schools (@Cat_Chowdhary on X), took when exploring ways to develop things for her students studying the English language IGCSE course.

Case study: Cat Chowdray

How Office 365 helped create an independent, flipped learning environment in English lessons

As an English teacher, I was frequently engaged in discussions about the balance between online work and traditional book-based methods. At my previous school, with each student having access to their own devices connected via **Office 365**, I initiated a project to assess the impact of this technology in fostering independent learning and reducing teacher workload.

The primary challenge was balancing engaging and developmental student activities with the extensive marking demands typical in English teaching. My focus was on the Year 9 KS3 English group, a linguistically diverse class with various levels of English proficiency. This diversity posed unique challenges, particularly with the increased writing requirements for the IGCSE language course.

Research into the benefits of ICT in education, influenced by works like M. Jarvis' *Brilliant Ideas for Using ICT in the Classroom* (2015) and Smith and Chickie-Wolfe's *Fostering Independent Learning* (2007), highlighted the complex nature of fostering independence in learning.

> Student feedback showed a preference for computer-based work, citing the ease and speed of writing and research. This feedback led to the creation of personalised Office 365 folders for each student, containing tailored resources and interactive **PowerPoint** presentations focused on the IGCSE English language exam. This setup allowed for real-time editing and immediate feedback, enhancing the learning experience both inside and outside the classroom.
>
> Lessons were designed to cater to the students' diverse needs. The use of Office 365 enabled me to efficiently monitor student progress and provide instant feedback. This shift to a more independent approach significantly enhanced the efficiency of my teaching.
>
> The method led to several positive outcomes. Students, particularly those who struggled with writing, found this approach beneficial as it facilitated easier access to online information and more sophisticated language use. The ability to provide immediate feedback fostered continuous improvement and reduced the need for extensive offline marking. The initial investment in setting up digital resources proved advantageous for future reuse and adaptation.
>
> The project emphasised the long-term importance of integrating technology into education. Looking ahead, there's a need for broader ICT integration across the curriculum. The forthcoming Office 365 CPD training is an ideal opportunity for staff development in this area. In the post-COVID-19 era, embracing ICT in education is not only beneficial but essential. Adequate training and resource-sharing can help establish a consistent and effective use of technology, enhancing the teaching and learning experience.

As the project shows, the benefits were numerous and helpful, all with just a bit of work to start things off: 'The initial investment in setting up digital resources proved advantageous'.

Summarising this, there were clear benefits:

- The learning process was improved, with students finding it easier and quicker to write while using technology.
- Using **Office 365** allowed students to access resources both in and out of school, which enhanced learning and progress opportunities.
- Workload and efficiency were improved, with more opportunities to monitor progress and to provide more timely feedback.

- The approach particularly supported students who struggled with their writing, as they could research and use more sophisticated language more easily.
- The initial effort was seen as being beneficial for future reuse, indicating a long-term positive impact.

It is also good to note from this case study that the project highlighted two key foci for the school:

1. The need for broader ICT integration across the school.
2. The importance of CPD sessions for staff to improve confidence in using technology.

Does this sound like something you might have read about before? We joke, of course, but it goes to reinforce the importance of using technology for purposeful means.

This case study is a great reminder and reinforcement of the messages shared in chapter 2 around TPACK and elsewhere in the book that, as practitioners, keeping our focus on teaching and learning and the content (PK and CK) and how technology can support those endeavours (TK) can help bring about those positive shifts we hope for.

Top tips

Mark's top tips

1. Technology use in English is as much about integration as it is about use. Technology shouldn't replace the need for reading from books or writing essays with a pen on paper. Use it to enhance the great learning and teaching already taking place.

2. Consider the benefits of allowing the use of dictation tools for students who struggle with their writing.

3. Consider technologically creative outputs such as podcasts, TV adverts or green-screening as a way to engage students in their writing for a purpose.

Olly's top tips

1. Offer regular CPD sessions for staff that build technological skills and reinforce pedagogy, and don't be shy to have students share their progress in those sessions.

2. Use the power of your network to see good practice in action. Why not ask #TeamEnglish on X what they are doing that's having a positive impact with effective technology use to support learning and teaching?

3. Train everyone in your community on the tools, like Immersive Reader, that will support them in accessing their work.

CHAPTER 11
Using technology in maths

'Nature is written in mathematical language.'

Galileo Galilei

11.1 Technology for the maths classroom

Maths has a broad curriculum that lends itself to many learning activities, such as:

- problem-solving
- critical thinking
- numerical literacy
- strategic planning
- communication
- reflection
- interdisciplinary connections
- decomposition which fosters algorithmic thinking
- spatial reasoning
- pattern and design thinking
- abstract thinking.

These skills empower students to think critically, solve complex problems, and approach challenges with confidence and creativity.

Just like we saw in the previous chapter with English, some activities transcend subjects, like some of those shown in table 10.1, such as presentations or podcasts, which could be a learning device in many classrooms. Just like the essay or newspaper article activities though, which would more often be associated with an English learning activity, there are some in maths which are more akin to activities in a maths lesson.

Equally, while there are some pedagogical approaches that can take place in most classrooms, such as 'pause, pounce, bounce' or 'think, pair, share', there are some which are subject-specific.

In English or a language class such as Spanish, you might, for example, use communicative language teaching strategies where you could see approaches that include role plays; this wouldn't necessarily be appropriate in a maths class. However, in maths, teachers often use manipulatives as part of a 'concrete, pictorial, abstract' approach to help convert abstract thinking to tangible learning experiences.

Let's consider activities in maths and their digital equivalents that can help with learning, teaching and workload reduction.

Type of output	Tools that can be used
Mathematical problem solving	▪ Desmos (www.desmos.com) ▪ Geogebra (www.geogebra.org)
Data analysis and graphing	▪ Microsoft Excel ▪ Google Sheets
Geometry and shape exploration	▪ SketchUp ▪ Geogebra ▪ Tinkercad
Algebraic expressions and equations	▪ Equatio ▪ Wolfram Alpha ▪ Photomath
Mathematical simulations	▪ PhET Interactive Simulations (https://phet.colorado.edu)
Visualisation of mathematical concepts	▪ GeoGebra 3D ▪ Desmos Graphing Calculator

Table 11.1: Technology tools for mathematics

It is clear then that all subjects have unique pedagogies and maths is no different.

In our first case study for this chapter, we hear from Emma Bell, Microsoft Innovative Educator Expert, FE CPD programme leader and experienced maths teacher. She explains how she tries to incorporate the technological knowledge of TPACK with her content and pedagogical knowledge.

Case study: Emma Bell
The Goldilocks effect using technology in GCSE maths

As part of my work teaching GCSE maths, I always try to pair my use of technology with what I call 'The Goldilocks effect', in that my choices have to:

- make content more accessible to students
- perfectly match the pedagogical strategies needed for students to make connections and progress
- be absolutely the appropriate tool for the content.

It's a difficult balance to strike, but over the years I've managed to work on a few easily translatable examples that work well with students.

Take algebra, for instance, where I want my students to understand the form $y = mx + c$ with respect to linear graphs. Drawing graphs by hand, over and over again, wasn't truly allowing my students to grasp the underlying mathematical structure. It seemed like a lot of time and effort was spent on the mechanics of drawing axes and plotting points, leaving little room for them to explore the effects of varying the gradient and y-intercept of a straight-line graph.

By using the online graph-drawing tool, **Desmos** (freely available to use), I was able to strip away the 'noise' of hand-drawing and empower my students to discover and investigate the graphs, meeting all three of the Goldilocks criteria.

It took my students three short steps to build a dynamic straight-line graph with the ability to change the values of the gradient and/or y-intercept:

1. Open www.desmos.com/calculator.
2. Type 'y = mx + c' into the input box.
3. Click the button 'all' to add sliders which vary the values of m and c within the equation.

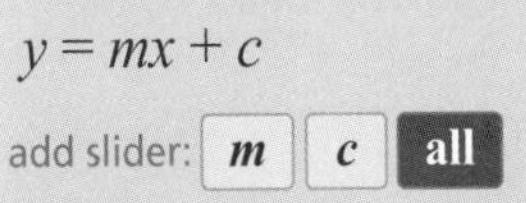

$$y = mx + c$$

add slider: | m | c | **all**

Figure 11.1: Example algebraic equation (1)

Students were able to change the graph by moving the sliders and, as a result, make connections between those changes and the appearance of the line.

1 $y = mx + c$ ✕

2 $m = 1$ ✕
   −10 ———●——— 10

3 $c = 1$ ✕
   −10 ———●——— 10

Figure 11.2: Example algebraic equation (2)

For formative assessment, using engaging technology to gather and collate responses is invaluable. I've used many online quiz tools in the past, but have encountered barriers to their success – like student devices running out of charge, or class-sets of hardware being booked for other lessons. **Plickers** gets around these kinds of obstacles as only a teacher device is needed.

Each student has their own five-by-five QR code which they orientate to give responses to multiple-choice questions. Turning the code through multiples of 90 degrees changes the appearance of the code, and changes the response that the student wants to give. I scan the room with my own device's camera and it quickly picks up and records each student's answer (as long as they don't have a stray finger covering the corner of the QR code!).

This tool gives every student a chance to participate in the task and helps with confidence – it's not easy for other students to see what responses are being given.

One augmentation that I made was to laminate the codes for my students with a sticky note showing each orientation on the back. This helps them show their answers to me more efficiently and increases accessibility for them all. I have one laminated set which can be reused class by class.

Figure 11.3: Example laminated QR code for classroom use

> Depending on the awarding body, up to two-thirds of the GCSE examination requires students to have the use of a calculator. I wonder how many of us maths teachers use calculators in two-thirds of our lessons?
>
> I aim to use calculators as much as possible, taking opportunities to hone the students' skills, knowing that each of them carries a calculator in their pocket outside the classroom – on their phones!
>
> There are many ways to incorporate calculators as a 'business as usual' tool in the GCSE maths classroom. They're instant feedback machines – I've seen my students motivated to go over errors when they've checked their calculations with a calculator. Calculators don't criticise or express disapproval of 'wrong' answers.
>
> I encourage students to play with their calculators, getting to know all of the appropriate functions and how they can help them. Calculators can reduce cognitive load during lessons too. If I want to explore applications of direct and inverse proportion, I don't want my students getting bogged down by the arithmetic. Calculators can do that work for them so that the students focus on the concept.

Emma's approach to using technology in the maths classroom is fantastic. She uses technology to enable students to focus on what is most important to develop their mathematical understanding. Her 'Goldilocks effect' is perfectly pitched to ensure that any technology she does choose to adopt, or have the student adopt, is purposeful and relevant to the objective(s) at hand. As Emma shows, technology doesn't need to be flashy to be highly effective. Take her use of **Plickers**, for example: it gives her in-the-moment formative assessment with real-time feedback which she can be responsive to at a class, group or individual level to bridge any misconceptions and enable progress for all students.

11.2 Using AI in the maths classroom

When it comes to maths, there are some great ways that AI can be used to help with learning and teaching.

AI maths tutors

Maths is a difficult subject with many specific equations to remember – such as πr^2 (which helps us remember how to calculate the area of a circle). So numerous are these that, just like we learned about Bloom's two sigma problem in chapter 9, the usefulness of having an AI tutor supporting us with our maths work in class would make for a superb, modern-day reckoner (a reckoner is a concise reference book of mathematical tables).

As we write, there are several tools available in the EdTech market that enable you to create your own AI tutors to help either with specific activities within your subject or the entire subject – think algebra versus maths as an entire subject. You can even create these GPT tutors to respond appropriately to the age range or specific content you want to be covered.

Helpfully, tools of this type such as **Mindjoy** (www.mindjoy.com) have 'Socratic' modes which means that rather than just answering questions students have, they prompt the child to work out the answer together.

Workload reduction

You'll know that one of our north stars for teaching and learning with technology is its propensity to help reduce workload. AI can massively help with this and maths teaching is no exception.

Lesson plan creation is one such idea which, from transcripts of videos such as those found on **YouTube** ('YouTube Summary with ChatGPT and Claude' is a useful Chrome extension to explore here) or other sources such as your syllabus or scheme of work, can significantly reduce your time spent preparing lessons.

From fast planning of differentiated maths questions to supporting adaptive teaching or cold calling/retrieval practice activities to have readily available useful and relevant questions for your classes, AI can help.

One way that AI has been helpful to maths teachers has been in creating resources that support independent learning. Students often have common queries on topics. AI can easily help to create FAQs for students to access, either in created knowledge organisers or in other spaces such as the resources sections of your learning platform. From Google **Classroom** to Microsoft **OneNote Class Notebook**, it's simple to add a PDF generated by AI containing common student queries. Here's a useful prompt to try:

> 'List common student queries on [Maths topic] for [Year group] following the [Insert course or curriculum] in [Insert your country] and generate simple explanations for each query.'

11.3 Managing resources in maths

Organisation can be a challenge for many teachers, especially when we have large classes. Technology can provide the solution to this and in our next case study we will see how it can be used to organise and structure the curriculum, along with enabling the teacher to customise and tailor their lessons to students' needs in the moment in any given lesson.

Case study: Orla Weaver

This case study comes from Orla Weaver, maths teacher and assistant headteacher at The Grammar School at Leeds (@orla_of on X).

If I were to consider the piece of education technology which has had the greatest impact on my teaching of maths over the last number of years, it would be Microsoft **OneNote**, without a doubt.

I switched to OneNote for lesson planning and delivery in 2018 when we first piloted one-to-one devices. Up to this point, I had been using other notebook software, which had some great features and mathematical tools for lesson creation; however, it was the option to easily share lesson resources with students to support and enhance their learning and organisation that convinced me to switch to OneNote.

For me, its power as a teaching tool lies in the ability to create a bespoke and dynamic textbook for my students, drawing on the very best electronic resources out there, generously shared by the likes of Jo Morgan on her carefully curated **resourceaholic** website (www.resourceaholic.com), the incomparable **Mr Barton** (www.mrbartonmaths.com), **Dr Austin maths** (www.draustinmaths.com) and John Corbett's extensive compendium, **CorbettMaths** (www.corbettmaths.com).

When training colleagues on OneNote, I often start by using the analogy of an old-style filing cabinet to explain its organisational structure, with separate tabs for each topic and pages of resources within each tab. But it offers so much more than that. I use it extensively for modelling as part of my lesson delivery and use the range of maths tools, including 'ink to math' (which I love!) and 'text to math'. I embed worksheets for practice with QR codes to link to answers so students can regularly check their understanding.

Outside of lessons, embedded videos and consolidation links can support revision, not to mention that my students have a clear chronological record of everything we have done to refer back to as they need – no more worrying about lost sheets or poorly organised folders! The class notebook Microsoft **Teams** integration means I can link OneNote pages to Assignments, use Grades as my mark book, and embed Reflect check-ins to check for understanding and assess confidence.

I have already mentioned a few go-to maths websites which can be relied upon for fantastic resources. I would add **Transum** (www.transum.org) and **Mathsbox** (www.mathsbox.org.uk) to this for interactive starters and various forms of routine and graduated practice and **Diagnostic Questions** (https://diagnosticquestions.com – another nod to Craig Barton) for powerful assessment for learning. I must also mention **DrFrost** maths (www.drfrost.org) here: a platform which ably supported many maths teachers, myself included, through lockdown learning and remains a wonderful resource, highly valued by students and teachers alike.

The new A-level mathematics specification places greater focus on using technology for learning, and not before time. Students are now required to have calculators with additional statistical features, and some students opt for powerful graphical calculators to support their learning. Graphical calculators remain stubbornly expensive, however, and beyond the reach of many students, so I am a huge fan of **Desmos**. This free website offers graphing software, a scientific calculator and a range of ready-made lesson resources, which I have used from the beginning of KS3 onwards for a range of geometry topics. I would not teach simultaneous equations, for example, without using Desmos and insisting that my students check their answers graphically as they go. Previously, I taught algebraic and graphical solutions sequentially and students often struggled to make and retain the connection between the seemingly abstract algebraic concept and the geometrical representation. Not any more, however, and students who might otherwise find the topic challenging can flourish and develop a solid understanding with the support of this powerful EdTech tool.

Geogebra is another hugely powerful free maths tool that can be used across key stages. I have found it particularly useful for demonstrating high-level concepts at A level, including further maths.

Finally, the maths manipulatives which can be found on a range of free websites, including **MathsBot** (www.mathsbot.com) and **Mathigon** (www.mathigon.org), place powerful online tools at students' fingertips to support understanding across a whole range of mathematical concepts. These can be used from Primary right the way through to challenging concepts at GCSE, such as completing the square. I have seen students, who might otherwise have difficulty accessing this advanced topic, use online manipulatives with great success to support them in producing their written solutions.

> There is little doubt in my mind that EdTech has been a game-changer for maths teaching, not only in terms of the range and availability of high-quality, dynamic resources and platforms, but also the powerful tools which can enable us to break down and demystify previously challenging abstract concepts for students to support and develop their understanding and increase their enjoyment of maths.

Orla's case study highlights the importance of organisation and demonstrates the many ways that EdTech can help. By showing this, plus the ways that tools can enhance and enable access to the curriculum as designed by the pedagogical decisions of the teacher, we can see the numerous benefits that technology can bring.

Tools that compile multitudes of resources into one place bring several benefits to students:

- No time wasted in trying to find resources.
- 24/7/365 access.
- Ease of access to different media types: worksheets, models, work solutions, videos.
- Ease of access to feedback by the teacher and in a variety of formats: voice, video, annotation and text.

The list goes on!

What strikes us here isn't necessarily the power of Microsoft **OneNote**, as this functionality is available in a variety of platforms, but how using tools that bring multiple marginal gains aggregate to bigger cumulative wins, particularly when you link it into what we know works about learning, i.e. direct instruction, timely feedback, retrieval practice, and so on. A helpful side-effect is that on top of that, these tools are particularly useful in helping reduce workload.

In our third and final case study for this chapter, Sara Tilley (@curious_maths on X) shares her journey with *virtual manipulatives*. Manipulatives are the cornerstone of any maths teacher's practice and here she talks about their benefits, helpful approaches to how you can use them and how she has done so throughout the context of her career.

Case study: Sara Tilley

I started teaching on a chalkboard. It was looped so you could write a few lessons up before school but you needed serious work at lunchtime to get the afternoon's learning up. Next came the whiteboard (not interactive), which posed similar issues with the added challenge of the pens running out! The move to SMART boards was significant. While time was needed to understand how to use them, this was balanced with the ability to save the screens and annotations, use squared backgrounds and be able to use the slides again. What a privilege!

This was also the decade that the National Strategies introduced 'ITPs' – interactive teaching programmes. They were an absolute revelation and changed the way that teachers modelled learning in the classroom. Before that, I had a hundred square in my classroom with plastic pockets and paper numbers (which I loved) but using the ITP number grid opened many more opportunities for pattern sniffing and reasoning. It didn't take long for me to notice the preparation time I was saving. I could hide cells and change the scale without having to write out a new set of paper numbers! Having a resource which could change at the click of a button gave me the flexibility to be a better teacher. I still recommend these ITPs to teachers, and they are available for free on **MathsFrame** (www.mathsframe.co.uk), which has updated them to work in modern browsers.

We are now in an era where there is so much choice with virtual manipulatives. Just like choosing a concrete manipulative, it is always important to ensure that the virtual manipulative you select is best suited for highlighting the structure of the maths you are exploring. If I am teaching multiplication, I will use Numicon because it has a structure which shows fixed groups. Children can see the same number being repeated lots of times which we can build on when we talk about division.

Virtual manipulatives do not replace the need for the use of concrete resources; I firmly believe they can enhance them. I still regularly advise using a visualiser or gathering all the children around a table to watch a demonstration using **concrete manipulatives**. My go-to websites for virtual manipulatives are **MathsBot** and **Mathigon**, which has a brilliant 'Polypad' tool. I also use **Toy Theater** (www.toytheater.com), although this is not UK-based and therefore some of the measures are different.

Here are some suggestions of approaches that have worked for me and the teachers I work with.

Whole-class teaching

One of the big advantages of using virtual manipulatives as a whole-class teaching tool is the beauty of the big screen! Everyone can see it, and everyone can reach it.

Recently, I was in a Year 3 class with a teacher who was using the 'fraction wall' from MathsBot. The class was gathered on the carpet, engrossed in comparing and ordering unit fractions, and this visual enabled them to predict, check and develop generalisations about the denominator sizes and their relationships with each other. We probed their thinking, and they confidently approached the whiteboard and proved their ideas using this tool. The teacher then used the virtual fraction wall to model how the children could use their concrete fraction walls to help them answer the questions they had been set. Some children benefited so much from the virtual manipulative and the maths chat that derived from it, they chose not to use the concrete resources. Those who did choose to use them did so with ease since the model had been so clear.

Mathigon is a fantastic website for whole-class teaching ideas. One of my favourite virtual manipulatives is the 'balance scale'. It has many versions to explore and there's a fun game called 'What are the 2 cards?' that goes with it. Alongside this, there is a task-in-action video which gives you an insight into how children might approach the game and the things you might encourage them to say. **Polypad** (https://polypad.amplify.com – part of Mathigon) has a collection of 3D solids which can be rotated on screen. There is also a function where you can unfold the shape into the net, which gets the whole class excited!

With an intervention group

One of the musts of effective intervention teaching is being able to get inside the children's heads. Sometimes it can be tricky to pinpoint misconceptions and, often, the children we are focusing on find it difficult to articulate their thinking. Just as we use concrete manipulatives, virtual manipulatives allow us to see the child's thinking in motion. Using 'dienes blocks' from MathsBot for column subtraction with regrouping is perfect because children just need to click the exchange button to convert one 10 into ten 1s and the learning flow is not interrupted by them having to count the blocks. This keeps them focused on the new learning since we know they can count to 10. I usually find children are keen to use the devices to practise their learning, so it is a good way to encourage them to be active mathematicians. Just like the concrete resource, it builds their confidence before they start recording in the maths book.

As a plenary

Using images is powerful. It enables children to say what they see, which is exactly what we want them to do when they reason and problem-solve. Virtual manipulatives can be great for activities like 'spot the mistake' because children can come up to the SMART board and prove the error through manipulatives. If they have been working on problem-solving, then you could go to Toy Theater and use the 'place value disks' to create an image to which the children could write their own problem. Put a few images up and children can match them to different problems or calculations.

Filling a spare 5 minutes

Virtual manipulatives are a great way to do some instant maths. It's enough time to get onto MathsBot and put up the tens frame for some number bonds or roll dice to generate numbers to calculate mentally. Ironically, there is never enough time to teach time, so those five minutes could be well placed on Toy Theater since it has a great interactive clock which merges analogue and digital. It's a very flexible tool, so you can remove the hour/minute hand or include dash lines for the children to read with accuracy.

Home learning

If you are lucky enough to work in a school with plenty of concrete apparatus, you may find that setting homework which mimics the learning at school is tricky. Take a Rekenrek, for example. The mastering number programme written by the NCETM uses Rekenreks as a teaching tool – not many homes will have one of those! MathsBot has an interactive Rekenrek that has fantastic flexibility built into it.

'Multiplication by heart' on **Mathigon** is a great resource for home-learning for Year 4 children preparing for the multiplication tables check (MTC). It uses images to help children remember the facts and personalises learning based on their answers. This enables parents to see how their child is progressing so they can target their support at the questions they are finding trickiest.

Virtual manipulatives are here to stay, helping us all become even better maths teachers. We've come such a long way, I'm excited to see what the next decade has in store for us.

It's clear, as we reflect upon what we've covered and read back the case studies from Bell, Weaver and Tilley, that technology can help in so many ways in maths teaching.

It's also clear though, just as in every subject, the tools and technologies we can use to enhance and support learning and teaching in maths aren't exhaustive. By keeping our eyes firmly on the pedagogies of teaching maths that we know work, then we will truly make a difference when applying technological approaches. As Mark often shares with his Bananarama principle, 'It ain't what you do, it's the way that you do it, and that's what gets results.'

From base ten blocks, fraction circles, geometric shapes, number lines, *Cuisenaire rods*, pattern blocks, tangrams, math balance and counters – all have their places as tools to be used by maths teachers in their teaching practice and all can be accessed digitally in a variety of ways. Just because we haven't included them here, doesn't mean their use in the classroom doesn't have value – it does. Apply the approaches shared in this chapter and others and consider how they can work for you beyond their analogue cousins to support your teaching and learning in the maths classroom.

Top tips

Mark's top tips

1. Value what you know works with teaching and learning in maths in an analogue way and consider ways technology can enhance or even improve the activity.

2. Consider how you can best manage your workload by using AI to support resource creation.

3. Don't throw the baby out with the bathwater; there are many occasions when physical and tangible objects can work just as well as their digital equivalents and sometimes even better than them. Technology should enhance, not dictate, learning.

Olly's top tips

1. You know your students best. Use tools which will support their learning rather than complicate it.

2. Select device-agnostic tools so all learners benefit from them and can make good progress.

3. Put yourself in the student's shoes. If the tool is complicated and unwieldy, don't use it with your learners.

CHAPTER 12
Using technology in science

'We cannot solve our problems with the same thinking we used when we created them.'

Albert Einstein

12.1 Technology for the science classroom

The sciences are full of awe and wonder. They are truly interdisciplinary subjects that seek to help us make sense of everything around us. They are the ever-curious pursuit of understanding our natural world across a trio of disciplines: biology, chemistry and physics. Each branch unlocks its own set of mysteries which balance the tightrope of life and death, the composition of matter and the fundamental forces that shape and govern our incredible universe.

The sciences help us decode and codify all that we know. They help to give us a glimpse into the breathtaking diversity and complexity we find in nature – from the microscopic world of cells to the macroscopic view of the cosmos. Science can capture our imagination and invite us to explore, engage, investigate and understand this place we call home and beyond. It also provides a framework for discovery and inquiry while fostering critical thinking, problem-solving, analytical reasoning and analysis.

Thanks to the breadth and depth of the sciences, there are plentiful opportunities to explore new learning, bring abstract ideas to life, make the abstract more tangible and, of course, use technology to support innovative approaches to learning across its interdisciplinary landscape.

Since the science curriculum is so vast across the three subjects, it enables a plethora of different learning opportunities that all feed into the curriculum, namely:

- the empirical method
- problem-solving
- critical thinking
- collaboration
- analytical thinking

- resilience and flexibility
- scientific literacy
- data collection
- creative thinking and innovation
- reflection
- numerical literacy
- interdisciplinary connections
- abstract thinking
- communication.

Many of the above featured on the World Economic Forum's 'Top Skills of 2025' (Whiting, 2020) list and highlight that a robust science curriculum extends beyond developing the four key skill areas in the report: problem-solving, self-management, working with people and the developed use of technology.

The empirical method helps bring sense, consistency and a unified approach to the sciences. This is especially important in an ever-developing field that moves human knowledge forward. Commonly, across the science curriculum, you will find a wide range of learning activities to help decode and then codify information to help students make sense of the area they are studying. These are typically underpinned by elements of the empirical method outlined below:

Key term	Definition	Tech to support collation and articulation
Hypothesis	The supposition or proposed explanation made based on limited evidence as a starting point for further investigation.	Diagnostic testing platforms such as: ■ PhET SIMS (https://phet.colorado.edu) ■ Java Lab (www.javalab.org/en) ■ SimPop (www.simpop.org) ■ Physics (www.ophysics.com/index.html) ■ LabXchange (www.bit.ly/labxchange_edu)

Key term	Definition	Tech to support collation and articulation
Estimations	Students make judgements giving an approximation of a value, predict the proportion of a value or calculate an expected/approximate of a value without having conducted any measurement(s).	Students can make their estimations in the platform the school typically uses; alternatively, they could use: ▪ Nearpod (www.nearpod.com) ▪ Showbie
Observations	Students take note of and perceive an outcome from a primary source. Data collection during an experiment is also an observation.	Students can log observations in the platform the school typically uses; alternatively, they could choose from Nearpod or Showbie, plus: ▪ Adobe InDesign ▪ Microsoft Publisher ▪ Microsoft Sway ▪ Book Creator
Scientific testing	This involves establishing what we would expect to observe if an idea was correct and comparing this expected outcome to what is observed. This is more commonly known as an experiment.	Data logging tools like Vernier (www.vernier.com)

Key term	Definition	Tech to support collation and articulation
Researching	The pursuit of knowledge through the process of discovery, inquiry and systematic observation of phenomena. Using a range of sources (primary/secondary) to help develop ideas and understanding.	▪ Google Scholar ▪ Perplexity.ai ▪ EBSCO (www.ebsco.com) ▪ Association for Science Education (www.ase.org.uk)
Classification and grouping	The process of arranging based on characteristics.	▪ Microsoft OneNote Class Notebook ▪ Padlet ▪ Kami (www.kamiapp.com) ▪ Pear Deck (www.peardeck.com) ▪ Wakelet (www.wakelet.com)
Data collection	Capturing, storing and processing measured information for variables of interest, enabling the student(s) to research and test a hypothesis, predict the future and evaluate outcomes.	▪ Phyphox (www.phyphox.org) ▪ BBC Micro:bit (www.microbit.org) ▪ Microsoft Excel ▪ Google Sheets ▪ Microsoft OneNote Class Notebook
Analysis and interpretation	The process of breaking down and examining data, or a topic, to gain a better understanding of it.	▪ Microsoft Excel ▪ Google Sheets ▪ Graph paper ▪ Canva for Education ▪ Adobe Express

Key term	Definition	Tech to support collation and articulation
Conclusions	Making statements based on measurement and observation, summarising results and discussing whether the results support/contradict the original hypothesis.	▪ Microsoft PowerPoint ▪ Google Slides ▪ Apple Keynote ▪ Microsoft Excel ▪ Google Sheets

Table 12.1: Technology to support learning activities in science classrooms

Students will undertake a range of activities in lessons which help to build scientific skills and knowledge, but how we sequence our science curriculum is pivotal to enable them to successfully make connections across the disciplines. A successful science curriculum promotes effective communication, incrementally builds complexity, connects and reinforces concepts and develops a deep understanding of the importance of the synergy between the application of scientific inquiry and problem-solving.

On this journey, students develop scientific skills in a range of contexts through iterative approaches which prepare and promote scientific literacy, cultivate inquiry skills, engage curiosity and wonder, develop them for future opportunities, address societal challenges (like public health) and offer opportunities for creativity and innovation. Technology can play a significant role in supporting the curriculum, enabling students to fulfil their scientific curiosity and literacy in a fast-paced industry.

12.2 Using AI in the science classroom

AI can help in many classrooms, such as with workload and lesson resource creation.

The maths-tutor approach mentioned in the previous chapter using **Mindjoy** can be applied just as easily in the science classroom. The team at Mindjoy markets the tool as one which is perfect for the STEM classroom and we couldn't agree more. Naturally, you can make it seem more relevant by having an Einstein tutor act as a learning coach for physics or Attenborough for the biology classroom; this is just the icing on the virtual cake. The support learners get from these chatbots is the point and the thing that helps with their learning and progress, not the virtual persona they take.

In science education, AI-powered tools and virtual labs are starting to make a big difference in how students engage with complex scientific concepts and how teachers share about them, offering a blend of interactive learning and practical application. Cambridge-based start-up **sAInaptic** offers a lovely AI-enhanced assessment for learning solution that marks extended answer questions (that traditionally have had to be marked by teachers), gives feedback on them and helps students improve on their responses.

It doesn't stop there. Here are several popular tools that educators can use to bring these experiences into the classroom, along with suggestions on how they can be integrated into teaching practices.

Virtual labs and simulations

PhET Interactive Simulations offers a wide array of free, interactive simulations for subjects including physics, chemistry, biology and Earth science. Developed by the University of Colorado Boulder, these simulations allow students to visualise and experiment with different scientific phenomena in a fun, game-like environment. PhET simulations are particularly useful for demonstrating concepts that are difficult to visualise or require expensive, complex setups, such as the states of matter, electrical charges and the greenhouse effect.

As an alternative, **LabXchange**[1] provides free, high-quality virtual lab simulations perfect for Key Stage 2 and Secondary science classes. These labs offer real-time feedback, allowing students to learn from mistakes in a safe, virtual environment. LabXchange simulations cover a range of topics and are designed to be compatible with various devices, making science education more accessible and enjoyable.

AI as a research assistant

While AI tools designed to act as research assistants in the science classroom are still emerging, the broader concept involves leveraging AI's capacity for data analysis, problem-solving and decision-making to support students' inquiry-based learning. For example, AI can help in designing experiments, analysing scientific data and even identifying relevant scientific literature based on the topics being studied.

---

[1] https://about.labxchange.org/types/virtual-lab-simulations

The ongoing data privacy concerns about children using large language models are beginning to be dealt with by technology companies. While this is not currently the norm, we envisage this will be a declining issue as more AI tools are developed to support learning and teaching in the classroom. Either way, as we will discuss in chapter 16, data protection impact assessments (DPIAs) will (and should!) always need to be completed before engaging with any EdTech tool in the classroom.

Use of AI image generators in the science classroom

While image generators can still be very useful in the science classroom, in our experience, it is time-prohibitive to create particularly useful diagrams such as those you might like students to label to demonstrate learning or understanding.

The tools that most educators would turn to, such as Adobe **Firefly** or **Dall-E**, still struggle to produce the exact images that you would need. These tools are great at creating representations of what you ask for, but their ability to understand and render exact images is still limited.

Generative AI models are known for their ability to create novel and unique outputs, but this creativity comes with a trade-off in terms of accuracy and reliability. Of course, as the models learn more, these will improve but, for the time being, if you want specific images, you will be better off keeping to specific resources that you know and trust.

Generic uses, such as representations of famous scientists, for example, would be perfect, but trying to get an image generator to create a specific image, let's say for a labelling task, would be challenging. Stick with the curriculum resources you already have, or alternatively stick to a (copyright-free) image from a Google search.

12.3 Science in Primary education

There are many different ways that technology can support teaching and learning in Primary science and we're excited to share many of these with you in this chapter!

Someone both Olly and Mark know who uses technology effectively in supporting learning and teaching in the Primary science classroom is Paul Tullock. In this case study, Paul shares practical ideas you could try in your Primary classroom to support your science curriculum while using technology.

Case study: Paul Tullock

Paul Tullock is an Apple Distinguished Educator, Apple Professional Learning Specialist, Google Certified (Levels 1 and 2), Microsoft Innovative Educator trainer, teacher of 14 years and Executive Lead of EdTech & Innovation at Laidlaw Schools Trust and can be found on Twitter/X as @MrTullock and YouTube as @Mr.Tullock.

Igniting the spark: unleashing the power of technology in science education

Teaching Primary science and igniting curiosity through investigations is incredible. However, the laborious process of writing up experiments often dampens the excitement. Students would lose interest, undoing all the initial curiosity. Using an iPad to record investigations and allow access to learning completely changed how I taught science – and how my students learned.

Capture the unseen magic with slow motion

Looking closely at scientific investigations can be a daunting task, let alone attempting to explain and make sense of what we observe. Enter the unsung hero of science education: the camera. Inspired by Simon Pile (@mrpielee on X), I took investigations to a different level with the slow-motion feature. Recording investigations and then adjusting the footage to slow motion opened up a world of exploration, questioning and discussion. This approach is a perfect fit for studying forces. One of our favourite experiments involved upturned nursery bikes, pedalling their wheels ten times. We then tested different materials against the wheels to observe the effects of friction. Slow motion allowed us to delve into the details, revealing the impact of each material on the motion and making explanations easier.

Tech recommendation: The slow-motion camera on the iPad is an incredible tool for examining intricate details. You can easily edit the slow-motion points within the Google **Photos** app. If further slowing down is needed, save the slow-motion video and import it into **iMovie**, where you can apply additional slow-motion effects.

Embrace digital portfolios

Investigation and analysis lie at the heart of scientific inquiry, but traditional methods may not be accessible to all students. In 2015, I had the privilege of teaching a boy who struggled with dyslexia. Putting pen to paper was a huge challenge for him. However, his scientific explanations were unparalleled. We began exploring alternative approaches, and that's when digital portfolios came to the rescue. Students create slides for each stage of their investigation, utilising text (including dictation if necessary), graphics, drawings and photos/videos. After creating the slides, they record audio explanations of their ideas, hypotheses, findings and conclusions. This enables deeper explanations and inclusive learning opportunities, allowing every student to flourish.

Tech recommendation: Explain Everything allows students to record slides with photos, videos and pointer tools. It's fantastic for pausing videos, zooming into key areas and making real-time annotations. Once students finish their work, they can export it as a project or a video. **Keynote** combined with screen recording is another great way to do this.

Animate and inspire

Showing understanding is fantastic using animations or GIFs. They are quick, easy and fun, and require students to demonstrate a process or concept. The possibilities in science are endless, and the outcomes are always personal and varied. Students select their own graphics and images, bringing them to life through animation. Animations or GIFs are great for illustrating how electrical circuits function, the pollination of plants, the stages of the digestive system, the water cycle and much more. GIFs can also serve as concise summaries of key lesson points or vocabulary, making them superb for quick recaps.

Tech recommendation: Keynote is perfect for creating effective animations. Use the 'create path' animation feature to move individual objects on a slide and the 'magic move' transition to animate multiple objects. This is a great way to help explain a difficult concept or to bring a topic to life. Once made, you can export your slideshow as a movie to create an animated video or, for GIF creation, use 3–5 slides containing key phrases, words and objects. Export the slideshow as a GIF and students have their personalised retrieval tool.

Building scientific foundations: scaffolding the process

Working scientifically has often been one of the most challenging aspects of teaching Primary science. Planning scientific inquiries with well-crafted questions and controlled variables can be daunting for many students. Apple **Numbers** helps to build scaffolds for learners. The sheets sections allow you to create sections (e.g. predictions, results, conclusion). Incorporating tables and pop-up menus enables students to select questions to explore and variables to change. For example, in a plant growth investigation, students can use pop-up menus to choose observations such as plant height, bud/flower count or leaf quality. Tables can then be used to record data and create charts, visually representing the findings.

> **Tech recommendation: Numbers** is the ideal app for scaffolding scientific inquiry. Students can enhance their work by using objects, images, videos, drawings and audio recordings, providing a comprehensive overview of their inquiry process and thoughts. Start by creating a template example with labelled sections, instructions and placeholder images. Export it to the Numbers template chooser, and now you have a blank outline that generates a new copy for each lesson, saving you hours of preparation time!

Paul's case study reinforces many of the approaches we advocate: leveraging technology to support and enhance the curriculum. Inform your use with the content you're covering, backed up by the pedagogies you know will work, and then apply your technological knowledge of the features and functionalities of software you have access to so that you enhance learning and teaching. Incorporating techniques, such as slow-motion, to enable students to focus on the granular details in an experiment or to allow students to codify their learning helps massively. Technology allows us to do things that wouldn't be possible without it. What shines through from Paul's examples and reinforces our messages is that it is not about the technology; it's about learning and teaching and how technology serves that.

It is important to remember that the approaches Paul uses with those technologies can be emulated in other ecosystems. **Keynote** and **Numbers**, for example, have their equivalents in the world of Microsoft and Google. It's the approaches we should focus on, not the tools.

12.4 Science across the broader curriculum

One of the key ways of ensuring the science curriculum is current and relevant in all curricula is by providing the opportunity for young students to explore the world around them. This helps them gain a better understanding of the world they live in. Christoffer Lindved Dithmer calls this the 'discover, learn, grow' model. In this case study, he explores how technology can contribute to a greater understanding of the world our children live in through exploratory and experimental activities that children can engage with in countless ways.

Case study: Christoffer Dithmer

*Christoffer is head of **makerspaces** and EdTech in Vallensbaek, Copenhagen, Denmark, and works across several schools and kindergartens to coach and support staff to use digital and makerspace technologies in teaching and learning. He takes a very collaborative approach to his work, developing ideas alongside the many educators he works with to ensure that digital technology is embedded in a meaningful way.*

Christoffer is another Apple Professional Learning Specialist and runs workshops and webinars for teachers in Denmark and Greenland, and has developed a huge bank of online resources and teaching materials for them to use.

Empowering young minds: EPUBs[2] for early childhood energy exploration

In the kindergartens I collaborate with, we work on helping our children understand the importance of not wasting energy resources. Before we begin the project, we start by covering what the children know about energy sources such as water, heat and electricity and how they use them in their daily lives, through drawings.

Then we go on photo hunts to gain insight into what uses electricity in our kindergartens, what water sources we have and how we are using heat. For example, the children use time-lapse videos on the iPad to investigate how the lights are turned on in different rooms in the kindergarten, even when no one is present.

Our children create short audio voice memos where they discuss their discoveries. Finally, they update their drawings from the start of the project to showcase their experiences and discoveries.

All of this is compiled in an *EPUB* template, where the children insert their photos, videos, audio recordings and drawings. The EPUB books are shared with families to demonstrate all the wonderful experiences the children have had using technology in meaningful ways.

Tech recommendation: Apple **Pages** is a login-free and pre-installed tool on iPads, making it a secure option for preserving children's data.

---

[2] EPUB (electronic publication) is a free, open eBook standard facilitating reflowable content for adaptable reading on different devices.

Creating local change: how pupils can build their own measurement devices and generate their datasets for creating impact

How can pupils contribute to taking care of their own mental and physical wellbeing? We have been working on this by detecting the physical conditions within the school environment.

The pupils developed hypotheses and conducted surveys among the school's students to identify areas that require physical improvements to create a better indoor environment. Afterwards, the pupils worked on creating measurement devices by developing unique codes, built physical holders by using paper, wood, colours and other materials, and used a datalogger to analyse the data, to gain insights into the positive and negative aspects of the indoor climate.

The data revealed challenges in temperature during the summer and light levels during the winter months – factors that undoubtedly impact pupils' physical wellbeing. Based on the pupils' documentation, there was support for applying films to the windows in selected areas of the school to reduce the temperature during the summer and purchasing individual lamps for students' desks to provide more intensive light for their work in winter.

This is an example of how technology empowers students to create genuine change in their lives.

Tech recommendation: Use **Micro:Bit** to make coding accessible for many students, so everyone can acquire the skills to create unique content targeted towards specific challenges.

The pupils have used Microsoft **Excel** as a datalogger to analyse the data to gain insights into the positive and negative aspects of the indoor climate.

Understanding complex concepts through technology: how augmented reality and virtual reality make concepts physical and more visual

Using the power of 3D modelling, pupils have actively participated in building and exploring the different elements of the periodic table. By incorporating graphical elements into the models, they have been able to illustrate the variations and differences. Through this hands-on approach, students have gained a deeper understanding of the complexity of atomic structures.

In addition, pupils have explored the world of block programming to make electron models more dynamic, allowing them to better understand their behaviour and interactions within atoms.

To further enrich their learning experience, we have integrated augmented reality (AR) and virtual reality (VR) technologies. Pupils have had the unique opportunity to experience their 3D models in AR or VR, immersing themselves in a virtual environment where they can explore and interact with their creations. This has empowered them to zoom in, rotate and dissect their models, fostering a deeper level of engagement and facilitating a connection between the concepts, the technology and the physical world.

Tech recommendation: Use **CoSpaces** (www.cospaces.io) to create classes, allowing you to track and explore pupils' progressions. Afterwards, pupils can choose whether they want to create productions that can be played on VR goggles or if they prefer to build on the **Merge Cube** template, which is played through AR using a phone or tablet camera.

Once the choice is made, pupils can insert shapes to construct the atom. They can add buttons, text boxes, images, videos, audio recordings and much more. CoSpaces is a powerful tool that allows students to express themselves in a variety of ways. Merge Cube adds a 'wow factor' to students' productions and makes challenging concepts more manageable.

Finally, pupils' productions can be shared with QR codes placed around the school, allowing other pupils and teachers to be inspired by experiencing the pupils' work in CoSpaces and Merge Cube.

What strikes us most about Christoffer's case study is not only his eye on sustainability and developing the scientific process with his learners, but also the approach he takes to ensure students see their work as being meaningful and relevant to their communities. Sharing their work outside of school means they won't simply make sure it is just 'good enough', but will aim to do their best as they know it is meaningful, has focus, is credible and strives to appeal to and reach an authentic audience.

12.5 Science in Secondary education

Now it's time to turn our attention to science in the secondary phase of education and how technology can support and enhance learning and teaching. Olly is sharing a case study, as is Alex Gray, a science teacher who, at the time of writing, is the head of science at Dubai British

School. First, we will see how Alex and his colleagues have adapted their pedagogy to incorporate technology so that they are harnessing the elements of the science of learning, streamlining efficiencies to support student learning and maximising curriculum time.

Case study: Alex Gray

Alex Gray is a science teacher of 15+ years and an RFU Level 3 coach. He holds an NPQTLD and an MA in Education, where he explored 'developing education through enhancing performance'. Alex doesn't stop there, hosting a variety of podcasts and vlogs via his website www.deepprofessional.com and YouTube channel.

Over the past three years, our science department has seen significant advancements in our teaching methodologies and student outcomes. This transformation is largely attributed to the integration of technologies into our pedagogical approach, primarily using platforms such as **Educake** (www.educake.co.uk) and **Formative** (www.formative.com).

Our journey began with the introduction of **Educake**. This tool has been instrumental in raising student attainment and progress across Key Stages 3 and 4. The platform has allowed our students to self-assess their understanding and progress, giving them a sense of ownership over their learning. The user-friendly interface and the extensive question bank have made it easier for teachers to set homework, classwork or revision activities that cater to individual student needs. The progress-tracking feature has also made it simpler for us to identify areas of strength and improvement, contributing to a more targeted and efficient teaching strategy.

We utilise Educake with our knowledge of the testing effect to reinforce students' memories and mastery of concepts by having them recall information frequently. In addition, instant feedback allows misconceptions to be rectified immediately. Consequently, the combination of Educake's online testing and the testing effect serves as an effective resource to raise pupil achievement and amplify retention in the long run.

Formative has changed the way we assess student understanding in the classroom. This technology has enabled us to transition from 'asks' to 'tasks,' ensuring every student is actively participating and demonstrating their understanding. The platform allows teachers to see every student's answers as they work. For instance, if a student makes a mistake, teachers can provide immediate corrective feedback, helping them to rectify their misconceptions on the spot. This real-time intervention not only prevents the consolidation of incorrect knowledge but also encourages a growth mindset, as students learn to view mistakes as opportunities for learning rather than failures.

The use of Formative was adopted during the pandemic, but we have continued to use it as our evidence has demonstrated that instant verbal feedback is superior to delayed written feedback in our classroom setting. Timely and specific feedback can greatly improve learning and performance. This form of feedback allows us to quickly correct misconceptions, preventing them from taking hold, as well as permitting students to apply corrections to their thinking right away. We found that written feedback was delivered too late to be useful or was less impactful due to its relevance being diminished by the fact that students had moved on from the material.

We have and will continue to use Formative, as it has proven to be an excellent way to reinforce learning, reduce misconceptions and instil confidence in our students.

As stated in chapter 8, timely feedback is key to student engagement. This should be a staple of all teachers' practice and has long been advocated by Mark – it's in his 2013 book, *Perfect ICT Every Lesson*. It's great that this is seen as being an essential cornerstone to the practice shared in Alex's science department.

Next, Olly shares some insights on how he and his colleagues have used technology in his classroom and those of his colleagues in the departments he has previously led.

Case study: Olly Lewis

Olly has taught science in state and independent schools in the UK and UAE for 17 years, alongside his various leadership positions. As the co-author of this book, it's safe to say he's certainly an advocate of, and for, impactful technology within his teaching. This isn't just the case in his classroom either. With his leadership experience, this is something he supports across the whole school/trust/district set-up. Great teaching and learning with technology isn't the big bells and whistles stuff; it's the thinking, practical application and cognisance of what works that makes the difference – and you'll see that in Olly's case study. Keep it simple, silly!

Models form an integral part of developing our understanding of the sciences. They help us to 'improve explanations, generate discussion, make predictions, provide visual representations of abstract concepts and generate mental models' (Chittleborough and Treagust, 2018). In recent years, more and more teachers and schools have moved towards live modelling of their explanations (as opposed to the default of using a presentation tool to relay the information), using a visualiser or Microsoft **OneNote** to build their lesson in the moment with students.

While it has evolved, I remember receiving lessons from the overhead projector as a student myself and it was effective for a range of reasons. The more modern equivalent is the visualiser, a technological tool that should be in every classroom across the globe. Visualisers offer the teacher dexterity, enable thinking aloud and modelling the learning process, show students what a good piece of work looks like (WAGOLL – what a good one looks like) and provide feedback to a whole class on a common misconception. They're extremely useful for demonstrations, live assessment, sharing a piece of text, zoning in on a small detail, practical demonstrations... The list goes on and on as there most definitely is not a 'one size fits all' when it comes to visualisers.

What's more important is how you use it, given the context of the learning taking place at the time in your lesson or cycle of learning. As a physics teacher, my modus operandi has been to use the visualiser for modelling worked examples of challenging concepts with students. I also ensure I have recorded those examples so that they are saved for future use, reducing my workload in the long run. Where, post an assessment, there are a few questions that were answered poorly across a class or classes, I will record an explainer video, using the visualiser, to work through the problem while re-teaching a concept. This increases the efficiency of class time as each student gets exactly what they need and when they need it, rather than waiting for 20-plus minutes in a lesson for me to get the question that they needed help with. This enables my feedback to be timely, pertinent to each individual, and builds time into lessons for reflection and follow-up activities.

In more recent years, I have fulfilled the above by using a combination of Microsoft **Stream** and **OneNote** to achieve the same goal. Here is a screenshot from my Year 12 physics class this academic year:

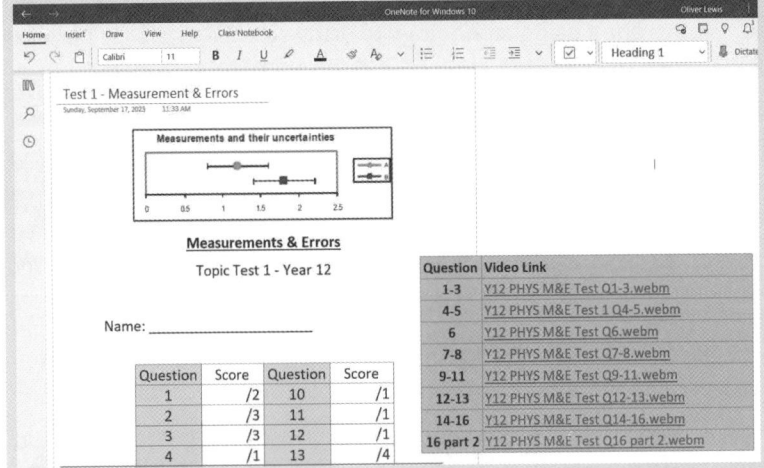

Figure 12.1: OneNote screenshot showing feedback for a student

Yes, this isn't exactly anything new or particularly innovative pedagogically speaking, but it capitalises on what works in a low-stakes and high-impact way using technology to support learning. With that in mind, I am still amazed at how few schools have invested in this instrumental piece of equipment that is so versatile across the age and curriculum range!

Here, as you can see, Olly has shared simple but effective ways of using technology to model in his classroom. These techniques work well in science classes and equally as well in any other subject where modelling is required. As the adage goes, there are many ways to skin a cat, although we don't think that's a science experiment you should be considering! When it comes to teaching and learning with technology in a science classroom, there are many approaches and tools you can consider using.

Multimodal uses of technology in the teaching of science

The very natures of the sciences lend themselves well to different types of media and technology, given the range of diverse information types and techniques that learners need to be exposed to, develop and demonstrate as a part of their learning.

For our final case study for this 'using technology in science' chapter, we thought it useful to share a case study demonstrating just that: approaches to science learning which feature a multitude of different linked but separate technologies, supported by a project-based learning approach. Shared by Australian educator Eleni Kyritsis, we'll see some of the many ways she's using technology to bring science to life for her very young learners. You can find Eleni on X @misskyritsis.

Case study: Eleni Kyritsis

Deputy head of a junior school at an independent girls' school in Melbourne, Australia, Eleni is an award-winning teacher with a passion for sharing her creative lesson ideas to enhance teaching and learning around the world. Recognised for her outstanding contribution and support of the education community by being awarded the 2017 ACCE Australian Educator of the Year and the 2016 DLTV Victorian Educator of the Year, Eleni has been honoured by the opportunity to facilitate keynote presentations and professional learning workshops across the globe.

To engage students in science concepts, we aim to design engaging and enjoyable learning experiences. Our Year 6 students are always excited to take part in the sustainability unit on energy. Throughout this unit, the students explore various types of energy and learn about the development of sustainable building materials. One of the highlights is the hands-on activity where students collaborate in small groups to design and create their own sustainable model homes.

Over the years, we have continuously improved the energy and sustainability unit by introducing new technologies and enhancing what the students produce. This year, we incorporated several components into the first simple 3D model of a sustainable home project. To start, students acquired knowledge about different forms of energy and examined modern home design techniques aimed at reducing energy consumption and environmental impact. They considered everything from building materials to the positioning of houses in the landscape.

To bring their ideas to life, students used a fantastic tool called **Splat3D** (www.splat3d.com) to create and visualise their 3D house designs. Each group had to include at least five sustainable and energy-efficient components in their designs. To showcase their knowledge, they used **Mote** to verbally explain the various elements they incorporated into their sustainable home designs. Recording the Mote explanations was a breeze through the Chrome extension, and they simply downloaded the Mote QR Codes and added them to their physical models.

For the construction of the model homes, students took an eco-friendly approach by using recycled materials. They also leveraged **LEGO Spike** (https://spike.legoeducation.com) and/or **SAMLabs** (www.samlabs.com/us) technologies to add moving parts to their models. Wind turbines, automatic light sensors and automatic blinds were just a few of the ingenious ways they integrated these technologies.

This year, we decided to take things a step further by incorporating **Minecraft Edu** (https://education.minecraft.net/en-us) and **MergeEDU**. After designing their model homes in Minecraft, the students exported the virtual creations to MergeEDU, allowing them to showcase their AR models alongside their physical models.

Through this comprehensive unit of work, we demonstrated the seamless integration of various technologies to enhance the learning experience. We hope this inspires you to explore incorporating these technologies into your classroom's curriculum, fostering creativity and innovation among your students.

Eleni's case study demonstrates how a typical activity and the associated learning and skills in schools can be transformed through the embedding of technology while incorporating an element of choice for her pupils.

The multimodal approach advocated for by Kyritsis demonstrates that by taking this approach, concepts and content are reinforced by being brought to life in a variety of ways to help detail student thinking and learning while they work towards completing their final product. There are plenty of positive digital skills and digital citizenship occurring in Kyritsis' classroom all while ensuring content and curriculum coverage.

There are commonalities of approach that work as well in science as they do in other subjects. Reflecting on the case studies from Lewis, Kyritsis, Gray and Dithmer, it's evident that the breadth and depth of opportunity for embedding technology, due to the vastness of the topics in its disciplines, is as wondrous as the universe that the subject seeks to explain. This makes teaching with technology in science a very exciting prospect indeed.

Remember though, as we shared in chapter 9 when thinking about XR, just because you can do things with technology doesn't necessarily mean that you should. Sure, if it was possible, you'd love to take your physics students on a trip to the Moon. The learning opportunities would be fantastic, but would they be the same as if you went on a virtual field trip there wearing VR headsets? The answer is unlikely. A real field trip would involve lots of preparation and learning about gravity, forces, atmospheres, oxygen-based life forms – and all sorts. The analogue can still be so much better than the virtual. Our north stars of asking:

- Will it help my teaching?
- Will it help their learning?
- Will it reduce my workload?

...ring as true as ever and should always be at the front of your thinking. Pedagogy first, as it should always be.

Top tips

Mark's top tips

1. Science is a subject that is rich with opportunities to embed technology. Remember, you don't have to use technology all of the time. Keep at the front of your thinking that gimmickry undervalues you and the subject. Keep the focus on uses that help and have impact!

2. Remember to share with colleagues when you find something that really works within your discipline within science. Not everyone will be a chemist, physicist or biologist, so support your non-specialists with the things that work within your discipline, as they might not have access to the same learning networks you do.

3. Some of the best technology to support learning in science might not be linked to the subject at all; just look at how many times Microsoft OneNote or quizzing tools have been mentioned. Keep this in mind when considering your technology uses.

Olly's top tips

1. Science has many intangible concepts; technology can serve to make these abstract concepts more tangible. Selecting the right simulation that marries with your explanations and modelling is the key to unlocking learning.

2. The unsung heroes in science education are lab technicians. Draw on their subject expertise to help you with demonstrations. They may or may not have a technological background but they will be able to guide you on how best to demonstrate a challenging concept – with or without technology being involved.

3. Don't forget to leverage collaboration tools to do the heavy lifting so that you don't have to reinvent the wheel. Remember, marginal gains!

CHAPTER 13
Using technology in humanities

'If working apart we are a force powerful enough to destabilise our planet, surely working together we are powerful enough to save it.'

David Attenborough

The humanities subjects offer a richness and depth to schools that transcend the physical spaces we occupy, given the global outlook that the subjects and schools are now more accustomed to adopting.

Knowing our place in this world, where we have come from, our family's history and how we can solve complex problems collectively has never been more important. Therefore, bringing the curriculum alive in humanities is crucial so that more young people are informed and can reform how we live, take action and adapt so that we can secure the future of our planet without compromising on our diverse historical past.

The humanities family of subjects can encompass courses such as geography, history, economics, psychology, political science, business, media studies, cultural studies, sociology and law. While some of these are often in the minority in schools, if they are even within a school's curriculum offering, their purpose is notable: to expand human cultural knowledge and help us understand the things that unite and differentiate us.

13.1 What can this look like in Primary geography?

James Fraser, computing specialist (@EatSleepICTRpt on X), offers us our first look into geography in the Primary classroom with seven exciting ways he incorporates technology into the curriculum at his school.

Case study: James Fraser

1. Google Earth and Google Maps narrated tour

Wherever your students are studying in the world, Google **Maps** (www.google.com/maps) and Google **Earth** (www.earth.google.com) are powerful tools for interacting and exploring maps in the twenty-first century. There's the ability to view in default map view, satellite view and view the land's terrain. There's also the facility to dive into street view – very useful when comparing environments around the world – and, on Google Earth, viewing the landmarks in stunning 3D. I set my Key Stage 2 students the task of using the screen record function on their iPads to record a tour of the area they are studying, whether that is their local environment or the Amazon rainforest. By holding down the screen record button in the control centre, they can turn the microphone on so they can narrate over the top of their tour. It's a fantastic way for them to present their learning and understanding of the topic.

2. Green screen using iMovie or Do Ink

Incorporating a green screen is an incredible way to transport students anywhere in the world. We have used it in multiple ways either through the free app, **iMovie**, or the paid app, **Do Ink** (www.doink.com). Children have created travel show reports, presented weather report broadcasts, transported themselves to different habitats just by clapping their hands, and created environmental awareness campaign videos. This was done by my Year 5s who were studying the availability of water around the world and used a green screen to create a WaterAid TV advert to raise awareness for the cause. Our school posted the campaign and the children's videos, which were liked and shared by WaterAid on X. The children were astounded and thrilled that their efforts were being recognised as part of a real-life campaign.

3. Exploring rivers in augmented reality using WWF Free Rivers

A must-have app for any year group studying rivers, **WWF Free Rivers** (www.worldwildlife.org) gives an incredibly detailed AR map of a working river flowing through a mountainous region, farmland and out to sea. Students get to see how the river changes and the environment is affected when heavy rainfall, dams and windfarms are introduced to the environment.

4. Creating a 3D environment using Tinkercad, SketchUp or Co-Spaces EDU

A creative and engaging way to showcase children's understanding of how environments compare is for students to create them in 3D. For Primary, there are a variety of sites that support this project. All need some training to use but are effective ways to create 3D environments. **Tinkercad** is aimed at Year 3 and up, **SketchUp** from Year 5 and up and **Co-Spaces Edu** has the feature to walk through a created environment from a VR perspective!

5. Exploring direction and basic mapping skills using Bee-Bots

A physical tool for exploring direction and learning basic mapping skills in Early Years and Year 1 is the **Bee-Bot**. Students learn the directional arrow commands to program the Bee-Bot around a grid. This could be a map of the UK, the shops in their local environment or through a drawn map of the buildings and outdoor areas in their school. They learn about spatial awareness and positional language and, linked to the computing curriculum, basic algorithms and computational thinking.

6. Fact files and labelling activities within Busy Things

A vast array of activities that can either be used as part of the input by the teacher or by the student for their task can be found within a subscription to **Busy Things** (www.busythings.co.uk). Activities range in challenge according to the year group selected and are categorised by the geography topic. So, whether students are learning about volcanoes, mountains, rainforests, settlements, trade or renewable energy, there are a range of digital activities including label matching, table sorting, customisable fact files and vocabulary matching games and quizzes.

7. Describing the changing seasons using markup on iPad Photos

Every few months, I take my Early Years and Year 1s outside with the iPads to take photos of the different seasons. They record the brown, crunchy leaves on the ground in autumn, the frosty mornings in winter, the blossom blooming in spring and the sun shining through the trees in summer. These photos are collected and compared over time and, with the addition of *markup* in the iPad's **Photos** app, students can label the features they have observed through each season using simple boxes, texts and arrows.

I hope you have found these examples of how geography can be enriched through technology helpful. We must continue to use the tools we have available to us to our advantage to make learning exciting, engaging, memorable and relevant.

What resonates about James' case study is how he uses technology to enhance learning with tools many of us use in our everyday lives, such as Google **Maps** and the **Photos** app. His approach to enhancing geography using technology highlights that it's not about the technology but about how technology can support and enrich learning. Students have the environment and tools to evidence their learning while also being able to use and curate digital artefacts to enhance and/or showcase it.

The best technology, as we hope you've come to realise in this book, is effortlessly deployed within a learning episode and is 'indistinguishable from magic' (as Arthur C. Clarke writes). It's not a bolt-on or 'fun' extra; rather, it is interwoven into the fabric of the journey which amplifies the great aspects of an already well-planned and sequenced learning episode. It enables students to enquire, solve problems, communicate well, collaborate, develop their thinking and evidence their learning in creative ways.

13.2 Using AI in the humanities classroom

This chapter, as you'll discover, concentrates quite heavily on two of the most popular subjects within the humanities (history and geography) and there are so many ways you can leverage AI to help you teach them.

As with other subjects, consider some of the ways you can use generative AI chat tools to help support resource creation, such as:

- timelines
- historical figure profiles
- quick-fire question lists
- multiple-choice quizzes
- lesson plans
- historical investigations
- geographical quick facts
- map quizzes

And for teachers of business studies and economics?

As a teacher of business and economics, Mark was quite determined to ensure we covered some of how technology and AI can help teachers of these subjects.

A cornerstone of these two subjects is case studies of businesses and economies which give real-life, practical applications for the different areas within the curriculum. From accounts analysis to the product life cycle, application of the marketing mix, examinations of push/pull economics and more, generative AI can help formulate case studies from both factual and fictional businesses/economies for students to examine. Add to this, once created, that AI can take things forward further by creating tests and quizzes (high- or low-stakes) based on the case studies they create *and* give you the answers to help with your assessment.

Naturally, business productivity tools are extremely useful in the analysis of data associated with these two subjects – particularly Microsoft **Excel**, Google **Sheets** and Apple **Numbers** (depending upon your ecosystem). Generative AI tools, however, with a Socratic mode built into them, will mean that students can spend more time interpreting the results than getting bogged down in repeatedly having to show each time they work through questions. Sure, students must know how to calculate an *acid-test ratio* based upon a set of accounts, but just as important is to know what the result tells them. Leveraging tools to support students' learning (that doesn't give them the answer but coaches them as they work through) will be of great help as they practise applying their learning.

What about media studies?

From considering and critiquing scripts to helping create campaigns to promote a project they have worked upon, AI has plenty of help for students. Sure, it will be important for them to know how to use and leverage tools such as Adobe **Premiere**, **iMovie** or **Final Cut**, but in a world where so much media is shared via social media, why not consider exploring tools with learners such as **OpusClip** (www.opus.pro). Here, powered by AI, the tool takes two inputs: the keywords you give it and a video clip you upload. From those two inputs, **OpusClip** will create short, punchy, social media-optimised video clips (with captions!) that focus on the areas you want to showcase.

It is, of course, important that learners know how to do these things themselves but, equally, they should learn about the tools available that can assist them. Both can work in tandem or be used to help support media creation, hand-in-hand.

It would also be remiss to not consider offerings from both Canva and Adobe with their tools **Canva for Education** and Adobe **Express**. Both are free for education and feature products that contain AI. They are perfect for helping with marketing campaigns, trailers and simple image and video editing. Both can, for example, edit videos, remove backgrounds, share templates, facilitate collaboration, and much more besides. Their uses go far beyond media studies courses, as is evident from the number of times they have been mentioned in our book.

Technology use in the Secondary geography classroom

With a lens on Secondary geography, we call on David Watkins, an ex-colleague and long-time friend of Olly's who has long been a fan of taking students out of the confines of school and onto national and international trips to truly immerse them in a range of extreme surroundings.

Case study: David Watkins

David Watkins (@mrdavidwatkins on X) is the assistant head for teaching and learning and a former head of geography at St Joseph's College, Reading, UK. He is a Founding Fellow of the Chartered College of Teaching, a fellow of the Royal Geographical Society and has a master's degree in educational leadership. He is a governor at his local Primary school, where he chairs the Curriculum and Standards Committee. As a geographer and expedition leader, David has led groups of young people into challenging environments all over the world. Increasingly, he navigates the digital ecosystem to maximise pupil learning.

Despite how much I like teaching geography in the classroom, there is no substitute for getting out in the field to gain first-hand experience of people, places and environments. Technology is the enabler that bridges the gap; it brings the outside world in and the subject to life. In its simplest form, the ability to integrate high-quality digital photographs (often sourced from the internet) of locations into PowerPoints provides a stimulus for our geographers to begin to understand the context of the lesson.

A good geographer is inquisitive: Where is this place? What is it like? Why is it like that? How may it change? Who is affected by the changes? How does it make me feel? The discussion around a simple image at the start of the lesson can activate prior knowledge, encourage pupils to think like a geographer and highlight misconceptions.

Elevating this is our use of video from sites such as **YouTube** or **Vimeo** (www.vimeo.com) to develop a sense of place, evaluate a geographical issue or hear from the stakeholders. In the past, our sense of faraway places has been dominated by the media, whereas the proliferation of smartphones has led to less sculptured views of the world and more real-time reporting of events.

Digital mapping tools, Earth viewers and geographic information systems (GIS) enable students to explore and analyse spatial data, maps and layers of information. For instance, platforms like **Digimap** (www.digimapforschools. edina.ac.uk), Google **Earth** and **ArcGIS** (www.arcgis.com/index.html) provide interactive maps, satellite imagery and layers of geographical data, allowing students to virtually explore different regions, analyse patterns and develop a deeper understanding of the geography. Additionally, pupils can upload their geolocated data for analysis in their coursework.

Using ArcGIS, pupils have shown the change in sediment size along a beach, environmental quality scores about the regeneration of Oxford City Centre and the urban heat island effect across Reading, Berkshire.

Cartographic forms of data presentation make it easier to see patterns, trends and anomalies. Increasingly, we have been using the ArcGIS StoryMaps feature which brings together maps, pictures and texts to provide a clear narrative for our case studies in the classroom.

Technology can be used to highlight change over time. We often use Google **Street View** to compare recently regenerated areas with previous images by clicking on the clock icon in the upper-left corner where the street name is displayed. We even use the images to collect primary data by carrying out an environmental quality or land use survey.

Lately, our pupils used Google Earth to calculate the recent rate of retreat for the Gangotri Glacier in India. The textbook only provided data for 1780–2001, yet we were able to use Google Earth to identify the position in 2001 and 2023 and the measuring tool to work out the distance of retreat; our results illustrated a worrying quickening of the rate. In a subject as contemporary as geography, technology keeps us up to date while the textbook quickly becomes history.

One of our departmental aims is to embed excellence. Our approach is based on Ron Berger's seminal book, *An Ethic of Excellence*, which suggests adopting the following principles: assign work that matters, study examples of excellence, build a culture of critique, require multiple revisions and provide opportunities for public presentation (Berger, 2003).

Visualisers allow us to display examples of excellence either modelled by the teacher or produced by the pupil, ensuring that pupils are aware of the success criteria before commencing their work. Integral to our approach has been building a culture of critique. For pupils to feel confident when their work is displayed to the class, we have worked on teaching pupils how to be constructive with one another, as well as ensuring a healthy dose of praise.

Once this culture is embedded, more work naturally finds itself under the visualiser. This also allows immediate feedback from the class and the teacher and is a great example of live marking, which provides support and guidance to help all learners attain excellence. The visualiser can also be used to break down complex models. When I teach the global atmospheric circulation model, I construct it slowly under the visualiser, explaining every step while pupils follow along and create their own. Understanding is aided through my metacognitive narrative as I think out loud and carefully explain every step of the process. We use the affordable, plug-and-play **HueHD** (www.huehd.com) camera and have heard good things about the quality of the **IPEVO** (www.ipevo.com) range too.

Technology can be an integral tool to help check for understanding within a lesson. Even when using such brilliant techniques as mini whiteboards, the cognitive load for teachers to compute what has been written by every pupil and how this may demonstrate their knowledge and understanding is too high. Whether it is using multiple-choice questions online (or the more engaging **Plickers** or an adaptive learning system[1] (such as **Seneca Learning** – www.senecalearning.com), I can gain a much quicker formative assessment of a pupil's learning. I'm confident AI will play a significant role here in the future.

When we do go into the field, a smartphone gives us a wide suite of apps that can be used to collect data. From taking photographs to geolocating study sites, measuring slope or aspect, and identifying plants or the geology, the list is endless. In their pockets, most pupils are now carrying in one convenient device an altimeter, compass, camera, calculator, clinometer, data collection sheets, geolocator, note-taker, sound recorder, stopwatch and theodolite. **ArcGIS** has a range of specialist apps for collecting data in the field.

Increasingly there are cost and environmental benefits in developing a digital ecosystem for our learners. This is important to us as geographers and I, for one, am pleased to not start every lesson on rainforest destruction by handing out multiple reams of paper. While I am certain that technology has contributed to the climate crisis, its powerful capabilities are surely going to be part of the solution too.

---

[1] Adaptive learning systems use the pupil's interactions and responses to generate new questions and content. This provides a personalised learning experience relative to the pupil's needs.

If 'currency is king', then what is real-time data to a geographer? In a subject as evolving and contemporary as geography, it is impressive to see the learners in David's school not just using real-time data to develop their understanding, but also contributing to it for the benefit of all ongoing studies.

Putting learners at the heart of their learning like this is both commendable and important. By employing some of David's strategies, whether using a visualiser for feedback and modelling, purposeful use of smartphones while in the field or using a range of tools to capture data so that learners have the most up-to-date evidence that they can later decipher and extrapolate meaning from, it is evident that technology can significantly enhance and improve both the teaching and learning experience in the subject of geography. (We discuss the appropriateness of mobile devices in school later on in chapter 16 and earlier in chapter 2.)

What about in history?

Our first history case study comes from Paul Grange. Paul has been teaching and leading humanities subjects in the UK and beyond for 12 years. You can find Paul on X @Pbgrange and his website is www.wolseyacademy.com.

Case study: Paul Grange

1. Historical debates

A large part of the attraction of learning history is the debating aspect. Being able to think critically, analyse evidence and consider different perspectives are crucial skills and can be a lot of fun. However, running an inclusive debate in a classroom setting can take great skill on behalf of the teacher, with a natural tendency for some students to take the lead – or bypass speaker rules by feeding notes to quieter team members for them to parrot. It can be an intimidating environment for many students who are uncomfortable with public speaking or confrontation.

Tech recommendation: Using online wiki platforms like **DokuWiki** (www.dokuwiki.org) or Microsoft **Teams** allows historical debates to thrive by removing that confrontational edge. Students can contribute ideas to the thread or the wiki and debate other people's suggestions on their own without feeling 'on the spot' to reply. You will be surprised how often students can come alive in these settings. It also allows you to get students to post their sources or evidence to support their claims. This creates a written record of ideas and evidence that is then the perfect launchpad for developing long-form arguments in essays or speeches.

2. Engagement

Part of effective history teaching is getting students to empathise with individuals and societies from the past. Great methods for that had always been role play – traditionally, this may have looked like a short play presented to the class – or a teacher fantastic at storytelling (I still have fond memories of my history teacher pretending to be multiple characters and arguing with himself). Technology has opened new methods for achieving this effect. Of course, with all role-play activities, teacher discretion needs to be applied to the subjects chosen; the activity by its very nature is designed to be interactive and fun and is therefore certainly not suitable for sensitive historical topics.

Tech recommendation: A huge credit here must go to Russel Tarr and his **Active History** website (www.activehistory.co.uk). For years now, his site has offered students the chance to ask famous historical characters questions and receive responses. This has made role play more interactive and immediate – it's not every day you get to ask Henry VIII why he divorced Catherine of Aragon.

More recently, generative AI has made this experience even more accessible and far-ranging, and spin-off AI sites like **HelloHistory.AI** (www.hellohistory.ai) give a huge range of characters and lifelike responses. As with all generative AI, however, note this word of warning about the reliability of some answers and the ethics of some characters the students may wish to talk to(!).

A more reliable and fun use of this tech in the classroom is to feed generative AI a list of the precise arguments and evidence you wish students to learn and ask it to turn them into a scripted conversation. Asking for a scripted play between medieval peasants on the points you wish to discuss results in great stage directions and character descriptions which students enjoy enacting. I usually ask students to use the play as a starting point and get them to add additional lines to further explain the causes and consequences of certain historical actions.

3. Gaming

When I started teaching, the very word 'gaming' was a Marmite issue in the staffroom. It evokes images of violent first-person shooters and students falling asleep at their desks after pulling an all-nighter on Fortnite.

That said, if done correctly, it can provide a hugely engaging starting point and shared cultural reference to aid student understanding. The video-game theorist

Steven Poole, on a simple level, breaks gaming down into two types: ludology (puzzle-based) and narrative (story-based). This is, in effect, what teaching is: skills and content. Gaming, by combining the two with instant feedback loops, can make learning highly addictive. I would argue, therefore, that it is not with suspicion but envy that teachers should view the world of gaming.

In the 1970s, a hugely influential game called the Oregon Trail took students through life as a 'pioneer' of the American West, balancing their settlers' supplies of food and other resources while overcoming the obstacles of Westward expansion. This was more popular in the US, for obvious reasons, but has been revived in the UK as 'The American West' and has become a popular GCSE module. Other games like Civilisation and Sim City are also excellent grounding for the humanities.

Using commercially successful video games to teach history does have its obvious limits and pitfalls. Assassins Creed creates fantastic replicas of ancient cities using the best archaeological evidence and guided by in-house historians – although it also lets you seriously injure or kill people, alas.

Tech recommendation: What if you could get students to design their own historical video games? (Ideally, free from time-travelling assassins.) Well, you can. Game engines like **RPG Maker** (www.rpgmakerweb.com) and **Smile Game Builder** (https://smilegamebuilder.com/en) are available at a low price point (around $70). They do not require any coding skills and the design elements are very much drag-and-drop in nature. What this creates is a hugely engaging historical project. Students have to design characters, maps, scripts and action sequences that draw upon their historical understanding.

I have had some fantastic results from groups of students managing their time and indulging their creativity. Giving students guidance on the content to cover is crucial but, if done effectively, this use of technology has been one of the most successful I have been involved in.

What we love about Paul's case study is that all of the different examples come from long-established approaches that help study the subject of history – from supporting debate to helping put learners in the shoes of historical figures by building empathy, and promoting relevant and meaningful learning opportunities (using games like Sim City and Civilisation). Paul's work highlights the many ways technology can help to bring his subject to life, by cleverly selecting tools that add value while simultaneously igniting interest in the topics (rather than the tech), driving inclusivity and relevance to the learners. Skilful stuff!

In our next case study, we have Sally Thorne, head of humanities and associate assistant headteacher at Montpelier High School, Bristol. Sally, someone whom Mark has known for years following her great shares at the Teachmeets he used to organise at Clevedon School, offers us her take on effective technology use in history.

Case study: Sally Thorne

I remember wondering, as we crashed into the pandemic, what online tools for learning would go the distance beyond remote teaching; it's safe to say that there is enough distance now for that to be clearer. Some tools faded quickly back into obscurity, while others proved themselves valuable enough to be adapted back into classroom teaching. In the main, these tools are the ones that tackle thorny issues in history teaching – specifically, working with historical materials and constructing evaluative arguments that go beyond the superficial.

Working with sources

While I was busy with my head in old textbooks, it seemed that a lot of museums and historic collections had been busy getting their treasures online, and it was quite joyful coming across these as I searched for digital materials to share with my classes.

My advice for improving student confidence in working with historical materials is to include a source of some kind in every lesson and to make a conscious effort to ensure these sources go beyond the written. Paintings, newspaper headlines, cartoons (political or otherwise) and photographs of artefacts, buildings and landscapes changed by human activity; all provide students with a window into the past – and their increasing availability in digital archives makes access even easier.

My first ports of call are usually the **British Museum collections** (www.britishmuseum.org/collection), the **National Archives** (www.nationalarchives.gov.uk) and, particularly good for landscapes and buildings, **Flickr** (www.flickr.com). The **Mary Evans Picture Library** (www.maryevans.com) is also a treasure trove – like Getty Images but with a focus on historical images.

Once I've chosen the sources for use in my classroom, my preferred method for annotating and zooming in on sources is still **Smartnotes** (www.smartnotesonline.com): using the magic pen tool to spotlight or enlarge key aspects helps with digging into the details in sources. Once annotated, the slide can be saved and printed – particularly useful for students for whom keeping up with board work is an impossibility.

Smartnotes is a free download and works without a smartboard, though it is becoming increasingly outdated. After 20 years of smartboard use, I will be bereft when mine is finally replaced, but I have been trying to train myself on other solutions.

Enter: the visualiser. These are becoming ubiquitous and mine is proving to be an excellent tool for breaking down my thought process when tackling a historical source. I can annotate and highlight on the fly and, much like the slide, am left with a record of the exercise to copy for students.

Visualisers come at all price points but I can highly recommend splashing out on one with Wi-Fi connectivity. This might seem a bit superfluous; however, what it means is that I can send the visualiser around the room so that students can share their annotations on the projector without having to leave their seats.

Extended writing

Forms have also been invaluable when it comes to tackling student evaluative writing. Students can be directed to certain aspects of an extended-writing task depending on where they need the practice. Following an assessment, I might set up three Google **Forms** for a feed-forward task: one focusing on applying knowledge to a question, one with some knowledge provided but asking students to analyse it concerning the question, and one with much of the argument provided but requiring students to write a conclusion.

Online software for homework setting (we use **Classcharts** – www.classcharts.com) enables different tasks to be assigned to different students. This makes the whole thing a breeze and ensures students are practising the specific aspect of extended writing that represents their next step to success.

One of my favourite tasks to build student confidence around extended writing remains the crowd-sourced silent essay. This requires students to use laptops or computers to work on a shared document that is displayed on the screen – for this reason, it needs to be a class you can trust not to stray away from the task.

What I particularly like about doing this is that students will work hard to come up with arguments and source evidence to prove their peers wrong – or support them. It also provokes discussion about what a good supporting argument looks like. A lot of students rely on arguing with logic (look out for the tell-tale conditional, 'This would have...' which is so often followed by supposition rather than fact) and so pausing the battle of words every so often to discuss the merits of the different arguments is a helpful exercise and stays low-threat as student contributions are anonymous.

Pragmatic as ever, what we love about Sally's contribution is that it is all about one of two things: the subject or the learning activity. None of what she shares is about the technology. Ever the historian, Sally also wisely points out the importance of focusing her classroom technology use choices around those that remained beyond the remote learning times of the COVID-19 pandemic. By taking a 'what works' tactic that best supports learning in her classroom, we can all take note of Sally's example and focus on the tools and methodologies which support learning.

Our final case study comes from Carole Stobbs, headteacher of EBACC at Unity Academy Blackpool and a long-standing teacher and head of history. Mark first came across Carole at a history conference where she was sharing strategies for teaching history and her innovative approaches stuck. So, when considering who to ask to share insights into using technology in history, she was someone who immediately came to mind.

Case study: Carole Stobbs
Virtual field trips

My first foray into a virtual tour was with castles and their development for Year 7. The location of the schools I have worked in for the last 20 years is not convenient for day trips. Even when we had done this previously, I was frustrated that just one castle did not give my students the understanding of change, numbers built and development over time I wanted. Of course, it is fantastic to see the buildings themselves and get an understanding of their size and location, but this was not always possible. We also wanted to link these castles to other elements of our Key Stage 3 course, to join the dots and extend their understanding of the period.

The castles were selected based on places we had been (building on our knowledge), places relevant to the course (both previous and future) and places that could show the development of castles. We always start our tours at school so that the students have a mental map of where places are in relation to where they live.

For each castle, we choose a map view for when they arrive but also jump to places within and around it that are relevant, using photographs. The information boxes accompanying the Google information can be edited, and pictures added to suit your needs.

One trip, for example, includes a visit to Hastings, where we arrive at a view of its position to show why it was a suitable location. This section of our trip has links to information from the official sites that run the castle, relevant or related images such as the Bayeux Tapestry, photographs including 360-degree views where available and questions to provoke discussion. It takes a lot of work to set one of these up but, once the main body is done, tweaks and updates are straightforward.

For an hour, we travel around Britain and visit seven castles, with a little freestyling if we have time at the end to go to castles our students have been to. The students complete field notes while we carry out our visits: plotting them on a map, sketching, making observations and noting questions they would like to research in a follow-up activity. These were discussed with our geography staff to complement how they carry out their local fieldwork.

Follow-up activities are varied but include independent research, student presentations to the class and even virtual tours. Students engage with the process and it is one of the types of lessons students always remember studying and can tell you what they learned. The work we have completed is then linked to previous and future lessons, and becomes a reference sheet for students.

We have created virtual tours for several units in Key Stage 3; some travel worldwide and others have links to the brilliant **NLS side-by-side maps** (https://maps.nls.uk). We know it doesn't replace the real thing and is always being improved upon, but it has encouraged students to drag their parents to castles on their holidays. Technology such as this is free and means we don't need to limit ourselves to what is in the textbook. When we combine tours like this with the increasing number of virtual museums and websites, it is possible to bring the past to life in a way the history classroom could only hope to do when I started teaching.

There can be a propensity with gimmicky activities in the classroom for the gimmick to be the long-standing memory rather than the learning activity. Craig Barton shares a lovely anecdote in his book *How I Wish I'd Taught Maths* when he remembers a lesson where he taught fractions using a Swiss roll to help explain to the students. Later, when asked about what they had learned, students remembered the Swiss roll rather than learning about fractions. Barton uses this as a means to explain episodic memory, where learners remember the things that happen around the learning rather than the desired learning outcomes the teacher had planned.

Stobbs' example is a great counter to this, as it ties in clear learning outcomes and activities that give context to the subject students are studying. They're not visiting these castles in lessons to simply have fun (albeit they may enjoy the activity). Yes, 'it is one of the types of lessons students always remember studying' but, importantly, students will and 'can tell you what they learned'.

This is a strong reminder of how critical it is to keep your choices around the use of technology squarely on your content (CK) and the best ways to teach it (PK), then apply technology to those two to consider whether or not it can add benefit to the learning activity (TK).

Top tips

Mark's top tips

1. Be mindful of bells and whistles. Technology can change everything or change nothing. It's the approaches you use, informed by what you have to teach and how you aim to teach it, that make the difference. Don't be blindsided by gimmicks.

2. Consider the benefits that technology brings to support modelling opportunities, from spreadsheet analysis in business and economics to extrapolate and consider trends, to using tools such as Google Earth and digital versions of artefacts, such as those found in Google Arts & Culture. Concrete examples help learning, and digital models can help students gain a better understanding of their topics when they use them.

3. Consider leveraging tools that enable students to immerse themselves in historical or geographical situations. By walking in the virtual shoes of those who've come before us, students can gain an additional appreciation of how things have developed over time.

Olly's top tips

1. In humanities subjects, there's no need to reinvent the wheel. Whether it's business, economics, geography or history, with a world of online sources such as Google Arts & Culture, the British Library and ArcGIS, make use of the fantastic resources at your digital fingertips.

2. Using live data is a way to make the opportunities for learning both memorable and authentic. By using real data and tying it to the learning taking place, it helps provide concrete examples alongside an authentic learning experience, and is much more likely to reside in memory than if it was packaged up just for use in a lesson.

3. Don't forget the value that collaborative platforms, such as Padlet, Microsoft Teams and Google Docs, can bring to support research, resource sharing and peer assessment. Just because they aren't humanities-specific, doesn't mean they can't help learning and teaching.

CHAPTER 14
Using technology in languages

'To learn a language is to have one more window from which to look at the world.'

Chinese proverb

Of all the subjects taught in schools and the subsequent sharing about the effective ways technology can enhance teaching and learning, it's fair to say that language teachers are some of the most innovative.

If you are reading this and have been using X (formerly Twitter) for any length of time, you can't help but notice the popular #MFLTwitterati hashtag (originally shared by Joe Dale @joedale). A quick perusal of the hashtag will reinforce what we have stated: on the whole, teachers of language love technology and they are creative and innovative in its use.

Over the years, Mark has had the good fortune of working with many language teachers, through webinars and inset days, as well as supporting departments in schools in the UK and internationally. In his experience, technology offers young people many opportunities to be creative as they express their knowledge of the target language they're studying.

Reading, comprehension, oracy and writing are cornerstones of all subjects; however, language subjects are the ones where the importance of these has added gravitas due to how they are assessed, particularly in summative assessments.

Language teachers already have a vast repertoire of technology-based activities at their fingertips:

- using animations (stop-frame, animated images or even green-screen) for students to demonstrate their language proficiency
- virtual tours
- voice notes and audio clips
- using chatbots in a target language to test, check and improve written work
- using AI to create fun stories in a target language to read and translate in class – and much more!

Type of output	Tools to try
Language comprehension	▪ Duolingo ▪ Rosetta Stone
Speaking and pronunciation	▪ Google Speech-to-Text ▪ Dictation tools such as Siri
Interactive role-playing	Role-play simulations, e.g. Minecraft
Vocabulary building, grammar practice and retrieval practice	▪ Quizlet ▪ Memrise ▪ Anki
Cultural exploration	▪ Google Earth ▪ Google Arts & Culture ▪ Google Street View tours ▪ Virtual tours in Minecraft
Collaborative story creation	▪ Google Docs ▪ Microsoft Word Online ▪ Book Creator
Reading and comprehension	Microsoft Reading Progress/Reading Coach
Listening comprehension	Podcasts or TV programmes in the target language with subtitles
Translation practice	Google Translate (for checking work)

Table 14.1: Technology tools to demonstrate learning in a languages lesson

With so many chances to use technology to enhance learning in the languages classroom, and given the breadth of assessment within the subject, providing students with broad and balanced opportunities is key. The ability to practise their use of the target language in as many ways as possible reinforces the subject in writing and verbally, which of course, helps with recall, fluency and the requirement of these when it comes to students succeeding in their summative assessments.

Moreover, language subjects are important in ways beyond academic study. From helping young people expand their knowledge about other cultures to better understanding their own language and its constructs, the subject opens doors to new worlds. Languages can be a gateway to unlocking cultural understanding, sensitivity, global citizenship and engagement, societal development, identity, individuality and, of course, social communication.

While knowledge can be a doorway to wisdom, the knowledge of languages gives you a key to the global community. Without this, we would live in a far less colourful, connected and expressive world.

So, now that we have hopefully started to convince you (if you weren't already there!) that languages are a fantastic and important element of your curriculum offering, let's delve into some case studies to highlight how technology supports their teaching and learning.

14.1 Using AI in the languages classroom

So, as you've probably already looked at the equivalents of this section in the other chapters, it would be remiss to just repeat ourselves to fill out the content in the book. If you are a languages teacher, however, and have just jumped straight to this section, please have a look at what we've talked about in the other chapters, as there are many cross-curricular ways that AI can help in all subjects beyond the ideas and approaches we will share here now.

Many educators have reported mixed reviews about the abilities of generative AI chat tools in supporting language teaching. There are, as always, pros and cons of all tools. We've seen them with things such as Google **Translate** for a long time. To help, we'll summarise some of the benefits and drawbacks:

Tool	Benefit	Drawback
Generative AI	**Real-time feedback:** Some AI models offer immediate feedback on grammar, pronunciation and fluency, encouraging self-correction.	**Accuracy and fluency:** Current AI models still struggle with complex grammar, slang and colloquialisms, potentially leading to unnatural or incorrect responses.
	Exposure to natural language: AI can generate conversations simulating real-world scenarios, providing exposure to natural variations in language.	**Lack of a human touch:** AI may not be able to adapt to subtle cues and nuances in conversation, limiting authentic interaction.

Tool	Benefit	Drawback
Translation tools	**Accessibility:** Tools such as Google Translate offer instant translation support, aiding comprehension and basic communication.	**Accuracy and context:** Translations can be grammatically incorrect, misleading or lack context, hindering true understanding.
	Vocabulary building: Students can discover new words and phrases while reading translated text.	**Passivity:** Overreliance on translation tools discourages active language practice and the development of speaking skills.

Table 14.2: Benefits and drawbacks of AI in a languages classroom

The truth is, currently, neither AI nor translation tools are a replacement for human teachers. They both have their strengths and weaknesses. They can help, for sure, but as with all technology used in teaching and learning, the choice to use them should be informed by your context and your cognisance of how they best support your learning goals. Strategic use rather than an overreliance is what appears to be best practice, blending their use, just like you might use a dictionary in an English classroom or a calculator in maths. Know when their uses are appropriate and apply or use as necessary.

Of course, AI for language learning and the research surrounding it is still ongoing. With the technology evolving so rapidly, your perception and that of your peers may change as AI models become more sophisticated and accurate.

It's also important to remember and consider the ethical implications of using AI in language learning. There have been many instances since its explosion on the scene where bias and a lack of ethics have been found in its algorithms; after all, it has learned from us! In a subject which at its core aims to make the world a more inclusive place, with better relationships built upon the understanding gained through conversation and writing in different languages, being mindful of ethical considerations should be front and centre in your thinking when considering the use of AI in a languages classroom.

Given the key domains of teaching languages in a languages class, we thought it would be useful to share some linked activities (while being mindful of the bias and ethical considerations) that you might like to consider for your classroom.

Speaking skills

1. Use AI to create language-challenge activities such as tongue twisters, quick debates or storytelling exercises to reduce workload and help improve pronunciation, fluency and complex sentence structures.
2. Create personalised pronunciation exercises using tools such as **Reading Coach** and **Reading Progress** from Microsoft. The tools listen to your speech and identify issues with pronunciation.

Reading comprehension

1. Use AI to create adaptive resources for your classes. AI can generate personalised vocabulary exercises based on the levels and learning gaps you identify. AI tools can create memory games, crosswords and quizzes, all focused on the specific vocabulary relevant to what you're focusing on in a class, with groups or individuals.
2. Consider using AI to create text passages to share with learners for reading comprehension exercises. This will save you time and you will be able to iterate these across different classes or within a class for children working at different levels.

Use of AI-generated images

Tools such as those we've mentioned previously, from the various derivatives of **Dall-E** to Adobe **Firefly**, **ideogram.ai** and more, are great at creating images featuring scenes that include examples of key vocabulary you may be studying in class. These are perfect for visual references, cold calling and checking knowledge in the moment, and for student labelling activities. Such is the speed with which you can create the images, they are a no-brainer for building high-quality resources, while helping make your life that little bit easier. Just remember to keep in mind any biases or other ethical issues that generated resources might bring up. We'd also recommend ensuring that the diversity of individuals in any images generated is representative of the community in which you work.

A popular way many teachers have been using these tools is to capture phrases, colloquialisms, idioms and more as images for resource creation. There are many more methods that can be applied to help elicit interesting approaches to supporting language acquisition and memorisation, such as for key vocabulary items. For example, if you were teaching about vocabulary for kitchen utensils, you could generate an image for this and then use it as the prompt for conversation around those items. Other potential uses include areas such as landmarks, festivals, traditional clothing and food items. If you can see it, you can say it, so think about relevant images you could create with these tools.

14.2 What can technology use look like in Primary?

Our first case study comes from Nicole Ferguson, a senior leader and experienced international educator who has taught in the UAE and Malaysia over the last decade. You can connect with Nicole on X @Fergusonteacher.

Case study: Nicole Ferguson

Around 2015, the languages department at my former Primary school embarked on a journey to innovate learning using **Seesaw** (https://app.seesaw.me). Having implemented a successful rollout with class teachers for the teaching of core subjects, Seesaw had already proved to be a powerful tool that inspired, created and engaged students in their learning. Over time, the platform's integration expanded to the languages department, resulting in remarkable improvements in oracy, fluency and vocabulary.

This case study outlines the successful rollout of Seesaw, its impact on language learning and the subsequent advancements made in the languages classroom.

Background

My former Primary school recognised the importance of leveraging technology to enhance language learning. By implementing Seesaw, an innovative digital platform, teachers sought to inspire students through engaging content and encourage collaboration with improved outcomes in their language-learning journey. The adoption of Seesaw in the school had already seen many positive outcomes, prompting the move to embed it further and effectively enhance learning in languages.

Implementation

Seesaw was implemented in languages to bring about improved language acquisition and fluency. It allowed teachers to create multimedia content to provide students with interactive lessons that fostered engagement and creativity. Through Seesaw, students from Years 1-6 were able to complete tasks, follow instructions and collaborate with their peers, both in the class and remote environments.

Impact on oracy, fluency and vocabulary

Seesaw is now playing a pivotal role in improving students' oracy, fluency and vocabulary skills. Through an intensive onboarding programme, the languages teachers immersed themselves in creating bespoke content; it is worth noting that Seesaw has an extensive library of pre-made lessons tailored to languages learning objectives. It provided educators with a wide range of resources to effectively support student progression. The platform's interactive nature enabled students to practise speaking and listening skills through recordings, and create oral presentations to enhance their oracy skills. Furthermore, their ability to create and share videos, audio clips and multimedia content helped to develop fluency by encouraging them to express themselves confidently in the target language.

Adaptation during the pandemic

The COVID-19 pandemic presented unforeseen challenges for educators worldwide, requiring a swift adaptation to remote and hybrid learning environments. Seesaw was already well-established in school which enabled the continuation and evolution of seamless communication, collaboration and assessment between teachers and students. This established approach to teaching and learning in languages ensured that lessons remained familiar. The platform's features allowed for the sharing of assignments, feedback and subsequent progress-tracking, ensuring continued engagement and improvement even in the face of unprecedented circumstances.

Collaboration and progression

Seesaw fostered a collaborative learning environment both in-person and online. Students were encouraged to work together on projects, share their language learning experiences through the blog and provide feedback on their peers' work. This collaborative approach enhanced language proficiency and fostered a sense of community among students. As a result, they were motivated to progress further and actively engage in their language learning journey.

Conclusion

By inspiring and engaging students, Seesaw prompted improvements in oracy, fluency and vocabulary. Its extensive library of pre-made lessons, teacher-led content and interactive features supported student progression and collaboration, ensuring effective learning pre- and post-pandemic. Seesaw's successful implementation in our school serves as a testament to the power of technology in enhancing language education and preparing students for a globalised world.

Nicole's approach highlights an important factor in successful digital transformation: a multimodal approach. This is essentially about leveraging the strengths of various educational tools and strategies to create a more dynamic, engaging and inclusive learning environment. Yes, the approach is framed around one tool, but it demonstrates multiple pathways for students to engage with the content, express their understanding and interact with their peers and instructors, thereby enhancing the overall learning experience.

Initially, the project set out to achieve increased student engagement, but it ended up doing far more than this by developing oracy, literacy and fluency, as well as offering choice and collaboration, improving feedback and giving students ownership of their learning.

Our next case study comes from Jane Basnett. Jane is the director of Digital Learning at Downe House School, holds a masters in digital technologies and is an MIE Master Trainer. Jane is on X @basnettj.

Case study: Jane Basnett

My experience is that languages have always been at the forefront of technology use in teaching. Whatever the demand, there is an appropriate technological solution.

A key factor in language learning is the need to drill vocabulary and phrases and several go-to tools fit the bill.

Let us start with **Quizlet**. At its basic level, Quizlet allows students to learn through flashcards. However, once the teacher has a subscription (look out for offers – I got mine for £3.99!), more functionalities tap right into the demands of language learning.

The tool that many teachers know is **Quizlet Live**, but to use just this is to overlook the ever-so-useful 'learn' feature which gives students the chance to type out the words or phrases and tests them again if they make a mistake. Students enjoy the process and can mix up their learning with a matching exercise or 'test out' when they feel ready. This low-stakes quizzing and drilling is perfect for language learners and teaches students about resilience.

Another invaluable EdTech tool for teaching languages is **Quizizz**. This interactive quiz platform allows language teachers to create engaging and gamified assessments for their students. With its user-friendly interface, there are a variety of question types, including opportunities to pose oral questions and receive responses orally (this feature is with a subscription only, but it is worth it). One of the reasons Quizizz features on my list of tools is that it provides great feedback reports which enable me to drill down into misconceptions at a student and class level, which is great for planning. I can set a Quizizz in class or I can assign it as homework with a request for students to complete the task many times, thus giving opportunities for students to build their knowledge over time. A neat feature of Quizizz is that you can make use of the many quizzes already in existence or you can 'teleport' questions from other previously created quizzes, thus adapting your quiz to suit your students' needs.

Next on my list is **Learningapps.org** (https://learningapps.org), which is like a well-kept secret because it does not get lots of mentions on social media and I cannot understand why this is the case. It is a free tool and requests a donation only. Like many online tools, you can design customised activities, such as matching exercises, gap-filling tasks and word scrambles, plus word or paragraph ordering to reinforce vocabulary, grammar and other language skills. Students can access these interactive activities through web browsers or mobile devices, enabling flexible learning both inside and outside the classroom. However, what taps right into the modern language brief is the ability to create listening tasks either by adding a YouTube video or by typing your text which is then converted to speech. As with most sites like this, there is a massive collection of resources already available for copying or editing.

I cannot finish this little article without mentioning **Textivate** (www.textivate.com). Textivate is an EdTech tool that focuses on language learning through text-based activities. It allows teachers to create a variety of interactive exercises, such as gap-filling, sequencing, matching and sorting tasks, using authentic texts. You can create your own texts or use pre-existing ones created by others. One of the unique aspects of Textivate is its 'text-to-speech' functionality, which allows students to listen to the text being read aloud in the target language. This feature can be particularly beneficial for improving listening skills and pronunciation. As the teacher, you can create sequences of activities, which I often do and assign to my classes, allowing me to see their progress and identify areas that might need further attention. Often, the final task I might set is one where students have to write out the whole text either as a translation or with a few clues, such as only the vowels of each word, the consonants or perhaps just the first letter. Students really enjoy the challenges. Textivate is not free, but in terms of value for money, I do not think it can be beaten.

Without a doubt, languages have embraced technology and the tools I have mentioned here are just some of my favourites that enhance drilling, vocabulary acquisition, collaboration and oral practice, fostering resilience and language proficiency in a safe and controlled environment.

We did say from the start of the chapter that teachers of languages have plenty of approaches and tools to innovate while supporting solid learning activities. There are no gimmicks in what Jane shares – just sound advice, grounded in many years of successful teaching of languages, while using technology (of course!).

Reinforcing Jane's approach, we love that she first selects tools to fit the learning she wants students to demonstrate while giving her useful metrics. Additionally, the fact that the tools Jane chooses offer dexterity to both the teacher and students in terms of their usage, whether that be collaboratively, individually, in class or independently, all adds value and serves as evidence as to how technology can positively enhance and support language learning.

Our next case study comes from Jérôme Nogues (@JeNoMfl on X) and he shares with us how he blends the use of different tools in his Primary languages classroom. Jérôme is head of digital learning and languages, an #MIEExpert and Wakelet Ambassador and an all-round sharer on his YouTube channel, @learnwithj.

Case study: Jérôme Nogues

In the realm of language teaching, harnessing the power of educational technology tools is key to fostering effective learning. I love using EdTech in my language classroom to enhance learning. One of the apps that I frequently use is **Canva**. In case you haven't heard of it, Canva is a versatile graphic design platform that offers various templates to create anything from Instagram posts to websites and slide presentations. By incorporating Canva into language lessons (or any other lessons), teachers can encourage students to think creatively. The platform is incredibly user-friendly and intuitive.

One of my favourite tasks is asking the children to create a postcard from a country where the target language is spoken. The first part involves designing the cover using cultural elements from the entire country or a specific city. This task is perfect for preparation before or reflection after a real visit!

Once the beautiful cover is complete (including a space for a QR code), it's time to put their writing skills into action. The children are supported with a sentence builder that they have previously studied. The task doesn't take too long, depending on the class level, and support is available for pupils with additional needs.

> Since this task comes at the end of a sequence, pronunciation skills are usually well-developed, but I always ensure that they practise before recording themselves. We use **Immersive Reader** and **Reading Coach** as we are Microsoft-based. Alternatively, some Chrome extensions can provide similar functionality to Immersive Reader.

Jérôme's multimodal approach in using versatile and user-friendly tools to curate and help students create a multifaceted artefact allows them to apply their linguistic skills while also exploring creativity and cultural elements – and simultaneously evidencing their understanding. Nogues' method of integrating multiple technologies to showcase different aspects of language learning, including those which are and aren't assessed, gives his students a broad, balanced and, we would argue, exciting learning experience. The adage that technology allows us to do things that wouldn't be possible without technology definitely rings true in this case study.

The teaching of languages can help provide a window to the world. How we choose to use technology in how we teach and how students learn can bring additional opportunities beyond the scope of the four walls of the classroom.

The various stories shared in our case studies align well with our belief that technology should serve pedagogy and content. Combining that with the competence, confidence, cognisance and consistency of approaches across the different case studies reinforces the supposition that our 5 Cs approach to teaching and learning with technology can truly work.

The case studies demonstrate a range of excellent examples for educators to try through the use of versatile technology, thoughtful and purposeful pedagogy, and creative approaches to learning. We hope you can try them too.

Top tips

Mark's top tips

1. Language-based subjects lend themselves well to many different types of technology, given that they cover oracy, writing, listening and reading. Remember the adage of keeping things simple and guided by a teaching and learning need.

2. Consider asking students to use dictation tools on their devices in classes, such as you find in Microsoft Word or Google Docs. Set a target language and try it! Similarly, suggest to students that they try this approach with home AI assistants such as Alexa or Siri to help improve their oracy and pronunciation.

3. Try using Reading Progress in Microsoft Teams assignments in target languages to improve reading and speaking fluency. It will have the side benefit of improving vocabulary knowledge too.

Olly's top tips

1. Think outside the box, just like Jérôme's postcard project, and give something different a try!

2. If you're thinking of an innovative AI tool, consider using www.udio.com or www.suno.ai, two tools which, from creative writing of lyrics in a target language, will create a song for you in a genre of your choosing. Free to use, these tools are great for helping memorise key target vocabulary, with great pronunciation in your desired language. You could even ask your students to write the lyrics!

3. Involve your team/department and the students. Trial a new technological tool described in this chapter to aid and enhance student practice.

CHAPTER 15
Using technology to manage learning

'Efficiency is doing things right; effectiveness is doing the right things.'

Peter Drucker

Peter Drucker is often referred to as the 'father of modern management' and certainly, many will recognise the famous quote attributed to him, 'Culture eats strategy for breakfast'; although, interestingly, it's a quote that was never actually written in any of his works, so its provenance is uncertain. There is wide acceptance that culture is the bedrock of what makes a strategy work and this quote often brings up plenty of discourse.

The same could be true when it comes to the choices of technology use – there are, indeed, many ways to make technology work across your school, trust or district, or organisation. The truth is, whether you use a Google Workspace or Microsoft ecosystem, laptops, Chromebooks, tablets or a mixture, ensuring you get impact at scale (whatever 'impact' means to you) is achievable in all of them. There is no 'one is better than the other'.

The same is often true with the apps we use. Let's take Google **Sheets** and Microsoft **Excel** as two tools for comparison. They both do similar things. Excel has additional functionality compared with Sheets, so that makes it better, right? Well, maybe not. With a cleaner user interface, with fewer confusing tools and ribbons compared to Excel, many would suggest that Sheets is more approachable and easier to use and therefore implement. Power users of Excel would disagree; for them, the ability to do things in Excel that simply wouldn't be possible in Sheets makes it the better choice. Again, no; context is paramount. The truth also lies in the fact that when considering technology and its uses across a broad implementation, it's what can work best at scale which is most important, not the number of things you can do with it.

The same is true when it comes to how you bring all of these things together into one place and space. The ways you use your technology to support teaching, learning and the workflow of bringing together all of these different digital artefacts and examples of learning for the activities of feedback, assessment and reporting is important. Consistency of approach is paramount, not just to help students be aware of these processes so that they can best access their feedback but, importantly, for ease of training, support, management and quality assurance.

Using technology to manage learning is a broad topic that includes more than just workflow solutions, albeit we'll discuss these later in the chapter. Technology can help manage learning in several ways, from behaviour management to classroom management, reward and sanction recording, device management and monitoring, firewalls – the options are many!

In this chapter, we are going to focus on just a few; namely, classroom management and workflow. So, let's get to it!

15.1 Technology to support classroom management

There have been many studies which show that metacognition and self-regulated learning have a positive impact on learning and progress. If we just take the Education Endowment Foundation's toolkit (EEF, 2021) as one source, we can see that, from its analysis:

> 'Evidence suggests the use of "metacognitive strategies" – which get pupils to think about their own learning – can be worth the equivalent of an additional +7 months' progress when used well.'

It is important to recognise that studies in these areas are looking at how teachers can support students. We won't labour on what metacognition and self-regulated learning are, as we've already covered that back in chapter 5 and there's a great case study there from Anoara Mughal.

Many studies (Attia et al., 2017) demonstrate that technology causes distractions which impact learning. Some try to share personal strategies to support self-regulation, such as the Harvard Business Review article, 'Conquering Digital Distraction' (Rosen and Samuel, 2015). These strategies could be shared with students; however, one way we can support learners in their positive use of technology in the classroom is to use classroom management software. As stated in the EEF's summary guidance (EEF, 2021):

> 'Carefully designed guided practice, with support gradually withdrawn as the pupil becomes proficient, can allow pupils to develop skills and strategies before applying them in independent practice.'

Point 6 of the summary guidance directs us to: 'Explicitly teach pupils how to organise and effectively manage their learning independently'. However, is it a stretch to say that we shouldn't use technology to manage a student's use of technology to enable them to organise and effectively manage their learning independently?

Studies show repeatedly that digital distractions have an impact on the quality of work undertaken and subsequent learning, such as this: '...the presence of digital distraction was particularly disruptive to the quality and quantity of laptop users' lecture notes relative to longhand note takers' (Flanigan and Titsworth, 2020). If this is the case, is it a stretch to suggest that using tools (classroom management software) that can scaffold the technology learners are using and helpfully shepherd them as they use it, while explicitly teaching them metacognitive and self-regulated learning strategies with technology, will have a positive impact on learning?

In the next case study, a previous contributor to the book, Jérôme Nogues, thinks about this and other ways that one such tool, **classroom.cloud**, can help counter this issue while helping learning and progress. He also shares other ways that tools such as this can be of help and support.

Case study: Jérôme Nogues

I have always believed technology has the potential to positively transform the way we do things in all aspects of our daily lives. As a teacher, this has meant I have always been enthusiastic about how we can incorporate technology into the classroom to improve the experiences of students and teachers alike.

As a teacher, **classroom.cloud** gives me complete control over what my students have in front of them. It means that rather than be distracted by things other than what I want them to focus on, they use the tools and resources *I* want them to use, when they need them. I can open and close windows and applications on all student devices, pushing out learning content directly in front of them when it is appropriate to do so. I can share my own screen during lesson demonstrations to ensure they are concentrating on my explanations. I can also limit which websites and applications pupils can access during lesson time, ensuring they can't simply surf the internet in class. When necessary, I can even remotely take control of a particular device to help set a student back on track. As I can view their screens and interact with them, I am also able to close the feedback loop quickly, by responding to issues and misconceptions in the moment.

The tool works in a hybrid fashion too, so when I was away with COVID, I was still able to check that the children were doing the work set during the cover lesson. One or two decided to play chess instead. I quickly managed to lock their machines, sent a message to the teacher in the classroom and added the chess game URL to the blocked website list.

Another evidence point for the benefits of EdTech is the wide-ranging possibilities these platforms can offer to increase student engagement and get them focused on the lesson and subject. From platform-specific functions to easily accessible multimedia resources, EdTech opens new ways for students to learn, enhancing and building upon existing curriculum plans.

Finally, the safeguarding module of the classroom.cloud app provides a crucial layer of protection and support for students in school. With its advanced features, the module ensures a safe and secure digital learning environment. It allows teachers to monitor online activities in real time, providing them with the ability to detect any potential risks or harmful content. The module also facilitates the implementation of internet filtering and blocking, preventing access to inappropriate websites or materials.

By promoting responsible and safe online behaviour, the safeguarding module actively contributes to creating a positive and secure educational experience for all students. I will always remember that when I received the first warning message, the word 'fighting' had come up a few times. Little did I know that the headteacher himself had been teaching Year 8 about gladiators in Latin!

Thanks to all these fantastic features, classroom.cloud has been one of the top apps in my everyday teaching to help keep my students focused on learning while helping me with my teaching.

15.2 Using technology to manage learning and assessment

There are many different types of digital artefacts that teachers can ask students to create. We went into this in more detail in chapter 6. To refresh your memory, here are some examples:

Type of artefact	Tool that can be used to create the artefact
Essay, notes, responses to extended answer questions, research proposals, summaries, collaborative documents.	▪ Microsoft Word ▪ Google Docs ▪ Apple Pages ▪ Microsoft OneNote
Annotated timelines, interactive infographics, product pitches/proposals, tutorials, storyboards, presentations.	▪ Google Slides ▪ Microsoft PowerPoint ▪ Apple Keynote
Explainer videos, product demonstrations, stop-motion animations, screencasts, tutorials, documentaries, news reports, virtual tours, musical performances, time-lapse videos, video reviews.	▪ WeVideo ▪ iMovie ▪ I Can Animate ▪ Explain Everything ▪ ClipChamp ▪ Adobe Premiere Pro ▪ DaVinci Resolve ▪ Final Cut Pro

Table 15.1: Technology tools for artefact creation

Of course, there are far more artefacts and activities to showcase learning that a teacher could ask a student to complete digitally. The above, however, should give a flavour of what is possible in the three main domains of text, mixed media and video. If you want more, flick back to chapter 6 (in particular, table 6.3), where we covered this in more detail.

The key to success with learning is, as we know, to ensure timely assessment and feedback. To support this, schools need a good assessment workflow solution. The next three case studies showcase workflows and ecosystems that support feedback across the three technology giants that schools choose to adopt, namely, Google, Microsoft and Apple.

A key takeaway that you'll discover in the first case study reinforces the principle of 'context' as part of our 5 Cs approach. While the core ecosystem is Google **Workspace**, 'we do not adopt a "one size fits all" approach. Our schools have complete flexibility in terms of the technology they use so they can tailor it to their own priorities.'

Emma Darcy (@darcyprior on X) is a former director of Technology for Learning at the Chiltern Learning Trust and director of technology for learning at Denbigh High School. A National Teaching Award Winner and Global EdTech 'Most Impactful Senior Member of Staff' award winner in 2023, Emma is a careful, yet innovative leader in education, renowned for her work around impactful digital strategy, particularly in supporting initiatives that are grounded in sustainability.

Case study: Emma Darcy
How we embedded our Digital Strategy at Denbigh High School and Chiltern Learning Trust

It took ten years to develop the Digital Strategy at Denbigh High School and Chiltern Learning Trust. I always mention both as during that time I had a dual role as director of technology for learning. I worked on the leadership team at Denbigh (as I still do), and also led and supported digital strategy at the other fifteen schools in the trust. This placed me in a unique position to experience the best of both worlds. I created a technology for learning strategy at central team level, while I also experienced first-hand the impact this had on our schools. During that time, there were several key initiatives we introduced at an early stage, first at Denbigh and then more widely across the trust which, looking back, were crucial to our success.

- We standardised the infrastructure and platform across all of our trust schools and central team. This meant moving all staff and students to Google Workspace.
- We made the effective use of technology a priority on both our Denbigh School improvement plan and our trust development plan to ensure it became a fundamental part of school improvement.
- We audited everything and everyone across our schools, not just the technology and infrastructure that was already in place, but also staff skills, confidence levels, CPD requirements and what access our learners had to technology at home.
- We made Google **Classroom** our core tool for the receiving of work from students and for assessing and feeding back to them.

- We made the effective use of technology a core part of the CPD programme for all staff, including support staff.
- We ran a year-long pilot at Denbigh to evaluate the impact of a one-to-one device model before introducing this as an optional (but highly successful) parental purchase scheme.
- We introduced 'no-cost' initiatives such as student digital leaders to support staff and the Apps For Good Programme (www.appsforgood.org) to bring tech industry engagement into the school and trust.

Ian Stonnell, assistant headteacher at Denbigh High School commented:

'Technology for learning has had a huge impact on the way we set homework at Denbigh. Using Google Classroom, we can give clear instructions, share resources and provide scaffolds that can support our students to complete homework independently. We can also set deadlines that help students prioritise their homework and completion. Furthermore, through Google Classroom, there are a range of ways we can provide meaningful feedback either using verbal recordings, or automated marking in **Forms** or **Rubrics** to mark written work. This has impacted on reducing teacher workload and has had a massive improvement in the rate of student completion of homework as well as homework quality.'

All the trust schools are different with diverse demographics and, with the exception of Google **Workspace**, we do not adopt a 'one size fits all' approach. The schools have flexibility in terms of the technology they use so they can tailor it to their own priorities. There are always going to be staff who are more 'tech-phobic' than others but, in my experience, the pandemic hastened the move to digital systems and we made a conscious decision to keep that momentum going.

I also developed our own evidence-informed practice within the trust by sharing what worked well in the schools that are more digitally mature. Critically, I ensured we were outward-facing, and utilised our previous membership of the DfE EdTech Demonstrator Programme along with conferences and visits to raise our awareness of the exemplary pedagogy in other schools and trusts.

Two years ago, we made a conscious decision to develop our technology for learning strategy in line with our climate change and sustainability strategy. The need to move to an increasingly paperless environment, coupled with the reduced carbon footprint of a mobile device as opposed to a desktop machine, made this synergy both inevitable and entirely appropriate. Sustainability leads were appointed in all trust schools, and we introduced climate change education through the Apps For Good 'Innovate for Climate Change Programme'. We were also one of the founding members of the Bedfordshire School sustainability network (https://beds.ukssn.org). Furthermore, we evolved our one-to-one device scheme so that five trees are now planted across the globe every time a Chromebook is purchased. In April 2023, we organised our first climate change and digital innovation summit (#CCADIS) in Luton, giving students from every school in the trust the opportunity to present their climate change app ideas from the Apps For Good programme to industry experts.

The emergence of AI is now one of my current focuses and at Denbigh High School we are meeting this revolution head-on. As a school, we introduced an AI steering group to keep pace with the rapid developments in this area and support training for both staff and students. Fundamental to this, we have been developing our digital character curriculum for students as we educate our young people on the appropriate use of this fast-moving technology and the imperative to always keep a human 'in the loop'.

Emma's case study is worthy of reflection, as we can unpick some key elements that will be helpful to others seeking to replicate the success at Denbigh and the trust:

1. **Strategic standardisation and infrastructure alignment:** Strategically standardising the infrastructure across the trust ensures consistency in key areas of communication, collaboration and education resources management. This helps reinforce the importance of a strategic approach to a cohesive digital environment that supports effective workflow, not just with assessment but with trust-wide activities.

2. **Prioritise technology in school improvement plans:** By integrating the effective use of technology into their school and trust's improvement and development plans, the trust is able to highlight the significance of technology as a core component of work within the various schools. This is important, as it ensures that technology integration isn't just a bolt-on, but is recognised and shared as a fundamental aspect of improving teaching and learning outcomes.

3. **Leverage core tools for pedagogical efficacy:** Adopting a central tool in Google **Classroom** for assignment submission, assessment and feedback streamlines processes. This makes training and sharing about what works simpler and means that the trust and the schools within it move forward as one. It isn't about one tool being better than any other, but by selecting that one tool, they gain the

benefits of utilising core tools that align with their educational and operational goals.

4. **Comprehensive audits for tailored CPD:** Conducting audits on technology, infrastructure and, critically, staff skills and CPD needs, allowed the development of targeted professional development. By doing this, the trust was able to see the current state of technology alongside its use and the competence of use – clearly working as part of the first 3 Cs of competence, confidence and cognisance of what works within their chosen tools. By approaching this strategically, colleagues are able to be supported with effective, personalised training that addresses specific needs and gaps, while simultaneously supporting learners with their needs.

5. **Innovation and sustainability:** The focus on aligning their strategy with climate change and sustainability initiatives helps to address many topical and relevant environmental concerns. Additionally, with so many schools seeking to reduce their carbon footprint while potentially saving on energy costs, there is much to take away and learn from considering sustainable approaches when considering your whole-school or trust digital strategy.

In our next case study, we hear from Olly's former colleague at the Thomas Deacon Educational Trust, Claire Rouse. As someone Mark has worked with too, Claire is passionate in her desire to integrate technology in both her practice and across the wider school and trust. Equally passionate about teaching and learning, Claire's approaches are always informed by what works best for learning and teaching, while seeking to innovate, reduce workload and improve the quality of assessment and feedback for learners. Claire (@MrsRouse17 on X) is the assistant principal at the Thomas Deacon Academy, part of the Thomas Deacon Education Trust.

Claire supported Olly during the digital transformation process at the Thomas Deacon Education trust, where Microsoft **Teams** and **OneNote Class Notebook** are now pivotal tools for sharing learning materials in the moment and for receiving artefacts for assessment.

Case study: Claire Rouse
Tools within Microsoft to support teaching and learning

Over the past two years, I have worked with Microsoft tools to support and enhance teaching and learning across my academy, utilising both Microsoft **Teams** and **OneNote** to facilitate workflow solutions, improving staff wellbeing and student accessibility.

As part of our blended learning approach, following the COVID-19 pandemic, we moved all staff and students to the real-world platform of **Teams** as a 'one-stop shop' to support learning. Predominantly, we used the features of **Posts**, **Teams**, **Files** and **Assignments** to help support blended learning, and this way of working continues to this day.

The partnership between staff and students grew digitally and, in September 2022, I was able to introduce OneNote to teaching staff; empowering them to build and set up their Class Notebooks to use with students. This was a game-changer, not only for offering student resources but also in terms of how staff personalised learning, balanced workloads and offered feedback.

I set up my Class Notebooks, personalising folders and using sections to organise different schemes of work and topics. I use OneNote to store and organise digital resources, such as literary texts and my own **PowerPoints**, so I have utilised resources from across the years, rather than rewriting planning. Each student has their section within the class notebook and within that section, I share documents with students through class distribution; this helps them to stay organised and for me to personalise their learning, differentiating lessons as needed.

Students can work together in OneNote on group projects. The collaboration space allows students to work in real-time, even if students are not in the same location, permitting a more collaborative approach to learning without the need to change seating plans in the classroom. This allows me, as a teacher, to support students remotely, both in class and at home, to monitor the level of work being completed by each one, offering support and guidance individually, either through written annotation or using audio feedback (another great feature!), as OneNote details which students have contributed to the work, so you have a clearer idea of student progress.

Other features I have found that enhanced the overall student learning are the use of digital inking and the ability to use OneNote as a whiteboard, which never erases! You can annotate texts alongside the class and adapt the texts for individuals by using the inclusivity tools, which has supported my EAL and SEND learners.

OneNote has enabled us, as an academy, to build on independent study in the sixth form. Its digital study booklets will be used academy-wide with the sixth form and are now embedded in our home-learning policies, utilising digital study-sessions booklets across all sixth-form lessons to bridge the gap between in-class and home learning (a digital personalised booklet which saves on reprographics too!). The digital booklets include features such as the subject handbooks, lessons, additional revision tasks for all aspects of their course and wider reading. It is expected that all A-Level students complete the tasks weekly, based on the in-class focus. This has enabled me to set pre-reading and independent tasks without the need for photocopying, and allows me to mark and offer individual feedback quickly through the Class Notebook tab. It's quick and easy to see who has completed the tasks set and I can offer the students feedback in real time, while they are working on a project.

At the end of last year, using Microsoft **Forms**, I asked my Year 11 students to give me their feedback on the useability of OneNote and its impact on their learning. Here are just a few of the comments I received from my students:

> 'OneNote has been very accessible and has allowed for me to gain feedback very quickly with knowing immediately what to improve on. It also is much faster to access than the use of paper that gets lost amidst the piles of work.' Izzah (Year 11)

> 'I enjoyed using technology for learning because it made my revision for English more efficient and better. Also, using technology meant I could take shorter notes in class (which meant revision for my actual GCSE exams was faster and more time-efficient) and if I needed to look at the topic in more detail, I could access the lessons on Teams.' Saher (Year 11)

OneNote has certainly changed how I use technology for teaching and learning. I use it as a vehicle to ensure learning is consistent across classes and that students feel confident in my ability to support and guide their learning. I have been able to offer much more personalised guidance, while also balancing my teacher workload and this, in turn, has enabled me to scale my successes to that of other members of teaching staff across the school.

As with Darcy's case study, there are some great reflections and takeaways from what Rouse has shared. Interestingly, despite different ecosystems, there are many similarities.

1. **Centralisation of the learning platform:** Moving to Microsoft **Teams**, which offered (similar to Google **Workspace** with Google **Classroom**) a 'one-stop shop' for learning, demonstrates the value of a centralised platform where staff, students and linked colleagues can easily access resources, assignments and communication tools. Simplifying and unifying the learning environment into one place and space makes activities both more manageable and accessible for all stakeholders. It also makes it easier for supporting staff CPD and for the central IT team to support when needed.
2. **Enhanced personalisation and organisation:** The introduction of OneNote allowed for significant personalisation in teaching and learning. By organising resources, schemes of work and those all-important individual sections for students, Rouse and her colleagues can tailor resources and experiences to meet diverse needs, supporting adaptive teaching, instruction and independent learning.
3. **Facilitation of collaborative learning:** The collaboration space of **OneNote** enables students to work and learn together in real time, regardless of their location. This helps with a variety of teaching and learning activities such as group work or peer feedback. It also supports peer interaction without the constraint of the physical classroom or timetabled lessons, meaning learning and collaboration can happen beyond the school day.
4. **Remote support and feedback:** The ability to monitor student work digitally, rather than waiting to collect in a physical book, means teachers can provide support in more timely ways. Additionally, that feedback can be done in ways that support teacher workload reduction (audio feedback) as well as in more traditional ways (inking and annotations), which enhances student–teacher interaction. These features help to ensure feedback is timely and personalised and aids students' progress by being so – a bit like Hattie said it should be (remember that quote?!).
5. **Professional development:** The case study highlights (like Darcy's) the importance of strategic professional development in the best way to use technology to promote positive impacts on teachers' workload and wellbeing. By reinforcing the importance of strategic continuous training and support, Rouse illustrates how confidence, competence

and cognisance of using these tools consistently within their context led to enhanced teaching methodologies and a more manageable workload for colleagues which, ultimately (and most importantly), helps with learning and progress across the school.

Lastly, but by no means least, we have John Jones, Director of Innovation at the RGS Worcester Family of Schools, sharing how staff there manage learning using **Showbie**. John is an Apple Distinguished Educator and Bett judge and can be found on X as @MrJones_Edu.

Case study: John Jones
Showbie at the RGS Worcester Family of Schools

In 2014, the RGS Worcester Family of Schools (RGSW) launched its digital learning programme (DLP) which involved one-to-one iPad provision for all pupils from Year 1 to Year 13, and an iPad and MacBook for each teacher. Our DLP has transformed the teaching and learning environments across our schools, helping us to personalise and adapt our pedagogy to the interests and needs of individual classes and pupils, reduce teacher workload and prepare pupils for their future. At the very heart of the programme is our workflow solution, **Showbie**.

From the very start, the relationship between RGSW and Showbie has been incredibly positive. Once it was rolled out across the schools and after an initial introductory training period, staff were soon able to access, navigate and use the software with ease. Chris Smith, our IT services manager, remembers that teachers took to Showbie well, saying:

> 'It wasn't long before teachers started to notice a real difference in their workload when they used Showbie effectively.'

Indeed, teachers across RGSW quickly discovered that it was starting to allow staff to focus more time, attention and effort on supporting pupils' academic and wellbeing needs. Speaking about their experience with Showbie, Matt Warne, head of digital learning and computing at RGS The Grange confirmed:

> 'Showbie saves us a huge amount of time. It makes the tracking, collecting of work, marking and feedback much quicker while massively reducing the need to spend time doing administrative tasks like scanning and photocopying.'

The platform has allowed teachers to easily share resources and lesson plans across classes, saving time on planning and preparation while still accommodating the individual requirements of each class. It has also made it easier to track attainment and progress by collecting all work in one central location. Teachers across the schools have been particularly impressed with how Showbie supports individual interventions and assessments. Head of computer science at RGS Dodderhill, Michelle Parton, explained:

> 'Showbie allows us to form a class overview from which we can ascribe tasks to individual pupils, if necessary, as a way of supporting and "scaffolding" their learning. For assessments, the incorporation of Socrative into the platform is brilliant as it allows us to set quick assessments to check progress with all results automatically collected alongside the students' other work stored on Showbie.'

Furthermore, for our Family of Schools, Showbie works as an incredibly effective tool to facilitate better communication with pupils and personalised learning, ultimately helping them become more engaged. Deputy head at RGS Springfield, Ian Griffin, commented:

> 'Using Showbie, alongside other digital tools, I can communicate with the classroom without interruption. I can provide tailored and meaningful one-to-one feedback, where pupils can respond individually, and I don't have to use classroom time to follow up on homework.'

During the COVID-19 pandemic, Showbie became even more indispensable to the RGS Worcester Family of Schools as an essential component of delivering remote learning. As a familiar platform, both our pupils and teachers found the transition and adjustment to full remote learning relatively easy, with our pre-existing digital culture playing a significant part in keeping learning alive. Throughout the lockdowns, Showbie's feedback functions were incredibly useful, allowing the continuation of personalised responses for each pupil. The support of their teachers in a recognisable manner helped to mitigate and prevent learning loss during a time of significant interruption to regular school life. Indeed, parents who suddenly had to play a much greater role in their children's learning noted what a 'powerful tool' Showbie is.

With many aspects of the learning process coordinated via Showbie, pupil engagement has increased. Additional feedback tools such as voice notes, recordings of lesson examples and other resources allow students to access teaching in a manner which best suits their requirements. Furthermore, the ability to use Showbie in conjunction with a digital stylus has revolutionised the feedback loop for many of our teachers. These factors have been particularly impressive when addressing pupils' weaker areas in a more efficient and personal way, with the option of also providing individual comments within shared work documents.

For all teachers and pupils across the RGS Worcester Family of Schools, Showbie has become an integral part of everyday teaching and learning, with many staff members now qualified as Showbie Certified Educators. Forming a core part of our education delivery, Showbie plays a pivotal role in our commitment to providing the best learning experiences for our students – offering engaging and flexible content while reducing teacher workload. It has become an irreplaceable part of RGSW life, with teachers claiming they 'would be lost without Showbie!' As Rebecca Roberts-Gawen, academic deputy head at RGS Worcester puts it:

> 'Teachers love Showbie! It's part of their "must-have toolkit"! It's a planner, a resource manager, a communication system and more. We have data that underlines how critical Showbie is for everyday practice across all RGS Schools – it's simply the most vital part of our digital workflow.'

As with Darcy and Rouse's case studies, it's also important to unpick the key elements of Jones' case study:

1. **Strategic standardisation and infrastructure alignment:** Standardising the approaches used at RGSW as part of its one-to-one provision, centred around a standard workflow solution, has had significant benefits: 'it's simply the most vital part of our digital workflow'.

2. **Prioritise technology in school improvement plans:** Deciding to prioritise technology with its DLP, RGSW has 'transformed the teaching and learning environments across our schools'. The long-standing implementation brought significant benefits during the COVID-19 pandemic; however, the centralised workflow of Showbie meant that remote learning was simply an extension of what the schools were already doing. Studies suggest (Abumalloh et al., 2021) schools that had robust ecosystems, device programmes and workflow solutions also performed better when thinking about learning loss, just as was experienced by RGSW. Reports from organisations such as the OECD (OECD, 2022) also highlight the advantages of pre-existing digital infrastructure in facilitating remote learning that mitigated learning disruptions.

3. **Effective workload management:** The adoption of Showbie significantly reduced administrative tasks for teachers, a benefit also shared by Rouse in her case study and Darcy in her trust's move to

go paperless. The benefits shared by Jones highlight the benefit of workflow solutions in streamlining teaching processes and enhancing teachers' efficiency.

4. **Enhanced communication and feedback:** As with others, Jones' case study highlights how the platform supports one-to-one feedback without disrupting classroom time, again reducing that all-important feedback loop.
5. **Personalised learning and feedback:** The workflow supports individual interventions and assessments that showcase the platform's ability to support personalised learning and helpful feedback. The platform enables teachers to tailor content and feedback to each student's requirements, which has helped to foster a more engaged and supportive learning environment.

The case studies help demonstrate and reinforce several key messages we've shared within the book, including two of our most important ones:

1. Competence, confidence, cognisance, consistency and context are key.
2. 'It ain't (so much) what you do, it's the way that you do it, and that's what gets results.'

When you compare the three case studies, there are some striking similarities in each, despite there being three distinctly different ecosystems in play. While Chiltern has Google **Workspace**, Thomas Deacon has Microsoft and RGSW has Apple utilising **Showbie** as its workflow, it's the commonalities that help ensure success.

All three case studies highlight the importance of the strategic integration of technology to enhance learning. Some of those key benefits shared include:

- reduction of teacher workload
- personalised learning and feedback
- enhanced teacher–student communication
- support for remote and blended learning
- increased student engagement
- streamlined resource sharing and collaboration.

Based on the insights shared from the three case studies, it is clear that, beyond some of the common benefits, there are some common approaches which are also worthy of note:

- implementation of a comprehensive digital strategy

- provision of devices and technology access
- strategic professional development and training
- streamlining administrative processes
- enhancing communication and collaboration tools
- supporting personalised and inclusive learning.

We covered these things in some detail in chapter 4 and, if you're looking for more on ways to create your digital strategy, you could do worse than check out the freely available *Guide to Creating a Digital Strategy in Education*[1] that Mark co-authored with Al Kingsley.

The key takeaway, we hope, is that if you want to have an impact with technology in your classroom, school or trust/district, you need to consider the things shared in this chapter.

Top tips

Mark's top tips

1. Keep it simple. By adopting well-established solutions that work within your ecosystem, you are more likely to achieve success.

2. Effective and supportive CPD is essential, and not just for teachers. Ensuring students and their parents/guardians know how work is collected, assessed and fed back on, is fundamental to success.

3. Ensure whatever you do, you aim to prioritise equality of access, accessibility and inclusivity in your strategy. If your users can't use it, it won't be used!

Olly's top tips

1. Consider how your systems can drive efficiency and effectiveness by saving every user time which can be better spent on other activities.

2. Make the development of technology a core part of your school/trust improvement plan, so that it is fundamental to your overall development objectives.

3. Audit, audit, audit. I know, it sounds accountable, but in reality if you don't measure and have your finger on the pulse, how will you know if you are heading in the intended direction of your strategy?

---

[1] www.netsupportsoftware.com/digital-strategy

CHAPTER 16
Online safety and digital citizenship

'Online safety and positive digital citizenship should be everyone's concern – because it is everyone's responsibility.'

Olly Lewis

Online safety is, as Olly says above, a strand that has such importance that it is everyone's responsibility within your educational setting. Just as the core aspects of the curriculum of spelling, grammar, numeracy and safeguarding run through every subject, so should online safety and digital citizenship.

We're all (hopefully) aware of the annual Safer Internet Day (www.saferinternetday.org) activity which has been running for many years. Annual focus or celebration days are important for shining a spotlight on many things but, as Mark always shares, 'Every day should be a safer internet day' because, well, it should!

Another issue that we both often see in schools is that online safety and digital citizenship are seen as things that only fall within the remit of the ICT or computing departments. This simply isn't true. In the same way that we are all teachers of literacy and numeracy, teachers have collective responsibility for online safety and digital citizenship, as highlighted in the 2024 'Keeping children safe in education' (KCSIE) statutory guidance (DfE, 2024a) which says, 'safeguarding and promoting the welfare of children is everyone's responsibility'.

'Children' includes everyone under the age of 18. Everyone who comes into contact with children and their families has a role to play. To fulfil this responsibility effectively, all practitioners should make sure their approach is child-centred. This means that they should consider, at all times, what is in the best interests of the child. Therefore, just like with literacy and numeracy, we should be strong role models and advocates of safe online practices, whether that's on our own social media, sharing on our blogs or wherever.

When a child sees you shopping in the supermarket at the weekend (or anywhere else for that matter), you don't stop being 'Miss X' or 'Mr Y' (although we did chuckle writing this, as children are often amazed that you actually have a life and exist outside of your classroom and/or school office). You are always a teacher and always 'on show'. Therefore, it should be the case that your behaviour in online places and spaces should mirror the professional conduct practices you adhere to in real life.

In this chapter, we share insights into best practices around online safety, the importance of digital citizenship, and the nuanced areas that fall within these two domains. Just like technology in education is too important (and expensive) to leave to chance, the safeguarding of young people is even more so.

16.1 Online safety

The Cambridge Dictionary defines 'online' as 'connected to and shared by a system of computers, especially the internet'[1] – and 'safety' as a 'state of being safe from harm or danger'.[2]

Children today are growing up surrounded by technology and the vast expanse of the internet, not to mention AI. While the online world presents incredible opportunities for learning, entertainment, exploration and communication, it also exposes young minds to a myriad of challenges and risks. It is therefore crucial that we, as educators, actively advocate for comprehensive education on online safety for children so that we empower them to safely navigate the virtual landscape.

'All staff'

As you'll know from reading this book, we are huge advocates for the use of technology. Reinforcing the importance of all in education being mindful of these areas, it was great to see in the 2023 update to the KCSIE guidance (DfE, 2024a) that it is now statutorily required that all staff must receive annual training and support in online safety and safeguarding – and, while not a requirement, we would advocate that digital citizenship and digital literacy also be a requirement. While the KCSIE guidance is aimed specifically at schools in England, the advice contained within is good practice wherever in the world you are. We recommend that all

---

[1] https://dictionary.cambridge.org/dictionary/english-arabic/online
[2] https://dictionary.cambridge.org/dictionary/english-arabic/safety

schools commit to annual training of both safeguarding and online safety as a bare minimum.

If you want a global opinion on this, the ISTE standards for educators[3] and students[4] have many similarities, showing a high level of demand for learning around digital citizenship, literacy and practice.

The KCSIE guidance (DfE, 2024a) contains some key points to ensure that schools have processes in place to protect students, including:

- All staff have to receive annual training on online safety.
- All schools need a clear policy for online safety.
- Schools need to meet the relevant standards for cybersecurity and appropriate monitoring and filtering systems.

The other key guidance that England's Department for Education shares is its 'Meeting digital and technology standards in schools and colleges' (DfE, 2022) manual, which communicates important aspects in a number of key relevant areas, particularly:

- cybersecurity
- governance standards
- filtering and monitoring standards

…alongside a number of technical key standards relating to levels of quality of your hardware and infrastructure.

The guidance helps emphasise effective and appropriate policies and processes linked to safeguarding children and works well alongside KCSIE. It emphasises continuous improvement, monitoring and review of practices that are key to safeguarding young people.

Building staff confidence

Many teachers lack confidence in raising issues around online safety (Vibert, 2023). The reasons are broad – from feeling unsure about technology due to its fast pace of development, to the curriculum already being crowded – so how can they find the time to squeeze it in? The best way to ensure teachers gain confidence is through professional learning opportunities and for there to be clear guidelines from within a setting on what to do when a concern is raised.

---

[3] https://iste.org/standards/educators
[4] https://iste.org/standards/students

Clear policy and approaches on this should be shared by leadership. Just as many will know the 'tell, explain, describe' (TED) approach around what to do when a child discloses, similar approaches around the difficult topics in this chapter should be shared with colleagues so that they know what to do when something happens.

Websites about staying safe online

To stay in the loop on the latest online safety developments and build your confidence and knowledge about the area, here are some useful websites you can refer to.

Name of resource	URL	Summary
Cyber Streetwise	www.cyberstreetwise.com	Offers practical advice and tips for secure online behaviour and protection against threats.
Get Safe Online	www.getsafeonline.org	Comprehensive resource for free expert advice on online safety for individuals and businesses.
Thinkuknow	www.thinkuknow.co.uk	Education programme from the National Crime Agency for online safety and protection for children.
e-Safety Adviser	www.esafety-adviser.com	Alan Mackenzie's superb website with a plethora of resources and an indispensable newsletter.
Internet Matters	www.internetmatters.org	A platform for helping parents keep their children safe online, offering tools, resources and advice.
Internet Watch Foundation	www.iwf.org.uk	A charity that works to remove child sexual exploitation and related content from the internet. It has lots of resources around online safety and safeguarding.

Table 16.1: Websites about staying safe online

16.2 Digital citizenship

Digital citizenship aims to equip students (and others in education) with the skills and knowledge to participate fully in society, both on and offline.

A great digital citizenship framework that has been developed over many years is the International Society for Technology in Education (ISTE) standards.[5] Available for students, educators, education leaders and coaches, the standards embed digital citizenship across the various strands and also have an explicit unit which focuses on what it is to be a good digital citizen. These can broadly be classified as understanding how to use technology effectively, ethically and safely. Mike Patterson, an ISTE contributor, shares the nine themes of digital citizenship (Patterson, 2015):

1. **Access:** Full electronic participation in society.
2. **Commerce:** Electronic buying and selling of goods.
3. **Communication:** Electronic exchange of information.
4. **Literacy:** Process of teaching and learning about technology and the use of technology.
5. **Etiquette:** Electronic standards of conduct or procedure.
6. **Law:** Electronic responsibility for actions and deeds.
7. **Rights and responsibilities:** Those freedoms extended to everyone in a digital world.
8. **Health and wellness:** Physical and psychological wellbeing in a digital technology world.
9. **Security (self-protection):** Electronic precautions to guarantee safety.

These nine themes provide a clear framework for educators to think about how both they and young people engage in the online world as digital citizens.

For example, in a world of fake news and the increasing use of AI, digital citizenship promotes the ideas of engaging respectfully and critically with technology and being highly mindful of our digital footprint – the premise being that whatever we do online leaves a footprint behind. Fake news impacts us all and ensuring children are critical consumers of the content they see online is essential, particularly with the ease with which lifelike content, video and imagery can be generated now with AI.

---

[5] https://iste.org/standards

Digital citizenship also includes ensuring an awareness of the rights and responsibilities that come with interacting online – encouraging people to be informed, engaged and responsible digital citizens who can navigate the digital world safely and thoughtfully, and make positive contributions to their communities (whether online or offline).

Online safety and digital citizenship go hand in hand. It's important that we recognise where and when we need to apply the knowledge they offer us – areas such as cybersecurity, social media use and the consumption and use of online tools and services. A collective and collegiate approach is necessary.

These online resources contain a wealth of information on both online safety and digital citizenship and are a great starting point for expanding your knowledge.

Name of resource	URL	Summary
South West Grid for Learning (SWGfL)	www.swgfl.org.uk	Provides resources for safe and effective use of technology in education and safeguarding.
National College Online Safety	www.nationalcollege.com/categories/online-safety	Offers online safety training courses for educators to enhance their understanding and practices.
ISTE Digital Citizenship	www.iste.org/digital-citizenship	Focuses on empowering students to think critically and use technology responsibly and effectively.
Childnet International	www.childnet.com	Dedicated to making the internet a safe space for children through education and resources.
Be Internet Awesome	https://beinternetawesome.withgoogle.com/en_us	Google's program for teaching children the fundamentals of digital citizenship and safety online.
Common Sense Education	www.commonsense.org/education/articles/23-great-lesson-plans-for-internet-safety	Offers a collection of lesson plans to educate students on navigating the internet safely.

Table 16.2: Websites to support teaching online safety and digital citizenship

16.3 What should we be worried about?

Parents and teachers alike worry about:

- exposure to inappropriate content
- cyberbullying
- privacy risks
- contact with strangers and grooming
- screen time and addiction
- impact on mental health
- misinformation and radicalisation
- online scams
- academic dishonesty
- legal and ethical concerns

...and more.

In a landscape where technology is advancing so quickly, it is difficult for parents and teachers to know what platforms and new tools are out there and what children are using them for and doing on them. We feel schools are engaging in curricula that are supporting these endeavours well, recognising the importance of working closely with parents or guardians of young people within that institution on topics around online safety and digital citizenship.

There is a lot of research (Butler et al., 2022) to suggest that good relationships between a school and the students' parents have a positive impact on supporting children's wellbeing, behaviour and progress. Positive relationships with parents are key to a child's wellbeing, as they contribute to fostering a supportive environment for the child's development. Taking that on board, a good approach to provide support to help children to navigate their online world safely is to hold digital parenting sessions where schools can answer questions parents may have and run training sessions about online safety, digital citizenship and all of its many facets, many of which we will discuss.

One activity Mark has engaged in with schools that he has supported in this area is to survey children to find out about their perspectives on the online world. Asking them for examples about their and their parents' use of technology often brings many smiles but also sparks interesting conversations around screen time, acceptable use, role modelling and much more.

Whichever way you look at it, everyone plays a part in students' online safety and anything we, as educators, can do to provide support for children in the communities we serve will always be beneficial.

Grooming

Grooming is an activity where an adult builds a relationship with a child with the intention to manipulate, exploit or abuse them, often in sexual contexts. Groomers will disguise their true identities and intentions, gradually building trust with their targets to isolate them from their real-life support networks. It continues to be a significant issue.

Cambridge-based charity, the Internet Watch Foundation (IWF), works to stop online child sexual abuse. It has found there is now more child sexual abuse imagery being discovered on the open internet than ever before. Its 2022 annual report (IWF, 2022) identified a 60% increase in child exploitation – and in 2023, almost every web page (92%) it worked to remove included self-generated material extorted from children who had been groomed or coerced by predators using webcams (IWF, 2024). These findings bring home the reality of individuals exploiting the anonymity and reach of the internet to connect with vulnerable young people for abusive purposes – and reinforce the importance of vigilance where children are concerned.

While a very difficult subject, the signs of grooming and child sexual exploitation are something we should all be aware of. The NSPCC has some fantastic resources around this for parents and those in loco parentis, such as teachers.[6] Writing this and other sections in this chapter are difficult, given the subject, but it's important to understand what happens and what we can do to mitigate it.

Groomers are clever and manipulative, using approaches that are framed around building trust. A great way that we can help with this, as parents, is to be involved in our children's online lives. As schools, we can educate young people about the signs that someone could be trying to groom them and share the importance of telling a trusted adult when they think something is wrong. As adults, we can look out for tell-tale signs that things *are* wrong, e.g. children using non-age-appropriate language

---

[6] www.nspcc.org.uk/what-is-child-abuse/types-of-abuse/grooming

or changing the way they dress (which is unusual for a child their age). Another sign is children being unusually secretive about their activities online or having money or items that they can't explain and won't have had the money to pay for themselves.

As with many of these things, vigilance and good relationships with young people are the foundation of good support.

Child sexual abuse material

Child sexual abuse material (CSAM) presents a whole new challenge to online safety. AI now enables those with ill intent to impersonate people and generate images and videos of an inappropriate and explicit nature to bully, intimidate or harass people. With the availability and access to AI generators, face cloning is now more accessible and widespread, presenting new safeguarding issues. Alan Mackenzie (mentioned above), known as 'The e-Safety Adviser' talks about this in his blog post on the topic (Mackenzie, 2023).

In the news, we read of young people using AI tools to generate these kinds of materials (Hedgecoe, 2023) and, beyond that, criminals are generating CSAM images/videos too (Tidy, 2023). This poses a significant risk and challenge, given the lasting nature of images/videos that find their way into the public domain. Not to mention when that media is of an explicit nature and involves children, the lasting negative impact it can have on young people and their families is hugely worrying.

It's vital that schools and organisations across the world are aware of the IWF's Report Remove tool and how it can be used to report any CSAM, including AI-generated imagery of children. Schools may even decide to share this tool with Secondary students (it is not appropriate to share it with Primary pupils). The IWF Report Remove can 'support a young person in reporting sexual images or videos shared online and enables them to get the image removed if it is illegal.' You can discover the IWF's Report Remove tool at www.iwf.org.uk/our-technology/report-remove.

A young person can make a report at any time without telling anyone who they are, as their identity isn't linked. Childline[7] also offers ongoing support through its website. Many young people will not report for fear of blame, shame, judgement and/or bullying. This is why the IWF's tool is so valuable; young people can report an issue themselves.

---

[7] www.childline.org.uk/info-advice/bullying-abuse-safety/online-mobile-safety/report-remove

In light of this, the IWF's approach is child-centred and done completely online by the online image/video being given a unique digital fingerprint, known as a hash. In the event of it being illegal, it is then shared with internet companies to prevent further online distribution or uploading of that item. If the young person has a Childline account, Childline will keep them updated and offer further support.

In the same way that they would report a safeguarding concern, Designated Safeguarding Leads (DSLs) should report a CSAM concern using the IWF's Report Remove tool, as well as following their own safeguarding policies. The overarching strategy here should be to educate all stakeholders about the severity and impacts of CSAM and how to find and use the appropriate reporting tools in the event they are needed.

The United Kingdom Council for Internet Safety (UKCIS) has lots of great advice and guidance (UKCIS et al., 2020) on responding to incidents and AI-generated imagery involving children along with safeguarding children and young people. This is another great resource for schools to tap into and even share with parents.

A concerning and worrying trend with the emergence of AI is the issue of 'deepfakes'. A deepfake is an AI-generated image or video which purports to be real but is, in fact, fake. These can be used in a wide variety of nefarious ways, the most concerning of which is CSAM; however, it is advocated that young people learn about deepfakes so that they are savvy to what is presented to them on social media. Discussion points could include the images generated of Taylor Swift supporting Donald Trump's presidency campaign[8] and a helpful example of a deepfake of Morgan Freeman[9] (brilliant for introducing the topic to children). If you are looking for more resources on this, Mark has made some great digital citizenship resources, including ones on deepfakes, which are all available for free at https://classroom.cloud/digital-citizenship.

Cyberbullying

Cyberbullying is the act of bullying online. It can happen in many online spaces, from chat rooms to social media and gaming sites. Online disinhibition (the act of people saying or doing things online that they wouldn't normally do in person) is often a factor here. The fact that perpetrators can't see the person they're being abusive towards can often

---

[8] www.theguardian.com/technology/article/2024/aug/24/trump-taylor-swift-deepfakes-ai
[9] www.youtube.com/watch?v=oxXpB9pSETo

mean they act in ways they probably wouldn't if they were with that person in real life. That said, just as bullying happens in every school, the reality is that it is more likely to happen in online spaces.

Combatting cyberbullying requires a multifaceted approach that should have education right at its heart. Strong digital citizenship programmes share what children should do if cyberbullying occurs – and schools (and parents working closely together) should have systems in place to know how to respond when (not if) these things happen. Just because things might happen outside of school, and often do, the problems from these activities will seep into everyday school life, even if it doesn't involve two (or more) parties from within the school.

Children who are being bullied in real life or online will display similar symptoms. They may be quieter than usual, withdrawn, quick to anger or upset – and whether the bullying is happening inside or outside of school, it shouldn't matter. If these issues are present, it will impact on a child's wellbeing and their learning progress. We should, of course, do everything we can to support young people in these cases.

How technology can help

Your school will have software that filters inappropriate content through your firewall so children cannot access it. There is, however, software you can use that tracks what children type into devices while at school. This helps safeguard them in lots of ways, not just by keeping an eye out for cyberbullying, but also for spotting inappropriate web searches, issues around county lines – all sorts. ('County lines' is the phrase used to describe the ways that gangs use phone lines to traffic drugs from urban to rural areas, recruiting young and other vulnerable people to move the drugs. This is relevant here as often these gangs will use technology to communicate and groom young people into this illegal activity.)

It is also a useful idea to have a 'report a concern' button available to your learners. Some schools have this as a link or button on their school website, or use tools that have the button available as an option on any school device, once logged in. Either way, having a technology solution that helps students type or share their worries with adults within your school is a good thing and something we both recommend considering for any setting.

Gaming

Online games, unfortunately, are sometimes used as a vehicle for grooming. Often (particularly post-pandemic, where many young people turned to online gaming for their social interactions), games provide the opportunity for those with ill intent to disguise their identities to exploit children.

A common recommendation given around gaming is for consoles to be in family areas rather than in children's bedrooms. This helps facilitate parental supervision, and having the devices in an open area helps parents to be actively engaged in the things that interest their children.

Just like films have a rating system for age-appropriateness, games have the Pan European Game Information system (PEGI) rating. We've put together this table to help explain the different ratings alongside some of the popular games that fall under each one.

PEGI rating	Explanation	Examples
PEGI 3	Suitable for all age groups. Games might contain very mild forms of violence in a comical context or a child-friendly setting.	Super Mario Odyssey, Animal Crossing: New Horizons
PEGI 7	May contain non-realistic violence in a child-friendly setting or context, and potentially frightening sounds or horror effects that are not intense.	Mario Kart 8 Deluxe, Splatoon 2
PEGI 12	Games that show slightly more graphic violence towards fantasy characters, non-graphic violence towards human-looking characters, mild sexual innuendo or minimal bad language.	Fortnite, The Legend of Zelda: Breath of the Wild
PEGI 16	Games depicting violence similar to real life, use of explicit language, or use of tobacco, drugs or alcohol.	Assassin's Creed Valhalla, Cyberpunk 2077
PEGI 18	Games featuring depictions of gross violence, motiveless killing, violence towards defenceless characters, explicit sexual activity or drug use.	Grand Theft Auto V (GTA), The Witcher 3: Wild Hunt, Call of Duty

Table 16.3: Game ratings and definitions

In many countries (as in the UK), these age ranges are legally enforceable, so a 12-year-old cannot purchase a PEGI 16-rated game. That isn't to say that parents won't buy them for their children. As parents ourselves, and as teachers of many years, we are aware of children whose parents allow them to engage in games that are rated above their age. This is not something that we can do anything about. However, we feel you must be aware that it happens and the potential impacts it can have on young people who may not be emotionally equipped to deal with some of the things that they see and experience. It can, of course, desensitise children to things such as sex and violence and make them more likely to accept them as normal.

Playing games meant for older audiences can cause nightmares and increased anxiety. Engaging in games with mature themes can impact children's social development, leading to difficulties in distinguishing acceptable social behaviour and potentially harming their interactions with peers and adults. There is also the concern that playing games with aggressive content may teach children that violence is an acceptable problem-solving strategy, potentially increasing aggressive thoughts and behaviours.

As we've mentioned, if you have a concern about a child's behaviour, a good place to start working around ways to support them is by talking with them – and their parents or guardians. Having good relationships with parents and finding out how you can help (or sharing some of the things we've mentioned around the appropriateness of games and the impacts that playing some of them underage can have on children) as part of ongoing digital parenting support is a good place to start.

A good resource to help identify the appropriateness of different games for your child is the **Family Gaming Database**[10] which is populated with independent reviews of different games. The reviews include screenshots, descriptions of the game itself and, helpfully for parents who think a game might be too mature for their child, an alternative suggestion of games which have similar themes and gameplay options.

Social media

Where do we start with social media? It is a huge topic and we can't cover all of the platforms in this chapter! You should know that while many social media apps have an age rating of 13 on the various app stores, this

---

[10] www.familygamingdatabase.com

was never anything to do with a collectively decided age where children are felt to be emotionally mature enough to use them. The truth is that the rating comes from the legacy of the USA's Children's Online Privacy Protection Act, 1998 (Federal Trade Commission, 1998), which states that it is illegal to collect or store the personal information of children under the age of 13.

As we've seen in the UK with the publishing of advisory material on mobile phones in schools (DfE, 2024b), there is increasing pushback about the suitability of smartphones and social media apps for children of school age. Certainly, many of the issues shared in this chapter would be mitigated if children didn't have access to technologies which can put them in vulnerable situations.

Advertising

Social media, artificial intelligence, gaming and XR present some risk to all who use them, not just young people. We need to recognise that these places, spaces and technologies are mostly created to generate revenue for businesses. They say there's no such thing as a free lunch and, when it comes to 'free' digital platforms, we pay with our privacy and our data. Companies use these to help curate information to help provide advertising.

In 2021, 44% of all global spending on advertising was with Meta[11] and Alphabet[12]-owned businesses. Facebook, Instagram and YouTube are machines to maximise engagement time on the platform to sell more advertising.

In 2023, Snapchat launched its 'My AI' chatbot (Snap Newsroom, 2023). As of 11 June 2023, two months after its launch and based on Snapchat's internal data, 150 million people sent over 10 billion messages to My AI, making it one of the largest consumer chatbots at the time. While many report that children use it purely for advice and help with their homework, it does beg the question: if children are using this kind of tool for education, what other questions are they asking it and what responses is it giving to them?

We cannot expect social media companies to act in children's best interests; they work in the best interests of their shareholders. They simply want to keep their users on their platforms as long as possible

---

[11] Facebook, Instagram, Threads and other platforms owned by Meta.
[12] The company that owns Google and all its subsidiaries.

to place ads in front of them. We would like to see more support and transparency around tools such as these.

Addiction

Social media is engineered to be as addictive as possible. Features such as infinite scrolling (with platforms sharing content they know you enjoy watching so you never reach the end of your feed) and algorithms designed to keep you on the platform as long as possible (to push advertising to you) make it difficult for you to put down your phone.

Young people often have what is known as FOMO (fear of missing out) in the notification-driven world, where there is even now such a thing as phantom pocket vibration syndrome (Henderson, 2016). This is the condition where people falsely feel that their mobile phone is vibrating or buzzing when it is not. This phenomenon is commonly associated with the overuse of mobile phones and can be characterised as a tactile hallucination, where the brain interprets a vibration that does not exist.

For young people who love all the likes, follows, reposts and everything else about social media that help give an adrenaline rush, it's a difficult world to navigate. Couple that with influencers sharing their perfect, glossy, airbrushed, filtered and photoshopped lives that are impossible to emulate, and there is a lot there that can make young people feel anxious, depressed and lonely. Remember that this can be a hive for cyberbullying and trolling.

Wellbeing

Studies have shown that social media use can lead to decreased attention spans, increased anxiety and lower self-esteem in young people (Deitchman, 2021).

There have been big pushes to ban mobile phones in schools. Many schools have been on top of this for a long time, but there are still significant issues surrounding their use, the impacts they can have on learning and the knock-on effects of their use on student wellbeing.

Social media can offer some benefits and opportunities to inform young people on learning about health issues and have a range of positive impacts on their health and wellbeing behaviours. It can also provide valuable opportunities to help them connect with friends and cope with problems. That said, the negative side effects give big cause for concern, with some significant drawbacks. Prolonged and active use of social media has been consistently linked with negative impacts on mental health (Zsila and Reyes, 2023), including increased feelings of anxiety, depression and stress among teens and students. The immediacy and pervasiveness of social media can exacerbate these issues, as students may engage almost constantly, leading to overexposure to stressors and negative feedback loops.

On top of this, the influence of social media on self-esteem, body image, misogyny, radicalisation and more have led to platforms potentially contributing to unrealistic body standards, engagement in inappropriate activities and unhelpful repetition of poor language or sexist or racist tropes pervaded by the popularisation of certain influencers on social media.

Mobile technology can make it difficult for young people to focus on tasks and can lead to multitasking, which can also be detrimental to learning. The constant stimulation of social media and mobile technology can make it difficult for them to relax and de-stress, which can also impact their ability to learn.

The combination of these factors makes for a heady and unhelpful mix, influencing developing minds and ultimately impacting young people's relationships, engagements with others and, of course, their wellbeing.

Stats

Almost all children use social media. Ofcom's 2023 Children & Parents: Media Use & Attitudes report (Ofcom, 2023) shared that:

- Nine in ten young people have at least one profile on social media.
- Half of teenagers have a device.
- One-third (32%) of children aged 8–17 years old believe all or most of what they see on social media is accurate and true.
- 23% of children aged 12–17 who claimed to be confident in their ability to spot fake profiles failed to identify profiles as fake. This overconfidence in their ability leaves them in a position of potential vulnerability.
- 75% of children aged 12–17 could recognise influencer online paid partnerships (read paid promotions) by Millie Bobby Brown (12 August 2022).[13] Yet, 30% thought that the influencer was likely posting to their feed as the product was *cool* or *good to use*.

---

[13] www.instagram.com/p/ChK6JmePOyg

- On average, across the UK, 33% of children aged 8–17 who go online have seen something worrying or nasty.

Most young people are drawn to social media but, just as we know metacognition and self-regulation are important in supporting teaching and learning, they are also useful here.

Digital citizenship programmes that are mindful of sharing about this, screen time and how to use these places and spaces responsibly, can hopefully help young people to mitigate risk and use these tools with an open mind and a critical lens, mindful of the issues these sites present.

Digital footprint

It is important at this point to highlight that all online activity leaves a digital footprint. Sometimes this is referred to as your 'electronic footprint' or 'digital shadow'. This is the trail of data you leave whenever you interact online, whether it's visiting websites, interacting on social media, sending emails, any information you submit, posts you share, newsletters you subscribe to, and so on.

Your digital footprint can be mindfully added to but it can also be less obvious that you are contributing to it, e.g. accepting cookies from a website you visit or the data you share with your favourite apps being sold on and shared with third parties. In the worst case, your personal data could be compromised as part of a data breach.

Your digital footprint can be used in ways many of us don't fully realise the implications of, from tracking your online activities or your device, to employers checking potential employees' social media accounts, to cyber criminals targeting you with phishing attacks, to misrepresentation of a person – and more.

It's always worthwhile reminding children (and ourselves!) that many of the apps and games we use on our mobile devices track and use personal data to whatever ends technology companies want, as agreed to in the terms and conditions. Take the game Pokémon Go, for example: in its terms and conditions, it states the company has the right to your geo-data, to track the use of other apps on your phone, the websites you visit and even other devices you connect to on your home network. Be mindful of what you give permission for. As we have previously shared, if something is free, you are often paying for it with your personal data.

Alongside this, we would share the reminder that we give an awful lot of our IP and data when engaging with large language models such as

ChatGPT. Our advice would be to make sure that you change the setting for data privacy on these platforms so that they are not able to learn from your interactions and harvest your ideas and data.

Once your data is in the public domain, as the owner, you often have little control over how it is used. There are now hundreds of items which make up our digital footprints, from online shopping, online banking, social media, browsing the web, reading news online, fitness apps and trackers, subscribing to newsletters and blogs, and any apps that you sign up to. This is all before we start on anything associated with our professional lives, so be careful and mindful of what you accept. A key point to remember here is that your digital footprint is permanent, especially on social networking sites.

It is becoming more commonplace that our digital reputations carry the same weight as our offline reputations. Many employers will investigate your digital footprint before making any employment offer. This is also common among further and higher education institutions before they offer students places on their courses.

Olly remembers well an assembly focusing on digital footprints in a school he worked in in the Middle East, where the head of computing did a live demonstration (with consent from two chosen students) as to how readily available information and data on them was, thanks to their digital footprints. This highlighted to the cohort the importance of thinking about not only what they are sharing online but who they are sharing their data with. The assembly was an excellent eye-opener for students and an important learning opportunity for us all.

So, how do you check your digital footprint? You can choose from many online digital footprint checkers, such as:

- www.npsa.gov.uk/resources/tracking-my-digital-footprint
- www.digitalfootprintcheck.com
- www.saymine.com/digital-footprint-assistant
- www.pipl.com
- www.whois.com
- www.google.com

Alternatively, you can complete a 'vanity search' by typing your name into Google and looking at the search results. If you want to delve further, check the 'advanced search' tab next to the search field, enabling you to narrow it. Google also allows you to sign up for Google **Alerts**. You can choose to be alerted on keywords of interest – or even your name – and receive alerts each time your name appears on the web. Another strategy for finding your name online is to search for 'intext:[first name] [last name]' (e.g. 'intext:Olly Lewis'). This will find specific instances of your name being used in text across social media and in publications by you or about you.

A firm favourite in the IT world is a website run by cybersecurity experts, called www.haveibeenpwned.com. This website helps you to find out if your email address has been leaked in a data breach and how it may have been used. If your data has been breached, the best resolution is for you to create a stronger password or use two-factor authentication (**2FA**).

Protect yourself

How do you protect your digital footprint?

- Check your privacy settings on all of the social media platforms you use; on most platforms, you can customise your settings between 'private' and 'public'.
- Delete any social media accounts you are not using.
- Set up a Google search alert for your name.
- Enable multifactor authentication (**MFA**) on all of your accounts. If you are happy to enable this for your banking details, you should also be happy to set this up for your personal data and school data.
- Avoid unsafe websites. The URL (https://) should have an 's' (for secure) within it.
- Do not disclose private data on public Wi-Fi networks.
- Use strong passwords made of at least 12 characters containing a mix of upper- and lowercase letters, plus symbols and numbers.
- Keep software up to date.
- Set a passcode for your devices.
- Consider using a VPN. These mask your IP address, making your actions almost untraceable and preventing websites from installing tracking cookies.
- Think before you post!

THINK and IDEAL frameworks

When thinking about your own digital footprint, what you share online and with whom – and how you make use of technology within education – it is always sensible to be mindful of your approaches. While there are many different ways to do things, Mark has long shared many great strategies, from his THINK framework (in 2013) to his IDEAL framework (in 2023).

Mark's THINK framework[14] came about when he was working with his student digital leaders in his school pre-2013 and they were focusing on sharing positive digital citizenship strategies. The THINK framework is still timely and relevant today across all aspects of our work online. THINK stands for:

- **T** – is it true?
- **H** – is it helpful?
- **I** – is it inspiring?
- **N** – is it necessary?
- **K** – is it kind?

While this was initially created over a decade ago, much like any great idea or tool, it stands the test of time – which is highly pertinent given the rate of acceleration in recent years.

A great way to be cognisant in your approaches and actions with technology, including AI, is to use Mark's IDEAL framework (Anderson, 2023):

- **I** – is it informative?
- **D** – is it deliberate?
- **E** – is it ethical?
- **A** – is it going to aid learning and is it accurate?
- **L** – is it helping you to learn?

Let's now dive into each part of this in greater depth:

- **Informative:** Does the information you are accessing improve and increase your knowledge? Does it add value to your work or the work of others? Does it aid the construction of learning and/or knowledge in your context? If the answer to these questions is yes, then keep going!

---
[14] https://ictevangelist.com/digital-citizenship

- **Deliberate:** Be crystal clear on why you are using the technology you are using. Think carefully and critically about the learning and how the technology supports the short-, medium- and long-term learning goals.
- **Ethical:** With repeated concerns of academic integrity and the integrity of the AI tools many of us are now using regarding bias and ethics, consider the moral implications, data privacy and integrity of what you are producing before sharing it, to ensure that it is ethically sound.
- **Accurate:** Is what is being generated or shared with you accurate? Is it true? Can you verify it from another source? Does it hold any inherent bias? Given that AI can hallucinate, it is important that we now fact-check information. We say this given that we would check our students' work, so we should also check AI's work, as well as our own, before sharing it publicly.
- **Learn:** Reflect on how technology is deepening your understanding and how you are using it as a tool to support learning, rather than a quick way of getting an answer without fully understanding the content.

These frameworks are helpful approaches to use as part of your online safety and digital citizenship curriculum with your students. Check them out via the references section at the end of the book.

Sharenting

'Sharenting' is a term that combines 'sharing' and 'parenting', referring to the practice of parents sharing information, photos and videos of their children on social media platforms or other digital spaces. This can range from posting pictures of milestones and everyday activities to sharing stories and details about their children's lives.

While sharenting is often done innocuously to connect with family, friends and online communities to celebrate children's achievements or to seek advice and support from other parents, it raises concerns about privacy, consent and the digital footprint it creates for children.

Concerns associated with sharenting include:

- **Privacy:** Posting personal information can infringe on the child's privacy and expose them to risks.
- **Consent:** Young children cannot give informed consent for their images or personal stories to be shared publicly.

- **Safety:** Sharing locations, routines or identifying features can inadvertently expose children to potential harm from predators or identity theft.
- **Digital footprint:** Content shared online can become part of a child's digital footprint, potentially affecting them in the future (e.g. during school admissions or employment screening).
- **Psychological impact:** As children grow, they may feel embarrassed, exposed or uncomfortable with the information shared about them without their consent.

Mitigating the risks of sharenting involves careful consideration by parents about what, how and where they share information about their children, ensuring that they prioritise privacy and safety, while considering the long-term implications of their and their children's digital footprint.

Screen time

The American Academy of Child and Adolescent Psychiatry (AACAP) found that children in the US aged 8–12 spend, on average, 4–6 hours per day using screens or watching videos, with teens spending up to 9 hours (AACAP, 2024). While this research is focused on children in the US, it is likely representative of children the world over who do have access to technology. They found that young people spent most of their time watching TV or videos, gaming, using social media, browsing websites or video chatting.

More recently, data from Data Reportal in 2023 (Binns, 2023) found that:

- The average screen time around the world for people aged 6–64, across different platforms and devices, was 6 hours and 37 minutes per day – a significant amount of time.
- The largest proportion of this was on mobile devices, with users averaging 3 hours and 46 minutes per day on their smartphones.
- Around the world, people spend – on average – 44% of their waking hours looking at screens.
- Since 2013, global daily screen time has increased by 18 minutes.

One of the key challenges of screen time is that parents (and educators) may not always know what is being viewed or how much time children are spending using a screen. Too much screen time can lead to a plethora of issues, such as sleep problems, spending less time with family and friends, mood problems, reduced self-image, not relaxing, and so on.

What doesn't help is many authorities offer differing advice on maximum screen time for children. The American Academy of Pediatrics and World Health Organization (WHO) recommend the following advice on screen time for parents:

Age	Screen time
Under 18 months	Zero screen time apart from video calls to an absent parent or family member.
18–24 months	Watch high-quality programmes together, if you introduce screens.
Age 2–5 years old	Limit to one hour per day.
Above 5 years old	Recommend that families create a family media plan that has rules which are consistently applied and enforced.

Table 16.4: Screen time recommendations (Common Sense Media, 2022)

While these times are recommended, we do champion consistent rules within a family concerning technology. That means avoiding using screens as a pacifier, removing all screens one hour before bedtime, consistently encouraging (and modelling) positive habits, and limiting activities that include screens. Parental controls are your friend and we recommend that you invest the time to learn how these can benefit you and your family. In the process, you may even wish to limit your own controls so you can use this as a vehicle to talk to your child(ren) about your screen-time habits and have a collective family push to build better habits.

While one size does not fit all, here are some strategies to help reduce your and your family's screen time:

- **Set limits:** Set clear limits on the daily use of your device itself and the applications on there.
- **Be smart about notifications:** By disabling non-essential notifications on some of your apps, you will be less likely to check your device or be distracted by the flow of notifications.
- **DND:** Start to enable yourself to focus by making use of the do not disturb (DND) function on your devices.

- **Track yourself:** Apple's 'screen time' will help you track and manage your usage (Android versions are also available). You can set limits for educational and non-educational applications on your phone and this is a great starting place for tracking your usage and giving visibility to your habits, whether good or bad.
- **Screen-free time:** Set agreed designated areas in your house where screens aren't allowed so you can spend quality time together.
- **Screen-free routines:** Set clear rules so that screens are not a part of lunch/dinner and bedtime routines.
- **Encourage non-tech activities:** Read, play board games, go for a walk, exercise, meditate, draw or make the time to do whatever it is that you enjoy that does not involve a screen or technology.
- **Space it out:** Many educators recommend the Pomodoro Technique[15] when it comes to working or revising; why not use focused intervals to give yourself structured time with and without technology?

Screens are certainly here to stay, in both our professional and personal lives, offering many positive and ever-expanding opportunities. It's always a good idea to share your ideas and concerns as a family or with friends, so that you focus and build positive behaviours.

Cybersecurity

Cybersecurity refers to the practices and processes designed to protect computers, networks, programmes and data from unauthorised access, damage or attack. While the implementation of cybersecurity will fall to those who work in your IT department, who are line-managed by someone on your senior leadership team, cybersecurity is everyone's responsibility.

It encompasses a broad spectrum of measures, techniques and technologies aimed at safeguarding IT systems from cyber threats such as viruses, malware, ransomware, phishing attacks and hacking – and effective cybersecurity is essential for protecting sensitive information, ensuring privacy and maintaining the trust and confidence of users and teachers.

It covers several key areas, including network security – the protection of network infrastructure and data from unauthorised access or attacks. Within this, there is the importance of ensuring a disaster recovery plan. It is likely your school will have a plan to ensure that, in the case of a

---

[15] www.pomodorotechnique.com/what-is-the-pomodoro-technique.php

disaster, it can continue to function. Just as you have fire drills to practise what to do in the event of a fire, your technical teams will practise how they will respond to a disaster that impacts your school's critical systems.

Data privacy emerges as a crucial concern, with you often having to handle sensitive information, ranging from student academic records to personal data. Teachers must ensure that such data is accessed and shared with the utmost care, being mindful of data protection laws and school policies. This includes being cautious about where and how student information is stored, ensuring that the digital platforms used comply with privacy standards. Much of this will be taken care of for you with school-approved systems, but things such as portable USB drives, for example, bring high levels of risk.

Another vital approach is the implementation of multifactor authentication (MFA) for accessing school systems. You should not only use MFA but also understand its importance as an approach to protecting against unauthorised access to platforms and data systems. By embracing it, you are playing your part in a more secure digital infrastructure within the school.

Beyond these measures, it's also important to be mindful of the broader digital ecosystem you engage with daily. This includes being cautious about clicking on links in emails, recognising the signs of phishing attempts, and understanding the importance of maintaining updated and secure software on all devices used for educational purposes.

The secure use of Wi-Fi networks, especially when accessing or inputting sensitive data, is another critical consideration, with a preference for secure, encrypted connections to protect against data interception. If you have a school-provided mobile device such as a laptop to use outside of school, be careful when connecting to insecure Wi-Fi locations. For sure, we all love a coffee shop, but only connect to its public Wi-Fi if it is allowable by your school, where systems such as virtual private networks (VPNs) have been set up on your device to make these locations more secure for you to access.

You should also consider your use of educational apps and platforms. Before adopting any new tool, it's essential to assess its security features and privacy policies. All schools should undertake a data protection impact assessment (DPIA) of any digital tool, ensuring it aligns with the school's cybersecurity standards and data protection policies. This isn't just us being overcautious; it's a statutory duty. Due diligence helps protect not only students' data privacy but also the integrity of what you're trying to achieve in the classroom.

So, while your primary focus will be on teaching and learning, your role in ensuring cybersecurity in schools is key. By being mindful of data privacy, adopting secure authentication methods, practising safe online behaviours, and scrutinising the digital tools you use, you play a pivotal role in safeguarding the digital ecosystem of your school.

This might all seem a little overwhelming, but we would share the advice given by our friend Gary Henderson (director of IT at Millfield School, @garyhenderson18 on X) in that 'we should all aim to be more secure tomorrow than we were today'.

16.4 How can you mitigate the risks?

Whether you are a parent, student, teacher or school, the advice on mitigating the risk is unanimous. While at a school level, much of this should be governed by the digital governance and security frameworks that the organisation deploys, outside of the remit of schools and in our personal lives, we don't mind repeating some of the advice that we have shared previously (along with some new points) in that you should:

- Limit the data you share.
- Think before you post on social media sites – are your posts/comments positive?
- Check your privacy settings so that you are only sharing with your friends/contacts.
- Don't share private data across public Wi-Fi networks.
- Don't use unsafe websites – the URL (https://) should have an s (for secure) within it.
- Use strong passwords (12 characters in length including upper- and lowercase, special characters, numbers and symbols) and multifactor authentication.
- Delete old or unused accounts (don't just delete the app!).
- Keep your software up to date.
- Avoid logging in with Facebook, Google, Apple where possible (as this gives the third-party companies direct access to your data).
- Create a Google **Alert** (www.google.com/alerts) for yourself so you know when things related to you are shared online.

The truth is, it all starts with education. In an area where the landscape can change on what seems to be a daily basis, the best approach is to try to stay ahead of the game by using your networks to know what's out there, what's coming up, sharing findings and learning to keep everyone aware and up to date. This is the challenge we all face, as staying on top of everything at all times is impossible. This is why strategy is important so that you can mitigate immediate risks and plan for preparedness.

In summary, there is a great deal to absorb from this chapter and, as time moves forward and the value of data as currency across the world increases, its themes will become increasingly important. We hope that it helps you to reflect and even act upon some of the themes to ensure you are safeguarding yourself and your data online. It also raises the importance of strong digital governance across your organisation, along with the importance of policies and procedures to help reinforce positive behaviours and actions. Digital governance covers your school/organisation's information systems and associated technology. Simply put, digital governance outlines policies to inform practices. It enables structures to be implemented that secure and safeguard all people, while also enabling compatibility and collaboration.

Hopefully, we haven't scared you off with all of this, but the scope and complexity of the online world reinforces why we all have a responsibility to help young people with online safety and digital citizenship.

One of the first steps is to ensure all school-based and learning devices are effectively managed through your MDM platform (which we covered in chapter 4, section 4.8). This will enable you, at scale, to enable or prohibit certain activities, applications, websites, etc., ensuring the safety of young people. In addition, you'll be receiving data that informs you of trends and patterns, plus the all-important safeguarding alerts.

Top tips

Mark's top tips

1. Every day is a safer internet day, so be mindful that we all have a duty to ensure student safety, whether that is online or in real life.
2. Role-model good screen time – it's good for you, too!
3. Continuing with the idea of role-modelling, we advise that you role-model good online behaviour, as it will always be likely that your learners will, at some point, find you online.

Olly's top tips

1. Have open, honest and challenging discussions with all stakeholders as early as possible when it comes to your safeguarding policies and MDM processes.
2. Teach your community about the impact that deepfakes can have and how this links to integrity.
3. Be a critical consumer. Just like you would share to your students about the importance of source validity and other critical aspects, mirror this in your own use of technology.

CHAPTER 17
Digital leadership

'When it comes to our students, as educators we are all digital leaders.'

Mark Anderson

17.1 *All* staff

When we say *all* staff, we mean *all* staff. Everyone. No opt-outs. No excuses. Just as everyone who is based in a classroom or works with classroom-based staff is responsible for literacy and numeracy, they are also responsible for digital literacy.

A development of Mark's 'achieving your digital vision' infographic (figure 4.1) that Olly produced in the light of the work in his trust, highlights the importance of whole staff buy-in.

Figure 17.1: Managing change in education (source: https://ollylewislearning.com/managing-change-when-change-is-hard)

In the same way as Mark's infographic works, Olly's highlights the importance of considering each of these priorities and the associated risks by excluding any of the important elements. (He goes into some considerable depth on the source link we've shared.)

So what?

Schools are inherently complex by their very nature and the breadth and depth of what goes on daily. Leaders influence many aspects of a school (or a group of schools), but it is the distribution of leadership that often leads to the highest levels of positive influence on school development and improved student outcomes. Bringing back the 'what' of what you do to your school values and goals is a surefire way to ensure that you keep the main thing 'the main thing'.

Digital should be on the table at every level and layer of the school. It isn't simply about devices or offering resources to learners in an additional format. It's everything from training to pedagogical decisions, to infrastructure, safeguarding, automation and more.

- How is technology enabling staff?
- How is it reducing workload and administrative tasks?
- How is it improving working practices?
- How is technology impacting organisational learning for staff and students?
- How often is digital on meeting agendas?
- Where are we with our digital strategy?
- Where are we with our IT refresh?
- How much money can we assign to research and development so that we can future-proof ourselves?
- What digital aspects are on our CPD cycle this year?
- Which digital subscriptions are we keeping/removing this year and why?
- What data supports all of the above?

These are just a few questions to get you going, but the truth of the matter is that technology is pervasive in our lives and our work and yet, still, digital skills are difficult to measure but are required in formal education and beyond.

Education has become a collection of yardsticks that we measure with relative frequency. The variable changes with the frequency of a metronome, but where and what are our control variables in a contextually rich and diverse setting? What are the common 'lines in the sand', what are your variants, classifiers and qualifiers, and how do you extract this information and with what frequency is it appropriate to extract the data?

These are important questions to ask because, if you do not know what your lines in the sand are, how do you know whether or not you've been successful? With this in mind, to measure our effectiveness, we must measure our output; we need metrics – some of these will be qualitative and some will be quantitative.

The purpose of this isn't to dissect the effectiveness of our measure of success in education, but to ask some questions, or even raise some provocations, to realign our thought processes. If it makes you reflect on your measures, that's a bonus.

It's no secret that digital technologies (EdTech) now have, and have had, an increasing spotlight within education, given the COVID-19 pandemic and our search for equilibrium in the face of being in school, out of school and simultaneously somewhere in-between, all at the drop of a hat for three years in many settings across the globe.

So, you might be thinking, 'What sorts of questions should we be asking and what is deserving of reflection?' Well, that, as with many things, is contextual and you will most likely be best placed to answer those questions, but here are some areas you might like to explore as you consider how to embed (or reflect on how you have embedded) effective digital technology in your setting:

Question	Why?
How are you measuring the impact of your digital strategy?	If you don't measure, you won't know if you've been successful.
What do you define as success?	By clearly defining success you will know whether you are being successful.
Can you benchmark data?	When so much data can be informed by contextual knowledge, consider the use of data being collected and how it can inform teaching or learning.
How does technology aid the efficiency and effectiveness of learning, teaching or reducing workload?	This can help unpick areas to consider continuing to support and those to not.

Question	Why?
What are the appropriate data streams that inform you?	By considering what data helps you, you can choose what data to track to support decisions both at a micro (classroom) and macro (whole-school) level.
What mechanisms have you put in place to support your community?	It takes a village to support digital transformation, so ensuring support for all stakeholders is essential to consider.
What research have you based these decisions on?	Whether it's your own qualitative and/or quantitative research or that from within the education sphere, it's important to know why you are doing these things. Knowing your starting points will help you understand why you are doing things the way you are.
What does 'good' look like in lessons, for departments, as a school and across your ecosystem?	By examining what 'good' looks like, it gives all stakeholders a clear roadmap of what success looks like for them to try to emulate.

Table 17.1: Evaluating effective digital technology

17.2 Students

In today's digital age, students need more than just academic skills and foundational literacies to succeed, as highlighted by the World Economic Forum's (WEF) twenty-first-century skills (WEF, 2016):

1. Literacy
2. Numeracy
3. Scientific literacy
4. ICT literacy
5. Financial literacy
6. Cultural and civic literacy
7. Critical thinking/problem solving
8. Creativity
9. Communication
10. Collaboration

11. Curiosity
12. Initiative
13. Persistence/grit
14. Adaptability
15. Leadership
16. Social and cultural awareness.

The WEF's Future of Jobs Report in April 2023 highlighted the top skills of 2023 (WEF, 2023b):

1. Analytical thinking
2. Creative thinking
3. Resilience, flexibility and agility
4. Motivation and self-awareness
5. Curiosity and lifelong learning
6. Technological literacy
7. Dependability and attention to detail
8. Empathy and active listening
9. Leadership and social influence
10. Quality control.

Number 6, 'Technological literacy', comes as no surprise given the rapid advancements of generative AI, which was also highlighted in the WEF's top 10 emerging technologies of 2023 (WEF, 2023a). While these technological skills are needed for today's workforce and those graduating from Secondary schools in the academic year 2023–24, how will we (the education sector) respond to this so that future generations in three, five or ten years leave us with technological literacy and digital skills ready for the future world of work?

When you compare the previous list to the skills that the WEF predicts will be in even higher demand in the future...

1. Creative thinking
2. Analytical thinking
3. Technological literacy
4. Curiosity and lifelong learning
5. Resilience, flexibility and agility

6. Systems thinking
7. AI and big data
8. Motivation and self-awareness
9. Talent management
10. Service orientation and customer service.

...and contrast that with the top 10 skills it suggests businesses will need by 2027...

1. Analytical thinking
2. Creative thinking
3. AI and big data
4. Leadership and social influence
5. Resilience, flexibility and agility
6. Curiosity and lifelong learning
7. Technological literacy
8. Design and user experience
9. Motivation and self-awareness
10. Empathy and active listening.

...it is imperative that we consider what and how we teach our young people.

While cognitive skills are involved in analytical and creative thinking, it is clear that technological literacy and digital skills must also make up a part of our curricula. It is possible, even probable, that, as the world becomes ever more digital, there will likely be an increase in the need for technological literacy and digital upskilling to maximise performance in all sectors.

As of the mid-point in 2023, AI and big data rank fifteenth in the WEF report on skills for mass employment and feature at number three in terms of priorities in company training strategies until 2027. For companies with more than 50,000 employees, it is the number one priority (WEF, 2023b). While titled as 'technology skills', this covers a broad spectrum of skills such as the efficient use of AI tools, computer networking, cybersecurity, general technological literacy skills, and user experience and design.

Learning a broad spectrum of technological skills in school must therefore be a priority. Our curricula should afford the time and opportunity to teach and learn such skills and literacies so that the children have not only the best starting point in life, but also transferable and employable skills that transcend sectors. This is in part why we feel there is a need to develop a digital cognition curriculum which encapsulates all of this, as shared back in chapter 4 (section 4.7). And while we are beating the curriculum drum here, we believe (technology aside) that even more curriculum reform is needed – in areas such as financial literacy.

According to the WEF, by 2027, 43% of work will be completed by machines and 57% by humans. That is in stark contrast to what we saw in 2022, with a split of 34% versus 66%. Inevitably, this will only increase, so ensuring strong digital literacy and leadership in ourselves, our schools and in the education we give our children should be our priority.

Digital leaders

Students should also be at the forefront of their educational experience and many schools make excellent use of student leaders. So, why don't all schools have student digital leaders?

Student digital leadership is something that Mark is particularly passionate about. As the co-founder of the UK's Student Digital Leader Network with Sheli Blackburn way back in 2007, student digital leaders have become a cornerstone for improving digital practice in schools across the UK.

Written in Mark's free book available on Apple Books,[1] *Digital Leaders: Transforming Learning with Students in the Lead*, student digital leaders are something he strongly advocates for as a key building block in every digital strategy in education – students working with teachers, TAs and parents to support them in their use of technology, where students lead with responsibility and purpose.

There are so many ways in which student digital leaders can support and contribute to school life, such as leader, manager, delivery technician, technician support, blogger, promotions and engagement manager, AI checker, and so much more!

---

[1] https://bit.ly/madigitalleaders

Here are a few examples of activities student digital leaders can support with:

- **Student school newsletter:** A monthly digest of what has happened in school, recommendations, apps, trends, etc.
- **Blogging:** A student-led school blog.
- **Screencasting:** Organise learning-driven screencasts and maintaining school YouTube channel(s).
- **Training and CPD:** Organise and deliver training sessions for staff, parents and students.
- **Whole-school assemblies:** Around responsible technology use, learning, digital citizenship, online safety and responsible use of AI, there are so many ways they can help.
- **Events:** Organise lunchtime and after-school sessions with a digital foci.
- **Genius bar:** Students and teachers can sign up for a 10-minute one-to-one session with a digital leader for support. Mark even used to have his student digital leader genius bars available to parents on parents' evenings!
- **Social media channels:** Students can support with curating and creating content for school social media channels. They could even have a student-driven channel for the school.
- **eSports:** Team players, promoters, hosts, commentators, game strategists and analysts, admin/referees, community managers, video editors, streamers, branding/design, business development, and not forgetting coaches.

Zareef Petkar (@Zareef_P), Senior Leader at Horizon International School, Dubai, offers us a case study on why and how student digital leaders can benefit your school.

Case study: Zareef Petkar

Education is constantly evolving and technology has become a powerful tool for transformative learning experiences. Integrating technology into the classroom not only enhances educational opportunities, but also fosters student leadership and empowerment.

Student digital leaders: empowering the next generation

As educational leader Michael Fullan once said, 'We need to prepare students for their future, not our past.' In the digital era, student digital leaders play a crucial role in shaping the educational landscape. These students are tech-savvy, passionate and adept at navigating the digital world. By empowering them as ambassadors of technology, we tap into their enthusiasm and expertise, creating a student-led culture of innovation within the classroom.

Microsoft OneNote: Student digital leaders can champion the use of tools like OneNote, transforming it into a collaborative platform. By guiding their peers in using it effectively, these leaders promote collaborative note-taking, resource sharing and project collaboration. As a result, students develop essential skills such as teamwork, communication and problem-solving, preparing them for the collaborative nature of the digital age. In addition, the use of OneNote improves time efficiency with the distribution of resources, alongside promoting the wellbeing and sustainability of teacher workload, as everything is centrally located. Through this, timely student feedback becomes much easier, with high purpose and impact.

Virtual Reality (VR): Student digital leaders can take the lead in exploring and creating VR content. By encouraging students to research, develop and share their own virtual experiences, these leaders foster a sense of ownership and engagement. Through student-created VR content, their peers can immerse themselves in personalised educational journeys, further enhancing their understanding and curiosity.

Educate for life

In the words of educational reformer John Dewey, 'Education is not preparation for life; education is life itself.' The integration of technology in education provides a platform for students to become active participants in their own learning journeys. By nurturing student digital leaders, we create a collaborative and innovative learning environment. These leaders empower their peers, fostering teamwork, communication and critical-thinking skills. As we embark on this technology-driven educational transformation, let us embrace the potential of student digital leaders to shape the future, where education becomes a dynamic and student-led experience.

17.3 Your wider community

Often, we see the term 'community' in education and, when we delve into the details, we see that schools mean 'teachers'. In truth, your school community is all stakeholders: teachers but also teaching assistants, admin and site staff, governors, students and parents.

Digital leadership should touch all of these groups, regularly. How often does your training cycle allow and enable all of these stakeholders in your setting? Training opportunities should be made available to everyone so that you are giving everyone a safe space to develop digital skills and digital literacy.

More often than not, from both Olly and Mark's experience, those who need the training the most will be the quietest in terms of requesting support. Make your training accessible to and for everyone. You can run digital training for admin and site staff during the school day; teachers, TAs, governors and parents after school; and students as a part of the curriculum. YouTube channels or your internal learning hub, such as you can create on Microsoft **SharePoint**, offer the opportunity for asynchronous learning opportunities.

The 'how' and the 'what' of your offer is also important; it should be tailored to the needs of the individuals within the organisation so that it is fit for purpose. A parent does not need training on your MIS, but they should be trained on your core platforms so they can support their child/children at home (something else you could add to your SharePoint).

Do your governors know what good digital leadership and teaching and learning look like? Are they confident enough to ask questions of students and teachers? This key group of people that help shape and guide your school should be part of the training and conversations too, so that they fully understand not only the journey, but also why you are heading in the digital direction you are heading.

The UNESCO Global Education Monitoring Report: Technology in Education (UNESCO, 2023) highlighted several contrasting outcomes, such as mobile phones and other devices being a learning distractor and having poor evidence of improving educational outcomes, while also stating that technology can also *improve* outcomes in some instances. While the majority of the negativity in this report is framed from the points of technology and social media use outside of school, it brings to the fore the need for digital parenting. Plus, it accentuates that which we hope has shone through in this book: not all technology use in schools is always positive and the context of its use is as important as the pedagogical rationale to use (or not use) EdTech.

eSports

Education is evolving and many schools are seeking innovative ways in which we can engage and prepare students for the challenges of tomorrow. While all schools offer traditional sporting opportunities, simultaneously, many educators are reflecting on their childhood and identifying how they developed collaboration, teamwork, discipline and problem-solving outside of school through gaming. Enter the world of eSports.

At its core, the essence of eSports is to build communities, collaborate, promote quick decision-making, problem-solving, strategising and effective communication. These are all traits and skills that employers highly prize and seek now (and will in the future).

Given that many of you reading this book will have likely grown up playing video games in your childhood, there are so many benefits to having an eSports club in school that go beyond just playing games or as a source of entertainment. Ofcom's media usage report from 2023 (Ofcom, 2023) found that about nine in ten children (89%) play video games. They also found that many 3–17-year-olds played games to 'hang out with friends' (24%), plus children aged 8–17 used games as a way of playing with (55%) and chatting (47%) with people they knew.

eSports offers an opportunity for inclusivity, an outlet for self-expression, developing cognitive skills, adaptability, communication, creativity, social interaction, and more. It also affords many students who are not traditional sportspeople to excel in a structured environment. Educators have a great opportunity to tap into students' existing passions and interests, and create social environments and new communities in their schools.

An eSports club will help students thanks to its multifaceted educational benefits, not to mention being a better alternative than simply passively absorbing media, such as social media and TV. eSports also have curricula links to subjects such as computer science, business and STEAM subjects, sports, and game development, while also developing digital literacy, digital skills and promoting team-based activities that foster character development.

What are the other benefits of eSports in education? They:

- foster an inclusive community
- develop social-emotional balance
- support a future digital career
- develop employability skills
- help students strategise and articulate plans
- promote leadership skills, teamwork and collaboration
- boost communication skills
- develop problem-solving and decision-making
- enhance multitasking abilities
- increase cognitive skills and perception
- enhance resilience
- act as a motivator
- encourage time management
- promote goal-setting
- enable task prioritisation
- foster sportsmanship.

All of these make a compelling case for why schools should be investing in their eSports programmes, as there are so many intended and unintended positives.

17.4 Digital parenting

We covered this in some detail in the previous chapter; however, we felt it worthy in its own right for us to spend time sharing how schools can triangulate support for children and homes around digital parenting. As we know, online safety and digital leadership are everyone's concerns. Children are exposed, in many countries, to technology almost as soon as they are born. While this can be beneficial, it also brings challenges for parents as they too need to be able to safely and securely navigate the digital world to help shepherd their child(ren).

Digital parenting not only helps to guide and support children in the safe and responsible use of technology, but it also involves supporting and teaching children about the risks of life online and how to use technology for positive means, such as communication, creativity and learning. Therefore, building these skills in parents is fundamentally important.

Parents need to have a developing understanding of the technology that their children are using, and its age-appropriateness, to ensure that they can effectively monitor online activity, provide guidance and be good role models.

This sounds almost impossible to keep up with, given that technology changes so rapidly. That is precisely why parents need to be willing to learn about new technologies so that they can adapt accordingly. Not only that, but the risks are real and parents need to be aware of the plethora of dangers in the online space so they can take the necessary protective steps.

No matter your context, all parents will benefit from some digital training and help when it comes to digital parenting. Even the most seemingly basic of tips and tricks will come in handy to (at least) reinforce your messages or (at best) help parents learn a new strategy/technique to support them and their child(ren).

Light-touch sessions, nudging through regular reminders in your newsletters, 'how to' videos, or more in-depth training and information sessions – these strategies are necessary to help and continue to foster a positive working culture towards appropriate use of technology (in school and at home), along with maintaining the triad of effective education between parents, students and the school.

Talking to children about the risks is a great first step, as is learning about the websites, apps and games they use so you can talk about their potential risks. By sharing with parents the importance of setting boundaries and how they can do this to limit how and when children can use their technology, parents will be able to set screen-time limits and age-appropriate limits that best support their children. Most technology has these parental features built into it; for example, on iOS (Apple) devices you can set screen-time limits for all apps on your child's device and restrict what they can/cannot do. This helps to mitigate any potential risks and is an easy parenting win!

We cannot also forget that perhaps, for many of us, the biggest challenge is modelling good use to our children. Olly says this is a big test as, all too often, he doesn't think he gets it right (and Mark concurs with his own two children): 'Just give me two more minutes', 'I'm nearly done', 'I'll be with you in a second', 'Sorry, Daddy's working' are all phrases he and Mark have caught themselves saying with their phones in hand or in front of a laptop while their children are vying for their attention (ironically, often when writing this book!). We don't always get it right, as many of us will likely attest to, but what is more important is that when we do stretch our own boundaries, we acknowledge being at fault and apologise, while also putting the device away.

There are plenty of great resources out there to help support digital parenting, such as:

Company	Link	Brief summary
Natterhub	www.natterhub.com	An online safety platform with resources for parents as well as schools (paid for and free options).
NetSupport	www.netsupportsoftware.com/online-safety-safeguarding-resources/	Online safety guides for parents (free).
The Family Online Safety Institute	www.fosi.org/good-digital-parenting	Resources to give parents and caregivers the tools to confidently navigate the online world with their families (free).
Common Sense Education	www.commonsense.org/education/family-resources	Prepare families to think critically and use technology in positive, creative and powerful ways; tips and activities for families (free).
Childnet	www.childnet.com/help-and-advice/parents-and-carers	Helpful information and guidance on a range of key online safety topics (free).
Digital Parenting	www.digital-parenting.com/digital-parenting-resources	The 3 M's of digital parenting and family media plans (free).
Schools Mobile	www.schoolsmobile.com/en-us	An MDM solution which brings parents and schools together to help manage student/children's devices in partnership between the key stakeholders of schools and home (paid for).

Table 17.2: Digital parenting resources

17.5 Where does wellbeing fit in?

One key element in successful individuals, teams, schools and systems that has been emphasised for several years (but is not always given the gravitas it deserves in some settings across the education landscape) is wellbeing. It has been fantastic in recent times to see more attention dedicated to this, such as a recent piece of research exploring the potential of **ChatGPT** as a teacher ally for workload relief and burnout prevention (Hashem, Ali and El Zein, 2023). Others note that:

> 'Psychological well-being is a core feature of mental health, and may be defined as including hedonic (enjoyment, pleasure) and eudaimonic (meaning, fulfilment) happiness, as well as resilience (coping, emotion regulation, healthy problem solving).' (Tang et al., 2019)

Seems obvious, no? Sometimes we cannot see the wood for the trees as we focus on the students and neglect ourselves, yet the evidence continues to accumulate to support the causal relationship between positive wellbeing, our overall health and outcomes.

It starts with 'I'.

This sounds selfish – but stick with us. While EdTech presents us with more opportunities and possibilities, we need a clear appreciation and understanding of both the positive and negative aspects of a digital action or activity. Thus, it starts with the personal: the individual: I, me, you, him, her, they. Why? Without a clear understanding of our wellbeing around digital activities then how can we understand, support or even mitigate for the digital wellbeing of those in our communities? We need a knowledge base from which to draw so that we can make informed decisions.

This is, again, where digital cognition can help. By having an understanding of how to use tools such as focus modes, calendars, scheduling of emails, timetabling, resource management, AI and more, digital cognition can help to make a difference to the wellbeing of students and teachers alike.

■----------------------■
METRICS   WELLBEING

The 4 aspects of digital wellbeing for individuals

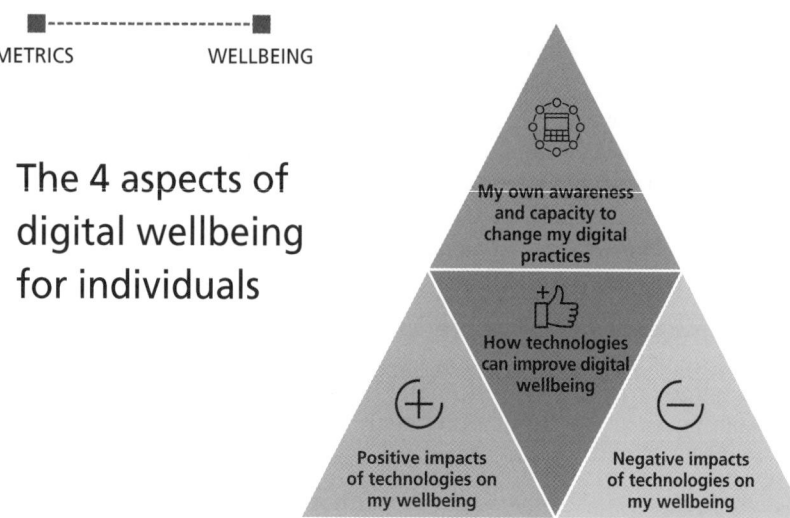

Figure 17.2: Digital wellbeing for individuals (image adapted and reproduced from the digital wellbeing element of Jisc's digital capabilities framework, see https://digitalcapability.jisc.ac.uk/what-is-digital-capability/digital-wellbeing/. Published with permission. Copyright © 2024 Jisc)

The Joint Information Systems Committee (Jisc) wrote a quick guide, 'Promoting digital wellbeing for learners' (Jisc, 2020), that highlights four aspects for individuals:

1. My own awareness and capacity to change my digital practices.
2. How technologies can improve digital wellbeing.
3. Positive impacts of technologies on my wellbeing.
4. Negative impacts of technologies on my wellbeing.

This leaves a few questions to help you reflect on the matter:

Question	Why?
Does everyone in your school know their role?	So that individuals know what their roles and responsibilities are with their use of technology.
Do they have a sound digital awareness?	Knowing whether or not individuals do have sound digital awareness will inform training, support and sharing around digital that is required within your context.

Question	Why?
Do stakeholders have digital cognition that helps them know how to use technology to support workload/ resource management/time management etc.?	By knowing how to use technology tools while using them appropriately, users will be more adept, efficient and productive. If they don't, then this highlights, among other things, a training need, while ensuring the digital ecosystem supports this with the tools they need to help.
Would they feel comfortable supporting learners with digital wellbeing?	If individuals are comfortable with this, it reflects that individuals have confidence in how to use technology to support teaching and learning in their environment.
Do you know what your digital skill baselines are?	It is essential to know what core knowledge and skills users at every level need to engage with the digital vision so that you can provide tailored ongoing CPD for all stakeholders.
Have you provided ongoing CPD to all stakeholders?	Ongoing CPD is essential in sustaining knowledge around essential systems to support and enhance teaching and learning.
How and what can you do to take out the detective work?	Considering what you can do to share what works and researching the best ways to use technology can save individuals time having to work this out for themselves.
What confidence/competence levels do key stakeholders have, such as teachers, students and the wider community?	By understanding this, you can gauge what support is required and provide tailored support where needed at the right level for the right audience.

Table 17.3: Digital wellbeing questions

From parents to students and colleagues, your overarching digital strategy should encompass and involve all areas of your overall education provision so that it improves digital literacy, outcomes, efficiency and overall effectiveness.

Any form of leadership, digital or otherwise, starts with the leading of ourselves and then the leading of our community. No matter where you start, take the first step and reflect on where you are, where you want to go and how you will get there through small, incrementally planned steps. Involve all the stakeholders in your community in the 'why' of all aspects of digital education.

Top tips

Mark's top tips

1. Digital leadership starts with the 'why'. Explaining this and supporting from the top to the bottom of your context is key to ensuring success.
2. Remember, while teaching and learning are an important facet of your digital leadership, other aspects of your school are important too – such as facilities, finance, admin and marketing.
3. IT takes a village (pun intended!).

Olly's top tips

1. When you plan your school calendar for next year, include a range of student- and parent-facing sessions that focus on digital education. Don't shy away from it, but meet it head-on in a positive light.
2. Audit the digital skills your school is developing across the curriculum so you can plan accordingly. Don't leave it to chance, as these skills won't happen by osmosis.
3. Offer more training than you think you need to!

CHAPTER 18
Ambassador roles

'Monsieur, with Ferrero Rocher, you are really spoiling us.'
Ferrero Rocher advertisement, 1993

18.1 What is an ambassador role?

Ambassador roles for educators have been around for some time. The ADE (Apple Distinguished Educators) programme, for example, started in 1994. At the time, it was launched to recognise K-12 educators who were effectively using Apple technologies in their schools, aiming to transform the teaching and learning process. Over the years, many more programmes such as Google Certified Innovators (previously Teachers) and Microsoft Innovative Educator Experts have sprung up.

The reference to the Ferrero Rocher advert above is due to the ambassador in the advert revealing lovely chocolates; the idea being that by sharing them at a high-society event, the chocolates gain credibility as a high-end treat. It's interesting that they chose to record the advert as a scene at the ambassador's ball. This has historical links to the roots of ambassadorial marketing.

During the late 1800s, the classic era of brand ambassadors emerged alongside the rise of large national and international companies, such as Cadburys and Coca-Cola. These companies experimented with sending products for free to influential people in the hope that they would share about their products. The idea is simple: if influential or well-respected people endorse a product, or perhaps were photographed using a product, others would likely follow suit.

Nowadays, we see it everywhere. On our TV programmes, we often see the actors all using phones or computers of a particular brand and then, in the show's credits, it will read, 'promotional consideration provided by Apple/Samsung/whoever'. Over the years, these activities have developed as specific marketing activities for companies that take place alongside what we know as more traditional activities, such as adverts on websites, newspapers and television.

Advertising is big business. In 2022, through its Google Ads platform, Google made $224.47 billion.[1] It is, in part, why Google pays Apple somewhere in the region of $18–20 billion a year to make Google the default search engine on its devices (Kunert, 2023). Ambassadorial marketing, therefore, is just one of many tools in the arsenal of big tech companies to help them in their sales of their products.

In today's society, ambassadorial marketing strategies have evolved to not just include individuals, but often groups of people, leveraging the power of community and shared experiences to promote a brand. With the explosion of social media in recent decades, influencers and brand ambassadors can reach huge audiences at a relatively low cost compared to traditional marketing methods (Geyser, 2024).

An ambassadorial marketing strategy offers a very cost-effective avenue for companies, as it leverages the credibility and personal connections of teachers within their communities. This is great for companies as it leads to high conversion rates, because trust is already established between the ambassadors and their online followers (Chung, 2021).

Of course, these schemes aren't all about the great advocacy teachers can put into practice to help with these companies' sales at a bargain price. (Don't forget, teachers don't – and neither do their schools – get any financial reward for all this work advocating for their products.) We felt it important, however, to share the elephant in the room about ambassadorial marketing.

Despite Mark and Olly holding – and having held – numerous badges from a wide variety of technology entities, including those from Microsoft, Google and Apple, at no point have any of the companies made it clear that these programmes were ambassadorial marketing. Sure, they talk about ethical compliance, but this is related to asking compliance officers in schools to sign off on us being able to participate in these schemes. They do not share any of the things we've said above. Should they?

Disclosure and transparency

Regulatory bodies, such as the Federal Trade Commission (FTC) in the US and the Advertising Standards Authority (ASA) in the UK, require ambassadors to disclose their affiliations when promoting products or services. Yes, some might have some of the overlays on their avatars

---

[1] www.statista.com/statistics/266249/advertising-revenue-of-google

which showcase their badge; the truth is, though, few rarely disclose their affiliations.

Not all companies are equal, that is for sure. We loved it when popular tool for learning **Book Creator** learned about these kinds of disclosures. It went above and beyond. At the time, founders Dan Amos and Dan Kemp shared an open letter for all to read.[2] In it, they stated their expectations about ambassadors meeting the requirements as we've outlined. They explained clearly their position; the fact that they love that people really want to share their product and how it's being used, but equally how they want to make sure that they are doing everything clearly and above board.

Shouldn't all companies do this, so that everything is transparent and on the level? For example, if you're on a board of governors in a school, you have to declare your pecuniary interests – but when an Apple Distinguished Educator shares about a feature of iPadOS (or equally those who are ambassadors for Microsoft or Google on features related to their ecosystems), do they disclose their affiliations and reasons for sharing that feature, when essentially they are advertising these products?

Conflict of interests

When educators, entrusted with the welfare and education of the students in their charge, endorse products from companies they have a relationship with, therein lies a conflict of interest. Educators are, as well all know, in loco parentis. Does being an ambassador for another company fit in with that?

One of the key concerns is whether these endorsements sway the impartiality of others, possibly influencing their choice of educational technology based on their affiliations and the benefits in kind they receive, rather than the educational merit of the products. It also begs the question: do these benefits sway how budgets are spent within schools when the choice of a competing product might be a better fit (for a whole host of reasons!)?

Take, for example, the experiences these companies put on for educators. They are fantastic! Sometimes they will put you up in a lovely hotel. They pay for your accommodation and supply lovely food. Often there's alcohol involved. What would the parents of the children in their schools say if

---

[2] Book Creator's open letter: https://bookcreator.com/2017/09/open-letter-ambassadors

they knew this was the case, bearing in mind again, they are acting in loco parentis?

Commercial versus educational interests

The problem, as the title above suggests, is that educators are at the centre of an ethical conundrum. For some, it might not even be on their radar, although we would suggest it should be. The potential for the benefits and commercial aspirations could be seen to overshadow educational or pedagogical benefits.

It can be a moral maze for educators. Some, keen to leave the profession and follow a career path such as Mark's, see them as an avenue and route out of the profession. Others see them as an opportunity to learn and develop their knowledge and skills, which ultimately get passed on to their colleagues and students. That's how (we feel) it should be and how it was for Mark. Yes, we realise so far in this chapter we have sought to point out some of the ethical issues around ambassador programmes. This is largely because we felt that someone should spend time shining a spotlight on it.

18.2 Risk versus reward

It really isn't all doom and gloom. Both from Mark and Olly's perspectives, they have gained significant insights from the collaborations and learning they've gained from being part of these networks. For many, they are essential and it is always good to learn beyond the boundaries of your school setting. Programmes such as these provide significant opportunities to do this.

Thinking back to when Mark and his colleagues deployed iPads in the school he was working in, there was very little help to be gained from Apple, but it was the networks across their ambassador programme that helped all to benefit; not just from things happening in the schools of others, but within Mark's school too. The network was, as they say, far more powerful than the node, in that sharing the things that were and weren't working led to making better decisions within the respective deployments in their schools.

It's also important to note that a closer relationship between yourself and these organisations allows you to have early insights into changes in how their products – both software and hardware – will impact your IT estate and, ultimately, what happens in the classroom. These are significant benefits to being involved. Therefore, could these programmes be seen as a symbiotic relationship?

So, while we have taken pains to discuss the ethical and moral considerations that ambassador programmes bring, there are benefits on both sides beyond that of hitting marketing goals.

Ambassadors have a closer relationship with these companies and can, therefore, give essential feedback on software and hardware that can result in improvements to them prior to major releases that can have benefits for all. The opportunity to influence technology evolution should not be overlooked.

Many educational technology companies (and this is seen by many as being best practice) like to co-create their software with their customers. By demonstrating agility in product development, by carefully listening to direct feedback from the end users and responding in kind by developing their products to match needs, technology solutions end up being better for all, and better for the company selling it. Users are ultimately far closer to the digital chalkface of the software and hardware, as they are the ones who have to interact with it as part of their everyday practice.

The opportunities provided across the networks you create help with professional growth and access to resources beyond those on offer from the company's websites and help forums. Access through the professional relationships you develop and a direct route to inboxes of others in similar positions to you are priceless. They are arguably an essential part of being able to successfully fulfil your roles and problem-solve many of the difficulties senior leaders and teachers face in their diverse settings.

Ultimately, balancing the benefits versus the potential conflicts of interest, commercial pressures (such as only promoting the software from a particular company) could divert attention from serving core educational priorities within your setting. It's a decision that should be made with clarity between individuals and the schools in which they work to decide if the risk is worth the reward.

Our advice would be to ask one simple question: will this help learning and the children in our classrooms? Rather than, will this help me to find a route out of the classroom into a new profession?

18.3 How to apply successfully

OK, so you've navigated the moral maze and have made the decision to apply for the ambassador programme that is, likely, closely aligned to the ecosystem that is already used within your school setting. It is likely that you will be most successful under the following circumstances:

- **Apple:** You are using Apple technologies, most likely iPad.
- **Google:** You are using Google technologies, most likely Chromebook and/or Google **Workspace for Education**.
- **Microsoft:** You are using Microsoft technologies, most likely Windows and **Microsoft 365**.

Most applications will ask you to verify your credentials as an innovative educator or leader using the tools in the ecosystem in which you work. Most will require you to have completed basic training in using their products.

Apple, for example, will expect you to have achieved Apple Teacher status[3] as a baseline. Microsoft will expect you to have achieved Microsoft Innovative Educator status.[4] If you'd like to become a Google Certified Innovator, then you need to have successfully completed both the Google Certified Educator level 1 and level 2 qualifications.[5]

It would seem anecdotally from conversations that we have had in recent years with successful applicants versus those who haven't been successful, that for some of the companies (mentioning no names), you are penalised for talking about the use of other or competing products, when the company which you're applying for has a product that does a similar thing (think Microsoft **PowerPoint** versus Google **Slides** versus Apple **Keynote**). So, while you may demonstrate that you are particularly innovative with one technology, if you share in your application that you use a different piece of software, such as an app that a competing company has made, you are likely to be scored lower than someone using the company's own product. That makes sense, as they want you to be an ambassador for them, not their competitor, however innovative or exciting your use of the competing tool on their technology might be.

---

[3] https://education.apple.com
[4] https://learn.microsoft.com
[5] https://edu.google.com/for-educators/certification-programs/professional-expertise/certified-innovator

Alongside this, remember that companies are looking for educators who are strong advocates with good social standing, particularly with a good following on social media, to be their ambassadors. So, if you're thinking of applying for one of these programmes, you might like to consider how you share and engage with your PLN, what platforms you use, the resources you might want to share (which may well have been created as part of your everyday work) that might be of benefit to others. An example of this might be Mark's periodic tables of apps[6] that he's created over the years. These started while in a role in a school as a resource to help students and colleagues, but given their universal appeal, Mark's sharing of them beyond his school helped many thousands of educators the world over to learn about new and exciting tools to support learning and teaching.

When it comes to finalising your application, we would recommend reaching out to a few educators in your PLN who have been through the process before, asking them for their advice and if they could check over your application. Some might decline because often, companies ask educators to be the people vetting and checking applications. It is likely, however, that you will have a good PLN and will be able to find others who can assist you. Asking colleagues in your school to provide a testimonial related to your application can also be a good way of bolstering it, as well as asking them to check it for you.

It should go without saying, but given what you are doing – while we might both come from the school of thought that it is easier to seek forgiveness than permission – we definitely recommend you seek approval from your line manager or headteacher before going ahead and applying for one of these programmes, particularly in light of the ethics around them. Clearly state your case and explain why you think your involvement would benefit the school.

18.4 Making the most of your ambassadorship

Congratulations, you've been chosen to become an EdTech Playbook ambassador! OK, maybe not; but if you get this far, then now is the time to really start capitalising on the opportunities you get.

The obvious best opportunity is networking. Soon after joining, you will gain access to ambassador-only platforms for communication and collaboration with others in your space. Get on there. Attend the virtual

---

[6] See Mark's periodic tables here: https://bit.ly/ictevangelistperiodictables

online meet-ups. Find out who your tribe is. Former ambassadors, usually referred to as alumni, are often used to coordinate these events. Befriend them quickly and use them to help you find those who can help you in your areas of interest.

Some of these programmes also require you to meet up at a face-to-face event, such as the Apple Distinguished Educator Institutes. You are required to attend these events, sometimes out of the country, to fully achieve your status. Apple tends to hold these within its three main geographical regions: the Americas, APAC (Asia/Pacific) and EMEA (Europe, Middle East and Africa). Often the Americas events take place in the US, APAC in Australia and EMEA somewhere in the UK. If you live further afield, expect to have to find the money for a flight to attend as Apple will not pay for these. This is something common to similar events with other companies too, such as the Google Symposiums that take place.

What else?

You will also find that you gain benefits such as access to free software, early access to features, and more – not just mugs and T-shirts, although these are likely to be handed out.

Don't be afraid to share your journey with your school either. This could be via in-school meetings or in an in-school teaching and learning magazine. After all, the reason why you likely engaged in the programme is for the benefit of the school, so sharing the insights you gain is going to benefit all, not just you – so share!

A great additional opportunity that this extended learning provides you is the opportunity to speak publicly. Some of the in-person events provide opportunities for ambassadors to share things happening in their schools. Equally, organising some training sessions in your school for colleagues is a great way to help develop yourself too. You'll soon discover that talking to students as a teacher is way easier than talking with other teachers about something. It is a difficult undertaking, so seeking out opportunities to speak publicly is great professional development for yourself.

Sharing your learning with others in your setting is a great way to ensure balance around ethics. Demonstrating that your engagement in these programmes has benefits for all ensures that the whole community profits from the professional learning you have gained and, as mentioned above, it's great for your own professional learning to share widely.

While we're on the topic, why not also sign up to speak at other events about what is going on at your school? There's a reason why you were picked for the programme and it's likely to be because you're doing awesome things in your school that the technology company is keen for you to share – so why not do it? Forget that you're promoting their product; in fact, you might like to not even mention their product, but instead focus on mentioning your school, your amazing colleagues and your fantastic students. It was them (and, of course, you) that helped you to achieve the 'accolade'.

By showcasing the great things going on with technology in your school, you will help others to achieve similar wins, further helping everyone – which is, of course, a commendable thing to do.

Top tips

Mark's top tips

1. Keep a diary of events or training sessions you've run and try to record some feedback from a colleague. This will make for great evidence when applying, whether you include the video or a key quote from your colleague's feedback.

2. Take photos or screenshots of excellent work created by students or colleagues linked to things you have helped them learn about.

3. Get feedback from stakeholders, such as students, teachers and parents, on the impact of the use of technology.

4. Bonus: If including the work or images of students, make sure you have consent from parents and/or guardians for you to include your student's work or images!

Olly's top tips

1. Keep a digital scrapbook using Microsoft OneNote whenever you create or share something helpful within your setting. When it comes to you then applying for a programme, you'll have a smorgasbord of evidence from which to choose.

2. Once accepted, make use of your new professional learning community, as members will have likely faced similar challenges as you and will have divergent solutions you may not have considered.

3. Make sure, speaking from experience, any evidence you share has accessible links.

CHAPTER 19
Working with vendors

'The network is more powerful than the node.'

Gapingvoid

19.1 Relationships, not transactions

From the offset, it is important to note that working with vendors is all about relationships, not transactions. You are working in partnership. By doing this as a collective responsibility, you are going to provide one another with the best possible expertise to enhance each stakeholder.

It is unfortunately the case that not all companies see or operate in this way, instead seeing the relationship between themselves and schools as transactional. We recognise that this is short-sighted. Seek clarity on a company's viewpoint on this before engaging.

From an education viewpoint, seeking relationships will benefit the education of all children and the knowledge of all educators. Vendors, on the other hand, will gain developing insights into the complexities of education, but also how and what works in differing contexts. This will assist product development to support current trends in the educational sector.

The strong affiliations and alliances formed between both parties ultimately determine the initiative's success and overall effectiveness. Education and EdTech vendors are both multifaceted; their partnerships can support transformative outcomes when sustained over the long term when they are co-produced, accessible, collaborative, credible, honest and operational, while also delivering on the intended impact. All of this is achieved in collaboration, not in isolation.

With that in mind, and with the aim of supporting you, we have put together some key questions for you to ask an EdTech vendor prior to agreeing to a potential partnership. But first, here's a contribution from Jodie Lopez on the importance of working with vendors.

Jodie Lopez (@jodieworld on X) is the founder of EdTech Ninja (@EdTechninjauk), a company that advises on all things EdTech from both school and business perspectives, with 20 years of experience in the education industry. Jodie is a regular sharer on social media and at conferences across the UK, an award-winning former Primary teacher and avid champion of the power of technology.

Case study: Jodie Lopez

The world of EdTech is awash with loyalty schemes, ambassador programmes and certified teacher badges. You may have been tempted by one already, for yourself or your school. We all love a badge – almost as much as 6-year-olds love a sticker! These programmes often come with attractive benefits too. These may include huge discounts on subscriptions (even 100% off) and payments for teachers to attend events or write blogs. The bigger the bonus, the more attractive this can seem. But it is worth stopping for a moment to consider the true cost and true benefits of these partnerships.

Working with an EdTech vendor could yield benefits you do not even think about to start with. Speaking opportunities can lead to further paid opportunities. Blogs written for a company website can then lead to writing articles for major news publications. However, there is a lot of time involved in these activities and they often rely on a sole teacher at a school. The school is often the one getting the benefit – in the form of a discounted invoice – and a teacher has their workload increased in their evenings and weekends. Therefore, it is important for schools to consider the impact that their discount is having on their staff. Be sure that the monetary value is not outweighed by teacher burnout.

But what, really, is the purpose of these engagements? Well primarily, for the vendor, they form part of a sales and marketing strategy. They know that if enthusiastic teachers talk about how they use the product, then more teachers are likely to buy their product. And that is very true: teachers buy from teachers. For the teacher, there is kudos involved – from a badge on the lanyard to the experience which may help when applying for their next promotion.

There is no doubt that a blog by a teacher helps other teachers to understand more about how they might use the same product in their classrooms. This is a huge benefit to the vendor and to other teachers too. But all too often, teachers are writing about the way they use a product even though there are loads of things about the product they would love to change. When they are working for a big-name company, they may be able to add some ideas in a focus group, but those ideas take a long time to become part of the product. Huge companies just take time to do things; smaller companies, however, are much more agile in their development.

Working with smaller companies often means that you can work more closely with teachers to help form the product – and this, in my opinion, is where the real EdTech magic happens. When you use an EdTech product, you will invariably wish it also did X, Y and Z. We don't tend to go directly to Google or Apple if we have a suggestion, but we would go to a small local company and tell them what we think, because we know that our one voice is more powerful in that smaller pond. The same is true in EdTech.

The best products on the EdTech market are from those who either are former teachers themselves, or who work very closely with teachers. They usually have former teachers on their team, and they are also engaging regularly with current classroom teachers. When these relationships work well, it means that schools get products which really meet their needs, and vendors get to sell to more schools. Everyone is happy.

Sadly, often the opposite happens – a real 'us versus them' situation – where schools just see vendors as people trying to sell to them and are wary of approaching them. Hand on heart, though, I would say that most people in EdTech just want the best for schools and their students. They need to sustain their business, of course, but they do care about schools and teachers.

The way to get the best EdTech product is for schools and vendors to work closely together. So, the next time you get an email or a call from an EdTech vendor, perhaps see if you can give a bit of your time to help each other out. Every conversation matters in EdTech. The big money deals are great, but make sure your teacher's voice is always heard within any size of company if you want the biggest impact.

19.2 Top questions to ask vendors before you buy

Throughout the book, we have been mindful to try to provide you with many take-aways to guide you and save you time. In the moment, when you are on a phone call with a salesperson, it is more often than not the case that you are speaking to a sales professional and not an educational professional. Not only are they paid to sell, but it is likely that they will be even further incentivised to sell on commission-based rates. They will, therefore, just as you in the classroom have an arsenal of teaching and learning strategies at your disposal, have a similar arsenal of sales strategies. It is useful to go into any of these types of conversations well-prepared with the questions you wish to have answered. Equally, take lots of notes and do not commit to anything on that call. Go away, consider their responses and speak with colleagues in other schools using their products to verify their claims.

Below, you will find a series of questions you may find useful to have answered. However, please be mindful that this list is not exhaustive and the most important questions to be answered are the ones which relate directly to yourself, your school and your context. Get these prepared well in advance of your meeting so that you know what your negotiables and non-negotiables are.

1. How have you used research to inform your product development?
2. What does ongoing support and adoption really look like at your company?
3. What support do you offer during implementation?
4. What impact should we expect to see from your product?
5. How does your product reduce workload?
6. How does your product improve teaching and learning?
7. How often do you update your product and what informs its development?
8. When was the last time your product was reviewed by a third party?
9. Can you share any product case studies with me from schools similar to my context?
10. How does your product allow me to import, export or synchronise information?
11. In what format can I do the above?
12. Does your product support a data standard such as Ed-Fi, IMS Global, Access 4 Learning or similar?
13. Do you adhere to secure student data privacy policies?
14. Are you a signatory of the Future of Privacy Forum Student Privacy Pledge or similar?
15. Has your development team received training about data privacy and security?
16. Does your architecture support student data security?
17. How does your application architecture support scalability to provide fast response times to high volume and product usage?
18. What is the process for incorporating your product into our curriculum?
19. How will we implement the new workflow with this product?

20. May I reach out to a customer who has incorporated your product into their curriculum to ask about their experience?
21. Does your product rely on research to demonstrate impact and inform product improvement?
22. If we chose not to continue with your product, what would happen to our data?
23. Have you signed the Project Unicorn Vendor Pledge?

NB: Some of these questions were taken from the Project Unicorn Vendor Pledge, www.projectunicorn.org/resources/10-questions-for-edtech-vendors.

One final piece of advice: don't be afraid to walk away. Follow up on their responses, don't just believe their case studies, and ask for the contact details of those who they have referenced so you can contact them yourself to validate any claims they may make independently.

With the above in mind, it's time to dig into a case study from Dave Smith. Dave had oversight for the content of the British Educational Suppliers Association's (BESA) partnerships and events, as well as leading on its EdTech Exchange and Bett Futures programmes. Formerly a teacher and local authority senior inspector in London, Dave has spent over twenty years specialising in computing, education technology and online safety support for schools in the UK and overseas. He is a former Bett and Education Resources Awards (ERA) judge and has also served as a member of the Bett Advisory Group. He recently worked with NAACE (the Education Technology Association) on the EdTech leadership briefing paper for school leaders. He is currently a member and governor of two Primary/Secondary multi-academy trusts in England, has been a governor of four Primary and Secondary schools and was previously a teacher/senior leader in three London schools and a UK university.

Case study: Dave Smith

My experience of advising schools on many EdTech projects in local authority and multi-academy trusts has always started with the key question, 'What will be the positive impact of the project you are planning once it is implemented?' Before reaching out to EdTech vendors, it's crucial to have a clear understanding of what you want to achieve and where EdTech fits in. This then allows you to look for EdTech solutions to address this.

Asking the right questions before making a purchase is essential to ensure that EdTech solutions align with your school's objectives. To begin, you should enquire about the vendor's experience in managing EdTech projects in schools. Request testimonials from other educational institutions that have worked with the vendor to gauge its past performance. What is the efficacy of its EdTech product or service – and how can it demonstrate this? It's also important to check the technical qualifications of the vendor's staff or company, and the support it can provide for staff training and implementation. Furthermore, ask about its systems for recording and resolving technical issues, as well as its data-compliance measures, especially when handling sensitive student and staff data.

Check that the vendor is listed on the Crown Commercial Services 'education technology' suppliers list or is a member of a reputable education sector trade association like BESA – this is an indicator of a reputable vendor. BESA's own code of practice[1] is a mandatory membership commitment that offers a good point of reference for schools to vendors abiding by them. It includes the following aspects:

- Quality and standards: We will seek to achieve the highest standards and will offer our products, advice and services honestly and honourably in a fair and transparent manner.
- Integrity: We value our customers and promise a high standard of customer service and to deal promptly with any complaints.
- Transparency and openness: We will be transparent about the costs and charges we make to our customers and these will be clearly stated in our T&Cs and the contracts we agree with them.
- Safeguarding and data security: We will ensure all staff are aware of safeguarding issues and will endeavour to comply with any educational institution's safeguarding rules and regulations.

These questions will help schools assess the experience, effectiveness, support and compliance of EdTech vendors before deciding.

What should you expect vendors to ask you?

Vendors should be willing to find out what your specific objectives are. I have worked with excellent vendors who have taken the trouble to read a school's inspection report, as well as checking school development and curriculum planning on the school's website to get an understanding of the school's context

---

[1] www.besa.org.uk/code-of-practice

and needs. This placed them at a distinct advantage when presenting their solution to the school. Doing this research matters, and certainly made the schools I worked with feel that the vendor was looking at their specific project through a bespoke lens. I would be concerned if a vendor arrived with a one-size-fits-all attitude.

As a governor, I had the misfortune of having a vendor, with no experience in the education sector, advising on the proposed Wi-Fi solution for the school, using an out-of-date satellite image taken from an online mapping platform. I asked why the vendor had not visited the school to undertake a wireless survey, including important factors such as the fabric of the school building. The vendor suggested that what it had proposed was 'the right solution for a school of that age and size'. Needless to say, it was not selected for the project.

What should you do to prepare for your first meeting with a vendor?

To prepare for your first meeting with a vendor, clearly define your expectations and objectives. If it's for a hardware project, consider holding the meeting in person, allowing the vendor to see your school's physical space and existing EdTech provision. Be realistic about potential discounts or support, as the vendor may not have the resources to offer free equipment, but it might provide support in terms of training and advice.

How do you establish what it is you are really looking for with a vendor?

I have seen vendors at close hand who have 'gone the extra mile' in handling issues. Ideally, you want the EdTech vendor to treat the project as if it was part of your school community and feed back on a regular basis. Ultimately, as the consumer, your school's needs and requirements should drive the decision-making process. Regular communication with the vendor, expressing concerns and celebrating successes, can lead to a successful EdTech implementation that benefits your school community.

Why is it important to have 'all cards on the table' before you make a purchase with a vendor?

Having 'all cards on the table' before making a purchase is crucial to avoid misunderstandings. Prepare a list of non-negotiables and draft a detailed contract with specific deliverables, timelines and penalties for missed deadlines. Consulting your school's procurement or legal advisers can provide additional assurance.

> **What a good relationship with a vendor looks like**
>
> Building an effective relationship is important in ensuring a successful EdTech project. A vendor following through on what it says is a good indicator. One headteacher with whom I worked would not countenance working with vendors who arrived late for meetings (without good reason), as they believed that this was an indication of a poor work ethic. Regular checkpoint meetings can help plan, implement and review the project's effectiveness. Remember, though, that there are two sides to the relationship; therefore, keeping on top of it on the school side is essential, as deadlines can be missed and this can be an issue when it comes to go-live dates, especially when it impacts negatively on teaching and learning.

Dave was also kind enough to share some key questions to ask vendors:

- What experience do you have managing the rollout of EdTech projects in schools?
- Can you provide testimonials from other schools regarding your company's past and present EdTech projects?
- What evidence do you have to demonstrate the efficacy of your EdTech product/service in schools?
- How will your solution address the issue we have?
- What technical qualifications do your staff members/company have?
- What systems do you have in place to record any technical issues?
- How do you ensure data compliance when managing my school's data?
- What support can you provide to help with training and implementation?
- Can you assist me with my EdTech strategy?
- Who will be supporting us and what is their relevant experience in doing so?
- Are you a member of a trade association which has a code of conduct guiding practice and approach to working in the education sector (e.g. BESA)?

19.3 Benefits for your school

Before you engage with any vendor(s), ensure you have completed your due diligence in line with your digital strategy: does this solution/software/tool align with and support it? If the answer to that question is no, then it is time to move on. And if you haven't got a digital strategy, then it's best to start constructing one!

As with every element in an education setting, one of the first ports of call is to consider the cost. Not all costs are financial in the first instance, but many will involve time, which is a resource in and of itself – and often an ill-afforded one. While vendors will likely offer you many different incentives, it is worth having in mind the cost that is associated with this, namely: time, training, implementation, feedback, guidance, meetings, reflections and more.

While you may well decide to be the innovator or early adopter and subsequent test-bed for a new EdTech tool and reap the reward(s), you will need to balance this against the possibility and increased probability that you don't reach the desired outcome, as it may simply not work. We are back to the risk versus reward paradigm: the earlier you are in adoption, the greater the risk, as the solution will likely not be fully developed at this stage. A sensible question to ask is: is it delivering on the deliverables? If not, why not?

19.4 Expectations versus reality

At this point, it may well feel like this chapter is coming across rather negatively. This is certainly not the intention, and both of us have worked with multiple EdTech vendors very successfully over the years. Our intention here is to ensure that you are doing it for all the right reasons, as opposed to it being another magpie moment because you are swayed by the new 'shiny thing' at the cost of the day-to-day stuff.

While many vendors will work well with you, it is important to ensure that, within your conversations, both parties are crystal clear on what is expected from each other. This will avoid any confusion and serve as a service level agreement (SLA) or benchmark as to how the relationship can and will operate moving forwards. While this may sound like a challenging conversation is needed, it is simply about transparency and knowing what you can and cannot do within the realms of being both realistic and achievable. It is better to under-promise and over-deliver than be faced with the opposite scenario (having both been there, it can get ugly). Identify what your shared communication and support strategies are and run with them. Remember, once you are partnered, you are on the same team and are working towards the same goal: improving outcomes.

19.5 You're in the driver's seat

As this heading says, you are indeed in the driving seat. Be mindful that being a verified organisation on X costs £1140 per month (as of August 2023) or that a stand with a table at an event costs upwards of £5000 per day – know thy worth!

It is fair to say that never before have we seen such a buyer's market in education when it comes to the relationship between schools and vendors. Therefore, given the moral duty you have to ensure that you get best value for money with your (often public) funds, everything should be on the table in the conversations you have with vendors.

Any EdTech vendor will tell you that it costs a fortune to advertise its products, whether that is online, at events, email marketing or adverts in magazines. But there is no better advertisement than word of mouth or a recommendation by a trusted person of influence: enter, you.

Try before you buy! Every EdTech company will (or at least should!) let you try its product before you buy it, so ensure that you negotiate a suitable timescale (a month at a minimum) for the trial so you can gain sufficient data to support your ongoing decision-making process – and if you're still not convinced after the trial, ask for an extension. If the vendor refuses, that helps your decision! While (often with cloud-based services) it will cost a company to give you that trial, so your trial can't last indefinitely, you should be given the opportunity to check out a product successfully. If the timescale isn't sufficient, then we would argue you aren't ready for that product (or any product) anyway.

Be clear about how you see the EdTech solution translating to solving a problem or supporting an initiative in your school setting. Ensure the evidence-based and context-specific needs are practical and translatable to the solution. Hold all parties to account and ensure this is all in support of your digital strategy. Control the variables as best as is possible, measure them frequently so you know the direction of travel – and when something goes off-piste, take the time to get to the root of it and adapt accordingly.

With the above in mind, be mindful of agreements! It is likely that you will have to sign a contract for the tool or service you are purchasing. Before signing anything, be very clear on what you are signing for and be very mindful of agreements that tie you into a service for longer than a 12-month period. Technology advances quickly and being tied into a 3-year agreement when a product doesn't end up being a good fit or isn't updated quickly enough to meet cybersecurity or other needs and demands can be problematic. It's only proper to have a quicker route out if you need it.

Just as on pricing, negotiate the terms of your agreement so that it benefits you rather than the company. If there's anything there you don't like, negotiate. Once you've signed something, the school is bound to it, so while you are in the driver's seat: drive – don't be a passenger!

Questions to consider
1. Is it a subscription basis or a one-off payment?
2. If it is a subscription, does it automatically renew?
   - When will it renew?
   - What notice needs to be given in the event of a cancellation?
   - Do you have a cancellation period after the initial purchase?
   - What are the terms of the get-out clause?
3. If it is not a subscription, how long is the term: 1, 2, 3 or 5 years? Remember, negotiate!
4. How often is the software/solution updated and will this impact learning/usage?
5. Can the contract/subscription be increased linked to inflation or is it a fixed price?
6. If a new version of the software is released, is this included in the original agreement or will a new contract and fee be required?
7. If you wish to add additional licences during the term of the contract, will this mark the start of a new contract or can it be bolted onto the original one?

When you are looking to strike a deal with a vendor (caveat: excluding the big three of Apple, Google and Microsoft, who use ambassador schemes – you can look back for more on this in chapter 18), every vendor should be open to a conversation about your potential relationship. There are many ways it can be mutually beneficial for both parties and these should always be on the table for discussion. For example, a discounted rate for a product can be achieved by the school undertaking activities such as providing case studies and other marketing collateral for the vendor. Also, make it clear that any such PR for the company is incumbent on the product being fit for purpose. You can only deliver on this if the product delivers on its use. These materials can come in the form of case studies, presentations at events about its products/services, interviews, social media sharing, podcasts, vlogs, being a lighthouse school, and more.

Hopefully, you will recognise the importance of only sharing things which are true; there is enough snake oil in the industry without being part of *that* problem, but if you are genuinely thrilled about the product/solution then why not seek to explore how you can work on a symbiotic relationship with a company that ultimately benefits your learners, colleagues, community *and* your budget?

Should you embark upon such a relationship, it is likely that the vendor will want to outline a friendly agreement which transparently sets out its terms. When it comes to this part of the conversation, as with the advice shared above, read the agreement carefully as, once you have signed it, you are bound to its terms. We are not legal experts, but it is likely that within your school/MAT/district you will have legal counsel within your structures, so it's probably wise to have any symbiotic relationship agreements checked by your legal team to ensure you are not opening yourself up to any potential conflicts.

While we don't actively advocate for these approaches, in a world where families are still choosing whether to heat or eat, you might like to think more creatively about how you can achieve best value with your EdTech purchases – because if you're not, somebody else will be!

With the above in mind, here are some more questions to help you capitalise on the situation:

1. How can we secure a discount?
2. What other activities can we undertake to receive a discount?
3. Are these discounts scalable? If so, how?
4. Will this initial discount be for year 1 only or transferable across the full term of the contract?

This is a great position to bring in a brilliant example from the fabulous Chris Dyson (@chrisdysonHT on X) of how to successfully work with EdTech vendors and what you can get. Chris was the headteacher at Parklands Primary, situated on one of Europe's largest council estates in Leeds. One of the most deprived schools in the city, with 64% pupil premium when Chris arrived at the school, it had been deemed 'inadequate' and had 150 suspensions in a year. In addition, results were at rock bottom. By the time he left, exclusions had dropped to only one in nine years, the school had the highest progress score for maths in the country and was in the top 5% in reading and writing. Ofsted judged the school 'outstanding'.

Chris's strength is changing the culture of schools, with the proverbial 'carrot' being used rather than a stick, coaching used with staff, and the wellbeing of staff and children becoming the driving force. Upon leaving for a new role, the succession planning was in place, with the deputy head becoming the new headteacher.

Chris was also an NLE (national leader in education) driving standards forward in schools across Yorkshire and worked with schools to achieve transformation and school improvement. Chris is now the deputy CEO of a trust in Birmingham with 3000 children, The Create Trust, where in March 2023 one of the schools moved from 'inadequate' (ungraded) to 'good' by inspectors.

Case study: Chris Dyson

23 March 2020 is a date that nobody will forget, when our country took the unprecedented step to go into national lockdown, in the wake of the WHO (World Health Organization) declaring COVID-19 a public health emergency of international concern.

Gavin Williamson had announced that all children would be doing online learning. The only problem with this is that we required 300 laptops or similar devices. The good old DfE (Department for Education) gave us three. Yes, three. If my own children were at home doing their lessons, so too would my children at Parklands.

So, working with LGfL, Let's Localise, Legal and General, Sky News, ITV News and BBC News, we set about the challenge of sourcing 300 laptops. The personal touch and the drive for equality saw us source 800 devices which we gladly shared with schools in a similar situation to us.

The obvious next problem was that the children had limited internet connections. Guarav and the team at Let's Localise did not let us down. A week after asking, 400 unlimited '*dongles*' arrived.

The results of having wonderful business partnerships saw my school benefit from £450,000 raised in 2022–23 from businesses (£1.6m in 5 years).

My top tips to you are:

- Use Google Maps to find the national or multinational companies that are close to you.
- Send a personal invitation to their community champions to showcase your school's niche. Mine was times tables with our Year 1 children.
- Don't send blanket emails. Make them personal and find the person who can help.
- Contact BITC (Business In The Community) – Google your closest partner. This organisation will find you volunteers, free of charge, for decorating or gardening projects.
- If you are lucky enough to be in the North of England, then do check out Shine Trust (www.shinetrust.org.uk) – we received £45,000 a year for projects.
- Voluntary action projects (Google) are a great source of help.
- Most importantly, value people and make them feel special.

Economies of scale

In business, when you purchase an item, it will have what is known as a unit price. This is calculated by taking the cost to produce the item plus whatever profit margin the company wishes to enjoy on top. It is often the case that when you buy multiple products, the unit cost per item reduces. We commonly see this in supermarkets; an individual item costs more comparative to that of each item in a pack of four. Businesses do this because it is far better to sell multiple products than just one; this price reduction is called an economy of scale. To illustrate, here are prices taken from Asda's website on 23 February 2024 at 11:09 BST:

Item	Cost	Cost/can
Single can of Coca-Cola	£1	£1
Multipack (8 cans)	£5.20	£5.20 ÷ 8 = £0.65
Multipack (24 pack)	£13.50	£13.50 ÷ 24 = £0.56

Table 19.1: Economies of scale using cans of Coca-Cola

When we purchase products from an EdTech vendor, it will have similar pricing tables, where a single unit will cost proportionately more than multiple items. With this knowledge, when in conversation with an EdTech company, be sure to find out what economies of scale you could look to enjoy for multiple purchases.

At this point, it might be good to talk about the benefits of collaborative purchasing. If you are in a MAT or school district, then leaders within your organisation will already be looking to purchase like items across each school. But if you are a school that's not part of a MAT or a district, then you might like to reach out to your local school networks to see if your peers are looking at similar purchases. If you were to join forces, you might be able to further reduce the unit price.

19.6 Financing the tech: buying versus leasing

For those schools/MATs/districts that provide work devices for staff, it is worth considering how you go about financing the technology itself as you have a couple of different options; namely, buying and leasing.

Buying requires an initial one-off outlay covering the cost of the items and, once procured, the organisation is in full ownership of the device(s). Leasing, however, sees the item cost split over the term of the agreement (which is negotiated at time of purchase). Typically, with leasing, the cost of a £650 device will be split over a monthly payment for, say, three years; so there will be a monthly or quarterly payment that covers the cost of the device over this term which equates to £650 over 36 months, giving a monthly payment of £18.06. Often, where finances are tight, leasing over the long-term enables organisations to access a higher specification of device than they could afford from a capital payment, due to the cost being spread out over a longer time.

The same theory and considerations also apply for those looking at one-to-one device provision for their learners. The only likely differences here will be that the cost of the technology may either be embedded into incurred costs for schools with a fee-paying structure, or there may be some form of parental contribution(s) towards the cost of the device(s).

The next table highlights some of the benefits and drawbacks for each of the two options. While it is not an exhaustive list, it is there to start the conversation and serve as a guide to support your thinking and discussions, giving you a 'starter for 10' to get you going on which option is best for your school/MAT/district.

Area	Buying	Leasing
Project costs	Economies of scale through aggregation, but large capital outlay at start.	Spread the cost over the timeline to suit your school/trust/district budget with fixed monthly/quarterly payments.
Cash flow	Full costs upfront.	Spread over an agreed term to suit the school/trust/district budget.
Ownership	Fully own the assets so you can use as you wish.	Assets remain property of the lease company rather than the school. At the end of the lease, you don't own the asset but can often buy them at 'current value'.
Maintenance	Control of assets and work within your own schedule.	Must return assets in a specific condition – can incur costs, so think about adding accidental damage insurance so there are no surprises at the end of the agreement.
Long-term planning	Great if you intend to keep the kit over a long time period, e.g. >5 years, then only paying for MDM. Can make some money back at the end by reselling assets but at reduced cost.	Great for replacing with a new device every few years to keep up to date. Can work out more expensive in the long term.
The extras	Need to purchase warranties and insurance, MDM and protective cases all separately.	Can often wrap warranties and insurance up into lease terms throughout the contract, covering faults/damage etc. Not all providers will offer this, so check T&Cs carefully. Occasionally, you can wrap MDM into the leasing fee structure along with device cases for a yearly annual charge.
Warranty	Most frequent range is 3–7 years, so covers device lifespan offering a cost saving over time.	Included in the leasing contract.

Table 19.2: Benefits and drawbacks for buying and leasing

So, how do you decide? Well, here are some further considerations to help guide you:

- The decision ultimately will be determined by your available budget for your procurement and IT refresh strategy: one big hit or small recurring payments? You may wish to try to be a little more creative in how you divert or reduce other funds to support this cost.
- Warranties and asset lifespan. Long-term, it is better to own the kit outright, but the trade-off is that the devices will become outdated. Leasing is a popular choice due to having access to the latest updates, but it needs consistent regular funding to support.
- Depending on your situation, the negotiation, the marketplace at the time of quotations and the reseller, each one can work out cheaper.
- Check in the T&Cs that the reseller isn't using a third-party finance underwriter, as this will cost you more!

Additional considerations to the device cost that will likely impact on your overall direction of travel:

- **Wrap-around costs:** What other costs will be incurred?
- **Support costs:** What will the support costs be for each device? All devices?
- **Textbook costs:** How could this be offset? Would digital textbooks be cheaper?
- **Book costs:** Exercise books. How could this cost be reduced? (You still need some!)
- **Printing costs:** What reduction in printing would you expect to see with a one-to-one initiative or even simply because more and more aspects of school are now digitised?
- **Planner costs:** Are they really needed with a one-to-one/digital project?
- **Stationery:** Will this need to be as extensive now you have one-to-one/more devices in the hands of learners?
- **Efficiencies from savings:** What efficiencies are you expecting to see and why? Is everyone aware of this and is it a part of the strategy?

19.7 IT MSP versus in-house service

Another area for us to delve into when working with vendors is that of IT services. While this might seem a little heavy for a book on EdTech, education and schools are becoming more businesslike in their financial foci to ensure they are getting a return on investment from all their resources: people, EdTech purchases and more.

Here, we are specifically looking at the provision of IT support within and across a school/MAT/district: from frontline support to how problems are dealt with and ticketed, to who manages this and who tells your technical support to deal with different problems, to strategic planning to ensure consistent uptime for all of your essential services – you name it, IT support does it!

Before we go any further, it's time to get familiar with three more acronyms:

- MSP = managed service provider
- SWOT analysis = strengths, weaknesses, opportunities, threats
- PESTLE = political, economic, social, technological, legal and environmental

It's important to be aware of these as they will likely form part of the frameworks you will use to determine your course of action.

Managed service provider

A managed service provider (MSP) is a company that provides managed services for your school/MAT/district where you do not have the requisite skills within your organisation or you need additional capacity.

There are benefits and drawbacks to using an MSP. The biggest drawback is the costs involved, which are significantly higher than what you would pay if you employed staff yourself. However, there are benefits to be had alongside these:

Benefits	Drawbacks
Clearly defined project work to support your digital strategy.	Increases challenge on fostering positive relationships.
Leverage potential cost reductions.	Risk of using an additional solution that is not in line with your existing ecosystem.
Scalable response.	Scaling the support increases the cost.
Compliance sits with the MSP rather than your organisation.	Potential hazard with communication timelines.
Opportunity to leverage additional training through the MSP.	

Benefits	Drawbacks
Opportunity to tap into highly specialised skills.	
Skilled staff who are trained to the latest standards (where you don't have to pay for their training).	

Table 19.3: Benefits and drawbacks of using an MSP

The IT services an MSP or third party company will provide are typically determined by the agreement you co-create but could include daily support and response mechanisms, project work, data hosting, strategic planning, ticketing support, procurement advice, auditing and more. The main point to be aware of here, when considering due diligence, is that an MSP will probably have employees who are experts in an area where your team may be lacking, so you could seek to leverage this as a part of your agreement. Having said that, our advice here would still be to reach out to others in your local area to find out about their experiences of working with the MSP you may wish to explore a relationship with.

Remember, don't be drawn into all of the additional extras you will likely be offered, as each MSP will have pecuniary interests. This means that it has affiliations with other companies and will be biased towards selling their products, so keep in mind the advice shared earlier in this chapter on procurement. As with all things procurement, it's likely that you will have undertaken some analysis, such as the following SWOT and PESTLE analyses. These analyses are equally as important when considering the adoption of an MSP.

SWOT analysis

A SWOT analysis is a technique used to assess four aspects of your organisational makeup. The framework is a tool to help you analyse what your organisation does well now, so you can devise a successful strategy that is future-facing. It is a realistic, fact-based and data-driven evaluative tool that helps you assess the current state of play at a micro level, while considering additional external factors that would support the development of strategic plans and actions.

There are four key areas in a SWOT analysis: strengths, weaknesses, opportunities and threats. Each area is designed to support the development of a truth-based and unbiased assessment of the current state of play.

- **Strengths:** This should describe what you are excelling at and in which areas of your organisation.
- **Weaknesses:** This identifies where you are not performing at your organisational best and pinpoints where improvements can be made.
- **Opportunities:** This refers to factors that are deemed to be favourable that would help drive an area of your organisation in line with its various strategic goals.
- **Threats:** This refers to factors that can cause harm to your organisation.

Benefits	Drawbacks
It's an easy-to-understand framework.	It can be seen as an oversimplification.
Holistic view of internal and external factors.	Might not capture all nuances specific to IT in your context.
Structured framework aids systematic analysis.	Requires regular updating as conditions change.
Facilitates strategic planning and resource allocation.	Overreliance on the framework might stifle innovative solutions.
Provides clarity for budgetary considerations.	SWOT's generalised approach may miss some IT-specific considerations.

Table 19.4: Benefits and drawbacks of a SWOT analysis

A successful SWOT analysis will involve you in determining your organisational objective and is achieved by gathering a range of voices and resources to contribute to the overall analysis. You will synthesise a range of internal and external factors and data for each category so that a broad range is covered and can later be distilled to the core components. You will filter these findings and rank them in terms of priorities and, finally, construct a strategic plan which makes a complex problem more manageable and actionable.

PESTLE analysis

A PESTLE analysis is a diagnostic framework that studies the varying external factors that influence an organisation, where the outcomes will ultimately guide strategic influences and decision-making processes. It is therefore an external and macro framework to support organisational thinking and strategic planning. The framework is made up of six different factors, namely: political, economic, social, technological, legal and environmental.

1. **Political:** These are the political factors that should be accounted for, such as government policies, regulations on industry and trade, inflation and political stability.
2. **Economic:** This includes factors such as economic growth/decline, interest and inflation rates, consumer rates, the cost of labour and the cost of living.
3. **Social:** This includes factors such as cultural norms, cultural expectations, attitudes, work–life balance, the stats across the populations and their demographics.
4. **Technological:** This focuses on how technology responds to service needs, along with how technology innovates and disrupts at micro and macro levels across society/industry, how social media and social networking drive and influence habits, and the roles of automation and AI.
5. **Legal:** This focuses on the legal landscape and, more specifically, labour law and how decisions impact working practices, legislation and, ultimately, regulations.
6. **Environmental:** This looks at how your organisation impacts the environment: how sustainable is your organisation? What social responsibility are you fostering and enacting? This covers everything from the supply chains that you use through to the processes and procedures in the organisation that reduce your carbon emissions.

As with the SWOT analysis, there are also benefits and drawbacks for a PESTLE analysis:

Benefits	Drawbacks
Aids the understanding over the wider organisational environment.	Can be a mechanism for oversimplification.
It encourages strategic thinking and thinking about how external partnership could lead to organisational benefit(s).	Too large a data set could cause organisational paralysis due to over-analysis of the data streams.
Leads to insights on potential future trends and therefore strategic plans.	The data may lead to unfounded and assumptive activities.
The framework is easy to understand.	Needs to be conducted regularly.

Benefits	Drawbacks
Enables opportunities to be identified.	It is difficult to anticipate developments due to the rate of change. (Just look at how fast AI is currently moving!)
Builds a clear and deep understanding of the current state of play.	The results are typically incomplete owing to external factors – industry/ political change being so frequent but not always transferable or appropriate to the education sector.
Cost-effective, as it draws on internal expertise and knowledge.	
Fosters a culture of organisational 'alertness'.	

Table 19.5: Benefits and drawbacks of a PESTLE analysis

Through a PESTLE analysis, the outcomes give your organisation contextual information that can support the redefinition of strategic planning, marketing, your workforce, opportunities for driving change in the organisation and its overall forward development. It is a framework that supports the exploration of future trends and ensures that 'the basics' and more complex facets of the organisation are all aligned and supportive of the broader organisational strategy.

PESTLE analysis example

An example of a weighting (or decision matrix) to support your PESTLE analysis might look like the following image. The caveat is that the weighting will need to be specific to your context, organisational vision and mission, and how the factors of the PESTLE model influence them.

Decision Matrix

CRITERIA	WEIGHTAGE	OPTION A RATING	OPTION A TOTAL	OPTION B RATING	OPTION B TOTAL	OPTION C RATING	OPTION C TOTAL
POLITICAL	15%	1	3.75%	2	7.50%	3	11.25%
ECONOMIC	20%	3	15.00%	1	5.00%	2	10.00%
SOCIAL	15%	3	11.25%	4	15.00%	2	7.50%
TECHNOLOGY	20%	2	10.00%	1	5.00%	4	20.00%
LEGAL	10%	1	2.50%	3	7.50%	2	5.00%
ENVIRONMENTAL	20%	1	5.00%	4	20.00%	3	15.00%
max	100%		TOTAL OPTION A 47.50%		TOTAL OPTION B 60.00%		TOTAL OPTION C 68.75%

Figure 19.1: Decision matrix to support a PESTLE analysis (adapted from TemplateLab – Best Business & Legal Templates – https://templatelab.com)

Making the case

When you're deciding which route is best for your school's IT provision, management and maintenance, there is a lot to think about! Consider:

- the advantages and disadvantages of an MSP
- the advantages and disadvantages of in-house
- the business case for each option
- the cost benefit for each option.

What are the UK commercial versus educational rates for IT roles?

- Vendor = IT technicians and developers can command £24–40k depending on their experience.
- MAT/district = IT technician roles typically command £22–30k.
- Technical manager = £40–55k.

(These rates are correct as of July 2023.)

MSP business case

Let's consider why your school/MAT/district should potentially use an MSP.

In the short term, this would likely drive changes in your IT; however, it would increase costs and not necessarily deliver the ROI (return on investment) you might expect to see. If the MSP misses deadlines and has its own capacity issues, it may have a negative knock-on effect on the school/MAT/district. Would you be at greater risk for service continuity and demoralisation of the workforce by going down the MSP route?

In the long term, you could employ an MSP to get great ROI for project-based jobs, like moving to a central domain or building onto Microsoft **SharePoint** to take pressure off your IT team, so it can maintain and build relationships, and improve service consistency with end users.

MSP SWOT analysis

Here is a baseline example of a SWOT analysis for having IT services supported by an MSP. Each organisation will have its preferences here and, quite often, many organisations will have a combination of an MSP and in-house central IT service.

Strengths	Weaknesses
▪ Ability to scale quickly to meet demands.	▪ Can be costly for 5-day/week MSP (especially for on-site presence).
▪ MPS responsible for staff training and skills.	▪ Potential lack of details within SLA leading to discrepancies in work.
▪ Specialist skills.	▪ Could generate some negativity in the team.
▪ Absence cover, so persistent coverage.	
▪ Build your own team around SLA/organisational IT.	▪ Off-site for much of their work so building relationships is difficult.
▪ Compliance built within SLA.	

Opportunities	Threats
■ Chance to save money on various channel partners (e.g. vendor SLAs).	■ Increased financial costs at points of high traffic.
■ Build SLA around your needs (pass through the legal team first).	■ Cost to maintain compliance for additional project work.
■ Create new systems and processes to be more time efficient.	■ Do you trust the MSP to make recommendations in the best interest of the organisation?
■ Free up a team member to be available as a local 'genius' at designated times (think the genius bar at Apple) to offer additional support structures.	
■ Curriculum-wise, take learners to the corporate space of MSP and possible work experience or apprenticeship.	
■ Develop the senior team members as leaders by increased capacity.	
■ Use money for other projects.	

Table 19.6: Example SWOT analysis for an MSP

In-house business case

What is your north star? The guiding principle should be that of the students in the classrooms – will in-house or MSP give you this at a faster pace? It's likely to be the MSP in some scenarios but, in equal measure, it will also be your own team. The MSP route could lead to reduced relationships with stakeholders; however, for in-house, you need clarity of expectations for everyone internally as to a realistic time frame for project delivery so that the team is not overburdened.

In the short term, retaining in-house will give less consistency during change management processes but improve return on investment (ROI) with relationships, etc. later on down the line. This will mean you have to continue to bear the compliance costs (which will also increase over time) and needs to be appropriately budgeted for.

In the long term, retaining an in-house service would give a greater service consistency and ROI along with fostering an organisational sense of home-grown talent.

In-house SWOT analysis

Strengths	Weaknesses
■ Potentially cheaper compared to MSP. ■ Know context and staff. ■ Independence and reduced vulnerability (compared to MSP cost increase(s). ■ Develop your in-house team. ■ Build stronger relationships. ■ Feed into digital strategy.	■ You are responsible for skills/training. ■ Absence cover falls to school/MAT/district. ■ Lose skillset and contextual knowledge through restructuring. ■ New SLA will highlight areas of skill deficit.
Opportunities	**Threats**
■ Restructuring team and operational model. ■ Develop a new SLA within IT. ■ Develop more senior team members as leaders (slower than the MSP route). ■ Drive change(s). ■ Fresh blood/ideas via recruitment process.	■ Loss of skill/context knowledge. ■ Continuation of poor relationships in areas across school/MAT/district. ■ You own all compliance. ■ Cost of maintaining knowledge and skills of the IT team for compliance (offset costs against MSP).

Table 19.7: Example SWOT analysis for in-house provision

Recommendation matrix

Recommendations are based on the analysis of price, ROI (considering relationships, vision actualisation, time cost, etc.), plus service consistency. Each area has been given a weighting from five to one (where five is highly positive and one is highly negative).

Foci	MSP weighting	In-house weighting
Price	1	2
ROI	2	4
Service consistency	3	4
Project work	4	2
Total	**10**	**12**

Table 19.8: Example recommendation matrix

A typical recommendation within education is to keep jobs in-house, but outsource project-based work to an MSP to achieve outcomes at a faster pace.

While the above takes into account Olly's thoughts, the scope and scale of a project run by an MSP will have a large implication on the overall price for project work; this will likely, therefore, change your weighting and, ultimately, the recommendation you may make. It is worth noting at this point that this task should not be done in isolation but be completed by a team of people (e.g. the IT Lead, a member of the executive group/leadership group from school/MAT/district, plus other key stakeholders).

Top tips
Mark's top tips

1. Don't be afraid to walk away from a vendor and never sign on the dotted line without having completed a DPIA. There's lots of salient advice in this chapter, but keep those two things at the front of your head above all else – that and negotiate, negotiate, negotiate!

2. Don't do these things in isolation. Remember, there's no 'I' in 'team', so seek thoughts from colleagues both within and outside your setting – this is where a solid PLN can help!

3. Financial planning is key. Just because your school or trust's business manager might say 'no', knowing what financial commitments a purchase takes gives you the opportunity to be creative, just as you saw in Chris Dyson's case study.

Olly's top tips

1. Before you meet with a vendor, know what it is you want to achieve and why. Do your research so that you know how any form of technology or vendor support can help you to achieve your goal(s) as an organisation.

2. Do your research! Reach out to your network and schools that are in a similar context to you to find out what has and hasn't worked for them and why; this will only help to further inform you about what's right for your school.

3. It's as much about them as it is about you. Keep yourselves and the vendor in check with clear communication so that you are realistic about achieving your deployment timelines.

CHAPTER 20
Personal learning networks

'I love it when a plan comes together.'

John 'Hannibal' Smith, *The A-Team*

20.1 What is a PLN and why should you have one?

Mark and Olly first met via social media a little over eight years ago, back in 2016. It was Olly reaching out to Mark via social media, asking him if he wanted to be interviewed for a UKEdChat podcast, that led to their meeting for the first time. This was at the 'EdTech Impact' conference Mark had organised, exploring impact with educational technology. Of course, this led to a great friendship between the two of them and this book would never have been written had it not been for that meeting!

For decades, educators have been coming together on social media platforms to share ideas, thoughts, woes and worries, seeking to find support, obtain new perspectives, find a mentor and gain insights. They find their tribes (and often their echo chambers) and gain insights from each other on these platforms; it is what is known as their professional learning network (PLN).

A PLN is a personalised network of individuals, resources, groups and companies that an individual curates, connects with and cultivates to improve their learning and professional development. Rajagopal et al. (2011) suggest that when a professional:

> '... intentionally builds, maintains and activates ... contacts within her personal network for the purpose of improving her learning – and uses technology to support this activity – [this] is creating a personal learning network.'

In the world we live in, there are many different platforms available for teachers to come together, and they do so in places such as X (formerly Twitter), Threads, Bluesky, LinkedIn, Mastodon, Facebook, Instagram, Reddit, Snapchat, YouTube – there are so many platforms available and, no doubt, in the future more will come to the fore.

It's not the platform that we should be looking at here; it's why educators reach out. Why do educators want, or possibly even feel the need, to find and connect with more educators? What is it about social media and a PLN that drives us to share? Why do we (mostly) see social media as a necessity in the modern day and age when it comes to professional learning and development?

Our places of work give us a natural collective of expertise to draw on, but in many ways this is finite and, by going to social media, we extend our staffroom to include all who we add to our network. There's a near infinite number of experts we can learn from across an array of contexts, which all serve to help us to learn and make more informed choices, enabling us to be as successful as possible in our own settings.

Social media platforms afford us the opportunity to connect with an author of a book we are reading, find the latest research paper with leading voices' views on it, learn from the latest advancement from a vendor and how to apply that to a school setting, learn about the work of governments and the latest policy developments, ask a question to an authority on a particular topic, find partners to collaborate with on a project, pose a question and receive a wider range of answers than we might find in our own setting, reach out to the entire network to seek advice – all from the click of a button. Learning, connecting and collaborating have never been easier.

20.2 What to do about inappropriate behaviour

As can be the case with many areas of life, there can be instances where less than savoury events, comments or incidences occur online. With a lens specific to social media, the following two examples are the most common, from our experiences. Firstly, comments which are inappropriate and/or hurtful which target an individual or group of people. Secondly, fake accounts posting materials which are unsavoury in nature or creating accounts that imitate an individual/organisation.

Either way, both instances highlight the importance of safeguarding yourself, your account(s), and your community, and ensuring that you take positive steps and actions towards maintaining a safer community. It's also worth remembering that anything we post online stays with us and forms a part of our digital footprint – a digital tattoo, you could say.

In recent years on X, there's been an increase in bots/fake accounts. Olly blogged about this in 2021 (Lewis, 2021) after his account was cloned; a fake account was created with a near identical handle (@) which mirrored all his details (photo, bio, etc.). There are typically a few indicators to look out for with accounts such as this, namely:

- **When the account was created (the join time):** Fake accounts are typically one or two months old.
- **What the account has engaged with:** Fake accounts typically do not engage with anything (be it likes, posts etc.).
- **Follower count:** Fake accounts typically have very low follower counts, if any followers at all.
- **Communication style:** Typically, fake accounts or bots won't have the same rhythm or language as what you'd expect from a professional educator.
- **Is what they are sharing too good to be true?** Have a critical mindset.
- **Evaluate the source's reliability and credibility:** Fake accounts typically have no link to a reputable website, secondary account or alternative source.

If, after checking all of the above, you believe the account to be fake, it is best to simply ignore it. If it is posting content that is hurtful, malicious or unkind, report it as either spam or targeted harassment and then block it. While educators are pressured for time the world over, there are tools out there to support you with this, such as @Botometer or @circleboom.

What about when it is a real human displaying inappropriate behaviour? In our experience, it is best to meet the person/account with kindness while still safeguarding yourself. When we decide to share online, we can follow the THINK framework we discussed earlier in the book, as outlined below:

- **T** – is it true?
- **H** – is it helpful?
- **I** – is it inspiring?
- **N** – is it necessary?
- **K** – is it kind?

As professionals, we must do our best to uphold and model that which we wish to see in our young people, no matter how polarising a statement or argument can be. While challenging at times, we need to be able to spot the difference between facts and opinions.

Information presented online can be biased or possess a slant towards one thing or another. Being mindful of this will help you not only form your own opinion, but also decide how you choose to respond. It is, of course, fine to ask questions and seek more information about what you are seeing. This can be achieved in a number of ways: ask the poster for more clarification, evidence, references and so on. Alternatively, you can conduct your own research into the matter, as we can find almost anything online.

20.3 Keeping it professional

There isn't necessarily a correlation through causation with how a person acts and behaves online versus how a person behaves in real life (we discussed online disinhibition in chapter 16, section 16.3). The online world can feel safer from the confines of your own home, potentially leading an individual to be more extreme in their viewpoints or comments.

No matter what you decide, we advocate for keeping your responses professional and courteous. Your online presence is a reflection of your professionalism and credibility, revealing insights into your character and values. A strong professional presence builds trust and confidence in who we are, what we stand for and our ability as an educator. Poor behaviour online can serve to undermine your credibility and reputation.

Given the very nature of all social media platforms, they are open public fora. Therefore, what we share has a lasting impact. What we hope we can all agree on is that the onus is on us as educators to uphold the integrity of our amazing profession, by demonstrating respect for everyone online through our interactions, and to be positive in those interactions even when we might disagree.

As a final caution, while it is entirely your decision, your social media privacy is vitally important. In keeping with the above themes, it is important to safeguard yourself so that should students find your profile, there is nothing there that can bring you into disrepute. Of course, you can consider making your account private; however, we would just like to share the same advice that was given to us when we first started using X:

- Keep it professional.
- Don't share anything you wouldn't want your mum or headteacher to see.

- Be mindful of privacy when sharing photos.
- Be kind.

There are a few clear reasons for this: firstly, you keep your personal and professional lives separate and, secondly, you are taking positive steps to ensure you are not putting yourself in a difficult position.

Before we get into the next section on this one, if you haven't already done so, now is the time to separate your professional and personal accounts. The rationale here is that you will keep the two worlds separate and your contributions appropriate to the authentic audiences you have curated.

20.4 How to make your profile stand out

Simply put, be of service to the education community by sharing things you consider helpful to your professional practice or helpful to the practice of others. Participate in professional learning communities, share your experiences in meaningful discussions, share ideas, share resources and share recent developments that you find in a particular field; the cumulative aggregation of all of these showcases you as someone who is committed to developing themselves *and* others.

Many educators will do this for the field of education as a whole or by focusing in on one particular aspect, e.g. assessment, behaviour, literacy and so on. Whichever you choose to do, you are contributing to the discourse in the field of education and social media is the lever which enables this. Knowing and following your passion within education is the important part and should remain your focus; not simply getting more followers. Increasing your follower count should be the by-product of your positive contributions and sharing.

Here are a few rules of thumb to get you going and some ideas for sharing:

- Make sure your posts showcase the positives in your current workplace.
- Don't include pictures of students' faces.
- Share what's working for you and your students.
- Share what hasn't worked and what your next steps are (it's OK to iterate).
- Share resources, an article, a research paper or something you have found useful and state why it has been useful.
- Share an initiative from your school.

- Share the events you are participating in and what learning you have captured.
- Engage with differing viewpoints so that you can see both sides of the coin.
- Be your authentic self.
- Shout out your fellow educators who are doing great things in the education sector (we all love to know we have had an impact, no matter how small/big).

20.5 All about the hashtags

One sure-fire way to extend and connect with a larger PLN is to use and follow hashtags. A hashtag is a word or keyword phrase with a hashtag in front (e.g. #EdTech) which is used within a post on social media to highlight your topic and make it easier for those who may be interested in your topic to find it.

Think of it as a spotlight that helps to draw attention to your post(s). The hashtag gives an index to your content so it is readily available to anyone, not just your followers. Hashtags help to give your content context and increase traffic which can, in turn, boost views.

What's the key to a successful hashtag? Keep it simple and accessible. Don't overcomplicate the hashtag, as this will reduce the likelihood of it being used, let alone found in the first place.

What do we mean by accessible? Use camel case; this is the capitalisation of the first letter in each word. For example, using #EdTech rather than #Edtech when referring to educational technology.

While hashtags come and go, below are a few to get you going, but this is by no means an exhaustive list!

Theme	Hashtags
Educational Technology	#EdTech, #EduTech, #iPadEd, #eLearning, #DigCit, #DigiStrat, #EdTechChat, #EdApp, #DigitalLiteracy #AIinEdu, #AIinEducation
Chats	#UKEdChat, #SatChat, #PrimaryRocks

Theme	Hashtags
Education	#EdChat, #Edu, #EduTwitter, #Education, #Wellbeing, #EduX, #Learning, #Teaching, #Students, #UKEdChat, #EducationForChange, #EquityInEducation, #HybridLearning, #RemoteLearning, #TeacherWellness, #Student, #CharacterEducation, #OutdoorEd, #SpecialEducation, #CriticalThinking, #K12, #Pedagogy, #FutureOfWork, #TeacherLife, #Curriculum, #DesignThinking, #FormativeAssessment, #GrowthMindset, #PBL, #PBLChat, #PlaceBasedEd, #ClassroomDesign, #StudentLed, #SchoolCulture, #StudentVoice, #InquiryBasedLearning, #ProjectBasedLearning, #DifferentiatedInstruction
Leadership	#SLTchat, #Leadership, #Leaders
Conferences	#GESSDubai, #ResearchED, #ISTE, #Bett
Subject or School Specific	#SciChat, #EngChat, #TeamEnglish, #MathChat, #PYPchat, #TESOL, #EFL, #STEM, #STEAM, #EarlyEd, #21stCenturySkills, #ArtEd, #CompSci, #Coding, #LangChat, #CommonCore, #HigherEd, #ElemSchool, #HighSchool, #K12, #PrimaryEducation, #SecondaryEducation, #EarlyChildhoodEducation

Table 20.1: EdTech social media hashtag list of examples

So, now you have a few potentially new spheres of social media to engage with through some of the hashtags above, it is competition time!

One of our favourite things about education is the unintended impact that we can have through sharing. We might never meet someone, but could read a blog or thread they've curated and this has a positive impact on what we do. With this in mind, here's our call to action.

Share on either LinkedIn or X (Twitter) a photo of yourself with our book and include in your post the hashtag that has had the biggest influence on your practice within education, and why this hashtag means so much to you and your practice. Also include the obvious hashtag **#EdTechPlaybook**! This will not only give a massive shoutout to your hashtag and community members, but also help to shine a positive light once more and attract more educators to engage with the hashtag.

20.6 Platform comparisons

In a world of marginal gains, we think the easiest and swiftest comparative tool we could use to share a comparison of platforms is to put them into a table. So here it is:

Platform	Typical uses	Advantages	Disadvantages
Facebook	Most commonly used for personal life sharing.	Oldest platform with largest user base.	Merging personal and professional lives by only using this platform. Least favourable platform with younger users.
LinkedIn	Professional work-like networking.	High audience reach due to professional nature of platform. Easy to build network connections.	Limited audience due to professional nature.
X (formerly Twitter)	Share and crowdsource information/ resources while also communicating.	Linked to Google so optimised for SEO. Targeted keywords attract extended audiences and increase traffic.	Cluttered feed due to content updates (similar to all platforms). Many bots of an inappropriate nature.
Instagram	Creative content sharing.	Analytics on demographics engaging with your content.	Time-consuming to keep current and up to date.
Mastodon	Sharing content, typically in text or image form.	Friendly and not advert-driven.	Mastodon is a collection of instances (read 'server' here) so anyone can create a new instance.

Platform	Typical uses	Advantages	Disadvantages
TikTok	Curating and sharing informal, short video clips.	Opportunity to involve yourself or your business in trending content.	Potential issues with aligning messages to business mission or brand.
YouTube	Video-sharing platform.	Potential for large reach.	Takes time to build authentic audience.
SnapChat	Messaging app with disappearing videos.		No metrics available from the app. Aimed at younger audience. Short video content.
Bluesky	Created by Jack Dorsey, the founder of Twitter, Bluesky works like Twitter used to but without all the bots and right-wing activities.	Good platform with similar features to X/ Twitter and a huge and growing teacher base.	You have to start your account from scratch but use Bluesky's 'starter pack' feature, often used by educators to help connect like-minded teachers and groups.

Table 20.2: Social media platform comparisons

Your PLN is exactly that; it is yours. How you choose to interact and positively engage with it is on your terms, and you will get out of it exactly what you put into it. You could draw an education parallel here and say that it's much like the student who actively and diligently engages in learning and asks for help when needed and who is more likely to achieve, compared to those who are passive.

Your investment in terms of time and effort is an investment in yourself, but must be met with a degree of balance. We say this given that social media can make you feel like you never do enough, as there's always another post to engage with. We are here to tell you that you are enough and you don't need to do everything to be successful. Focus on what you need, when you need it, for as long as you need to.

Top tips

Mark's top tips

1. When sharing online, align your purpose for using social media to your educational aims – to learn. You don't need to share everything all the time; share that which is most pertinent to you and your practice.

2. Be a critical consumer. Much like we ask students to have a critical approach to their learning, we should also do the same by analysing and evaluating the content we consume and share online.

3. Be the role model and always be kind.

Olly's top tips

1. Got a question? Ask someone or, better still, ask everyone! Run a poll or ask an open question on your platform of choice to get responses from a larger number of people.

2. You can verify information by evaluating the source of information; check reputable websites, verified accounts, news sources, etc.

3. Engage in and with your PLN – you own who appears on your timeline. Curate a balanced set of educators so that you can see and learn from across the spectrum of education.

CONCLUSION

Congratulations, you've reached the end of the #EdTechPlaybook! Now the real work begins!

The book brings together our collective experiences from more than 50 years of working in education and education technology. It offers a practical synthesis of what we have found to work, why it works, and how to engage with stakeholders to ensure success with your digital transformation in education.

Next Steps

Well that's down to you! It all depends on where you are in your digital journey. Obviously, beyond the book, Mark and Olly are able to work with you and help you, but strategy starts with asking the right questions, finding the gaps, and then working together with stakeholders to build your journey. There's lots to consider.

We won't summarise it all here, you've got the book for that, but we'd love to hear how you get on. Please do reach out to us via our social media, and website contact forms or say hello at the conferences at which we speak.

Want to stay in touch?

Mark	LinkedIn	https://www.linkedin.com/in/themarkanderson/
	Bluesky	https://bsky.app/profile/ictevangelist.bsky.social
	X/Twitter	https://x.com/ictevangelist
	Instagram	https://instagram.com/ictevangelist
	Website	https://ictevangelist.com/blog
Olly	LinkedIn	https://www.linkedin.com/in/ollylewis
	Bluesky	https://bsky.app/profile/ollylewisedu.bsky.social
	X/Twitter	https://x.com/olewis_coaching
	Instagram	https://www.instagram.com/ollyl
	Website	https://www.ollylewislearning.com

As well as our direct details above, Mark and Olly have been working on a website to accompany the book: https://edtechplaybook.co.uk/ where, over time, resources and news related to the book can be found.

If you'd like to reach out directly, you can do so easily by emailing us at mark@ictevangelist.com or olly@ollylewislearning.com.

What's next for us?

We'll all know the phrase 'Are we nearly there yet?' but when it comes to teaching and learning with technology, the journey is never over. So as this book is going to press, Mark and Olly are working on their upcoming playbooks focusing on more in-depth playbooks focusing on key teaching and learning activities. We can't wait to share them with you.

Our final call to action! Please do share what has resonated from within this book on your social channels and use the hashtag #EdTechPlaybook

Mark and Olly

GLOSSARY

2FA: Two-factor authentication (2FA) is an identity and access management security method that requires two forms of identification to access resources and data.

Acid-test ratio: An accounting analysis tool that helps evaluate a company's ability to meet short-term obligations with its most liquid assets. Calculated as (current assets – inventory)/current liabilities, it indicates short-term financial health. Beyond business, 'acid test' metaphorically means a way of determining the likely success or viability of something.

Adaptive practice: An educational approach where tasks and activities are adjusted to match a learner's individual skill level and learning pace, ensuring optimal challenge and supporting personalised learning and mastery of subject matter.

ALN: Additional learning needs.

Asynchronous: Asynchronous learning is an approach where teaching materials and assessments are available online, allowing students to access content, engage in learning activities and complete assignments at their own pace, without the need for real-time interaction with instructors or peers.

British Educational Suppliers Association (BESA): BESA is a trade association representing educational suppliers in the UK. It supports the education sector by providing market information, insights and networking opportunities to its members. BESA advocates for quality and innovation in educational products and services, ensuring that schools and educators have access to effective tools and resources for teaching and learning.

Bett (or The Bett Show): (formerly the British Educational Training and Technology (BETT) Show) An annual UK trade show that focuses on technology in education. It brings together educators, industry leaders and technology providers to showcase the latest innovations, share best practices and discuss trends in educational technology. Bett provides a platform for networking, professional development and exploring new tools and resources to enhance teaching and learning.

Blended learning: Similar to hybrid learning, involving in-person, remote and independent work. It is different to hybrid learning in that all learners participate in both in-person and online learning.

Bloom's two sigma problem: This proposes that one-on-one tutoring and mastery-based learning can significantly improve students' performance by two standard deviations (sigma) compared to conventional classroom instruction. This highlights the opportunity to scale personalised learning approaches effectively, an area where AI chatbots may be of great help to learners at a low cost.

Chatbot: An AI-driven piece of software that simulates a conversation with users via text or voice. Most commonly used for customer service and information retrieval, it processes user queries with natural language processing (NLP) to deliver automated responses.

Choice Theory: A theory that explores the impact of our choices on our lives and the relationships we have with others.

Chunking: A cognitive strategy for breaking down information into manageable units, enhancing the ability to process, understand and recall by leveraging working memory's limited capacity for more efficient long-term memory storage and retrieval.

Clinometer: A clinometer is an instrument used for measuring the elevation angle of a slope.

Cognitive load: The amount of mental effort required to process information and perform tasks. It encompasses intrinsic load (the complexity of the task itself), extraneous load (how information is presented) and germane load (effort devoted to learning). Managing cognitive load effectively is crucial in education to enhance learning and prevent overwhelm.

Cognitive Load Theory (CLT): This theory, developed by John Sweller, posits that learning is optimised when instructional design considers the limitations of human cognitive architecture. Sweller's research suggests effective learning occurs by managing the working memory's capacity to process new information without causing overload, thereby enhancing comprehension and retention.

Collective teacher efficacy (CTE): The collective belief of the staff in a school or faculty in their ability to positively affect students.

Computer-assisted instruction (CAI): A method of teaching where computers are used to present instructional material and monitor the learning process. It's a form of e-learning that involves direct interaction between the student and the computer.

Computer-supported collaborative learning: A pedagogical approach where learning occurs through social interaction facilitated by technology. In essence, it's about using computers to help groups of people learn together.

Concrete manipulatives: A concrete manipulative is physical and not digital, such as actual beans, coins, blocks or shapes. These tools are designed to help students understand abstract concepts by manipulating physical objects.

CPD (or PD): Continuing professional development (CPD), known as professional development (PD) in some contexts, involves systematic, ongoing learning activities designed to enhance professionals' knowledge, skills and effectiveness.

Cuisenaire rods: Colourful, rectangular blocks used in maths to help teach arithmetic, geometry and algebra concepts by representing numbers and their relationships visually and tactilely, allowing for hands-on learning.

Deliberate practice: A highly structured activity specifically aimed at improving performance. A term coined by Ericsson, this practice is characterised by its explicit goals, sustained effort and the receipt of feedback, designed to push abilities beyond current levels towards mastery.

Digital citizenship: In education, digital citizenship is crucial for teaching students how to use technology responsibly and ethically. It covers online safety, privacy, digital etiquette, and understanding the impact of their digital footprint. By promoting digital citizenship, schools equip students with the skills to navigate the digital world confidently and responsibly, fostering a positive and respectful online community.

Digital cognition: How humans think, act and respond in digital environments.

Direct instruction: *See* deliberate practice.

Dongle: A mobile Wi-Fi dongle is a small, portable device that connects to a mobile network to create a Wi-Fi hotspot. This allows multiple devices, such as laptops, tablets or smartphones, to access the internet via a mobile connection. Particularly popular during the pandemic.

Dual coding: The cognitive science theory that emphasises optimal learning occurs when information is presented both visually and verbally. It encourages careful consideration of layout, white space and cognitive load to ensure improved comprehension, retention and recall.

Dyscalculia: A specific learning difficulty that affects an individual's ability to understand and perform mathematical tasks. Characterised by challenges in number sense, memorising arithmetic facts and performing calculations, it can impact daily activities requiring numerical skills.

Dyslexia: A common learning difficulty that primarily affects reading and spelling abilities. Individuals with dyslexia often struggle with accurate and fluent word recognition, decoding and writing, despite having average or above-average intelligence and educational opportunities.

Education Endowment Foundation (EEF): A UK charity focused on improving the education of disadvantaged students. It funds research into effective teaching methods, shares findings with schools and provides support to help them implement evidence-based practices.

EPUB: EPUB is the shortened version of 'electronic publication'. EPUB is an e-book file format that has the '.epub' file extension.

Forgetting curve: Ebbinghaus's forgetting curve refers to the decline in memory retention over time.

Forgetting gap: The forgetting gap, a concept derived from Ebbinghaus's forgetting curve, refers to the rate at which information is lost over time when there is no attempt to retain it. This gap highlights the critical importance of revisiting learned material at strategic intervals to combat memory decay and enhance long-term retention.

Formative assessment: An assessment technique used during teaching to monitor student learning, provide feedback and guide teaching strategies. It aims to improve student understanding and outcomes by identifying strengths and areas for improvement, allowing for timely adjustments in teaching methods, hence 'formative'.

Games for learning: This is a pedagogical approach that utilises game mechanics and design to facilitate learning. It's a method of instruction where educational content is integrated into interactive and engaging game formats, such as with Minecraft.

Gamification: *See* Games for learning.

Generative AI: Generative AI is a technology that acts like a highly skilled person who can absorb vast amounts of information from texts, images and sounds. It uses complex computer algorithms to recognise patterns and styles. Then, drawing on its extensive 'training', it generates new, original pieces of content, mirroring the creativity found in human-made works. An issue to consider is that the outputs mirror the inputs, which can of course, based upon how it has been 'trained', have human traits of bias, including racism, ableism, sexism, classism, ageism and more. We always advocate for careful thinking about any inherent bias that may come from any AI-generated content.

Green screen: A technique where subjects are filmed against a green backdrop, allowing for easy removal and replacement of the background using chroma-keying software. This enables the insertion of any desired backdrop in post-production. It's ideal for educational projects, such as creating virtual tours of remote locations or exploring the inside of a human cell, encouraging students to creatively demonstrate their learning.

Growth mindset: Growth mindset is a term championed by psychologist Carol Dweck, which suggests that one's abilities and intelligence can grow through a mindset of dedication, hard work and persistence. It contrasts with a fixed mindset, which assumes that you can't develop, grow and get better.

Hashtag: A hashtag is a word or phrase preceded by a # symbol on social media. It categorises posts and makes them searchable, allowing people to find content related to specific topics or events. For example, #EdTech or #AIinEdu.

Hybrid learning: An educational approach combining traditional face-to-face classroom methods with online activities, allowing students to benefit from direct interaction with teachers and the flexibility of remote learning. This model supports personalised learning paths and fosters a more adaptable and engaging learning environment.

International Society for Technology in Education (ISTE): A global organisation focused on improving teaching and learning through technology. ISTE provides standards, resources and professional development to help educators use technology in the classroom effectively.

Internet Watch Foundation (IWF): A UK-based organisation that aims to make the internet safer by identifying and removing online child sexual abuse images. www.iwf.org.uk

Joint Information Systems Committee (Jisc): A not-for-profit organisation supporting the UK's higher education, further education and skills sectors. It provides digital services and solutions to help institutions improve learning, teaching and research. Jisc is a membership organisation that works collaboratively to address the sector's shared challenges and opportunities.

Keeping Children Safe in Education (KCSIE): KCSIE is a set of guidelines for schools and colleges in England to protect children from harm. It covers areas like child abuse, neglect and online safety. All staff in schools and colleges must be familiar with KCSIE to ensure children's wellbeing.

Lighthouse schools: Schools that showcase their successes (and failures) while offering advice and support to other schools.

Makerspace: A collaborative workspace equipped with tools and technology for design, prototyping and creation. These spaces often house a variety of equipment such as 3D-printers, laser cutters, vinyl cutters, sewing machines, soldering irons and computer workstations with design software. Makerspaces encourage experimentation, problem-solving and the development of technical skills.

Marginal gains: This theory suggests that making small, incremental improvements in multiple areas can lead to significant overall gains. It's like adding tiny amounts to a pot; eventually, it makes a big difference. This concept has been applied successfully in sports and business and, as shared by Dr Zoë Elder, can be helpful in education too.

Markup: In IT, markup refers to adding metadata or annotations to data. This can involve adding HTML tags to text for formatting, adding comments to code for explanation or labelling objects for feedback or other purposes. Markup enhances the understanding and usability of data.

MDM (mobile device management) profile: A file or small program that sits on a mobile device and helps technical teams manage that device for the purposes of updating, safeguarding and ensuring its safe use.

Metacognition: This refers to the awareness and understanding of your thought processes. Introduced by John Flavell, it involves monitoring, regulating and directing oneself towards effective problem-solving and learning, enabling individuals to plan, evaluate and adjust their approaches to learning more effectively. It has been found to have significant impacts on learner progress, making it a highly successful strategy in teaching and learning.

MFA (multifactor authentication): An electronic authentication method in which a user is granted access to a website or application only after successfully presenting two or more pieces of evidence to an authentication mechanism.

MSP (managed service provider): A company that provides IT services on a contractual basis to other organisations. These services can include network management, data backup, cybersecurity and technical support.

NLP (natural language processing): A sub-field of artificial intelligence and computer science that uses machine learning to enable computers to understand and communicate with human language. Not to be confused with Neuro Linguistic Programming.

Oak National Academy: An online learning platform created in response to the COVID-19 pandemic to provide high-quality, sequenced video lessons and resources for teachers, students and parents. There has been some opposition to Oak, suggesting that it puts forward ideological approaches supported by the Government which do not align with the students' best interests. Further to that, some have suggested that its resources lack personalisation and do not represent students' diverse cultural backgrounds. Notwithstanding that, they were seen by many as a lifesaver during the pandemic.

Online safety: This means protecting yourself from harm when using the internet. This includes keeping personal details private, being careful about what you share, and knowing how to spot and avoid scams or cyberbullying. It's about staying safe while enjoying the online world.

Oracy: Through dialogue, students deepen understanding, identify knowledge gaps and build on each other's thoughts. This collaborative learning fosters problem-solving and creativity. Ultimately, oracy empowers students to become confident, articulate individuals, ready to engage in the world.

PESTLE: PESTLE is an acronym for political, economic, social, technological, legal, and environmental factors. It's a framework used to analyse and monitor the macro-environment that may have an impact on a school or other organisation. By understanding these external factors, you can identify potential opportunities and threats.

PICRAT (passive, interactive, creative, replacement, amplification, transformation): A matrix that analyses higher-order thinking paired against technology use.

Professional (or personal) learning network (PLN): A group of people and resources connected through technology to share information and foster professional learning. A PLN can include colleagues, mentors and online communities.

Prompt: The text you write as a user to get the generative AI tool to create your output. It serves as an instruction or query, guiding the AI to generate specific content. We advocate both the STAIR model and to think about GIGO, the computing term which stands for 'garbage in, garbage out'; namely, that the quality of the output from a system you are using is only ever as good as the input you put in.

QR code (quick response code): A type of barcode that can be scanned by a smartphone or camera-enabled device. It contains information such as a website link, contact details or text. QR codes are square-shaped with black and white patterns. Scanning a QR code quickly directs you to the stored information and using them in the classroom can speed up access to online resources.

Remote learning: An educational process where teaching, facilitated by technology, occurs outside of the traditional classroom environment. It allows students to access educational materials, engage in learning activities and communicate with educators online, supporting continuous education irrespective of geographical constraints.

Retrieval practice: A study method that enhances learning by encouraging the recall of information from memory, thereby strengthening long-term retention. For more insights, www.learningscientists.org offers comprehensive resources on this effective technique.

SAMR: A model for using technology put forward by Dr Ruben Puentedura. Not reinforced by an evidence base, the SAMR framework outlines different approaches to using technology across what it calls substitution and transformation levels across substitution, augmentation (substitution levels), modification and redefinition (transformation levels).

SEND: Special educational needs and disabilities.

Self-regulation: The ability to control one's emotions, thoughts and behaviours to achieve goals.

It involves managing impulses, delaying gratification and adapting to changing circumstances.

Single sign-on (SSO): This allows users to access multiple educational tools and resources with one login. It simplifies access for students and educators, reducing password fatigue and enhancing security.

Social and emotional learning (SEL): An educational approach that focuses on teaching students the skills to manage emotions, build positive relationships, make responsible decisions and achieve personal goals. It helps students develop the skills they need to succeed in school and life.

Socratic questioning: Socratic questioning is an inquiry-based teaching and learning strategy aimed at stimulating critical thinking and deeper understanding through guided questions, rather than direct answers. This approach encourages students to develop independent thinking and problem-solving skills by exploring and discovering solutions on their own through guided conversation. In the context of EdTech, increasingly, AI chatbots incorporate a 'Socratic mode', using it as a means of enhancing learning through digital inquiry, thus connecting traditional teaching methods with contemporary EdTech tools.

SOLO taxonomy: A framework that categorises learning outcomes from simple to complex levels: pre-structural, uni-structural, multi-structural, relational and extended abstract. Developed by John Biggs and Kevin Collis, it aids in designing curriculum and assessing students' understanding, for example, moving from knowing facts (uni-structural) to applying them in new situations (extended abstract).

Spaced practice: A learning technique that entails spreading learning activities across several intervals, rather than massing them in a short period. This method improves retention and recall by leveraging the psychological spacing effect. For more insights, see www.learningscientists.org.

STAIR model: An approach to how you create your AI prompts to help achieve the best output. Created by Mark, it advocates that you should be SPECIFIC in your instruction, TELL the tool exactly what is needed, including all ACTIVITIES involved, be open to ITERATE for improvement, and give the AI tool you are using a ROLE to help it understand the output required. Through extensive testing, the STAIR model has been found to help generate good outputs when used across a broad range of AI tools such as Perplexity, Gemini, Claude and ChatGPT.

Stop-frame animation: A digital animation technique where objects are manipulated frame by frame to create motion, much like the technique you see in films such as those made by Aardman Animations. It is an effective technique for creating explanations of processes, where you create each frame for the process, or for recording things that take a long time to move, such as the movement of a plant towards the sun for photosynthesis, or the movement of a slug.

Summative assessment: An assessment technique used at the end of a period of significant teaching, such as at the end of a unit, year or course, to determine the level of understanding a student has gained against a set of predetermined criteria.

SWOT analysis: A planning tool used to identify an organisation's strengths, weaknesses, opportunities and threats. It helps assess internal capabilities and external factors to develop strategic plans.

Synchronous: An approach to teaching and learning where teaching happens in real time online, which allows for immediate interaction, feedback and discussion. It closely mirrors the traditional classroom experience, albeit in a digital environment.

Technology Acceptance Model (TAM): TAM predicts how people will adopt technology. It suggests that two main factors influence technology use: perceived usefulness (how helpful it is) and perceived ease of use (how easy it is to use). These factors impact a person's attitude towards the technology, which ultimately affects their decision to use it.

Theodolite: A surveying instrument used to measure horizontal and vertical angles.

Technology integration matrix (TIM): This is a framework that guides educators in integrating technology effectively into teaching. It combines five interdependent characteristics of meaningful learning environments (active, collaborative, constructive, authentic and goal-directed) with five levels of technology integration (entry, adoption, adaptation, infusion and transformation). TIM helps educators evaluate and enhance their use of technology to promote student engagement and learning outcomes.

Technology integration model (TIM): This TIM is a framework that guides educators in effectively using technology to enhance teaching and learning. It outlines different levels of technology use, from basic substitution to transformative redefinition of tasks, helping teachers to make informed decisions about how to integrate technology into their classrooms.

TPACK: The technological, pedagogical, content knowledge framework.

Vendor: A vendor is a person or business that sells goods or services. They can be a manufacturer, wholesaler or retailer. For example, a company that supplies software to schools is a software vendor.

Virtual manipulatives: An online equivalent of an in-class manipulative. Often used in maths, a manipulative should be a physical, tangible object, such as beans, coins, blocks and more. These tools are designed to help students understand abstract concepts by manipulating physical objects. Virtual manipulatives serve the same purpose as physical ones but are in a digital format.

Visualiser: A digital camera that displays objects or documents onto a screen. It's like an overhead projector but with higher quality and more flexibility. You can show anything from a book page to a small insect, making it a versatile tool for teaching and presentations.

Worked examples: Worked examples are step-by-step demonstrations of how to solve a problem or perform a task, used to guide students by showing both the process and reasoning involved, effectively reducing cognitive load and enhancing problem-solving skills and understanding.

XR: An umbrella term to cover all forms of virtual realities, be it mixed, virtual or augmented reality.

REFERENCES

Chapter 1 – Why EdTech hasn't worked historically

Blume, H. and Ceasar, S. (2013), 'L.A. Unified's iPad rollout marred by chaos', *Los Angeles Times* [website], 1 October 2013. Retrieved from: www.latimes.com/local/la-xpm-2013-oct-01-la-me-1002-lausd-ipads-20131002-story.html [Accessed: 25 May 2024]

Education Endowment Foundation (2020a), 'Remote Learning, Rapid Evidence Assessment', London: *Education Endowment Foundation* [website], April 2020. Retrieved from: https://d2tic4wvo1iusb.cloudfront.net/production/documents/guidance/Remote_Learning_Rapid_Evidence_Assessment.pdf?v=1688757690 [Accessed: 25 May 2024]

Global Education & Training Expenditure, *Holon IQ* [website], January 2021. Retrieved from: www.holoniq.com/edtech-in-10-charts [Accessed: 25 May 2024]

Hattie, J. (2018), 'Collective Teacher Efficacy (CTE) according to John Hattie', *Visible Learning*. [website], March 2018. Retrieved from: https://visiblelearning.org/2018/03/collective-teacher-efficacy-hattie [Accessed: 1 August 2024]

Chapter 2 – Models for learning with technology

Anderson, M. (2013), *Perfect ICT Every Lesson*, Carmarthen: Crown House Publishing

Education Endowment Foundation (2020a), 'Remote Learning, Rapid Evidence Assessment', London: *Education Endowment Foundation* [website], April 2020. Retrieved from: https://d2tic4wvo1iusb.cloudfront.net/production/documents/guidance/Remote_Learning_Rapid_Evidence_Assessment.pdf?v=1690278154 [Accessed: 25 May 2024]

Education Endowment Foundation (2020b), 'Using Digital Technology to Improve Learning', London: *Education Endowment Foundation* [website], 27 October 2021. Retrieved from: https://educationendowmentfoundation.org.uk/education-evidence/guidance-reports/digital [Accessed: 25 May 2024]

Education Endowment Foundation (2018), 'Working With Parents To Support Children's Learning', London: *Education Endowment Foundation* [website], 27 October 2021. Retrieved from: https://educationendowmentfoundation.org.uk/education-evidence/guidance-reports/supporting-parents [Accessed: 25 May 2024]

Higgins, S. (2010), 'The Impact of Interactive Whiteboards on Classroom Interaction and Learning in Primary Schools in the UK' in Thomas, M., and Schmid, E.C., eds. *Interactive Whiteboards for Education: Theory, Research and Practice*. Hershey, PA: IGI Global; pp. 929–938

Hughes, J. E. and Roblyer, M. D. (2023), *Integrating educational technology into teaching: Transforming learning across disciplines* (9th ed.). Boston, MA: Pearson.

Reynolds, D. and Muijs, D. (1993), 'The effective teaching of Mathematics: A review of research', School Leadership and Management, 19 (3), pp. 273–288

Shaw, H., Ellis, D.A. and Ziegler, F.V. (2018), 'The Technology Integration Model (TIM). Predicting the continued use of technology', *ScienceDirect* [website], June 2018. Retrieved from: www.sciencedirect.com/science/article/abs/pii/S0747563218300591 [Accessed: 1 August 2024]

UserSense, 'Technology Acceptance Model (TAM Model)', *UserSense* [website]. Retrieved from: www.usersense.io/knowledge-base/usability-metrics/technology-acceptance-model-tam [Accessed: 25 May 2024]

Wittwer, J. and Renkl, A. (2010), 'How effective are instructional explanations in example-based learning? A meta-analytic review', *Educational Psychology Review*, 22 (4), pp. 393–409. Retrieved from: www.researchgate.net/publication/225335923_How_Effective_are_Instructional_Explanations_in_Example-Based_Learning_A_Meta-Analytic_Review [Accessed: 25 May 2024]

Chapter 3 – Instructional delivery methods with technology

OECD (2015), 'Foreword and Acknowledgements', in *Students, Computers and Learning: Making the Connection*, OECD Publishing, Paris. Retrieved from: www.oecd-ilibrary.org/docserver/9789264239555-1-en.pdf?expires=1723061765&id=id&accname=guest&checksum=7C7275A52339300D168DE8DAF00C5489 [Accessed: 6 August 2024]

Chapter 4 – Effective digital transformation

Darling-Hammond, L. and Hyler, M. (2017), 'Effective Teacher Professional Development', *Learning Policy Institute* [website], 5 June 2017. Retrieved from: https://learningpolicyinstitute.org/product/effective-teacher-professional-development-report [Accessed: 1 June 2024]

Department for Education (2022), 'Meeting digital and technology standards in schools and colleges', *gov.uk* [website] 23 March 2022. Retrieved from: www.gov.uk/guidance/meeting-digital-and-technology-standards-in-schools-and-colleges/digital-leadership-and-governance-standards [Accessed: 1 June 2024]

Education Endowment Foundation (2021), 'Effective Professional Development', London: *Education Endowment Foundation* [website], October 2021. Retrieved from: https://educationendowmentfoundation.org.uk/education-evidence/guidance-reports/effective-professional-development [Accessed: 1 June 2024]

Education Endowment Foundation (2017), 'Lesson Study', London: *Education Endowment Foundation* [website], November 2017. Retrieved from: https://educationendowmentfoundation.org.uk/projects-and-evaluation/projects/lesson-study [Accessed: 1 June 2024]

Hamilton, A., Wiliam, D. and Hattie, J. (2023), 'The Future of AI in Education: 13 Things We Can Do to Minimize the Damage'. *EdArXiv* [website], 10 August 2023. Retrieved from: www.researchgate.net/publication/373108877_The_Future_of_AI_in_Education_13_Things_We_Can_Do_to_Minimize_the_Damage [Accessed: 5 August 2024]

Pjanić, K. (2014), 'The Origins and Products of Japanese Lesson Study', Teaching Innovations, Vol 27 (issue 3), pp.83-93. Retrieved from: https://scindeks-clanci.ceon.rs/data/pdf/0352-2334/2014/0352-23341403083P.pdf [Accessed: 1 June 2024]

Seleznyov, S. (2021), 'Learning Through Research: The Case For Japanese Lesson Study', *Impact MyCollege* [website], 12 February 2021. Retrieved from: https://my.chartered.college/impact_article/learning-through-research-the-case-for-japanese-lesson-study [Accessed: 1 June 2024]

Weston, D. (2017), 'Does Lesson Study work? A look at the new EEF trial', *Teacher Development Trust* [website], 10 November 2017. Retrieved from: https://tdtrust.org/2017/11/10/lesson-study-work-look-new-eef-trial [Accessed: 1 June 2024]

Chapter 5 – Cognitive science with technology

Caviglioli, O. (2019), *Dual Coding With Teachers*, Suffolk: John Catt

Coe, R. (2019), 'EEF Blog: Does research on "retrieval practice" translate into classroom practice?', EEF [blog], 5 December 2019. Retrieved from: https://educationendowmentfoundation.org.uk/news/does-research-on-retrieval-practice-translate-into-classroom-practice [Accessed: 28 May 2024]

Dunlosky, J., Rawson K., Marsh, E., Nathan, M. and Willingham, D. (2013), 'Improving Students' Learning With Effective Learning Techniques: Promising Directions From Cognitive and Educational Psychology',

Association for Psychological Science [online PDF], 2013. Retrieved from: https://pcl.sitehost.iu.edu/rgoldsto/courses/dunloskyimprovinglearning.pdf [Accessed: 28 May 2024]

Education Endowment Foundation (2021), 'Metacognition And Self-regulated Learning', London: *Education Endowment Foundation* [website], October 2021. Retrieved from: https://educationendowmentfoundation.org.uk/education-evidence/guidance-reports/metacognition [Accessed: 26 May 2024]

Education Endowment Foundation (2020), 'Using Digital Technology to Improve Learning', London: *Education Endowment Foundation* [website], 27 October 2021. Retrieved from: https://educationendowmentfoundation.org.uk/education-evidence/guidance-reports/digital [Accessed: 25 May 2024]

Jisc (2020), 'Promoting digital wellbeing for learners', *Jisc* [website] 2 April 2020. Retrieved from: www.jisc.ac.uk/guides/promoting-digital-wellbeing-for-learners [Accessed: 2 June 2024]

Lewis, O. (2020), 'Top 5 Online Learning Tips', *Olly Lewis Learning* [website] 23 May 2020. Retrieved from: https://ollylewislearning.com/top-5-online-learning-tips [Accessed: 2 June 2024]

Rosenshine, B. (2012), 'Principles of Instruction: Research-Based Strategies That All Teachers Should Know', ERIC [website] 2012. Retrieved from: https://eric.ed.gov/?id=EJ971753 [Accessed: 28 May 2024]

Rosenshine, B. (2012), 'Principles of Instruction: Research-Based Strategies That All Teachers Should Know', American Federation of Teachers [website] 2012. Retrieved from: www.aft.org/sites/default/files/Rosenshine.pdf [Accessed: 6 August 2024]

Simon, B. (1981), 'Why no pedagogy in England?', *Education in the Eighties: The Central Issues*, London: Batsford

Sweller, J. (2011), 'Cognitive Load Theory', *ScienceDirect* [website], 2011. Retrieved from: www.sciencedirect.com/topics/psychology/cognitive-load-theory [Accessed: 28 May 2024]

Chapter 6 – Using technology to demonstrate learning

Wiliam, D. (2011), *Embedded Formative Assessment*, Indiana: Solution Tree Press

Chapter 7 – Accessibility for all

Jackson, N. (2015), *Of Teaching, Learning and Sherbet Lemons: A Compendium of Careful Advice for Teachers*, Carmarthen: Independent Thinking Press

Ofsted (2019), 'Education inspection framework: overview of research', *gov. uk* [website], 16 January 2019. Retrieved from: www.gov.uk/government/publications/education-inspection-framework-overview-of-research [Accessed: 26 May 2024]

Chapter 8 – Feedback and assessment with technology

Australian Government Tertiary Education Quality and Standards Agency (2023), 'Assessment reform for the age of artificial intelligence', *teqsa.gov.au* [website], November 2023. Retrieved from: www.teqsa.gov.au/sites/default/files/2023-09/assessment-reform-age-artificial-intelligence-discussion-paper.pdf [Accessed: 26 May 2024]

Furze, L. (2023), 'The AI assessment scale', *leonfurze.com* [website], 18 December 2023. Retrieved from: https://leonfurze.com/2023/12/18/the-ai-assessment-scale-version-2/comment-page-1 [Accessed: 6 August 2024]

Hattie, J. (2011), *Visible Learning for Teachers: Maximizing Impact on Learning*, London: Routledge

Norden, J. (2023), 'AQA plans for digital GCSE exams from 2026', *TES Magazine* [website], 17 October 2023. Retrieved from: www.tes.com/magazine/news/secondary/aqa-plans-digital-gcse-exams-2026 [Accessed: 26 May 2024]

Wiliam, D. (2011), *Embedded Formative Assessment*, Indiana: Solution Tree Press

Woolcock, N. (2023), 'Pupils will take GCSEs on laptops by 2026, says exam board', *The Times* [website], 17 October 2023. Retrieved from: www.thetimes.co.uk/article/pupils-will-take-gcses-on-laptops-by-2026-says-exam-board-m98wsn8jj [Accessed: 26 May 2024]

Chapter 9 – Artificial intelligence and XR

Anderson, M. (2023), 'The Little Book of Generative AI Prompts for Teachers', *ICT Evangelist* [blog], 6 October 2023. Retrieved from: https://bit.ly/littlebookofgenerativeaiprompts [Accessed: 26 May 2024]

Clarke, A. (1962), *Profiles of the Future (New Edition): An Inquiry into the Limits of the Possible [1999]*, London: W&N

Education Endowment Foundation (2020), 'Using Digital Technology to Improve Learning', London: *Education Endowment Foundation* [website], 27 October, 2021. Retrieved from: https://educationendowmentfoundation.org.uk/education-evidence/guidance-reports/digital [Accessed: 25 May 2024]

Hamilton, A., Wiliam, D. and Hattie, J. (2023), 'The Future of AI in Education: 13 Things We Can Do to Minimize the Damage'. *EdArXiv* [website], 10 August 2023. Retrieved from: www.researchgate.net/publication/373108877_The_Future_of_AI_in_Education_13_Things_We_Can_Do_to_Minimize_the_Damage [Accessed: 5 August 2024]

Milmo, D. et al., (2023), 'Two US lawyers fined for submitting fake court citations from ChatGPT', *The Guardian* [website] 23 June 2023. Retrieved from: www.theguardian.com/technology/2023/jun/23/two-us-lawyers-fined-submitting-fake-court-citations-chatgpt [Accessed: 1 June 2024]

Pontefract, D. (2023), 'Harvard and BCG Unveil the Double-Edged Sword of AI in the Workplace', *Forbes* [website], 29 September 2023. Retrieved from: www.forbes.com/sites/danpontefract/2023/09/29/harvard-and-bcg-unveil-the-double-edged-sword-of-ai-in-the-workplace [Accessed: 5 August 2024]

Chapter 10 – Using technology in English

Jarvis, M. (2015), *Brilliant Ideas for Using ICT in the Classroom: A Very Practical Guide for Teachers and Lecturers*. London: Routledge

Smith, V. and Chickie-Wolfe, L.A. (2007), *Fostering Independent Learning*. New York: Guilford Press

Chapter 11 – Using technology in maths

Anderson, M. (2023), 'The Little Book of Generative AI Prompts for Teachers', *ICT Evangelist* [blog], 6 October 2023. Retrieved from: https://bit.ly/littlebookofgenerativeaiprompts [Accessed: 26 May 2024]

Chapter 12 – Using technology in science

Anderson, M (2013), *Perfect ICT Every Lesson*, Carmarthen: Crown House Publishing

Anderson, M. (2023), 'The Little Book of Generative AI Prompts for Teachers', *ICT Evangelist* [blog], 6 October 2023. Retrieved from: https://bit.ly/littlebookofgenerativeaiprompts [Accessed: 26 May 2024]

Chittleborough, G. and Treagust, D. (2018), 'Why Models are Advantageous to Learning Science', *Science Direct* [website], 2 February 2018. Retrieved from: www.sciencedirect.com/science/article/pii/S0187893X1830003X#:~:text=Models%20are%20useful%20tools%20in,Chittleborough%20and%20Mamiala%2C%202003 [Accessed: 26 May 2024]

Hattie, J. (2011), *Visible Learning for Teachers: Maximizing Impact on Learning*. London: Routledge

Whiting, K. (2020), 'These are the top 10 job skills of tomorrow – and how long it takes to learn them', *World Economic Forum* [website], 21 October 2020.

Retrieved from: www.weforum.org/agenda/2020/10/top-10-work-skills-of-tomorrow-how-long-it-takes-to-learn-them [Accessed: 26 May 2024]

Chapter 13 – Using technology in humanities

Berger, R. (2003), *An Ethic of Excellence: Building a Culture of Craftsmanship with Students*, New Hampshire: Heinemann Educational Books

Chapter 15 – Using technology to manage learning

Abumalloh, R., Asadi, S., Nilashi, M., Minaei-Bidgoli, B., Nayer, F., Samad, S., Mohd, S. and Ibrahim, O. (2021), 'The impact of coronavirus pandemic (COVID-19) on education: The role of virtual and remote laboratories in education', *ScienceDirect* [website], November 2021. Retrieved from: www.sciencedirect.com/science/article/pii/S0160791X21002037 [Accessed: 26 May 2024]

Attia, N., Baig, l., Marzouk, Y. and Khan, A. (2017), 'The potential effect of technology and distractions on undergraduate students' concentration', *National Library of Medicine* [website], July–August 2017. Retrieved from: www.ncbi.nlm.nih.gov/pmc/articles/PMC5648953 [Accessed: 26 May 2024]

Education Endowment Foundation (2021), 'Metacognition and Self-regulated Learning', *Education Endowment Foundation* [website], 27 October 2021. Retrieved from: https://educationendowmentfoundation.org.uk/education-evidence/guidance-reports/metacognition [Accessed: 26 May 2024]

Flanigan, A. and Titsworth, S. (2020), 'The impact of digital distraction on lecture note taking and student learning', *ResearchGate* [website], October 2020. Retrieved from: www.researchgate.net/publication/343853594_The_impact_of_digital_distraction_on_lecture_note_taking_and_student_learning [Accessed: 26 May 2024]

OECD (2022), 'How Learning Continued during the COVID-19 Pandemic' OECD [website], 24 January 2022. Retrieved from: www.oecd.org/education/how-learning-continued-during-the-covid-19-pandemic-bbeca162-en.htm [Accessed: 26 May 2024]

Rosen, R. and Samuel, A. (2015), 'Conquering Digital Distraction', *Harvard Business Review* [website], June 2015. Retrieved from: https://hbr.org/2015/06/conquering-digital-distraction [Accessed: 26 May 2024]

Chapter 16 – Online safety and digital citizenship

American Academy of Child and Adolescent Psychiatry (2024), 'Screen Time and Children', *www.aacap.org* [website] May 2024. Retrieved from: www.aacap.org/AACAP/Families_and_Youth/Facts_for_Families/FFF-Guide/Children-And-Watching-TV-054.aspx [Accessed: 1 June 2024]

Anderson, M. (2023), 'AI In Education: The IDEAL Framework For Informed Learning', *ICT Evangelist* [website] 10 November 2023. Retrieved from: https://ictevangelist.com/ai-in-education-the-ideal-framework-for-informed-learning [Accessed: 1 June 2024]

Binns, R. (2023), 'Screen time statistics 2024: Global increases/decreases, mobile vs desktop, and screen time's effects on children', *The Independent* [website], 5 September 2023. Retrieved from: www.independent.co.uk/advisor/vpn/screen-time-statistics [Accessed: 1 June 2024]

Butler, N., Quigg, Z., Bates, R. et al. (2022), 'The Contributing Role of Family, School, and Peer Supportive Relationships in Protecting the Mental Wellbeing of Children and Adolescents', *School Mental Health*, vol 14, pp.776–788. Retrieved from: https://link.springer.com/article/10.1007/s12310-022-09502-9 [Accessed: 1 June 2024]

Common Sense Media (2022), 'How Much Screen Time Is OK for My Kids?', *Common Sense Media* [website] 11 March 2022. Retrieved from: www.commonsensemedia.org/articles/how-much-screen-time-is-ok-for-my-kids#:~:text=They%20recommend%20the%20following%20for,day%20of%20high%2Dquality%20programs [Accessed: 1 June 2024]

Deitchman, A. (2021), 'Wait, What? On Social Network Use and Attention', *Applied Psychology Opus* [website]. Retrieved from: https://wp.nyu.edu/steinhardt-appsych_opus/wait-what-on-social-network-use-and-attention [Accessed: 1 June 2024]

Department for Education (2022), 'Meeting digital and technology standards in schools and colleges – Summary', *gov.uk* [website], 23 March 2022. Retrieved from: www.gov.uk/guidance/meeting-digital-and-technology-standards-in-schools-and-colleges [Accessed: 6 August 2024]

Department for Education (2024a), 'Keeping children safe in education', *gov.uk* [website], 26 March 2015. Retrieved from: www.gov.uk/government/publications/keeping-children-safe-in-education--2 [Accessed: 1 June 2024]

Department for Education (2024b), 'Mobile phones in schools', *gov.uk* [website], 19 February 2024. Retrieved from: www.gov.uk/government/publications/mobile-phones-in-schools [Accessed: 1 June 2024]

Federal Trade Commission (1998), 'Children's Online Privacy Protection Rule ("COPPA")', *Federal Trade Commission* [website], 1998. Retrieved from: www.ftc.gov/legal-library/browse/rules/childrens-online-privacy-protection-rule-coppa [Accessed: 1 June 2024]

Hedgecoe, G. (2023) 'AI-generated naked child images shock Spanish town of Almendralejo', *BBC News* [website], 24 September 2023. Retrieved from: www.bbc.co.uk/news/world-europe-66877718 [Accessed: 1 June 2024]

Henderson, E. (2016) 'Phantom vibration syndrome: Up to 90 per cent of people suffer phenomenon while mobile phone is in pocket', *The Independent* [website], 10 January 2016. Retrieved from: www.independent.co.uk/life-style/health-and-families/health-news/phantom-vibration-syndrome-up-to-90-per-cent-of-people-suffer-phenomenon-while-mobile-phone-is-in-pocket-a6804631.html [Accessed: 1 June 2024]

Internet Watch Foundation (2024) 'Under 10s groomed online "like never before" as hotline discovers record amount of child sexual abuse', *IWF* [website], 17 January 2024. Retrieved from: www.iwf.org.uk/news-media/news/under-10s-groomed-online-like-never-before-as-hotline-discovers-record-amount-of-child-sexual-abuse [Accessed: 1 June 2024]

Internet Watch Foundation (2022) 'Annual Report 2022', *IWF* [website]. Retrieved from: https://annualreport2022.iwf.org.uk/?gad_source=1 [Accessed: 1 June 2024]

Mackenzie, A. (2023), 'AI Sexually Generated Images of Children and the IWF Report Remove Tool', *esafety-adviser.com* [website], 14 September 2023. Retrieved from: www.esafety-adviser.com/ai-sexually-generated-images-of-children-and-the-iwf-report-remove-tool [Accessed: 1 June 2024]

Ofcom (2023), 'Children and Parents: Media Use and Attitudes', *ofcom.org.uk* [website], 29 March 2023. Retrieved from: www.ofcom.org.uk/__data/assets/pdf_file/0027/255852/childrens-media-use-and-attitudes-report-2023.pdf [Accessed: 1 June 2024]

Patterson, M. (2015), 'The 9 Elements of Digital Citizenship & How to Embrace Them', *EdTech Magazine* [website], 1 September 2015. Retrieved from: https://edtechmagazine.com/k12/article/2015/09/embracing-9-themes-digital-citizenship [Accessed: 1 June 2024]

Robins-Early, N. (2024), 'How did Donald Trump end up posting Taylor Swift deepfakes?', *The Guardian* [website], 26 August 2024. Retrieved from: www.theguardian.com/technology/article/2024/aug/24/trump-taylor-swift-deepfakes-ai [Accessed: 16 October 2024]

Snap Newsroom (2023), 'Early Insights on My AI', *Snap Newsroom* [website], June 2023. Retrieved from: https://newsroom.snap.com/early-insights-on-my-ai?lang=en-GB [Accessed: 1 June 2024]

Tidy, J. (2023) 'Charity wants AI summit to address child sexual abuse imagery', *BBC News* [website], 17 July 2023. Retrieved from: www.bbc.co.uk/news/technology-66129575 [Accessed: 1 June 2024]

UKCIS and Department for Science, Innovation and Technology (2020) 'Sharing nudes and semi-nudes: advice for education settings working with children and young people', *gov.uk* [website], 23 December 2020. Retrieved from: www.gov.uk/government/publications/sharing-nudes-and-semi-nudes-advice-for-education-settings-working-with-children-and-young-people [Accessed: 1 June 2024]

Vibert, S. (2023), 'The role of schools in keeping children safe online', *Internet Matters* [website], 21 June 2023. Retrieved from: www.internetmatters.org/hub/research/the-role-of-schools-in-keeping-children-safe-online [Accessed: 1 June 2024]

Zsila, Á. and Reyes, M. (2023), 'Pros & cons: impacts of social media on mental health', *BMC Psychology*, vol 11, 201 (6 July 2023). Retrieved from: https://doi.org/10.1186/s40359-023-01243-x [Accessed: 1 June 2024]

Chapter 17 – Digital leadership

Hashem, R., All, N. and El Zein, F. (2023), 'AI to the rescue: Exploring the potential of ChatGPT as a teacher ally for workload relief and burnout prevention', *ResearchGate* [website], September 2023. Retrieved from: www.researchgate.net/publication/374024140_AI_to_the_rescue_Exploring_the_potential_of_ChatGPT_as_a_teacher_ally_for_workload_relief_and_burnout_prevention [Accessed: 28 May 2024]

Ofcom (2023), 'Children and Parents: Media Use and Attitudes', *ofcom.org.uk* [website], 29 March 2023. Retrieved from: www.ofcom.org.uk/__data/assets/pdf_file/0027/255852/childrens-media-use-and-attitudes-report-2023.pdf [Accessed: 1 June 2024]

Tang, Y., Tang, R. and Gross, J. (2019), 'Promoting Psychological Well-Being Through an Evidence-Based Mindfulness Training Program', *PubMed* [website], July 2019. Retrieved from: https://pubmed.ncbi.nlm.nih.gov/31354454 [Accessed: 28 May 2024]

UNESCO (2023), 'Technology in education', *UNESCO.org* [website], 2023. Retrieved from: www.unesco.org/gem-report/en/technology [Accessed: 1 June 2024]

World Economic Forum (2023a), 'Top 10 Emerging Technologies of 2023', *World Economic Forum* [website], 26 June 2023. Retrieved from: www.weforum.org/publications/top-10-emerging-technologies-of-2023 [Accessed: 1 June 2024]

World Economic Forum (2023b), 'The Future of Jobs Report 2023 – 4. Skills Outlook', *World Economic Forum* [website], 30 April 2023. Retrieved from: www.weforum.org/publications/the-future-of-jobs-report-2023/in-full/4-skills-outlook/#4-skills-outlook [Accessed: 1 June 2024]

World Economic Forum (2016), 'Ten 21st-century skills every student needs', *World Economic Forum* [website], 10 March 2016. Retrieved from: www.weforum.org/agenda/2016/03/21st-century-skills-future-jobs-students [Accessed: 1 June 2024]

Chapter 18 – Ambassador roles

Chung, E. (2021), 'Why Ambassador Marketing Is More Effective Than Paid Social Ads', *ConvertOut* [blog], [no date]. Retrieved from: www.convertout.com/blog/why-ambassador-marketing-is-cheaper-and-more-effective-than-paid-social-ads [Accessed: 26 May 2024]

Geyser, W. (2024), 'What is Ambassador Marketing?', *Influencer Marketing Hub* [website], 29 August 2024. Retrieved from: https://influencermarketinghub.com/what-is-ambassador-marketing [Accessed: 26 May 2024]

Kunert, P. (2023), 'Google pays Apple $18B to $20B a year to keep its search in iPhone', *The Register* [website], 10 October 2023. Retrieved from: www.theregister.com/2023/10/10/google_pays_apple_18_20_claims_bernstein [Accessed: 26 May 2024]

Chapter 19 – Working with vendors

Chuang, R., Coflan, C., Giraldo, J-P., Attfield, I. and Tungatarova, A. (2022), 'National EdTech strategies: what, why, and who', *EdTech Hub* [website], 18 February 2022. Retrieved from: https://edtechhub.org/2022/02/18/national-edtech-strategies/#:~:text=When%20we%20say%20%27national%20EdTech,%2C%20equity%2C%20and%20learning%20outcomes [Accessed: 26 May 2024]

Chapter 20 – Personal learning networks

Lewis, O. (2021), 'Safeguard yourself on Social Media', *Olly Lewis Learning* [website], 7 August 2021. Retrieved from: https://ollylewislearning.com/safeguard-yourself-on-social-media [Accessed: 1 June 2024]

Rajagopal, R., Joosten-ten Brinke, J., Van Bruggen, J. and Sloep, P. (2011), 'Understanding personal learning networks: Their structure, content, and the networking skills needed to optimally use them', *First Monday* [website], 23 December 2011. Retrieved from: https://firstmonday.org/ojs/index.php/fm/article/view/3559/3131 [Accessed: 1 Aug 2024]